Knowledge Management

Edited by
Pasi Virtanen and Nina Helander

Knowledge Management

Edited by Pasi Virtanen and Nina Helander

Republished by InTech

Janeza Trdine 9, 51000 Rijeka, Croatia

Technical Editor Sanja Mujacic

Cover Designer Dino Smrekar

Additional hard copies can be obtained from orders@intechopen.com

Knowledge Management, Edited by Pasi Virtanen and Nina Helander
p. cm.
ISBN 978-953-7619-94-7

For EU product safety concerns:
IN TECH d.o.o., Prolaz Marije Krucifikse Kozulić 3, 51000 Rijeka, Croatia,
info@intechopen.com or visit our website at intechopen.com.

Preface

Knowledge is nowadays recognized as a significant factor of production. However, as the area of interest is still relatively new, there are multiple views and angles to the phenomenon. This book is a compilation of writings handpicked in esteemed scientific conferences that present the variety of ways to approach this multifaceted phenomenon.

The challenge in all research is to know where to draw the line, to make limitations for what to include and what to exclude in one's study. It is often seen as a sign of a good scholar when the borders of the subject in one's study are clear to see. Quite often the writer has to define the outlines for the study artificially, for example, in management there is no management without the organization and on the other hand there is no organization without people and structures. All this falls beneath the umbrella of knowledge management. The question remains, which are the relevant parts in accordance with one's own study and its focus. One has to theorize on something that is both tangible and intangible as well as their interactions.

Knowledge management as a research field divides further into several schools including such orientations or focusing areas as intellectual capital, information systems, communal direction (communities of practice), social networks and complexity, to name but a few. It is also extremely important to recognize that also the roots of knowledge management lie on several disciplines and focus areas, like general management, human relations management and information systems management and their respective literature.

First studies in leadership and management arose among the military issues and date back centuries. One of the first ones, if not the first one, was written some 2300 years ago. This refers to Sun Tzu's The Art of War (Sun Tzu 1993), which is quite widely read especially among the eastern leaders (Wee 1994), but also in the western hemisphere. After that there are names such as Machiavelli (1993, orig. 1531) and von Clausewitz (1998, orig. 1832) that surely ring a bell among those interested in these matters. However, this area is still not finished.

Knowledge management might also be seen as a descendant of the so called human relations - school that dates back to the nineteen twenties and thirties. Up until then the dominant way of how management was seen, had been the classic theory of management in which the labor is looked upon an asset like all the other assets for manufacturing businesses, the employee could even have been thought of as a part of a machine. The so called scientific management is one the best known examples of this movement. In 1924 General Electric's plant in Hawthorne near Chicago, US, authorized a group of scholars from Harvard to conduct a study on the effects of lighting on productivity. The results of these experiments were somewhat surprising and although later at least some of the implications were questioned, they still gave a start to more human-centered viewpoint to management and began to clearer divide management and leadership from one another.

Since the thirties this more humane approach has been attracting scholars in certain amount but not en masse. After the war in the forties and later in the fifties the human side began to win on popularity also among academia. This may be seen for example in the increased amount of literature that goes in this direction.

In all, it can be argued, that the roots of the scholars in knowledge management are mostly to be found in the human relations school. There are quite a few overlapping and shared elements in human relations schools writings and in writings that may be later defined to be knowledge management literature. Penrose (1958) wrote already in the late fifties about a new way to regard a business enterprise and knowledge management as a discipline is being born. Later Peter F. Drucker introduced the term knowledge worker (1970). The early years were perhaps neither easy nor successful but the thoughts remained in the under current. They may be seen as re-emerged at the latest in 1995 when the Knowledge-Creating Company was published by Nonaka and Takeuchi (1995).

Although the role of human relations and leadership, i.e. the softer side of knowledge management, is highly important and can be seen as the origin of knowledge management approach, we cannot ignore the fact that effective knowledge management in practical business life needs also solid understanding and utilization of information systems. In fact, in some occasions this kind of "harder" side of knowledge management is more concrete thing for the managers to grasp the big umbrella of knowledge management - there needs to be a solid starting point for every new idea and approach.

In this book, knowledge management is seen as an integral part of information and communications technology (ICT). The theme is approached firstly from the more general angles, starting by discussing knowledge management's role as a medium towards increasing productivity in organizations. This also relates to the discussion of intellectual capital and its measurement methods, without forgetting the viewpoint of manufacturing operations. In the starting chapters of the book, the duality in between technology and humans is also taken into account. In the following chapters, one may see the essence and multifaceted nature of knowledge management through branch specific observations and studies. Towards the end of the book the ontological side of knowledge management is illuminated. The book ends with two special applications of knowledge management.

We hope that this book gives fresh ideas for applying and practicing knowledge management in different organizations, especially those operating in the ICT sector, as well as opens new directions for future studies in the growing field of knowledge management research.

Editor

Pasi Virtanen and Nina Helander

Contents

1

Cutting costs and making profits through knowledge management

Nina Helander (Ph.D.), Marianne Kukko (M.Sc.)
and Pasi Virtanen (M.Sc.)
Tampere University of Technology
Finland

1. Introduction

The commonly recognised primary idea of a business enterprise is to make a profit for its owners. There are three conditions that a company must meet in order to survive: it should be financially sound and solvent, it should have liquidity, and it should be profitable. Making a profit means that the enterprise should be viable; it should be capable of maintaining a certain amount of income and keeping costs down. Furthermore, in order to be successful it should do this in some way better than its competitors. Today, as most companies possess or at least may gain access to the infrastructure generally used in their chosen field of operations, they have to seek a competitive edge elsewhere. That advantage can be achieved by finding a unique way of combining the more traditional tangible assets with intangible ones such as individual and organisational knowledge (Spender & Grant 1996). It is exactly this combination of different types of knowledge that makes each and every company different from its peers, as there simply are no two companies exactly alike.

Knowledge is widely recognised as an asset, but it is also a vital factor of production (Zack 1999a). This means that the general perception of knowledge is changing. Knowledge is no longer seen as something one needs, or even is allowed to, hold on to oneself; instead, personnel are encouraged to share it. Companies will have to alter their ways of thinking about knowledge and start to look at it as they looked upon raw materials or finances some decades ago. The state of affairs is somewhat contradictory, since the financial means, flows of money, are in general kept under rather good control while knowledge, which is often even more important - as it may control and aid in monitoring the other flows - is only just reaching this point. One feature of knowledge is that it multiplies when shared (Allee 2000). One can only hope that this would apply also for financial assets.

As indicated above, knowledge is an essential resource for contemporary organisations (Penrose 1995, 79-80), especially according to the knowledge-based view of the firm, under which theory knowledge is seen even as a critical element in many organisations' success (see, e.g., Grant 1996). The modern company must evaluate its assets and resources, which include knowledge, and where there is shortage, they must acquire the deficient or entirely lacking asset so that production, whatever its nature, can commence anew, or continue efficiently and economically. One way to utilise this resource is to optimise the use of existing knowledge in the company. As knowledge is a focal component of an organisation's success, critical knowledge should first be recognised, after that it may and should be utilised effectively. Knowledge management (KM) is the tool for recognising and utilising this knowledge. In this chapter, KM is elaborated upon through a real-world example. The chosen example is a software company operating in business-to-business markets; i.e., the company produces software solutions and sells these to other organisations. In this company, the business unit management realised that there is a large amount of overlapping work, as the software production teams tend not to be aware of the big picture. Thus, the teams start their software production with a clean slate regardless of the work already done and knowledge created elsewhere in the company. All projects have more or less the same costs, because each team creates software code covering all aspects of the functionality, whether or not the same features already have been created by another team for another project or software product. If the latter features could be thought of as a common component in and of software rather than merely lines of code relevant to a single project, a significant amount of working costs could be saved. The company's management sought a solution in componentisation - which translates into codification in the language of knowledge management. To be more precise, this chapter is meant to clarify the use of componentisation as a way and example of putting codification strategy to use as part of KM in the context of software production.

2. What is knowledge management?

On a general level, knowledge management can be seen as managing the sharing and application of knowledge, as well as improving knowledge creation (Marchand & Davenport 2000). Essential elements in knowledge management are administration and goal-oriented management of knowledge, skills, competence, and communication (Suurla 2001). On the basis of these statements, it may be concluded that, as these concepts cover the whole enterprise and its operations, they belong to the jurisdiction of the board of directors. Basically it can be said that one of the main ideas in knowledge management is effective diffusion and promotion of the reuse of existing resources (Wah 2000) throughout the organisation. Thus, to move knowledge and experience in the organisation from their origin to places where they are novel can be seen as one of the tasks of knowledge management (Ainamo 2001). The knowledge should be shared openly, which, in turn, means that, from the organisation's point of view, the only proprietary view is that of the company itself. However, getting people to talk and share their knowledge could be considered to be the greatest obstacle to effective knowledge management (Desouza 2003). It has been stated that an attitude of wisdom is required within an organisation (i.e., the members of the organisation willing to search for knowledge inside the organisation and also willing to share their own knowledge) if knowledge management is to work well there (Hansen et al. 1999). This implies that knowledge management also is a function that has a close connection or an interface with human resource management and leadership in companies.
The attitude of wisdom inside the organisation can be enhanced and encouraged by social interaction. Through social interaction, organisational units have more opportunities to share their resources and ideas. Social interaction also promotes trust and reduces uncertainty among employees (Tsai 2000). Despite all this, many companies lack an attitude of wisdom, as the employees see their knowledge as their personal capital rather than something benefiting the whole work community. Still, exactly this attitude of wisdom would be

needed for unrestricted knowledge flows to occur more commonly. One reason for this lack might be that even if the different organisational units are expected to collaborate with each other, in fact they still quite often compete with each other (Tsai 2000). It can be said that it is exactly social interaction that is indispensable in creation of the attitude of wisdom that is needed for sharing knowledge among the various units in companies. Among the benefits cited for inter-unit knowledge-sharing are innovativeness (Tsai & Ghoshal 1998) and efficiency in project completion times (Hargadon 1998a); these, in turn, are among the success factors of a modern enterprise. A question may arise as to whether an organisation can perform knowledge management without knowing it. We state that the distinction in this context is to be drawn between implementing carefully planned operations in KM and doing things that match the definition of KM. In the first case, we say that KM is being applied; in the latter case, we claim that the organisation in question is simply managing its knowledge. Problematics with knowledge management and knowledge acquisition especially are sometimes divided into two: sharing knowledge and creating new knowledge. Sharing of knowledge may on some occasions also be called knowledge transfer. This question is further elaborated upon later in this chapter. Concerning the creation of new knowledge, the founding fathers of KM, Nonaka & Takeuchi (1995), wrote that it is to be divided into a fourfold table, which they named the SECI model. This model shows that knowledge is created in different ways between different actors in organisations. The model derives its name from these means of transfer: socialisation, externalisation, combination, and internalisation. In brief, socialisation occurs when two knowledgeable persons share experiences (i.e. tacit knowledge, not previously explicated) and both learn something new from the combined knowledge base. Externalisation happens when a knowledgeable person makes his or her tacit knowledge explicit for the rest of the organisation. Combination refers to the situation in which there are two separate explicit sources from which facts can be drawn together to create new knowledge. Internalisation describes the situation wherein an individual takes in explicit knowledge and processes this within the framework of his or her experiences and creates new tacit knowledge. (Nonaka & Takeuchi 1995) Each of these processes can be found in organisations; they may be realised in an orderly manner or spontaneously. It may well be said that knowledge management consists of carefully designed operations in which these forms can be realised through proper planning and management, rather than just to choose the *laissez-faire* policy of not trying to influence knowledge utilisation and creation but instead just letting them happen if they occur at all. In effect, knowledge management may also be said to be there to channel and govern the human capital and intellectual properties of an organisation (Ståhle & Grönroos 1999) to maximise performance and to make the most of the efforts of the organisation.

According to Ansoff (1965, 5), the main problem of an enterprise is how 'to configure and direct the resource conversion process in such way as to optimize the attainment of the objectives'. This problem for decision-makers involves all sub-segments of the company and their functions. As most businesses are meant to be continuous endeavours, they need to carefully plan their actions on a day-to-day basis but also in the long term. Daily operations are run in terms of operational tasks. The tool for long-term planning is strategy, where strategy refers to 'the determination of the basic long-term goals and objectives of an enterprise, and the adoption of courses of action and the allocation of resources necessary for carrying out these goals' (Chandler 1966, 16).

As already shown, knowledge is an important part of the asset repertoire of an enterprise, so it and its use must be included in these plans. This also means that knowledge management should be grounded within the context of business strategy (Zack 1999b, 142). Whether there is need for a specific KM strategy or KM should be part of the overall business strategy is debatable. Whichever approach is chosen, such strategy should include the actual activities that are needed to embed knowledge management in the organisation (Seeley & Dietrick 1999). This also should include a timetable for actions, so that the actual tasks become scheduled and not only planned. With proper strategic grounding, the investments in knowledge management will be better focused and prioritised, providing competitive advantage (Zack 1999b, 142).

The main idea of KM is to make the reuse of existing resources effective (Wah 2000). A quite commonly known way to put knowledge management into practice is to apply either a codification or personalisation strategy (Hansen et al. 1999). The main idea in codification strategy is to concentrate on codified knowledge and information technology. The purpose is to codify knowledge carefully and store it in databases. Through this, anyone in the company can access and use the knowledge easily. In implementation of the codification strategy, the focus is on technology-oriented issues. The other perspective in executing knowledge management is to employ personalisation strategy; here, the main idea is to concentrate on tacit knowledge and person-to-person contacts. Information technology is used to help people network and communicate. (Hansen et al. 1999) In a personalisation strategy, the emphasis is on human-related issues.

It has been claimed that an organisation should make a choice between these two strategies. At the same time, however, when one strategy is chosen, the other should not be totally neglected. The ideal balance between these two strategies has been suggested to be 80/20. (Hansen et al. 1999) In spite of this, some suggest that in software companies the balance could be different from this. The suggestion is that codification and personalisation strategies should go more hand-in-hand and there should be a dual-core process, of codification and personalisation. (Mukherji 2005) Software companies' core competence often lies in software development. The software development process is typically characterised as rather knowledge-intensive. Also, the actual outcome of the process, software, is very much a knowledge-intensive product.

One wise choice for software development is component-based software engineering (CBSE), called componentisation in this chapter. Componentisation means in this context the way of not using unique code written specifically for each and every project and product but instead always keeping in mind the broader opportunities to reuse the code once it has been written. The other side of componentisation is that when writing the code, one must always bear in mind the wider possibilities for using the code throughout the organisation and in all of its teams and products. The actual components are always independent entities, and they may vary from a few lines of code to larger functional units. Either way, the component must possess one or more interfaces via which it may be used also in other contexts. It has been stated that componentisation is one way to increase the effectiveness of software development (see, e.g., Meyers & Oberndorf 2001), as it decreases the amount of overlapping work, which, in turn, corresponds with Wah's (2000) main idea of KM making the best of reusing the knowledge in organisations. Through componentisation, existing knowledge can be used more effectively. The emphasis in componentisation is typically on codified knowledge. Still, to be able to create unique solutions to meet customer needs, the human side of knowledge management (tacit knowledge) should not be neglected.

One of the challenges for organisations is the difficulty of recognising what knowledge is needed in which situation (Lave 1988; Reeves & Weisberg 1994; Thompson, Gentner & Loevenstein 1998 as cited by Hargadon 1999). Organisations typically face a big problem in employees not knowing about all of the available knowledge existing in the organisation. Therefore, they cannot look for it or utilise it in their own work. The creation of new ideas would be most effective if old knowledge could be attached to new situations and in this way be cultivated and developed (Hargadon 1999, Hargadon 1998b, Hargadon & Sutton 1997).

Whilst working in componentisation mode, in addition to completing their day-to-day tasks as before, the teams must try to identify potential components - i.e., products, subparts, or features - that could also be used in other teams and environments. The components created must be made available for the organisation's use. Exchange of resources and interaction among the people developing and using reusable software is an important factor for enabling componentisation (Sherif et al. 2006).

While one of the goals of knowledge management is effective reuse of existing knowledge, KM can be seen as an integral element in the shift to componentisation. The choice to renew software development in the direction of componentisation can be seen as a choice leading toward a codification-based strategy of knowledge management. Despite the emphasis on codification strategy, it should be remembered that personalisation strategy should not be totally neglected. Through this division it is quite easy to recognise the elements that are important in knowledge management. Only by noticing both aspects (despite the fact that the emphasis might be on codification strategy) can one discern an approach to knowledge management that is appropriate for software development. No matter what the knowledge management strategy is, both technology and human issues should be considered.

It is still worth noting that it is estimated that as many as a third of software reuse cases fail. The lack of processes dedicated to reuse and adaptation of existing processes are the main reasons for the failure. In such cases, the processes do not support reuse; i.e., there is no means or time for reuse and componentisation (Morisio et al. 2002). By drawing up and implementing a proper KM strategy, these challenges might be tackled. In accordance with this, in order to work, componentisation requires very careful planning and adjustments (Morisio et al. 2002). It has also been stated that often componentisation projects fail because, it is thought, they are implemented in the existing structures with little motivation and technical training. Often, the human factor has been neglected. (Morisio et al. 2002) Typically, also pressure from various sources (related to the customers, the management, and financial goals) takes the attention away from componentisation. Another potential challenge is that independent or physically dispersed units may even compete with each other (Lynex & Layzell as cited by Kunda & Brooks 2000), leading to a situation in which there is no willingness to share software code. There is some evidence that social interaction enhances inter-unit knowledge-sharing (see, e.g. Tsai 2002). Thus the role of social interaction might be crucial when one is introducing componentisation, as its point is to get people to share knowledge in the form of components that are creations of others' knowledge. After reflection on the above-mentioned aims of knowledge management, one can state that the idea of componentisation - i.e., reuse of work already done and existing resources - is very closely tied to the central idea of knowledge management.

3. A practical example of an organisation and its operating environment

Let us consider a large software company operating in business-to-business markets. In the segmentation of the software industry devised by Hoch et al. (1999), this company stands mostly in the enterprise solutions sector, although it also has characteristics of professional software services (e.g., tailoring the software for specific customer needs is typical for the company) and of software products (e.g., there are 'product categories' visible to customers). It provides large and complex information and communication technology (ICT) systems and solutions for its organisational customers. The company is quite dispersed. The operations of the company are based on independent teams, which differ in many ways. They have different organisational backgrounds on account of mergers and acquisitions, different technologies in use, and different products and customers. Each of these teams is responsible for its own software development, production, and sales. In addition, the teams can be quite separated from each other even physically and geographically. This makes it difficult to know what others in the organisation are doing. For the most part, even the team leaders do not know what those on an equal level in the organisation are working on. Because of this, the teams mainly create the software from scratch. This also leads to the problem that too often the teams do overlapping programming and software development work. The unnecessary redundancy in the software development process naturally causes extra costs for the company.

The toughening competitive situation is forcing the company to review and renew its software development process to form a more efficient way of working. The aim is to root out redundancies and to improve productivity. To get to that point, full utilisation of the knowledge within the organisation is needed. Thus, improvements in knowledge flows and closer collaboration between teams and individuals throughout the organisation are a necessity. The organisation is tackling its problem by switching to component-based software engineering. In this organisation, work has been strictly team- and project-based. Thus, the current organisational structure does not support the interactions required by componentisation. Nor has there been time or motivation to create code that works for the common good. Hence, the transition from a team-oriented way of working to a productised, more holistic software development process is a great challenge for the whole organisation.

In addition to a change in the organisational structure, the organisation has now decided to take advantage of a single shared technology by applying the same programming environment and language across the organisation. The chosen technology is already in use in a few teams but is new to most. As this field is not the focus of the chapter, it is not addressed further here.

Two stages of progress have been identified for the renewal of the company's software development practices: the design and preparation phase and the implementation phase. The design and preparation phase include preliminary assessment of the available, and thus possible, technologies; analysis of the current process; the revision of practices; division of responsibilities; preliminary allocation of resources; and, finally, the technological decisions. Early on, in preparation of the componentisation shift, a dynamic, well-functioning cross-team group of specialists, the architect group, is to be set up. The task of the architect group is to critically monitor the actions and needs of the teams. The group will scrutinise these and decide whether a suggested part is suitable as a component, on the basis of the team leaders' suggestions. Each member of the organisation so authorised can use and reuse components. To be fully usable and developed further for and by other teams, a component must be well documented. Therefore, carefully planned specifications for the documentation must be completed. The planned practices are put into action and anchored in the organisation in the implementation phase. In this phase, the architect group should monitor the process and support the correct actions. The aim of these two phases will be to ensure appropriate implementation of new practices and technologies.

Renewal of the software development process by introducing componentisation comprises many challenges from a knowledge management perspective. The fundamental idea in renewal for componentisation is to share knowledge effectively, in order to be able to reuse it. Before that point can be reached, several knowledge management challenges can be identified. By renewing the software development process by introducing componentisation, the organisation emphasises a technology-oriented KM strategy. The focal element is a repository, also called a component library, where the knowledge is explicated. Alongside utilisation of components from the repository, the programmers still need a lot of their own and others' expertise and tacit knowledge to effectively develop and produce software. Thus, the human side should never be neglected in the organisation. Accordingly, the knowledge management challenges (and their eventual solutions) for the renewal may be described by dividing them into technology-oriented and human-oriented challenges (and solutions).

The amount of redundant work and the great diversity of the teams in their initial situation are the main sources of the need for implementation of knowledge management in renewal of the organisation's software development process. Both technology- and human-oriented challenges can be seen to derive mainly from the diversity of the teams. It was clear even in the design and preparation phase that the heterogeneous nature of the teams makes it challenging to find an appropriate common technological solution that could fit all the technological demands of all the teams. It is a difficult and trying task to find a technology to support the existing software produced and maintained by the teams, because of the different nature of the software developed in the various teams. Also a tricky question is that of how the component library should be structured such that it is truly usable and exploitable by the members of the organisation.

For the implementation phase there is a great challenge of making the chosen new technology fit with the initial technologies used in different teams when the initial technologies are still in active use. The aim of making a transition to the new chosen technology throughout the organisation creates a challenge, as there is a lack of competence in the new chosen technology. The challenge of making the component interfaces general enough when the components are created can also be considered a technology-oriented challenge in the implementation phase. There is also a lack of time for training and experimenting related to the new technology. When there is insufficient time for training and experimentation with a new technology, the members of the organisation do not have enough knowledge to utilise the new technology properly. Overall, the technology-oriented challenges in the shift to componentisation impose great demands.

The design and preparation phase too features human-oriented challenges. There are prejudices related to the new chosen technology. People have questioned the superiority of the chosen technology, and many people would like to continue with the old and familiar technology that they are used to. Some members of the organisation even feel afraid as they feel that through the change the future is blurred and unknown. One phenomenon perceived in practice is the change in internal power/value structures. This change stems from the fact that, with the new technological choices, the competence and know-how of some individuals are becoming more valuable whereas those of some others is becoming less significant or even obsolete. Also, in the implementation phase there exists the challenge of activating the information and knowledge flow between teams. The heterogeneous nature of the teams in the organisation also has an effect from a human perspective by adding some contradictory or controversial notions to the knowledge-sharing between the members of different teams. People are not used to sharing knowledge with members of other teams. The social interaction between the teams is weak or even non-existent. Prejudices and attitude problems such as lack of trust and a 'love' for the code they themselves have written are significant reasons for this. Overall, attitude problems pose an obstacle to the change. Questions have been raised in relation to, for example, the whole idea of componentisation and whether the technological decisions are right.

4. Generalisations and managerial implications

The general goal in management is to get the company to make a profit. One way to achieve this is to produce low and sell high. As customers are becoming more and more price-conscious, there is nearly always the need, and room, to cut costs. One way to do this cost-cutting is to make the best of existing resources. As knowledge is recognised as a resource and as it is seen to be in a strategic position for contemporary organisations, its full utilisation and reuse becomes vital. This requires a conscious decision at the strategic level to implement organised knowledge management in the organisation.

In our example organisation, the main idea behind the componentisation is, as noted above, an attempt to avoid overlapping work and to utilise existing knowledge better across team and project boundaries. Thus, the role of effective knowledge management and especially of knowledge-sharing is recognised in the organisation. However, there remain several knowledge-management-related challenges that should be considered more carefully. From the facts presented, we argue that by recognising these challenges and reacting to them more proactively, starting in the design and preparation phase of the renewal process, the knowledge management magic can happen more effectively and the shift to CBSE be easier.

In the subchapter three of this chapter there were described some KM-challenges that the example organisation faced in the change-over to componentisation. Based on these examples and existing KM-frameworks the generalisation of challenges that are most typically found in a team-oriented organisation implementing a codification strategy are presented in the following table 1. To aid in examination of the process of implementing the codification strategy, the process is divided into two phases here also: the design and preparation phase, in which the process is mainly being planned, and the implementation phase, in which actual procedures are carried out. The challenges are divided into two categories, technology-oriented and human-oriented challenges, according to their primary sources.

	Design and preparation phase	Implementation phase
Technology-oriented challenges	· Different kinds of teams and demands · Agreement on viable tools that meet the needs of different teams · Usability and exploitability of the knowledge repository	· Compatibility between the initial and new knowledge · Assuring sufficient familiarity with the new knowledge · General enough usability of the knowledge · Lack of time for training and experimenting
Human-oriented challenges	· Prejudices against change from the present state · Fear and uncertainty caused by not knowing the future · Change in the competence-related power/value structure	· Information and knowledge flows between teams · Social interaction between the teams · Attitude problems related to change · Attitude problems related to the new technology

Table 1. KM challenges in different phases of the renewal process

Naturally, the first step toward efficient KM is analysis and identification of the potential obstacles present within the organisation and its practices. Often one can identify multiple challenges that are present at several organisational levels and related to many central business processes of the organisation, as can also be seen in Table 1. There are, however, also many possible solutions to these challenges. The most interesting feature of knowledge management is that the effects of the actions taken are multiple and sometimes even difficult to pinpoint. This is why the solutions to KM challenges cannot all be matched against a certain challenge presented in Table 1. The purpose is that, by applying the suggested solutions, the organisation creates the right circumstances for meeting the challenges. This is fairly natural, as KM is not a single organisational tool but an overall management philosophy. Possible solutions based on the ideas of codification and personalisation strategies are represented in following Table 2.

	Design and preparation phase	Implementation phase
Technology-oriented solutions	· Strategic-level decision to go through with the project · Proper planning and scheduling of the implementation · Implementation of the chosen strategy according to plan · Approval of parallelism of the old and new way of working in some situations for the agreed time · Designing of the knowledge repository with experts and representatives of different teams	· The new way of working being adaptable and agile enough to accommodate the needs of the teams · Allocation of enough resources and opportunities for training · Clear architectural design and structure
Human-oriented solutions	· Strategic-level decision to go through with the project · Proper planning and scheduling of the implementation · Implementation of the chosen strategy according to plan · Proper communication of the change · Training for the chosen approach	· Publishing of pilot cases to serve as an example · Creation of both formal and informal communication areas and of spaces for work between teams · Pursuit of cultural change toward a more open and sharing work environment

Table 2. Solutions to KM challenges in different phases of the renewal process

In the design and preparation phase, one of the main issues from the technology-oriented perspective is to plan well the implementation and the schedule for implementation of the new chosen technology. Experts and members of different teams should be involved in this process. In addition, as early as in the design and preparation phase, it would be wise to consider letting some teams use old technologies as long as required for maintaining software that has been created with old technology and that will not adapt to the new technology. This should be allowed only in situations where the integration of old and new technology is impossible and only if it is truly necessary. In the choice of the new technology, the knowledge of the experts inside the organisation should be utilised to ensure that the choice is right from a technological perspective (and from different teams' perspective) and so also to rationalise and justify the choice. The experts should also be involved in the design and preparation of a knowledge repository. This aids in building a knowledge repository in which usable and exploitable knowledge can be found.
The choice of new technology in the design and preparation phase has a direct effect on the implementation phase. In relation to the technological side of the change, it should be considered that the chosen way of working must be agile enough to enable the work of the individual teams to continue. The new techniques should also be such that they mesh at least on some level with the old way of working. Only this guarantees that the old and new knowledge go hand-in-hand and no knowledge is missed out. In choosing of the technology, it should be made sure also that the members of the organisation are either already familiar with it or have the ability to learn how to use it. For learning how to use the new technology, there must be sufficient training possibilities to match people's different ways of learning. The managers should also allocate time and money for the employees to adapt to the new technology. In the implementation phase, the usage of the existing knowledge is the main focus. Thus, to ensure the usability of the newly created knowledge, clear definitions and guidelines for this knowledge that is placed in the knowledge repository should be prepared. This aforementioned should be done by means of which it could be ensured that the knowledge is general enough for everyone to use.
The human-oriented challenges of the design and preparation phase that are related to prejudices, fear, and uncertainty could be met with proper communication. Through appropriate communication about the change, the various grey areas may be elucidated and the uncertainties eliminated. It is important to communicate the message of the renewal clearly all the way down to individual teams and groups within the organisation. It is also wise to provide training for the chosen approach already in the design and preparation phase. Through training, various types of prejudices may be diminished.
What is essential at the beginning in all situations involving a change is short-term success. A counterbalance to the human resistance to change is needed. The organisation and its members need to see positive examples if they are to overcome the difficulties. Successful pilot cases should be promoted on the company level (e.g. via the intranet). To make sure that information and knowledge will flow between the teams in the implementation phase, different kinds of spaces where people can meet and create mutual trust, along with similar opportunities, would be useful. Examples are job rotation among the teams, formal and informal meetings of team members, regular team leader meetings, shared coffee rooms and game rooms, and visits of a team member to meetings of other teams. The communication of the renewal should be handled well. This way, a better and more thorough picture of the process can be given to the members of the organisation. The change needs promotion

through well-executed organisation-wide communication. Promotion is more likely to be taken care of properly and to remain functional if dealt with by dedicated personnel, even if their main tasks lie elsewhere. It is also wise for a known and appreciated person inside the organisation to be nominated to be a leading figure in the change. Additionally, the opinions and ideas of the members of the organisation on all levels should be better taken into account. Also, the team leaders' meetings could be visited (at least occasionally) by a member of the top management for promotion of the process. In turn, the team leaders could promote the message of the management to their own team members. In these middle-level meetings, various training needs could be discussed and developed also. To put it simply, if the people know what is going on and they are able to be active about it, they are less concerned and are more confident and trusting in a better future.

Leadership carries immense weight in knowledge management. The 'people skills' of the management have an essential role in winning the employees over to the new *modus operandi*. Thus it can be said that leading the change systematically is critical also in the kind of endeavour discussed in this chapter. Often the individual teams in the organisations of this kind all have their own 'business as usual' modes. In the organisation wide renewal process they are typically expected to renew these and, at the same time, their thinking patterns. A major adjustment can be seen on a mental level. All teams and individuals need to adjust their functions and even change the technology that is being used. Some must learn and adapt to a wholly new technology and way of working. To achieve these changes, a new way of thinking and readiness to adapt to change are needed. Thus, the attitude of wisdom is needed. This can be brought about properly and at all functional levels only if leaders create the right circumstances and provide all necessary resources for successful social interaction. This also supports the claim that reuse in the absence of means or time typically fails. Hence it can be said that leading and leadership in this kind of undertaking and setting are crucial for a successful outcome.

5. Conclusion

This chapter has discussed the challenges of knowledge management on the basis of an actual example. We analysed the software development renewal process of a large software company from a KM perspective. The aim was to track the KM challenges that appear during the renewal process and, by reflecting the example on the basis of the KM literature, propose possible solutions to the challenges identified. While we identified several challenges related to the renewal process from the knowledge management standpoint, still it can be said that knowledge management is also a key to helping renewal go forward. By identifying knowledge management challenges, these challenges can be faced and handled. It can be argued that companies that are renewing their ways of working would benefit a great deal from applying KM practices even in starting the design and preparation stages of the renewal process; KM practices should already be considered in the design phase of the change, to ensure smooth progress of the change. Another significant issue that should be raised is that both technological and human perspectives of KM need to be recognised in renewal process. Also proper technological KM solutions may be needed and are worth taking into consideration for making things easy and efficient. To master the technological side of the whole change process is a great challenge already, but the organisational and human side may be an even bigger one to handle. The key element is to have the right attitude towards knowledge-sharing. This has already been stated in many KM studies. For example, Desouza (2003) has stated that 'The biggest obstacle to effective knowledge management is not implementing a cutting-edge IT solution, but getting people to talk and share their know-how'. Monitoring and guiding the change and persons involved in it is extremely useful. Some control is needed or even vital if a renewal process is to bear successful fruit and especially for the new approach to actually become the usual way of working. The role of the management is that of a facilitator of this knowledge sharing forum. The qualifications and traits required of leaders in this kind of situation are not necessarily easy to find in one person. It is very challenging to fully consider which organisational changes are needed, and it is even harder to figure out how they should be implemented and presented. This all can also be seen as taking up of knowledge management practices as everyday functions inside the company. In this kind of situation, one should always bear in mind that it is typical that such a procedural change may well take up to two or three years or even be continuous, a sort of ongoing change. The ultimate goal of all this fuss in an organisation is a permanent change in the ways of working so that abundant and overlapping work is cut to the minimum. This way the company may be able to significantly cut the costs and make profits.

6. References

Ainamo, A. 2001. Tietämyksen välitystoiminta: Näkökulma uusien tuotteiden ja kulutusmallien syntymiseen, kehittymiseen ja vakiintumiseen. Hallinnon tutkimus 20 (4): 347-357.

Allee, V. 2000. Knowledge Networks and Communities of Practise. OD Practitioner. Fall/Winter.

Ansoff, H. I. 1965. Corporate Strategy. McGraw-Hill. New York. 241 p.

Chandler, A. D. Jr. 1966. Strategy and Structure: Chapters in the History of the Industrial Enterprise. Doubleday. New York. 580 p.

Desouza, K. C. 2003. Facilitating Tacit Knowledge Exchange. Communications of the ACM. Vol. 46, No. 6 (June), 85-88.

Grant, R. M. 1996. Toward a Knowledge-based Theory of the Firm. Strategic Management Journal. Vol. 17, Winter Special Issue, 109-122.

Hansen, M. T., Nohria, N. & Tierney, T. 1999. What's Your Strategy for Managing Knowledge? Harvard Business Review. Vol. 77, No. 2 (March/April), 106-116.

Hargadon, A. 1998a. Firm As Knowledge Brokers: Lessons in Pursuing Continuous Innovation. California Management Review. Vol. 40, No. 3 (Spring), 209-227.

Hargadon, A. 1998b. Group Creativity: Interpersonal Cognition in New Product Development Projects. Gainesville, University of Florida 40 (working paper).

Hargadon, A. 1999. Brokering Knowledge: A Field Study of Organizational Learning and Innovation. Gainesville, University of Florida 58 (working paper).

Hargadon, A. & Sutton, R. I. 1997. Technology Brokering and Innovation in a Product Development Firm. Administrative Science Quarterly. Vol. 42, 716-749.

Hoch, D., Roeding, C., Pukert, G., Lindner, S. & Mueller, R. 1999. Secrets of Software Success: Management Insights from 100 Software Firms around the World. Harvard Business School Press. Boston, MA.

Marchand, D. A. & Davenport, T. H. (eds). 2000. Mastering Information Management. Prentice Hall. London.

Meyers, B. C. & Oberndorf, P. 2001. Managing Software Acquisition. Open Systems and COTS Products. SEI Series in Software Engineering. Addison-Wesley.

Morisio, M., Ezran, M. & Tully, C. 2002. Success and Failure Factors in Software Reuse. IEEE Transactions on Software Engineering. Vol. 28, No. 4, 340-357.

Mukherji, S. 2005. Knowledge Management Strategy in Software Organisations: Straddling Codification and Personalisation. IIMB Management Review. Vol. 17, No. 3 (September), 33-39.

Nonaka, I. & Takeuchi, H. 1995. The Knowledge-creating Company: How Japanese Companies Create the Dynamics of Innovation. Oxford University Press. New York.

Penrose, E. 1995. The Theory of the Growth of the Firm, third edition. Oxford University Press. Oxford. 272 p.

Seeley, C. & Dietrick, B. 1999. Crafting a Knowledge Management Strategy. Knowledge Management Review. No. 11 (November/December).

Sherif, K., Appan, R. & Lin, Z. 2006. Resources and Incentives for the Adoption of Systematic Software Reuse. International Journal of Information Management. Vol. 26, 70-80.

Spender, J.-C. & Grant, R. M. 1996. Knowledge and the Firm: Overview. Strategic Management Journal. Vol. 17, Winter Special Issue, 5-9.

Ståhle, P. & Grönroos, M. 1999. Knowledge Management - tietopääoma yrityksen kilpailutekijänä. WSOY. Porvoo.

Suurla, R. 2001. Teknologian arviointeja. 6: Avauksia tietämyksen hallintaan: helmiä kalastamassa: loppuraportti.. Tulevaisuusvaliokunta, Oy Edita Ab. Helsinki.

Tsai, W. 2002. Social Structure of 'Coopetition' within a Multiunit Organization.Organization Science. Vol. 13, No. 2 (March-April).

Tsai, W. & Ghoshal, S. 1998. Social Capital and Value Creation: The Role of Intrafirm Networks. Academy of Management Journal. Vol. 41, No. 4, 464-476.

Wah, L. 2000. Behind the Buzz: The Substance of Knowledge Management. In Cortada, J. W. & Woods, J. A. (eds), The Knowledge Management Yearbook 2000-2001. Butterworth-Heineman. Boston.

Zack, M. H. 1999a. Managing Codified Knowledge. Sloan Management Review. Vol. 40, No.4, 45-58.

Zack, M. H. 1999b. Developing a Knowledge Strategy. California Management Review. Vol. 41, No. 3.

Knowledge Management (Intellectual Capital) Assessment using Fuzzy Expert System

Mehdi Fasanghari
Iran Telecommunication Research Center (ITRC)

1. Introduction

The economy of the world is changing fast, and the knowledge assets and the process are become the primary source of the organization. This is clear when we browse the stock market websites and see the companies with unequal physical assets and stock market value. Also, this notion of knowledge management, as a corporate resource, has been looked to deliver sustainable core competencies in the future (Jans B. D. & Prasarnphanich P., 2003, Khoshsima G., 2003).
Companies today are facing important challenges such as the need to reduce the time-to-market, the development and manufacturing costs, or to manage products with more and more technology. Thus, this current situation is encouraging the implementation of new management techniques such as knowledge management to increase competitive advantages (Gholamreza Khoshsima et al., 2004). Knowledge is an intangible asset, and measuring the effectiveness of knowledge management solutions is challenging. This paper attempts to address the challenges. In order to achieve competitive sustainability, many firms are launching extensive knowledge management efforts. To compete effectively, firms must leverage their existing knowledge and create new knowledge that favorably positions them in their chosen markets (Gold A. H. et al., 2001).
The first step in developing knowledge management is to determine the current position of knowledge management systematically or, more activities and organizational conditions (Gholamreza Khoshsima et al., 2004).
Even if there are some modules and techniques for measuring intellectual capital (IC) (Sveiby, 2003); but, lack of such systems which improve our ability for measuring is observable. The designed expert system act based on three categories: knowledge Capital (KC), management capital (ManC), and market capital (MarC).
Fuzzy numbers, average, mathematics, and inference have been embedded in our system in order to enhance the efficiency and effectiveness of our expert system.
In this paper, we will propose a fuzzy expert system to measure the intellectual capital via fuzzy mathematics. So, in the next section we will discuss more about the literature of subject and determine the Intellectual Capital Measures. Next, the

basic concepts of fuzzy set theory for fuzzy expert system design have been presented. The expert system structure has been illustrated in the next section. A numerical example for four Intellectual Capitals of ITRC has been shown the accuracy of designed system; finally, Conclusion has been determined the results of the employing of designed fuzzy expert system in measuring the Intellectual Capitals.

2. Intellectual capital measures

The intangible property mainly comes from the demand of market and formed by the legal right (Reilly R.F. & Schweihs R.P., 1998). Since the intangible assets are valued as a type of property, it will be appropriate for us to discuss the meaning of a property, and then the meaning of intangible assets is elucidated. There are kinds of rights, while the traditional concept is related mostly to those of real estate. However the intangible assets in accountancy, citing from the general business accounting law, trademark, patents, copyright, permits. Some experts add computer software and organizational cost (Edvisson L. & Malone M., 1999).
Intellectual property rights consist with the industrial property right, copyright, trademark right, and patent right etc, which are created by the human knowledge. Copyright includes the right of copy, issue, public display, selling, artistic performance and translation etc. Edvisson and Malone suggested that the IPR consist with knowledge capital, non-financial capital, concealed property capital, non-visible property, or intangible assets (Edvisson L. & Malone M., 1999). Brooking, Board and Jones (1998) indicates that IPR include market assets, intellectual property assets, infrastructure assets, human-centered assets. Such intellectual property, being the difference between the company market value and the book value, is the counterpart of visible entity capital and finance capital (Brooking Annie et al., 1998).
Reilly and Schweihs, and Edvisson and Malone propose that intellectual capital includes three basic classes, such as human capital, structural capital, and relationship capital. Human capital represents the individual skills applied to satisfy customers (Edvisson L. & Malone M., 1999, Reilly R.F. & Schweihs R.P., 1998). Structural capital is the organizational capabilities of the enterprise, demanded by the market. Relationship capital is the strength of a franchise afforded by a business's ownership of rights. While Mar (2000) surmise the literature and suggest that the intellectual capital in the wide sense, including Knowledge Capital (KC), Management Capital (ManC), and Market Capital (MarC) (Mar S., 2000).

3. Fuzzy set Theory

Fuzzy set theory provides a framework for handling the uncertainties. Zadeh initiated the fuzzy set theory (Zadeh L. A., 1965). Bellman presented some applications of fuzzy theories to the various decision-making processes in a fuzzy environment (Bellman R. E. & Zadeh L. A., 1970). In non-fuzzy set every object is either a member of the set or it is not a member of the set but in fuzzy sets every object is to some extent member of a set and to some extent it is member of another set. Thus, unlike the crisp sets membership is a continuous concept in fuzzy sets. Fuzzy is used in support of linguistic variables and there is uncertainness in the problem. Fuzzy theory is widely applicable in information gathering, modeling, analysis, optimization, control, decision making and supervision.

4. The Basic Concepts of Fuzzy Numbers

A fuzzy number is a fuzzy set $\tilde{A}$ on R which possesses as the following three properties:
$\tilde{A}$ is a normal fuzzy set;
Special cases of fuzzy numbers include crisp real number and intervals of real numbers. Although there are many shapes of fuzzy numbers, the triangular and trapezoidal shapes are used most often for representing fuzzy numbers. The following describes and definitions show that membership function of triangular and trapezoidal fuzzy number, and its operations (Mehdi Fasanghari & Farzad Habibipour Roudsari, 2008a, Mehdi Fasanghari et al., 2008).
A fuzzy number $\tilde{A}$ is convex, if

$$\mu_{\tilde{A}}[\lambda x_1 + (1-\lambda)x_2] \ge \min[\mu_{\tilde{A}}(x_1), \mu_{\tilde{A}}(x_2)]. \qquad x_1, x_2 \in X,\ \lambda \in [0,1] \tag{1}$$

Alternatively, a fuzzy set is convex if all α-level sets are convex.
A fuzzy set $\tilde{A}$ in the universe of discourse X is normal if (A. Kaufmann & M.M. Gupta, 1988, S. Mabuchi, 1988)

$$\sup_x \mu_{\tilde{A}}(x) = 1 \tag{2}$$

A nonempty fuzzy set $\tilde{A}$ can always be normalized by $\mu_{\tilde{A}}(x) / \sup_x \mu_{\tilde{A}}(x)$.

A fuzzy number is a fuzzy subset in the universe of discourse X that is both convex and normal.
One of the most important concepts of fuzzy sets is the concept of an $\alpha-\mathrm{cut}$ and its variant. It is a bridge from well-defined structure to fuzzy environment.
A triangular fuzzy number can be defined by a quadruplet $\tilde{A} = (a_1, a_2, a_3)$, where $a_1 \le a_2 \le a_3$, its member function represented as follows.

$$\mu_{\tilde{A}} = \begin{cases} 0 & x < a_1 \\ (x-a_1)/(a_2-a_1) & a_1 \le x \le a_2 \\ (x-a_3)/(a_2-a_3) & a_2 \le x \le a_3 \\ 0 & x > a_3 \end{cases} \tag{3}$$

Let $\tilde{A}$ and $\tilde{B}$ $\tilde{B}$ be two fuzzy numbers parameterized by the quadruplet (a_1, a_2, a_3) and (b_1, b_2, b_3), respectively. Then the operations of triangular fuzzy numbers are expressed as (S.J. Chen & C.L. Hwang, 1992):

$$\begin{aligned}\tilde{A}(+)\tilde{B} &= (a_1,a_2,a_3)+(b_1,b_2,b_3)=(a_1+b_1,a_2+b_2,a_3+b_3)\\ \tilde{A}(-)\tilde{B} &= (a_1,a_2,a_3)-(b_1,b_2,b_3)=(a_1-b_1,a_2-b_2,a_3-b_3)\\ \tilde{A}(\times)\tilde{B} &= (a_1,a_2,a_3)\times(b_1,b_2,b_3)=(a_1\times b_1,a_2\times b_2,a_3\times b_3)\\ \tilde{A}(\div)\tilde{B} &= (a_1,a_2,a_3)\div(b_1,b_2,b_3)=(a_1\div b_3,a_2\div b_2,a_3\div b_1)\end{aligned} \tag{4}$$

Triangular fuzzy numbers are appropriate for quantifying the vague information about most decision problems (C.H. Cheng & Y. Lin, 2002). And the primary reason for using triangular fuzzy numbers can be stated as their intuitive and computational-efficient representation.

In this paper, the triangular fuzzy number is used for measuring Intellectual Capitals. More details about arithmetic operations laws of trapezoidal fuzzy number can be seen in (Lee et al., 2004).

Considering experts E_i provide the possible realization rating of a certain Intellectual Capital. The evaluation value given by each expert E_i are presented in the form of a triangular fuzzy number

$$\tilde{A}^{(i)}=(a_1^{(i)},a_2^{(i)},a_3^{(i)}),where \quad i=1,2,\dots,n \tag{5}$$

The average $\widetilde{A}_m$ of all $\widetilde{A}^{(i)}$ is computed using average means

$$\tilde{A}_m=(a_{m1},a_{m2},a_{m3})=(\frac{1}{n}\sum_{i=1}^{n}a_1^{(i)},\frac{1}{n}\sum_{i=1}^{n}a_2^{(i)},\frac{1}{n}\sum_{i=1}^{n}a_3^{(i)}) \tag{6}$$

5. Fuzzy Expert DSS

Fuzzy expert decision support system is an expert system that uses fuzzy logic instead of Boolean logic. It can be seen as special rule-based systems that uses fuzzy logic in its knowledge base and derives conclusions from user inputs and fuzzy inference process (Kandel A., 1992) while fuzzy rules and the membership functions make up the knowledge-base of the system. In other words a "fuzzy if-then" rule is a "if-then" rule which some of the terms are given with continuous functions (Li-Xin Wang, 1994).

Most common fuzzy systems are: pure fuzzy systems, Takagi-Sugeno-Kang (TSK) and fuzzy system with fuzzifying and defuzzifying parts (Li-Xin Wang, 1994).Since in the system developed in this paper the input and output are real numbers, the last kind is used. This system has a fuzzifier module in the input that changes the real numbers to fuzzy sets and a defuzzifier module in the output that changes the fuzzy sets to real numbers. The architecture of system is described in more detail in the next section.

6. Architecture of Fuzzy Expert System

System architecture defines the system function, System blocks and the way they interact with each other (Mehdi Fasanghari & Farzad Habibipour Roudsari, 2008b). The architecture of the system is composed of three main blocks as shown in figure 1.

6.1 Fuzzy Inference Engine

A program which analyzes the rules and knowledge aggregated in the database and finds the logical result. There are different selection for the fuzzy inference engine depending on the aggregation, implication and operators used for s-norm and t-norms (Li-Xin Wang, 1994). Mamdani inference is used as equation 7 cause of its local rules and appropriate inferences among the collected rules.

$$\mu_{B'}(y) = \max_{l=1}^{M}[\sup_{x \in U} \min(\mu_{A'},...,\mu_{A'_n}(x_n),\mu_{B'_y}(y))] \tag{7}$$

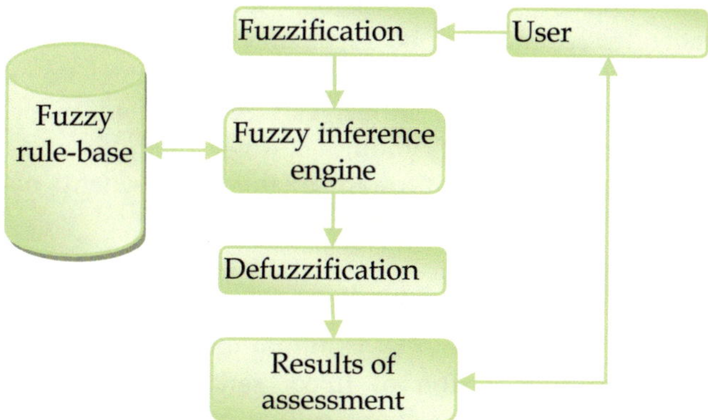

Fig. 1. Process of intellectual capital assessment

6.2 User Interface

Users of this system are organizational decision makers that enter the real number of all linguistic variables via user interface. Also, user interface shows the result scoring of all vendors; therefore, as providing this aim in the designed system, Matlab user interface is used.

6.3 Fuzzy Rule Base

Experts' experience is used to build up the fuzzy rules. These rules are conditional statements and in general can be represented as
IF x is X_i and y is Y_i and … THEN o is O_i.

Where x and y are linguistic input variables. X_i and Y_i are possible linguistic values for x and y; respectively. They are modeled as fuzzy sets based on reference sets containing x and y: Similarly the output or decision variable, o is a linguistic variable with a possible value, O_i modeled as a fuzzy set. The clause x is X_i and y is Y_i can be interpreted as fuzzy propositions delivering partial set membership or partial truth. Consequently the partial truth of the rule premise can be evaluated, modifying the fuzzy set parameters of the output fuzzy sets (Matthews C., 2003).
The language value for each one of the selected parameters in fuzzy expert system (KC, ManC,and MarC) are combined by: *Low, Medium,* and *High.* Therefore, there will be $3^3=27$ rules out of our depth interviews as below:
Rule 1: IF "KC" is *High* AND "ManC" is *Medium* AND "MarC" is *Low* THEN "Intellectual Capital" is *Medium.*

6.4 Fuzzification

Fuzzification refers to the process of taking a crisp input value and transforming it into the degree required by the terms. We do this by simply recognizing that many of the quantities that we consider to be crisp and deterministic are actually not deterministic at all: They carry considerable uncertainty. If the form of uncertainty happens to arise because of imprecision, ambiguity, or vagueness, then the variable is probably fuzzy and can be represented by a membership function. If the inputs generally originate from a piece of hardware or drive from sensor measurement, these crisp numerical inputs can be fuzzified in order for them to be used in a fuzzy inference system (Timothy J. Ross, 2005). So, as our inputs data are manually, we use singleton Fuzzification method to benefit of its simplicity and speed of calculations in our fuzzy expert DSS.

6.5 Defuzzification

The inference process is complete the resulting data for each output of the fuzzy classification system are a collection of fuzzy sets or a single, aggregate fuzzy set. The process of computing a single number that best represents the outcome of the fuzzy set evaluation is called defuzzification. There are several existing methods that can be used for defuzzification. These include the methods of maximum or the average heights methods, and others. These methods tend to jump erratically on widely non-contiguous and non-monotonic input values (Diego C. E. S., 1999). We chose the centroid method, also referred to as the "center-of-gravity (COG)" method, as it is frequently used and appears to provide a consistent and well-balanced approach (Klir G. J. & Folger T. A., 1998).
For each output using this defuzzification method illustrated in equation 8, the resultant fuzzy sets are merged into a final aggregate shape and the maximum or the average heights of the aggregate shape computed to smooth the procedures and decrease the complexity of expert system calculations for its acceleration.

$$y^* = \frac{\int_{hgt(B')} y\,dy}{\int_{hgt(B')} dy} \tag{8}$$

whereas

$$hgt(B') = \{y \in V \mid \mu_{B'}(y) = \sup_{y \in V} \mu_{B'}(y)\} \tag{9}$$

7. Case Study

In order to evaluate the applicability of the proposed system, we implemented it in telecommunication research center in Iran (ITRC) in order to measure some Intellectual Capital of its projects.
All linguistic values KC, ManC, and MarC are fuzzy sets. We then conducted a group that included 4 experts in the field of Information and Communication Technology to determine the factors value for 4 projects, which has been done in ITRC in last year (2006), while the values have been signified in triangular fuzzy numbers that is illustrated in Table 1.
At first level one system is designed to assess Intellectual Capital, which has three components, at IF-part a triangular fuzzy number scale is used, therefore with respect to three linguistic variables and three linguistic terms and all of 3^3=27 rules should be fired to the expert system be able to measure the intellectual capitals. After the data of questionnaires was aggregated degree of each component was determined (Table 1). The aggregate data (Table 1) can enter Fuzzy system as either crisp or fuzzy. In the first procedure, fuzzy numbers were embedded into rules through singleton fuzzification and entered fuzzy system designed at MATLAB 7.04. The scores of Intellectual Capital has been computed and changed to crisp numbers by maximum of heights defuzzification method. The following results were acquired (Table 2).

	Expert's number	KC	Management Capital	Marketing Capital
Intellectual Capital of project 1	1	(2.2,4,5.5)	(3.4,4.5,5.6)	(6.1,7.2,8)
	2	(1.2,2.3,4.6)	(4,4.1,4.5)	(5,6.2,6.5)
	3	(3,3.5,4)	(3,3.5,4)	(3,3.5,4)
	4	(1.7,2.1,3.2)	(2.4,3.5,6.2)	(1.2,4.3,5.7)
Intellectual Capital of project 2	1	(6.2,7.6,8.8)	(5.4,7.2,7.9)	(4.4,6.2,7.4)
	2	(7.2,8.1,8.9)	(3.2,4.3,5.8)	(5.2,6.8,7.2)
	3	(2.2,3.5,4.2)	(1.2,3.4,6.6)	(5.7,6.8,9)
	4	(3,5.3,6.8)	(5.2,4.6,8.9)	(6.5,7.5,8.6)
Intellectual Capital of project 3	1	(4.2,5.1,5.4)	(2.3,4.6,7.2)	(4.2,6.2,6.8)
	2	(4,5,6)	(4,5,6)	(4,5,6)
	3	(3,3.5,4)	(3,3.5,4)	(3,3.5,4)
	4	(6.4,7.9,9.2)	(3.5,6.5,7.8)	(2.5,3.4,4)
Intellectual Capital of project 4	1	(1.4,2.5,3.2)	(1.9,2.5,3)	(3.2,3.5,4.8)
	2	(4,5,6)	(4,5,6)	(4,5,6)
	3	(0.4,0.5,1.2)	(3.4,4.1,4.8)	(0.3,0.8,0.9)
	4	(3.4,4.2,4.7)	(5.2,6.7,6.8)	(2.2,3.1,3.3)

Table 1. The experts score for selected Intellectual Capitals of ITRC

As shown in Table 2, Intellectual Capital of project 2 is better than project 3, and respectively Intellectual Capital of project 1 and 2 are in the next stages.

	Final Score
Intellectual Capital of project 1	4.43
Intellectual Capital of project 2	6.31
Intellectual Capital of project 3	5.02
Intellectual Capital of project 4	3.76

Table 2. The final output results of fuzzy expert system

8. Conclusion

In this study, the proposed fuzzy expert system is a flexible system that: (a) simultaneously considers all the different criteria in determining the most suitable Intellectual Capital, (b) takes advantage of the best characteristics of the existing methods, (c) involves the full participation of the users in deciding the number of experts, alternative Intellectual Capitals, and evaluation criteria and sub-criteria, and (d) provides that users can investigate the impact of changes in certain parameters on the solution and quickly receive feedback on the consequences of such changes. The implementation of the proposed fuzzy expert system for a Intellectual Capital Measuring undertaken by telecommunication research center in Iran confirmed the above considerations. The experts of the telecommunication research center in Iran were pleased and agreed with our recommendations since the fuzzy expert system can reduce the decision-making time, and are a practical tool for dealing with the uncertainty problem of linguistic terms.

9. References

A. Kaufmann & M.M. Gupta (1988). Fuzzy Mathematical Models in Engineering and Management Science, North-Holland, Amsterdam

Bellman R. E. & Zadeh L. A. (1970). Decision making in a fuzzy environment. Management Sciences, Vol. 17, 141-164

Brooking Annie; Peter Board & Sue Jones (1998). The Predictive Potential of Intellectual Capital. Int. J. Technology Management, Vol. 16, 115-125

C.H. Cheng & Y. Lin (2002). Evaluating the best main battle tank using fuzzy decision theory with linguistic criteria evaluation. European journal of operation research, Vol. 142, No. 2, 174-176

Diego C. E. S. (1999). The Fuzzy systems handbook: a practitioners' guide to building, using and maintaining fuzzy systems, CA: AP Professional

Edvisson L. & Malone M. (1999). The wood is big to permit the intelligence capital- how to measure the information ages immaterial assets, City Culture, Taipei

Gholamreza Khoshsima; Caro Lucas & Ali Mohaghar (2004). Assesing Knowledge Management with Fuzzy Logic, Proceeding of Springer-Verlag, pp. 425-432, Berlin Heidelberg, Berlin Heidelberg

Gold A. H.; Malhotra A. & Segars A. H. (2001). Knowledge management: An organizational capabilities perspective. Journal of Management Information Systems, Vol. 18, No. 1, 185-214

Jans B. D. & Prasarnphanich P. (2003). Understanding the antecedents of effective knowledge management: The importance of a knowledge-centered culture. Decision Sciences, Vol. 34, No. 2, 351-384

Kandel A. (1992). Fuzzy expert systems, FL: CRC Press, Boca Raton

Khoshsima G. (2003). A model for measuring organizational agility in Iran television manufacturing industry: a fuzzy logic framework, Proceeding of Proceedings of International Engineering Management Conference, pp. 354- 358, Albany, New York USA, Albany, New York USA

Klir G. J. & Folger T. A. (1998). Fuzzy set ,Uncertainty ,and information, Prentice-Hall

Lee, J. W.; Hong, E. & Park, J. (2004). A Q-learning based approach to design of intelligent stock trading agents. Engineering Management Conference, Proceedings. IEEE International, Vol. 3, 1289-1292

Li-Xin Wang (1994). A course in fuzzy systems and control, Prentice Hall

Mar S. (2000). The research of the information software immaterial assets price evaluation system, Taiwan Stock Exchange Incorporated Company

Matthews C. (2003). A formal specification for a fuzzy expert system. Information and Software Technology, Vol. 45, 419-429

Mehdi Fasanghari & Farzad Habibipour Roudsari (2008a). The Fuzzy Evaluation of E-Commerce Customer Satisfaction. World Applied Sciences Journal, Vol. 4, No. 2, 164-168

Mehdi Fasanghari & Farzad Habibipour Roudsari (2008b). Optimized ICT Project Selection Utilizing Fuzzy System. World Applied Sciences Journal, Vol. 4, No. 1, 44-49

Mehdi Fasanghari; Farzad Habibipour Roudsari & S. Kamal Chaharsooghi (2008). Assessing the Impact of Information Technology on Supply Chain Management. World Applied Sciences Journal, Vol. 4, No. 1, World Applied Sciences Journal

Reilly R.F. & Schweihs R.P. (1998). Valuing Intangible Assets, McGraw-Hill, New York

S. Mabuchi (1988). An approach to the comparison of fuzzy subsets with an α-cut dependent index. IEEE Transactions on Systems, Man, and Cybernetics SMC, Vol. 18, No. 2, 264–272

S.J. Chen & C.L. Hwang (1992). Fuzzy Multiple Attribute Decision Making: Methods and Application, Springer, New York

Sveiby (2003) Methods for Measuring Intellectual Assets.

Timothy J. Ross (2005). Fuzzy Logic With Engineering Applications, John Wiley & Sons

Zadeh L. A. (1965). Fuzzy sets. Information and Control, Vol. 8, 338-353

3

The Knowledge Management Strategic Alignment Model (KMSAM) and Its Impact on Performance: An Empirical Examination

Yue-Yang Chen[1] and Hui-Ling Huang[2]
I-Shou University
Chang Jung Christian University
Taiwan

1. Introduction

Recently, firms have started to realize the importance of the information technology (IT) for effective KM activities (Alavi & Leidner, 2001) or interorganizational learning facilitating (Scott, 2000). It is found that the high coalignment quality of KM and IT (i.e., their high-high fit) achieved high KM performance and satisfaction than those whose quality fitted low (Sher & Lee, 2004). More specifically, effective KM project alone can't lead to success without the support of IT (Kim, 2001; Sabherwal & Sabherwal, 2005); IT alone also can do nothing without good KM initiatives (Kim, 2001) in attaining KM success thus leads to organizational performance (Bhatt & Grover, 2005). Accordingly, the strategic alignment between KM and IT with other resources or strategies must be considered for business performance (Asoh, 2004). However, their high-high fit doesn't always yield positive organizational outcomes since enough exceptions are found to indicate that business strategy and knowledge strategy (e.g., Asoh, 2004), as well as human resource management strategy (e.g., Shih & Chiang, 2005) are interdependent.

It has been realized that research regarding the integrated investigation of various strategies is not sufficient. Furthermore, the analysis and design of the organization as a whole is critical to achieve efficient organizational benefits. In the practical terms, the basic alignment mechanism is "strategy", and it is though that a match between strategy and organization is the key driven to effectiveness at realizing intended strategies. Therefore, this study focused on three types of strategies discussed above that are critical to business in today's knowledge-based organizations, namely knowledge management (KM) strategy, information technology (IT) strategy, and human resource management (HRM) strategy. We posit that performance constructs including growth and profitability are affected by strategic alignment bilaterally among these strategies.

2. Theoretical background: Alternative perspectives of alignment (or fit)

The concept of alignment (or fit) is a key issue in structural contingency theory (Drazin & Van de Ven, 1985). Its commonly basic proposition is that "organizational performance is a consequence of fit between two or more factors; such as, the fit between organization environment, strategy, structure, system, style, and culture (Van de Ven & Drazin, 1985). In this study, the terminology of fit and its concept are analogical with the term of strategic alignment. According to (Venkatraman, 1990), fit has three approaches: selection, interaction, and systems approaches; whereas six different perspectives are proposed by Venkatraman (1989): matching, moderation, mediation, gestalts, covariation, and profile deviation. The six perspectives can be classified into two categories according to the number of variables being simultaneously examined. Accordingly, fit as matching, moderation, and mediation can be categorized into the reductionistic perspective, whereas fit as gestalts, covariation, and profile deviation can be regarded as holistic perspective (Venkatraman, 1990).

3. Research model and hypotheses

3.1 Strategic alignment between KM strategy and IT strategy (H1)

The other main purpose of the present research project is to develop a KM strategic alignment model (KMSAM) in the strategy-related MIS area. Consistent with the perspectives mentioned earlier, the emerging body of literature on KM depicts strategic alignment or congruence among properties of KM, units, relationships, and environment leading to better organizational performance and better KM and IT outcomes than those achieved when alignments are misfit. Additionally, the relative effectiveness of the type varies with context. In this vein, we describe the reductionistic-level (or bivariate-level) model briefly, so as to provide a rationale for the more detailed discussion about the underlying meanings of KM strategic alignment that follows.

The rapid progress of IT provides a good solution to answer the question: why does a KM project alone not always lead to enhanced business performance when firms overlook its links to other resources? That is, firms with excellent IT capabilities allow them to cope with the present competitive and dynamic environment well (Bhatt & Grover, 2005). Accordingly, strategic IT management has been regarded an enabler in business performance, when it fits with certain aspects of the KM context, helping companies to survive in the highly-competitive business environment (Alavi & Leidner, 2001).

IT also is regarded to be a critical enabler for KM (Alavi & Leidner, 2001). Choosing the right ITs for different KM strategies is critical for organizations (Kim, 2001). Using various IT solutions to comply with KM strategy will contribute to the creation of corporate knowledge directories, via knowledge mapping or the building of knowledge networks. Therefore, the relationship between KM strategy and IT strategy is highly relevant. Meanwhile, according to Asoh (2004), as an enabler for KM and IM/IS, IT strategy serves as the delivery-oriented component that must be aligned with KM strategy to improve organizational performance.

In the past, a few scholars have developed conceptual models that attempt to describe how organizations can match different technologies to their KM practices, in order to achieve firm value (Abou-Zeid, 2003; Sabherwal & Sabherwal, 2005). The basic notion of these models is that a proper fit and alignment between technology and KM in an organization will result in high performance. In the context of the KM development environment, higher KM capability requires a high quality of IT relatedness, which, in turn, depends upon how well their relationships have been modeled (Sher & Lee, 2004; Tanriverdi, 2005; Tippins & Sohi, 2003). That is, an organization's KM strategy should provide direction in determining how IT can support knowledge activities within the organization.

IT strategies can be classified into two general categories: IT environment scanning and strategic use of IT (Bergeron et al., 2004). System KM strategy requires IT tools that allow for explicit knowledge to be formalized and articulated in documents, and shared electronically through IT infrastructures such as intranets. In this manner, organizations should invest in an extensive IT system to codify knowledge. Therefore, a firm's IT strategy should focus on paying more attentions to strategic use of IT internally, in order to improve the quality and quantity of electronic repositories or databases.

In contrast, human KM strategy draws upon interpersonal relationships to exchange and share tacit knowledge across the organization. Thus, firms need a moderate investment in IT to connect experts in the organization. The technologies may include an e-mail system, on-line discussion networks, videoconferencing, and other collaborative tools (Scheepers et al., 2004). A firm's IT strategy, therefore, should aim at scanning the external IT environment, searching for communication tools and other interactive technologies to support person-to-person knowledge-sharing in organizations.

Accordingly, IT strategies vary depending upon KM strategies. Hence, the following hypotheses are proposed:

H1: The strategic alignment between KM strategy and IT strategy has a positive direct effect on business performance, as measured in growth and profitability

H1-1a: The strategic alignment between human KM strategies and IT strategies for IT environment scanning has a positive direct effect on business performance, as measured in growth.

H1-1b: The strategic alignment between human KM strategies and IT strategies for IT environment scanning has a positive direct effect on business performance, as measured in profitability.

H1-2a: The strategic alignment between human KM strategies and IT strategies for the strategic use of IT has a positive direct effect on business performance, as measured in growth.

H1-2b: The strategic alignment between human KM strategies and IT strategies for the strategic use of IT has a positive direct effect on business performance, as measured in profitability.

3.2 Strategic alignment between KM strategy and HRM strategy (H2)

Classifying KM strategies into centralized and de-centralized, which are analogous to the perspectives of 'people-to-document' and 'people-to-people' approaches, respectively, a case study of 4 international consulting firms with different models and KM strategies was conducted by Grolik et al. (2003). They asserted that with a centralized KM approach to training programs, the implementation of an incentive system for successful use of the knowledge repository was the important HR technique; whilst in a de-centralized KM strategy, a 'peer-group feedback' system for sharing implicit knowledge was the focus. The recruiting policies that such a strategy employ involve seeking out candidates who either

fall into a skill portfolio defined in terms of knowledge goals or have outstanding skills and experience in related domains. Furthermore, mentors or coaches and suitable rotation programs are ways to structure a de-centralized policy well. Again, it has been found that both of these KM strategies are considered to have high correlations with human resource flow, employee training, and reward systems. Additionally, according to Hansen et al. (1999), different KM strategies should reflect different drivers of their human resources. In the system KM strategy, adequate HR policies consist of hiring persons who are well suited to the reuse of knowledge and the implementation of solutions, training people in groups and through computer-based distance learning, and rewarding people for using and contributing to document databases. Additionally, with the human KM strategy, suitable HR policies are hiring persons who like problem-solving and can tolerate ambiguity, training people via one-on-one mentoring, and rewarding people for directly sharing knowledge with others. Therefore, both system and human KM strategies highlight the importance of recruitment and selection of employees (HR flow), training and development employment security, teams and job redesign control (work systems), and reward systems.
Furthermore, Shih and Chiang (2005) also assert that a satisfactory HRM strategy, that is the HR flow of hiring or promoting polities and training programs, the work systems of tasks and assignment, and reward systems of wage level and appraisal, should be compatible with KM strategy to optimize organizational performance. Therefore, we contend that a certain degree of alignment must exist between KM strategy and HRM strategy. Hence, the following hypotheses are proposed:

H2: The strategic alignment between KM strategy and HRM strategy has a positive direct effect on business performance, as measured in growth and profitability.

H2-1a: The strategic alignment between human KM strategies and HRM strategies for HR flow has a positive direct effect on business performance, as measured in growth

H2-1b: The strategic alignment between human KM strategies and HRM strategies for HR flow has a positive direct effect on business performance, as measured in profitability.

H2-2a: The strategic alignment between human KM strategies and HRM strategies for work systems has a positive direct effect on business performance, as measured in growth.

H2-2b: The strategic alignment between human KM strategies and HRM strategies for work systems has a positive direct effect on business performance, as measured in profitability.

H2-3a: The strategic alignment between human KM strategies and HRM strategies for reward systems has a positive direct effect on business performance, as measured in growth.

H2-3b: The strategic alignment between human KM strategies and HRM strategies for reward systems has a positive direct effect on business performance, as measured in profitability.

H2-4a: The strategic alignment between system KM strategies and HRM strategies for HR flow has a positive direct effect on business performance, as measured in growth.

H2-4b: The strategic alignment between system KM strategies and HRM strategies for HR flow has a positive direct effect on business performance, as measured in profitability.

H2-5a: The strategic alignment between system KM strategies and HRM strategies for work systems has a positive direct effect on business performance, as measured in growth.

H2-5b: The strategic alignment between system KM strategies and HRM strategies for work systems has a positive direct effect on business performance, as measured in profitability.

H2-6a: The strategic alignment between system KM strategies and HRM strategies for reward systems has a positive direct effect on business performance, as measured in growth.

H2-6b: The strategic alignment between system KM strategies and HRM strategies for reward systems has a positive direct effect on business performance, as measured in profitability.

Consequently, the reductionistic perspective of the strategic alignment model between KM strategy and IT strategy, and between KM strategy and HRM strategy is proposed and illustrated in Fig. 1. Because of their mutual reinforcement, and serving as the basis for business performance, we will conduct a bivariate analysis (Drazin & Van de Ven, 1985) to verify the specific dimensions of interest.

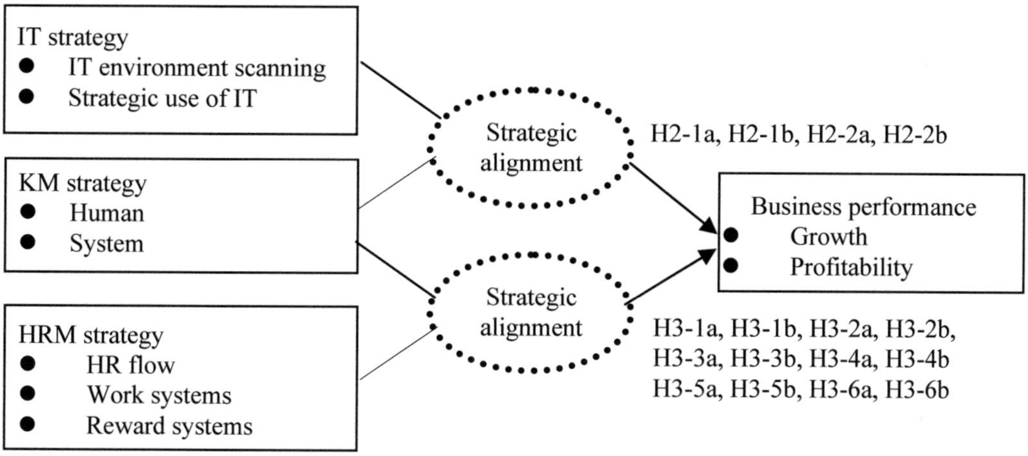

Fig. 1. A reductionistic perspective of strategic alignment

4. Research methodology

4.1 Sample characteristics

The characteristics of the sample are described as follows. The largest number of respondents is from the manufacturing industry, representing 57.1% of the responding companies. Most of companies have 100 to 499 employees (37.9%). Approximately 60.2% of the respondents have experiences more then 6 years.

4.2 Hypotheses testing

The actually patterns of the alignment were been assessed by matching approach. It is used to specify the various functional forms between any two related variables. As Venkatraman (1989) stated, the most common technique used when adopting the matching perspective is the deviation score model (Hoffman et al., 1992), which has been used with great success by

many researchers (e.g., David et al., 1989; Lai, 1999). We employed a deviation scores approach as our fit assessment method. Meanwhile, according to Venkatraman (1989), the underlying premise of deviation score analysis is that the "absolute difference between the standardized scores of two variables indicates a lack of fit" (p. 431). In this vein, fit or lack of fit is presented by one independent variable being subtracted from another.
To operate this method, in practice, the deviation score is entered into regression equations and the performance implications of fit are tested by examining the impact that this difference score variable has on performance. The regression equation would be written as follows:

$$Y = \alpha_0 + \alpha_1 X + \alpha_2 Z + \alpha_3(|X - Z|) + e \quad (1)$$

If the coefficient α_3 is statistically significant, then the hypothesis, regarding the performance effects of fit, is supported (Venkatraman, 1989).
To minimize bias in the scaling of questionnaire items, the item scores first were standardized using Z scores prior to computation of the difference scores. SPSS was used to run linear hierarchical regression analyses. Therefore, the hierarchical procedure required that the independent variables were entered into the regression model in a specific order. In our study, the performance factor initially was regressed on KM strategy. Next, the two IT strategy variables were added to access their incremental contribution to the performance factor. Third, the two HRM strategy variables were entered into the equation. Finally, the KM-IT and KM-HRM strategic alignment (fit) variables were added to the previous regression equation, to test firm performance.
The results of hierarchical regression analyses are presented in Table 1. The importance of a given independent variable as a predictor of performance is indicated by a ΔR^2 symbol, representing the increment in unique variance it explains. Model 1 contains all variables, including fit variables, in the equation; this model demonstrates that system-HR flow fit (β = -.33, $p < .01$), system-work systems fit (β = -.19, $p < .1$), system-reward systems fit (β = -.27, $p < .01$), human-reward systems fit (β = -.23, $p < .05$), system-strategic use of IT fit (β = -.20, $p < .05$), and human-IT environment fit (β = -.17, $p < .05$) all are significant determinants (adjusted R2 = 0.34, F-value = 5.85, $p < .001$) of business growth. Furthermore, the value of ΔR^2 (= 0.11) in step 4 of Model 1 is higher than that of step 3 (ΔR^2 = 0.08), demonstrating higher explanatory power of variances of the various fit variables on growth.
In step 4 of Model 2, system-HR flow fit (β = -.20, $p < .1$), system-work systems fit (β = -.18, $p < .1$), and system-strategic use of IT fit (β = -.18, $p < .05$) were found to have significant impacts on profitability (adjusted R^2 = 0.34, F-value = 5.93, $p < .001$). Furthermore, the value of ΔR^2 (= 0.10) in step 4 of Model 1 is larger than that of step 3 (ΔR^2 = 0.08), demonstrating more explanatory power of the variances of the various fit variables on profitability.

5. Discussion and conclusions

In summary, the reductionistic perspective, using the approach of fit as matching, definitely recognizes the bivariate patterns of impact upon business performance. The results show that the firms which are good at aligning IT strategy and HRM strategy with KM strategy demonstrating a high performance level. Observing their relationships in more detail, some of the fit patterns show a significant direct effect on growth or profitability. Hence, firms must employ the right IT and HRM practices with the right KM strategies. In other words, successful firms that use a system-oriented (codification) KM strategy utilize extensive selection and training procedures and have relatively high job security in their HR flow practices; compensation and promotion decisions tend to be tightly connected to employees' work performance; these companies generally use broadly defined jobs with enriched design; they utilize team-based work organization; and they usually rotate jobs among employees to familiarize them with their colleagues' work. All this is done to ensure that the reused codified knowledge can store abundant expertise derived from different employees. Furthermore, firms that use system-oriented (codification) KM strategies focus their IT strategies on strategic use of IT, meaning that they not only collect operational knowledge to connect people with reusable codified knowledge, they also focus on generating large overall revenues.

	Dependent variable: Business performance							
	Growth (Model 1)				Profitability (Model 2)			
Independent variables	Step 1	Step 2	Step 3	Step 4	Step 1	Step 2	Step 3	Step 4
KM strategy								
System	0.17+	0.11	0.06	-0.02	0.20*	0.16	0.10	0.04
Human	0.33***	0.28**	0.17+	0.25*	0.31***	0.28**	0.14	0.21*
IT strategy								
IT env. scan.		-0.01	-0.04	-0.11		-0.08	-0.13	-0.18
Str. use of IT		0.14	0.11	0.08		0.18	0.15	0.13
HRM strategy								
HR Flow			0.32**	0.26			0.40***	0.36***
Work systems			0.02	0.08			0.02	0.06
Reward systems			0.03	0.15			0.02	0.11
Strategic alignment								
S-HR fit				-0.33**				-0.20+
S-work fit				-0.19+				-0.18+
S-reward fit				-0.27**				-0.12
H-HR fit				-0.13				-0.13
H-work fit				-0.12				-0.03
H-reward fit				-0.23*				-0.15
S-ITE fit				0.05				0.07
S-SU IT fit				-0.20*				-0.18*
H-ITE fit				-0.17*				-0.12
H-SUIT fit				-0.03				-0.04
R^2	0.21	0.22	0.30	0.41	0.21	0.23	0.31	0.41
ΔR^2		0.01	0.08	0.11		0.02	0.08	0.10
F	20.76***	10.88***	9.57***	5.85***	21.53***	11.46***	12.07***	5.93***
ΔF		0.99	6.34***	2.56**		1.30	9.19***	2.41**
Adjusted R^2	0.20	0.20	0.27	0.34	0.20	0.21	0.32	0.34
D.W.				2.14				2.05
C.I.				11.84				11.84

Notes: 1. Standardized regression coefficients are shown. + p<.1; *p<.05; **p<.01; ***p<.001

2. S-HR fit: System-HR flow fit; S-work fit: System-work systems fit; S-reward fit: System-reward systems fit; H-HR fit: Human-HR flow fit; H-work fit: Human-work systems fit; H-reward fit: Human-reward systems fit; S-ITE fit: System-IT environment scanning fit; S-SUIT fit: System-strategic use of IT fit; H-ITE fit: Human-IT environment scanning fit; H-SUIT fit: Human-strategic use of IT fit

Table 1. Results of hierarchical regression analysis (n=161)

On the other hand, firms that use human-oriented (personalization) KM strategies must have reward systems that encourage workers to share knowledge directly with others; instead of providing intensive training within the company, employees are encouraged to develop social networks, so that tacit knowledge can be shared. Such companies focus on 'maintaining' not 'creating' high profit margins, and on external IT environment scanning, supporting the latest technologies, so as to facilitate person-to-person conversations and knowledge exchange.

Contrary to our expectation, neither human-HR flow fit nor human-work systems fit have found to have a significant impact on performance in terms of both growth and profitability. That is, when human KM strategy is adopted, only the strategic alignment between human KM strategy and reward systems of HRM strategy is found to have a significant impact on business performance in terms of growth. One possible explanation may be that the strategy a firm used on knowledge sharing in human KM strategy is mainly by members' face-to-face conversation in private. The informal dialogues between organizational members are just encouraged through appraisal and compensation systems related to tacit knowledge sharing, accumulation, and creation. No matter how much training about the jobs a firm offered to their employees, or how often the employees rotated to another jobs, the person-to-person social network for linking people to facilitate conversations and exchange of knowledge would never be diminished.

6. References

Abou-Zeid, E. (2003). Developing business alignment knowledge management strategy, In: *Knowledge Management: Current Issues and Challenges*, Coakes, E., (Ed.), 157-173, Idea Publishing Group, Hershey.

Alavi, M. & Leidner, D.E. (2001). Review: knowledge management and knowledge management systems: conceptual foundations and research issues. *MIS Quarterly*, Vol. 25, No. 1, 107-136.

Asoh, D.A. (2004). *Business and Knowledge Strategies: Alignment and Performance Impact Analysis*, Ph.D. thesis, University at Albany State University of New York.

Bentler, P.M. & Bonett, D.G. (1980). Significance tests and goodness of fit in the analysis of covariance structures. *Psychology Bulletin*, Vol. 88, 588-606.

Bhatt, G.D. & Grover, V. (2005). Types of information technology capabilities and their role in competitive advantage: an empirical study. *Journal of Management Information Systems*, Vol. 22, No. 2, 253-277.

Bierly, P.E. & Daly, P. (2002). Alignment human resource management practices and knowledge strategies: a theoretical framework, In: *The Strategic Management of Intellectual Capital and Organizational Knowledge*, Choo, C.W. and Bontis, N., (Ed.), 268-276, Oxford University Press, Oxford.

Cabrera, E.F. & Bonache, J. (1999). An expert HR system for aligning organizational culture and strategy. *Human Resource Planning*, Vol. 22, No. 1, 51-60.

David, F.R.; Pearce, J.A. & Randolph, W.A. (1989). Linking technology and structure to enhance group performance. *Journal of Applied Psychology*, Vol. 74, No. 2, 233-241.

Delery, J. & Doty, D.H. (1996). Modes of theorizing in strategic human resource management: tests of universalistic, contingency, and configurational performance predictors. *Academy of Management Journal*, Vol. 39, No. 4, 802-835.

Drazin, R. & Van de Ven, A.H. (1985). Alternative forms of fit in contingency theory. *Administrative Science Quarterly*, Vol. 30, No. 4, 514-539.

Grolik, S.; Lehner, D. & Frigerio, C. (2003). Analysis of interrelations between business models and knowledge management strategies in consulting firms, *Proceedings of the 11th European Conference on Information Systems*, Naples, Italy, June 2003.

Guest, D.E. (1997). Human resource management and performance: a review and research agenda. *The International of Human Resource Management*, Vol. 8, No. 3, 263-276.

Hoffman, J.J.; Cullen, J.B.; Carter, N.M. & Hofacker, C.F. (1992). Alternative methods for measuring organization fit: technology, structure, and performance. *Journal of Management*, Vol. 18, No. 1, 45-57.

Kankanhalli, A.; Tanudidjaja, F.; Sutanto, J. & Tan, B.C.Y. (2003). The role of IT in successful knowledge management initiatives. *Communications of the ACM*, Vol. 46, No. 9, 69-73.

Kim, S.K. (2001). An empirical study of the relationship between knowledge management and information technology infrastructure capability in the management consulting industry. Ph.D. thesis, University of Nebraska.

Lai, V.S. (1999). A contingency examination of CASE-task fit on software developer's performance. *European Journal of Information Systems*, Vol. 8, No. 1, 27-39.

March, J.G. (1991). Exploration and exploitation in organizational learning. *Organization Science*, Vol. 2, No. 1, 71-87.

Marsh, H.W. & Hocever, D. (1985). The application of confirmatory factor analysis to the study of self-concept: first-and higher-order factor models and their invariance across groups. Psychological Bulletin, Vol. 97, 562-582.

Sabherwal, R. & Sabherwal, S. (2005). Knowledge management using information technology: determinants of short-term impact on firm value. *Decision Science*, Vol. 36, No. 4, 531-567.

Scott, J.E. (2000). Facilitating international learning with information technology. *Journal of Management Information Systems*, Vol. 17, No. 2, 81-113.

Sher, P.J. & Lee, V.C. (2004). Information technology as a facilitator for enhancing dynamic capabilities through knowledge management. *Information & Management*, Vol. 41, No. 8, 933-945.

Shih, H.A. & Chiang, Y.H. (2005). Strategy alignment between HRM, KM and corporate development. *International Journal of Manpower*, Vol. 26, No. 6, 582-602.

Van de Ven, A.H. & Drazin, R. (1985). The concept of fFit in contingency theory. *Research in Organizational Behavior*, Vol. 7, 333-365.

Venkatraman, N. (1989). The concept of fit in strategy research: toward verbal and statistical correspondence. *The Academy of Management Review*, Vol. 14, No. 3, 423-444.

Venkatraman, N. (1990). Performance implications of strategic coalignment: a methodological perspective. *Journal of Management Studies*, Vol. 27, No. 1, 19-41.

Venkatraman, N. & Prescott, J.E. (1990). Environment-strategy coalignment: an empirical test of its performance implications. *Strategic Management Journal*, Vol. 11, No. 1, 1-23.

Tanriverdi, H. (2005). Information technology relatedness, knowledge management capability, and performance of multibusiness firms. *MIS Quarterly*, Vol. 29, No. 2, 311-334.

Tippins, M.J. & Sohi, R.S. (2003). IT competency and firm performance: is organizational learning a missing link? *Strategic Management Journal*, Vol. 24, No. 8, 745-761.

Bergeron, F.; Raymond, L. & Rivard, S. (2004). Ideal patterns of strategic alignment and business performance. *Information & Management*, Vol. 41, No. 8, 1003-1020.

Scheepers, R.; Venkitachalam, K. & Gibbs, M.R. (2004). Knowledge strategy in organizations: refining the model of Hansen, Nohria and Tierney. *Journal of Strategic Information Systems*, Vol. 13, No. 3, 201-222.

Hansen, M.T.; Nohria, N. & Tierney, T. (1999). What's your strategy for managing knowledge? *Harvard Business Review*, Vol. 77, No. 2, 106-116.

This study is funded by the Taiwan National Science Council under project number NSC97-2410-H-366-006

4

The Intelligent Manufacturing Paradigm in Knowledge Society

Ioan Dumitrache and Simona Iuliana Caramihai
POLITEHNICA University of Bucharest
Romania

1. Introduction

The today society has to face great challenges due, ironically, to its own development capacity and speed, that resulted in phenomena like globalization and competition, in a more and more rapidly changing environment.

The development of Information & Communication Technologies (ICT), which was intent to solve usual problems, became actually a driver for the increased complexity of socio-economical advance.

In this context, especially in manufacturing, the role of human resources was, for the last century, ambiguous, with balances between the trends that relied mostly on technology and those that trusted human superiority.

Actually, it is the role of knowledge management, as a relatively new discipline, to find a way by which humans and technology could optimally collaborate, towards the benefits and satisfaction of whole society.

This work intends to propose some functioning principles for knowledge management architectures, where human and software agents could coexist and share knowledge, in order to solve new problems.

The authors have taken into account researches in the fields of manufacturing system, as well as from the area of knowledge management, control systems, organizational research and complexity analysis, in order to develop a model for the imbricate development of manufacturing and knowledge.

The first part presents the evolution of manufacturing paradigm, underlining the parallel development of ICT and knowledge management.

The second one focuses on the paradigm of Intelligent Manufacturing and presents some of the developed control approaches based on complexity theory and multi-agent systems.

The following part presents some developments in the field of the knowledge management and the last ones introduce the authors view on the subject.

Finally, some future trends towards a knowledge society where humans and software agents will symbiotically work through their mutual progress and satisfaction are suggested.

2. Historical evolution of manufacturing and knowledge management concepts

From very long time ago people knew that information means power and that good decisions critically depend on the quality and quantity of analysed data, as well as on a good reasoning capacity.
Wisdom and intelligence were always considered to be necessary qualities for success, even if not always sufficient, and procedures to acquire them were studied since the beginning of human civilisation. ("*By three methods we may learn wisdom: First, by reflection, which is noblest; second, by imitation, which is easiest; and third, by experience, which is the bitterest*"- Confucius)
There were identified subtle differences, between information and knowledge ("*Information is not knowledge*" - Albert Einstein) for instance, or between erudition and wisdom. Links between learning and reasoning capacity ("*Learning without thought is labour lost; thought without learning is perilous*"- Confucius), the genesis of new ideas and the triggering events for great inventions, the good balance between expertise and innovation - were and still are goals of study for educators, philosophers, scientists and even managers.
But the real need of a formal approach and understanding was triggered by the technological qualitative bound and its implications.
After the Second World War, tremendous changes arrived both in the industry and society (Figure 1). The computer era was at its beginning and, together with its implication in industry, human resources management took also a new shift.

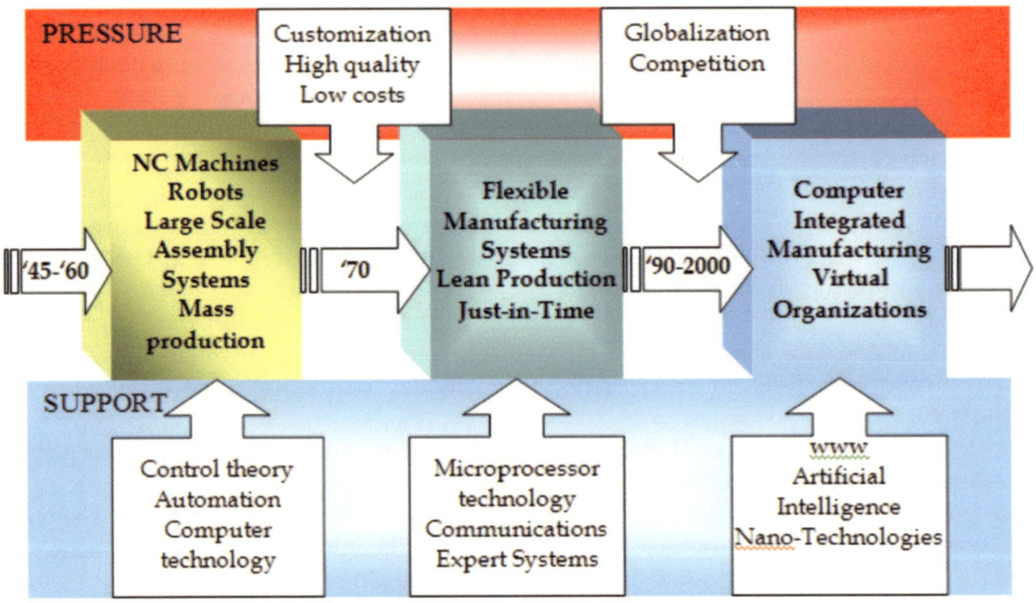

Fig. 1. Evolution of manufacturing paradigms

Indeed, the era of control and automation can be dated from the middle of the XX century, as some of the most important connected events in science and engineering occurred between years '45 and '60 (Mehrabi et al., 2000): first electronic computer in 1946, invention of transistor in 1946-47, integrated circuits and the first electronic digital computer, as well as first applications of automatic control in industry in 1949-50; development of numerical control (NC) and NC languages, invention of machining center and first industrial robot between 1950-60. Especially after 1956, an important role in leading the research in the field of control was played by the International Federation of Automation and Control.

New management challenges were also brought by the increased market demands for products, that resulted into a rapid development of new enterprises and, subsequently, into an increased competition for customers and profit. Large scale assembly systems and mass production shop floors expanded and improved until it became obvious that a new manufacturing approach was necessary.

With customers realizing to be real drivers of the industrial development, the quality of products and the high productivity, though extremely important goals for manufacturing enterprises, were no more sufficient: in order to attract new customers and to keep the old ones, diversity of products as well as the capacity to bring new desirable products on the market became key factors in an enterprise success.

This evolution resulted not only in supplementary attention for technologies and automation, but also into new managerial concepts with regard to human resources and to knowledge assets, and also into an increased complexity of the manufacturing enterprise as a system, demanding new concepts and theories for control and performance evaluation.

The first shift of manufacturing paradigm (fig.1) was brought by new control concepts: Numerical Control Machines, Industrial Robots, and, later on, whole Automated Manufacturing Systems, have operated the change from mass production to customization and, more than affecting the customer position in the product life-cycle, required new views of human resources management (Seppala et al., 1992; Adler, 1995). As manufacturing is an activity where the importance of the quality of man and machines is overwhelmed only by the importance of their interaction, it is interesting to note that automation imposed two contrasting views on human resources: the first one consider humans as the source of errors and relies on machines and extensive automation, and the second regards people as a source of fast error recovery.

Nevertheless, as repetitive tasks were more and more assigned to machines, though increasing the speed and the reliability of the production, human resource became more creative at the design level and more skilled in order to operate at the shop floor level, as a result of training and instruction, and thus becoming a valuable asset for the enterprise. Moreover, with the increasing importance of computer-aided techniques, high qualified personnel needed complementary training in computer use.

The need of a change was underlined also by the oil crisis (1973) which continued with a major depression in USA machine tool industry and the recession of automotive industry. At that moment, the Japanese manufacturing enterprises, which have emphasized the importance of human resource and of discipline of production, based on an accurate definition of design and manufacturing processes, proved their superiority on the international market by achieving high-quality products at low costs.

In years '70 the paradigm of "Flexible Manufacturing System" was defined, as a machining system configuration with fixed hardware and programmable software, capable to handle changes in work orders, production schedules, machining programs and tooling, so as to cost-effective manufacture several types of parts, with shortened changeover time, on the same system, at required (and variable) volume and given quality. The capability of storing and retrieving information and data proved to be one of the key factors for the efficiency of

those new (and expensive) systems. As a consequence, the development of new disciplines as computer-aided document management and database management was highly stimulated. First difficulties arisen in the transfer of information between software applications, as CAD and CAM, that had different approaches to integrate the same data.
On the other hand, another of the key factors of enterprise success became the capacity to shorten the duration of product life cycle, especially in the design and manufacturing phases. One of the approaches used for accomplishing this goal was found to be the detailed enterprise process decomposition and specification allowing re-use, analysis and optimisation and anticipating the concurrent engineering paradigm.
This new paradigm can be considered as a pioneer for the evolutionary approaches in intelligent information systems with direct applications in manufacturing.
From the manufacturing point of view, terms and procedures should be more precisely defined, in order to allow the different kinds of flexibilities, as they were defined by (Browne, 1984) and (Sethi and Sethi, 1990)

- **Machine flexibility** - The different operation types that a machine can perform.
- **Material handling flexibility** - The ability to move the products within a manufacturing facility.
- **Operation flexibility** - The ability to produce a product in different ways
- **Process flexibility** - The set of parts that the system can produce.
- **Product flexibility** - The ability to add new products in the system.
- **Routing flexibility** - The different routes (through machines and workshops) that can be used to produce a product in the system.
- **Volume flexibility** - The ease to profitably increase or decrease the output of an existing system.
- **Expansion flexibility** - The ability to build out the capacity of a system.
- **Program flexibility** - The ability to run a system automatically.
- **Production flexibility** - The number of products a system currently can produce.
- **Market flexibility** - The ability of the system to adapt to market demands.

From the informational point of view, two main trends can be identified: One, which takes into account storing and retrieving data and information, as well as more complex structures as NC programmes, part design documents, software libraries a.s.o. Its aim is to allow cost reduction by reusability of problem solutions and to shorten product life cycle by using computer aided activities and automatically exchanging product details between different software applications. In time, this trend resulted in developing disciplines as document management, database design and management etc. that can be considered a precursor of first generation knowledge management.
Some drawbacks already appeared: even if the number of information technologies (IT) providers were still reduced comparatively with today, difficulties arise when data and information had to be shared by different applications or transferred on other platforms. Investing in IT was proved not to be sufficient for increasing manufacturing efficiency over a certain limit, exactly because of these information portability problems. Having the right information at the right place and at the right time seemed to be less obvious, despite (or even because of) increasingly extensive databases.
Even today there are no generally acknowledged definitions for data and information, but the extensive development of computer aided manufacturing was one of the first occasions to discriminate between content directly observable or verifiable, that can be used as it is –

data - and analyzed and interpreted content, that can be differently understood by different users - information - even if they work in the same context.
The accumulation of those drawbacks, combined with the increasing tendency of customization (resulting, for enterprises, in the need of extended flexibility) started a sort of spiral: more flexibility required more automation and more computer-aided activities (design, planning, manufacturing etc.), more computers, NC equipments and software application thus requiring more data & information sharing and transfer, meaning more interfacing between applications and eventually hardware, and consequently more specialized people - all those things implying elevated capital and time. On the other hand, due to the socio-economical continuous progress, more and more producers entered the market, competing for customers by highly customized products, lower process and shorter delivery times. In other words, the diversification and complexity of manufacturing production resulted in the complexity of manufacturing enterprises as production systems.
The other trend was re-considering the importance of human resources. Not only new kinds of specialists entered the labour market - software specialists whose contribution to product cost reduction and quality increase was indirect and which were rather expensive, but high level specialists from different other areas needed training in computer use for being more efficient. However, even with those added costs, it became obvious that expert human resource was an extremely valuable asset for the enterprise, especially in the manufacturing area, where innovation capacities, as well as the possibility to rapidly solve new problems with existent means were crucial. One problem was that such experts were rare and expensive. Their expertise was augmented by their experience into a company, by what is now called organisational knowledge and this raised a second and more important problem: when an expert changed the company, one brought in the new working place some of the knowledge from the old one.
This is the reason for this second trend developed in expert systems theory and knowledge engineering, cores of second generation knowledge management.
The concepts of expert systems were developed at Stanford University since 1965, when the team of Professor Feigenbaum, Buchanan, Lederberg et .all realised Dendral. Dendral was a chemical expert system, basically using "if-then" rules, but also capable to use rules of thumb employed by human experts. It was followed by MYCIN, in 1970, developed by Edward H. Shortliffe, a physician and computer scientist at Stanford Medical School, in order to provide decision support in diagnosing a certain class of brain infections, where timing was critical.
Two problems have to be solved in order to build expert systems: creating the program structure capable to operate with knowledge in a given field and then building the knowledge base to operate with. This last phase, called "knowledge acquisition" raised many problems, as for many specialists were difficult to explain their decisions in a language understandable by software designers. It was the task of the knowledge engineer to extract expert knowledge and to codify it appropriately. Moreover, it was proven that something exists beyond data and information - knowledge - and that is the most valuable part that a human specialist can provide.
Expert systems started to be used despite the difficulties that arise in their realization and despite the fact that an "expert on a diskette" (Hayes-Roth et al, 1983) was not always a match for a human top-expert: but they were extremely fast, not so costly and could not leave the company and give to competitors its inner knowledge. Moreover, learning expert

systems could improve their performances by completing their knowledge bases and appropriately designed user-interface allowed them to be used for training human experts.

Even if expert systems and their pairs, decision support systems are now considered more to be results of artificial intelligence, techniques used in extracting and codifying knowledge are important parts in knowledge management policies.

As Feigenbaum pointed in (Feigenabum, 1989) it was a concept that complemented traditional use of knowledge, extracted from library resources as books and journals, waiting as "passive objects" to be found, interpreted and then used, by new kind of books that are ready to interact and collaborate with users.

Both trends had to converge finally in order to overcome the expanding spiral of technological drawbacks underlined by the first trend and to adapt management techniques to the ever increasing value of human resources, emphasized by the second one. (Savage, 1990)

And, effectively, consortiums of hardware and software suppliers, important manufacturers interested in flexibility, research institutes and universities, such, for instance AMICE, managed new shift in manufacturing paradigms - shift concretised especially in the concept and support of Computer Integrated Manufacturing (CIM) - Open System Architecture (OSA) (CIM-OSA, 1993)

CIM-OSA defines a model-based enterprise engineering method which categorizes manufacturing operations into Generic and Specific (Partial and Particular) functions. These may then be combined to create a model which can be used for process simulation and analysis. The same model can also be used on line in the manufacturing enterprise for scheduling, dispatching, monitoring and providing process information.

An important aspect of the CIM-OSA project is its direct involvement in standardization activities. The two of its main results are the Modeling Framework, and the Integrating Infrastructure.

The Modeling Framework supports all phases of the CIM system life-cycle from requirements definition, through design specification, implementation description and execution of the daily enterprise operation.

The Integrating Infrastructure provides specific information technology services for the execution of the Particular Implementation Model, but what is more important, it provides for vendor independence and portability.

Concerning knowledge management, the integrationist paradigm in manufacturing was equivalent with the ability to provide the right information, in the right place, at the right time and thus resulted in defining the knowledge bases of the enterprise. Moreover, all drawbacks regarding the transfer of data/ information between different software applications/ platforms in the same enterprise were solved by a proper design of the Integrating Infrastructure and by the existence of standards.

It still remains to be solved the problem of sharing information between different companies and the transfer of knowledge (Chen & Vernadat, 2002).

3. Intelligent Manufacturing Systems: concepts and organization

The last decade has faced an impressive rate of development of manufacturing organizations, mainly due to two driving forces in today's economic:

- *Globalization,* that has brought both a vast pool of resources, untapped skills, knowledge and abilities throughout the world and important clusters of customers in various parts of the world
- *Rapidly changing environment* which converges towards a demand-driven economy

Considering these factors, successful survival in the fast pace, global environment requires that an organization should at least be able to:

- Discover and integrate global resources as well as to identify and respond to consumer demand anywhere in the world.
- Increase its overall dynamics in order to achieve the competitive advantage of the fastest time to market - high dynamics of the upper management in order to rapidly develop effective short term strategies and planning and even higher dynamics for the operational levels
- Dynamically reconfigure to adapt and respond to the changing environment, which implies a flexible network of independent entities linked by information technology to effectively share skills, knowledge and access to others' expertise

The CIM-OSA approach and the paradigms derived from the integrationist theory in manufacturing insisted on very precise and detailed organization of the enterprise as a key factor of success.

However, research exploring the influence of organizational structure on the enterprise performance in dynamic environments, already indicated (Burns and Stalker, 1961; Henderson and Clark, 1990; Uzzi, 1997) that there is a fundamental tension between possessing too much and too little structure.

As a general result, organizations that have too little structure do not possess the capability of generating appropriate behaviours (Weick, 1993), though lacking efficiency, as those using too much structure are deficient in flexibility (Miller and Friesen, 1980; Siggelkow, 2001).

Real-life market development and manufacturing systems performances have confirmed this dilemma for organizations competing in dynamic environments, as their sucess required both efficiency and flexibility.

New manufacturing paradigm arised, from Concurrent Engineering and Virtual Organizations to Intelligent Manufacturing Systems, and networked enterprises, each of them trying to make use of collaborative autonomous structures, simple enough to be versatile, but connected by ellaborated protocols of communications, ready to ensure efficient behavior.

To manage these new kinds of complex systems, a new approach has to be developed, integrating Computer and Communications in order to reinforce the analysis power of Control theory. This can be viewed as the C3 paradigm of control, for collaborative networks. (Dumitrache 2008)

A Virtual Organization (VO) is, according to a widely accepted definition: "a flexible network of independent entities linked by information technology to share skills, knowledge and access to others' expertise in non-traditional ways". A VO can also be characterized as a form of cooperation involving companies, institutions and/or individuals delivering a product or service on the basis of a common business understanding. The units participate in the collaboration and present themselves as a unified organization. (Camarinha-Matos & Afsarmanesh, 2005).

In the framework of increasing effectiveness and quality of service in a global e-economy, networked, collaborative manufacturing paradigm includes: design, programming, operation and diagnosis of automation behaviour in distributed environments, system integration models, configuration and parameterization for communication connected devices, heterogeneous networks for automation-based quality of services, life-cycle aspects for distributed automation systems and remote maintenance. (Thoben et al, 2008)
The enterprise itself is regarded as a network integrating advanced technologies, computers, communication systems, control strategies as well as cognitive agents (both humans and/or advanced intelligent systems) able not only to manage processes and products, but also to generate new behaviours for adapting themselves to a dynamic market. The study of the emergent behaviour of those cognitive agents imposes new theories, as the theory of complexity.
Collaborative networked organizations (CNO) represent a new dynamic world, based on cooperation, competitiveness, world-excellence and agility. They are complex production structures - scaling from machine tools, robots, conveyors, etc., to knowledge networks, including humans - and should normally be designed as hives of autonomous but cooperative/ collaborative entities.
The problem is, one cannot design such a structure, provided they are highly dynamical and result from changing market necessities that can bring former "business foes" to become associates on vice-versa. In order for an enterprise to be a sound candidate for a CNO, it has to solve at least the following aspects of its functioning:

- Increased autonomous behaviour and self-X ability (self-recovery, self-configuration, self-organization, self-protection etc.),
- Increased abstraction level, from signals to data, to information, to knowledge, to decision or even wisdom;
- Integrated solutions for manufacturing execution systems, logistics execution systems a.s.o.
- Coherent representation of interrelations between data-information-knowledge

This is the reason for the great focus on problems like enterprise interoperability and especially a new kind of knowledge management, allowing to structures virtually different to coherently exchange true knowledge. Intelligent Manufacturing Systems (IMS) is a paradigm that reflects the concern for those problems.
The above mentioned C3 paradigm of control has shifted, for this new class of systems, to a C4 one, integrating Computers, Communications and Cognition and resulted in the emphasis of the great importance of knowledge in attaining intelligent behaviour. (Dumitrache 2008)
However, the nature and the basic characteristics of "intelligence" are still subject for endless debates and there is no widely recognized ontology of the field. Usually, it is associated with some abilities, as problem solving, communication and learning capabilities.
In fact, adaptation is probably one of the first identified phenomenons linked to intelligence and it can be viewed as a sort of common factor in different approaches of intelligence definitions. The adjustment of behavioral patterns is one of the clearest acts of adaptation. This correction is the result of applying different methodologies, concepts, approaches, logical schemes, etc. that finally represent the ability of reasoning and logical deduction. On a higher level of adaptation, intelligence requests also the capacity of dynamical self-

organization of communities of agents into common goal-oriented groups, in answer to new problems.

At the level of abstract systems, adaptation can be viewed as following: a system that adapts well can minimize perturbations in its interaction with the environment and behaves successfully. As a simple case study, this adaptation can be done by a system that reacts to external stimuli by appropriately enacting different predefined processes. If the system has not a sufficient capacity of discerning between external events or it has no appropriate process to trigger as a response to a given stimulus, it is unable to adapt anymore. This is the reason for the learning capacity is one of the most important factors for adaptation and thus for intelligence. There is a wide set of applications that involve system adaptation, such as communication systems, banking, energy management, transportation, manufacturing, a.s.o. Besides the necessity to have an adaptive behavior, all those systems have in common, in different degrees, other similarities, like the high dynamics, multiple solutions to a given problem, high heterogeneity.

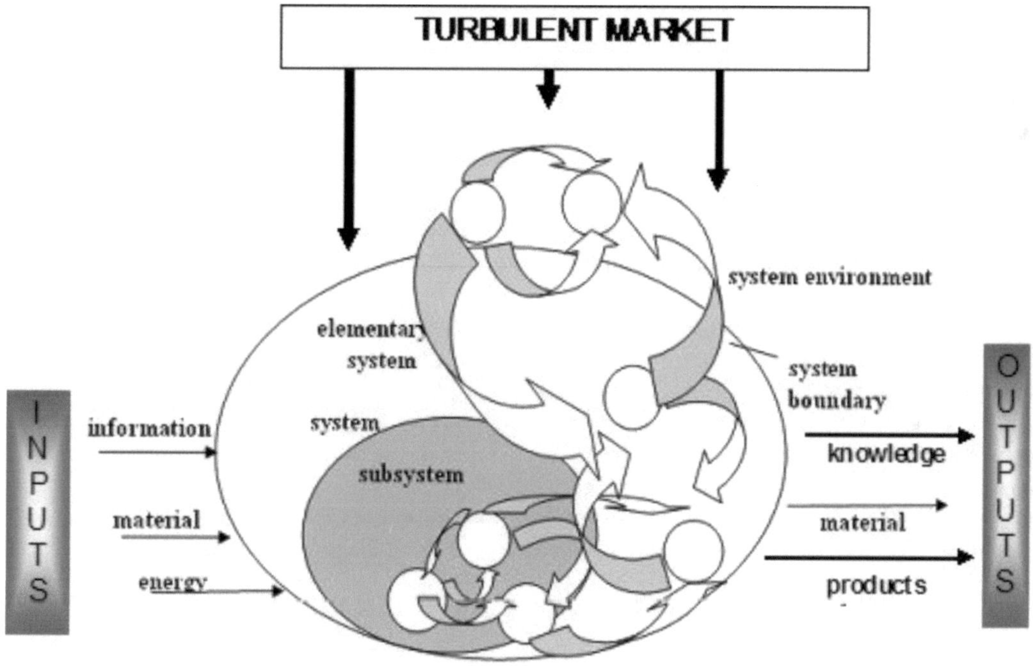

Fig. 2. A systemic view of enterprise

Intelligent Manufacturing Systems (IMS) can be viewed as large pools of human and software agents, with different levels of expertise and different local goals, which have to act together, in variable configurations of temporary communities in order to react to dynamically changing inputs (Figure 2.) and to accomplish dynamically changing objectives.

As systems acting in unpredictable and turbulent environments, IMS have to solve problems as:

Integrated production planning and scheduling (mathematical models and combinations of operation research, estimation of solution appropriateness, parametric scalable modules for

production optimisation, integration of intelligent technologies as hybrid intelligent systems)
Real-time production control (recognition situations and related problem solving, decision support, reactive and proactive rescheduling algorithms and production control support systems).
Management of distributed, cooperative systems (multi-agent systems in hierarchical and heterarchical architecture, models for describing production networks, behaviour networks analysis and negotiation mechanisms and communication protocols for efficient behavioural patterns involving inter-related spatial and temporal effects)
Manufacturing enterprise intelligence should then encompass features as:
Adaptivity - as a primary intelligence level, implying the capacity of acting on rules "if-then-else"
Reasoning - as a higher level that includes preparation of new possible scenarios and strategies "what if..."
Knowledge representation and processing (including focusing, feature identification and organization in connectionist structures)
Considering the problematic and the structure of Intelligent Manufacturing it became obvious that it corresponds to at least some definitions of Complex Adaptive Systems:
Definition 1: A **CAS** is a complex system that includes ***reactive*** units, i.e., units capable of exhibiting systematically different attributes in reaction to changed environmental conditions.
Definition 2: A **CAS** is a complex system that includes ***goal-directed*** units, i.e., units that are reactive and that direct at least some of their reactions towards the achievement of built-in (or evolved) goals.
Definition 3: A **CAS** is a complex system that includes ***planner*** units, i.e., units that are goal-directed and that attempt to exert some degree of control over their environment to facilitate achievement of these goals.
The balance between control and emergence is a real challenge for designing CAS involving non-linear phenomena, incomplete data and knowledge - a combinatorial explosion of states, dynamic changes in environment.
It is easy to discern that there is a strong similitude between CAS characteristics underlined in the above definitions and the main features of intelligent agents, as they are widely recognized (Wooldridge & Jennings, 1995) :

- *reactivity*: agents should be able to perceive their environment and respond timely and accordingly to external events, in order to satisfy their *design objectives*
- *pro-activeness*: agents should be able to exhibit goal-directed behaviour by *taking the initiative*
- *social ability*: intelligent agents should be capable of interacting with other agents in order to exchange information and knowledge susceptible to support the accomplishment of their objectives

Consequently, it is only natural the fact that control approaches for CAS are mainly based on multi-agent structures (MAS) and theory.
Starting with the well-known Albus model (Albus, 1997) of an intelligent agent, their structure includes, implicitly or explicitly, the following modules:

- World Model (WM) - which includes the information and knowledge detained by the agents and that acts both as a knowledge manager in problem solving and as an integrator of environmental information;
- Behaviour Generation (BG) which ensures the *pro-activity* of the agent by planning different scenarios of activities to be performed by the agent in order to accomplish a given goal and its *reactivity* by scheduling a scenario conforming to external events occurred;
- Value Judgement (VJ) which evaluates scenarios generated by BG module, estimating their effects accordingly with WM knowledge and taking into account the agent designed objectives by cost-objectives functions
- Decision Making (DM) which finally choose the scenario to be executed by the agent

The WM module is the core of an agent and even if its performances can be improved by modifying evaluation procedures in VJ and decision criteria in DM, the real problem solving "power" of an agent resides in the quality and quantity of knowledge it possess.

Autonomous manufacturing and logistics systems integrate mathematical models of hybrid systems with intelligent agents into hierarchical multi-purpose architectures, solving all problems of effectiveness and optimal delivering products to customers.

As a system, the enterprise (or a network of enterprises) will be considered as a complex system, integrating materials, resources, technologies, not only by information technologies infrastructures and management, but especially at knowledge level. The behavior resulted by the appropriate and synergic functioning of all enterprise active components and processes are criteria of enterprise success.

An intelligent enterprise should be characterized by the capacity to be flexible and adaptive in the market environment, but, in addition, it has also to cope with complexity, as it has to process an enormous quantity of information and a comparable amount of processes to trigger. Moreover, the environment itself - the global market that includes not only customers and providers, but also competing enterprises - is highly perturbed and unpredictable.

This context requires from the enterprise the ability to sense unbalances, perturbations and threats, react and adapt quickly, anticipate and predict developments and finally, actively influence the environment. The enterprise as a system has to refine its behavior within timescales much shorter than its employees can do it.

Moreover, the enterprise can be included in cooperative networks that, as meta-systems, should attain the same performances, but on a greater level of complexity.

Consequently, it is necessary to adapt the system theory to such challenges, in order to deal with system abstractions that are extremely large and complex.

The complexity management paradigm is challenging the traditional management assumptions, by considering that the behavior of the system is not predictable, based on previous information of its evolution, but, on the contrary, it is highly non-linear. As a consequence, the behavior of a complex system is emergent, in the sense that it results from the interaction of many participant's behaviors and cannot be predicted from the knowledge of what each component does. Moreover, an action can lead to several possible outcomes, some of them being disproportionate with the action itself, and it became obvious that the "whole" is very different from the composition of parts.

As a consequence, it results that directing an organizational network towards a given behavior, expressed in inter-related goals, represents an objective that requests other tools than mathematical modeling, behavior prediction and linear control. Alternative modeling and analysis approaches include hybrid and heuristic techniques, agent-based models, knowledge management and simulation, that seem to represent a more proper way of study.

Digital manufacturing implies intelligent control and integration of micro-electromechanical systems, mechatronics, manufacturing execution systems, multi-agent systems, human-machine systems and e-technologies to digitally control with increased agility the entire manufacturing chain, from design to manufacturing, to maintenance and service, over the whole product and processes life-cycle.

4. Evolution of Knowledge Management in manufacturing

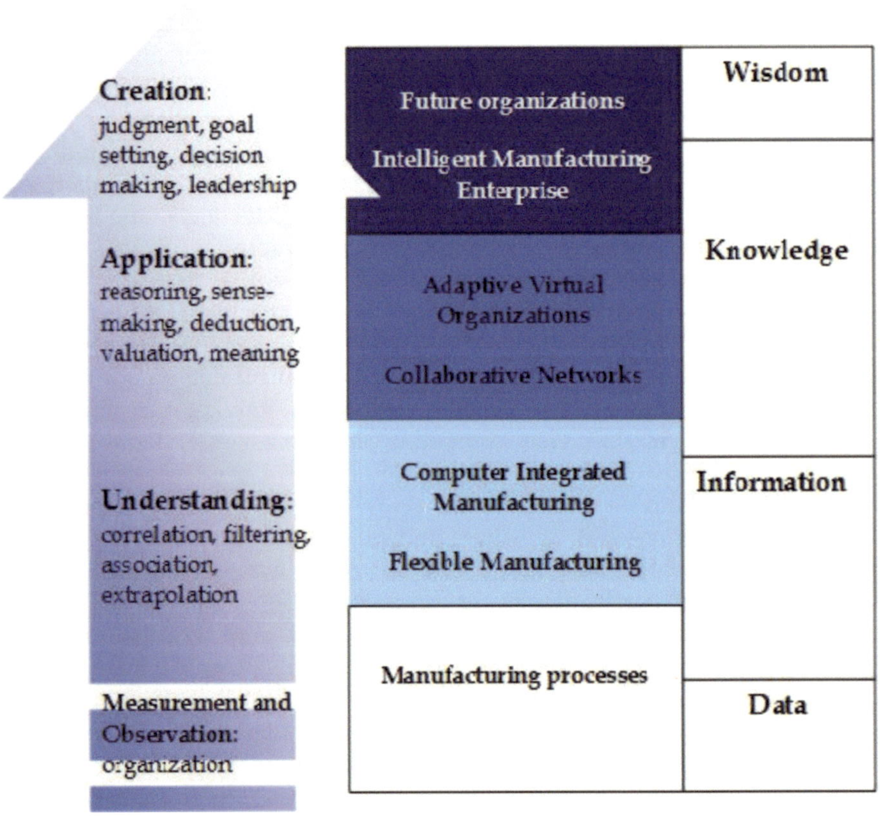

Fig. 3. Evolution of Knowledge Management

Modern manufacturing (Figure 3) has started in extensively using data, which are the first level of knowledge, in order to ensure a constant quality of products and an optimization of manufacturing processes in terms of time. Sometimes referred as *raw intelligence* or *evidence* (Waltz, 2003), data result from observation and measurement and can be retrieved in primitive messages of low level automation. In order to properly use data for analysis and

optimization, they have to be organized: sorted, classified, indexed a.s.o. and this contextualization transform data in information.
Information needs understanding and information management implies not only filtering and correlation of data, but also association and extrapolation of new obtained information.
As manufacturing paradigms evolved through Flexible Manufacturing Systems and Computer Integrated Systems, procedures of information management were improved until, from models that synthesized static and dynamic relationships between information, a new level of intelligence arise: knowledge.
Knowledge is, for data and information, what is integrated enterprise for flexible manufacturing. This notion, together with standardization supported by the Integrated Infrastructure, has marked a shift in knowledge management - a discipline that started to be recognized and developed. Knowledge engineering and data mining, supporting first generation of knowledge management, brought their support in developing new types of manufacturing systems.
CAS theory holds that living systems (i.e. organizations made up of living, independent agents, such as people) self-organize and continuously fit themselves, individually and collectivelly, to user-changing conditions in their environment.
Knowledge (in the form of theories and „mental models") according to CAS theory, can be represented by „rules"that agents (or people) follow in their ongoing attempts to adapt themselves sucessfully to their environment.
It is expected from the complexity theory to understand how knowledge forms at the level of individual agents and then influences knowledge processing at the level of the collective to produce shared organizational knowledge. The application of complexity theory to a broad range of business and organizational development issues is widening in practice.
There is a profound connection between complexity theory and knowledge management.
At the end of '2000, the process of knowledge management mainly implies the identification and analysis of knowledge, the purpose being the development of new knowledge that will be used to realize organizational goals. Because knowledge is usually gathered from a geographical and informational distributed system, knowledge management architecture should fulfill the following:

- detection and identification of knowledge
- storage and modeling of knowledge
- inference of conclusions
- retrieval and visualization of knowledge
- decision making

This view is representing what was called "first generation knowledge management" and can already be retrieved at the core of modern manufacturing paradigms, supporting concepts as concurrent/ collaborative engineering, virtual factory, and extended enterprises.
However, things will not stop here: challenges and pressure from the "outside" of manufacturing systems became stronger - including extreme customization, necessity of low production costs and short delivery times as well as necessity of networking enterprises, on short or long time horizon.
Actually, the most important driver of the evolution of both manufacturing and knowledge management paradigms seems to be the necessity of enterprise collaboration, with approaches at ontological level for knowledge sharing.
There are two main philosophical orientations in knowledge management (Sanchez, 1997):

Personal Knowledge Approach - that assumes knowledge is personal in nature and very difficult to extract from people. It must be transferred by moving people within or between organizations. Learning can only be encouraged by bringing the right people together under the right circumstances.

Organizational Knowledge Approach - implies that knowledge can be articulated and codified to create organizational knowledge assets. Knowledge can be disseminated (using information technology) in the form of documents, drawings, best practice models and so on. Learning processes can be designed to remedy knowledge deficiencies through structured, managed, scientific processes.

The Intelligent Manufacturing paradigm takes into account a synergic combination of these orientations and hopes to lead and attempts to realize a new shift in knowledge management: wisdom. Wisdom means not only using existing knowledge for solving new problems, but mainly the capacity to issue new problems to be solved.

5. Knowledge management and intelligent enterprise

In (Davis et al, 2007) is presented a very interesting study emphasizing the effect of the balance between organizational structure and enterprise efficiency for different kind of enterprises and environments. The conclusions of the study have revealed the following:

There is an inverted U-shaped relationship between structure and performance, that is *asymmetric:* too little structure leads to a catastrophic performance decline while too much structure leads to only a gradual decay

The key dimension of the market dynamism is *unpredictability* that underlines the tension between too much and too little structure. The *range* of optimal structures varies inversely with unpredictability: in unpredictable environments, there is only a very narrow range of optimal structures with catastrophic drops on either side that are likely to be difficult to manage.

Other dimensions of market dynamism (i.e. velocity, complexity, and ambiguity) have their own unique effects on performance

Similar to organization studies, network research presented in the mentioned paper indicates an environmental contingency such that the optimal structure decreases within increasing market dynamism. As in organization studies, the logic is that flexibility becomes more valuable than efficiency as market dynamism increases because of the more pressing need to adjust to environmental change.

The balance of organizational structure is also important for the complexity approach. Complexity theory seeks to understand how system level adaptation to environmental change emerges from the actions of its agents (Anderson, 1999; Carroll and Burton, 2000; Eisenhardt & Bhatia, 2001).

The common conceptualizations of an enterprise as a network of business units, partially connected by commonalities such as the same brand and innovation processes (e.g., Galbraith, 1973; Galunic & Eisenhardt, 2001; Gilbert, 2005), and strategy consisting of unique, yet intertwined decisions such as manufacturing and marketing (e.g., Rivkin, 2000) are also more concrete operationalizations of the abstract concept of a complex adaptive systems.

Intelligent Manufacturing Systems require new solutions based on the know-how from control engineering, software engineering and complex systems/ artificial life research.

New design promise scalability, reusability, integrability and robustness, based on the concepts of emergent and self-organizing systems, inspired by biological ones (living organisms).

Production structures can be considered as Complex Adaptive Systems (CAS), as manufacturing systems presently work in a fast changing environment full of uncertainties.

Autonomous manufacturing and logistics systems integrate mathematical models of hybrid systems with intelligent agents into hierarchical multi-purpose architectures, solving all problems of effectiveness and optimal delivering products to customers.

Complex adaptive systems are to be considered as being rather probabilistic than deterministic in nature and factors such as non-linearity can magnify apparently insignificant differences in initial conditions into huge consequences. It means that the long term predictions for complex systems are not reliable. A reliable prediction procedure should be one based on iteration with small increments.

On the other hand, solving a problem into the framework of a complex system is not, for enterprises or enterprise networks, a task with an infinite time horizon. Sometimes, the solving time is almost as important as the solution.

Bearing this in mind, the approach presented in this paper will allow to start with different evolutions, that will be eventually eliminated when they will prove inappropriate.

In short, the complexity theory has attested that complex systems are highly dependent on their initial state and their future evolution cannot be forecasted based on the past. Moreover, the scaling factor of a non-linear system is highly important for the prediction accuracy

An answer to the double challenge imposed by the intelligent enterprise as a system and by the complexity of problems it has to solve is a representation that uses both functional and managerial autonomous units (Dumitrache & Caramihai, 2008), (Dumitrache et al, 2009). There is no more question to control such a system in order to accomplish a given objective, but to structure its composing parts so as to allow to every one to act when the appropriate context appears.

Reconsidering the intelligent manufacturing enterprise, as mentioned above, as a pool of agents that have to accomplish both explicitely defined goals of themselves and implicitely defined global goals of the enterprise, it can be deduced that they also have to reach a balance between goal-directed and reactive behavior.

More precisely, as stated in (Wooldridge, 2000) we want agents to attempt to achieve their goals systematically, but not blindly executing their scenarios even when the goal is no longer valid. An agent should react to a new situation, in time for the reaction to be of use, but it should not continually react, never focusing enough on a goal to finally achieve it.

This balance can be obtained, as in the case of an manufacturing enterprise, by actually combining the functioning principles of the multi-agent architecture - that shapes the dynamic grouping of agents in global-goal oriented comunities - and the decision making inner mechanisms of agents.

Our approach is considering people as particular enterprise resources: even if the particular knowledge of an individual about "how to accomplish" a goal cannot be extracted, ones skills can be systematically taken into account and used as a primitive action, incorporated in more complex ones.

Actually, knowledge management is recognizing and taking into account two main kind of knowledge co-existing in an organization (Dalkir, 2005): *explicit knowledge*, which is the only form of knowledge possessed by non-human agents, and which has been codified and structured and *tacit knowledge,* which is the intangible knowledge that only human agents can have.

Organizational knowledge management approach focus especially on procedures to transform tacit knowledge into explicit, but as it is widely recognized the fact that such an objective will not be completely fulfilled, we will present in the following and multi-agent knowledge management architecture that takes into account both kind of agents (human and non-human) and both king of knowledge, focusing only on communication and grouping of agents.

It will be denoted by "knowledge" or by "knowledge module" a sequence (partly ordered) of primitive actions and/ or activities that are necessary to fulfill a given objective. Every action/ activity can have assigned - if necessary - resources, costs, duration, parameters a.s.o.

It will be also considered that by an activity (as a managerial unit) is denoted the implementation of knowledge (as a functional unit) and, respectively, at a lower level of granularity, by a task, the implementation of a primitive action.

It results from here that:

- the definition of a "knowledge module" is iterative (it can include other knowledge modules);
- it is always important for solving a problem to define primarily a list (part of a common dictionary) of primitive actions - implying, at the organizational level, an important focus on generating, articulating, categorizing and systematically leveraging organizational knowledge assets.

Figure 4 represents a problem solving approach in the following circumstances: a new problem is raised, eventually by the strategic level of a manufacturing enterprise. At this level, problem specification is made taking into account very general knowledge, as enterprise purpose, technologies and theories that are available a.s.o. Problem specification is made in terms of initial conditions and final results.

The operational level is the one where different stakeholders (individuals, departments), with diverse skills, store and share knowledge.

The problem solving is performed by a technique of puzzle "trial and error": activities that start with the specified initial conditions are considered to be potential parts of the solution. Their results are simulated and analyzed and will be the initial conditions for the step two of the iterative process of solution generation.

The procedure will continue until the desired final conditions will be attained or until no advance could be made. A solution will be a sequence of activities where the first one has the initial conditions of the problem and the last one has the desired outcomes.

It is clear that in an appropriate context, a problem could have several solutions. On the other hand, the state space of possible solutions could explode, imposing the necessity of a control mechanism that will eliminate trajectories which are obviously false. This mechanism is represented by a value judgment block.

Criteria for eliminating unpromising partial solutions could reside in implementation conditions (unavailable infrastructure, for instance), or in more complex and flexible domain-dependent structures, that can improve by learning.

Obviously, a very important problem is the implementation of such a knowledge architecture. Some of the implementation requirements include distribution, capacity of decomposition and aggregation for knowledge modules as well as knowledge hierarchy and classification.

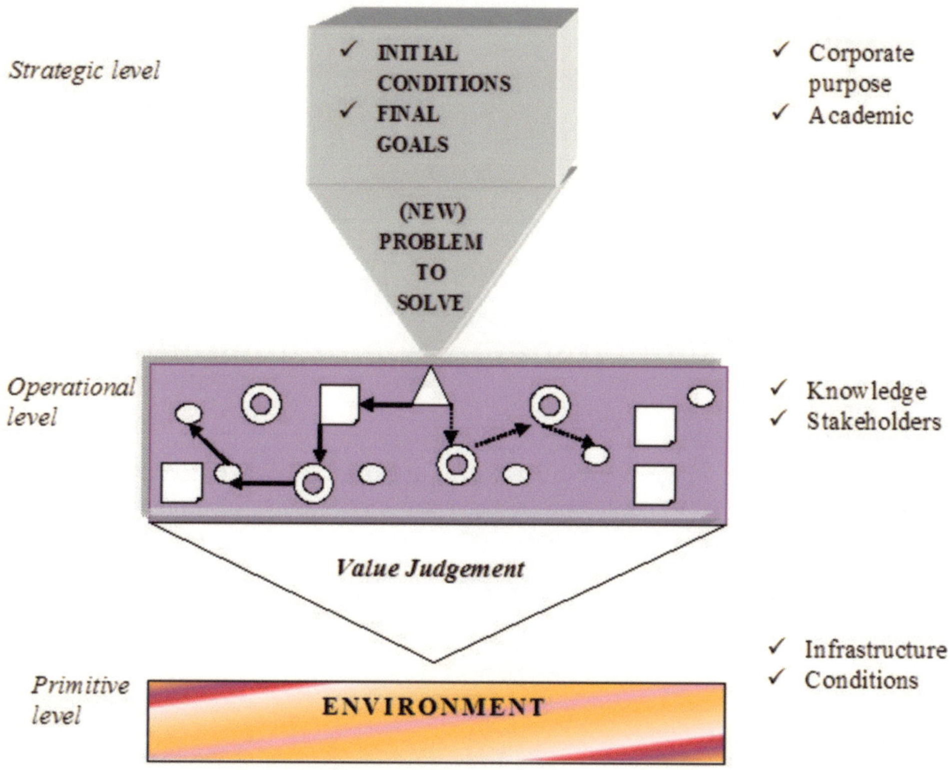

Fig. 4. Problem solving approach

6. Intelligent Systems Architecture for Manufacturing Enterprise – ISAM

The main attributes of intelligent architectures for manufacturing, as perception, reasoning, communication and planning (or behaviour generation) are organized on different layers and need a large, distributed knowledge base. On the other hand, they necessary include several levels of abstraction.

Usually, strategic goals are relatively unclear, with respect to the practical aspects concerned by the shop-floor on-line activities, and they need stepwise decomposition and reformulation in order to be achieved. Moreover, it is not sure enough from the beginning if the system can fulfil strategic specification.

Although those considerations, knowledge can emerge from knowledge and the generic process is the same, even if formal specifications are different. The process of knowledge management is following a spiral, as presented in figure 5.

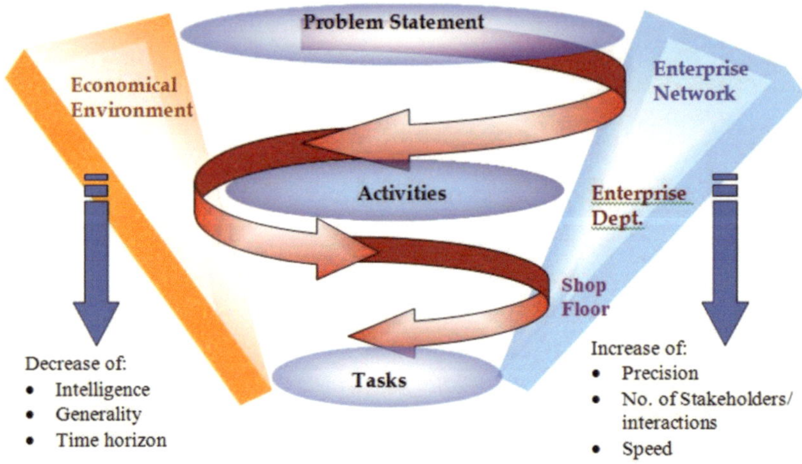

Fig. 5. Knowledge spiral

The ISAM model allows a large representation of activities from detailed dynamics analysis of a single actuator in a simple machine to the combined activity of thousands of machines and human beings in hundreds of plants.

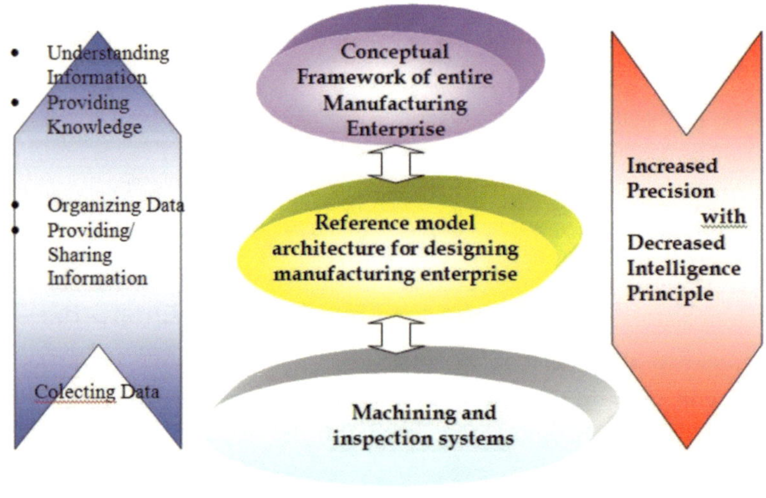

Fig. 6. ISAM architecture

First level of abstraction of ISAM (Figure 6) provides a conceptual framework for viewing the entire manufacturing enterprise as an intelligent system consisting of machines, processes, tools, facilities, computers, software and human beings operating over time and on materials to create products.
At a second level of abstraction, ISAM provides a reference model architecture to support the development of performance measures and the design of manufacturing and software.
At a third level of abstraction, ISAM intend to provide engineering guidelines to implement specific instances of manufacturing systems such as machining and inspection systems.

To interpret all types of activities, ISAM adapts a hierarchical layering with different range and resolution in time and space at each level. In this vision could be defined functional entities at each level within the enterprise such that each entity is represented by its particular responsibilities and priorities at a level of spatial and temporal resolution that is understandable and manageable to itself.

The functional entities, like as agents, receive goals and priorities from above and observe situations in the environment below. Each functional entity, at each level has to provide decisions, to formulate plans and actions that affect peers and subordinates at levels below.

Each functional entity needs access to a model of the world (large knowledge and database) that enables intelligent decision making, planning, analysis and reporting activity into a real world with large uncertainties and unwanted signals.

A large manufacturing enterprise is organized into management units, which consist of a group of intelligent agents (humans or machines). These agents have a particular combination of knowledge, skills and abilities.

Each agent is expected to make local executive decisions to keep things on schedule by solving problems and compensating for minor unexpected events.

Each unit of management has a model of the world environment in which it must function. This world model is a representation of the state of the environment and of the entities that exist in the environment, including their attributes and relationships and the events, includes also a set of rules that describes how the environment will behave under various conditions.

Each management unit has a set of values or cost functions, that it uses to evaluate that state of the world and by which its performance is evaluated.

Future manufacturing will be characterized by the need to adapt to the demands of agile manufacturing, including rapid response to changing customer requirements, concurrent design and engineering, lower cost of small volume production, outsourcing of supply, distributed manufacturing, just-in-time delivery, real-time planning and scheduling, increased demands for precision and quality, reduced tolerance for error, in-process measurements and feedback control.

These demands generate requirements for adaptability and on-line decision making.

The ISAM conceptual framework attempts to apply intelligent control concepts to the domain of manufacturing so as to enable the full range of agile manufacturing concepts.

The ISAM could be structured as a hierarchical and heterarchical system with different level of intelligence and precision. For each level, the granularity of knowledge imposes the operators Grouping (G), Focusing Attention (F) and Combinatorial Search (S) to get an optimal decision.

For a representation of knowledge into categories like $C_{k,i}$ for each level of the hierarchy we have to define a chain of operators G, F and S (Figure 7) :

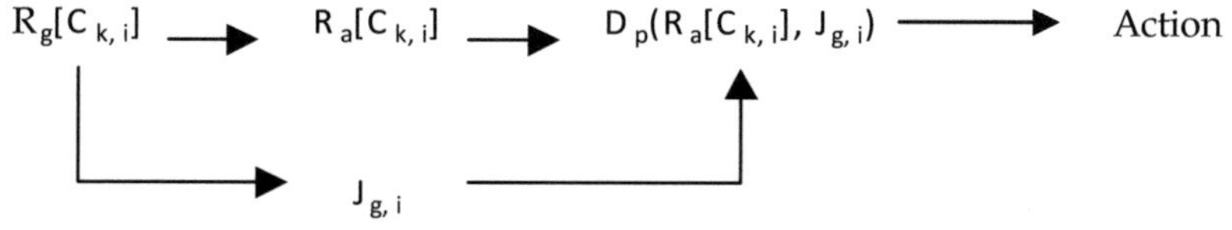

Fig. 7. Grouping-Focusing and Searching loop

where
$R_g[C_{k,i}]$ – is a knowledge representation of grouping
$R_a[C_{k,i}]$ – is a representation of focusing attention
$D_p(R_a[C_{k,i}], J_{g,i})$ - decision-making process
$J_{g,i}$ – represents a cost function associated for each level i
Knowledge is represented on each level with a different granularity and by using GFS (Grouping, Focusing Attention, Combinatorial Search) operators which organize a decision process. At each level of the architecture is implemented a dual concept-feed-forward and feedback control and the GFS operators are implemented on different levels.

7. Future trends

„Recent developments in manufacturing and logistics systems have been transformed by the influence of information and communication, e-Work and e-Service collaboration and wireless mobility, enabling better services and quality to consumers and to communities, while bringing new challenges and priorities" (Nof et.al, 2008) – such was the beginning of the milestone report presented by the IFAC Coordinating Committee on Manufacturing & Logistics Systems at the last IFAC Congress. And indeed, last years have seen a tremendous technological development, best reflected in manufacturing, which necessitates new approaches of management in order to cope with.

Knowledge management in particular, owing to its evolution that parallels that of manufacturing paradigms, is expected to issue new methods allowing humans to both benefit from - and increase the value of – technological advances.

It can be foreseen a hybrid knowledge structure, where the interaction between human and non-human knowledge stakeholders will became transparent and will allow creation and use of meta-knowledge.

Until then, some of the following developments could be expected, combining knowledge management advances with technological ones:

- Integration of human and technical resources to enhance workforce performance and satisfaction
- „Instantaneous" transformation of information gathered from a vast array of diverse sources into useful knowledge, for effective decision making
- Directing of manufacturing efforts towards the realization of ecological products, though contributing to sustainable development
- Development of innovative manufacturing processes and products with a focus on decreasing dimensional scale
- Collaborative networks, including human and software agents as an hierarchical and heterarchical architecture
- Development of a new theory of complex systems, taking into account the emergent and hybrid representation of manufacturing systems

Finally, the agility for manufacturing, and the wisdom, for knowledge management, will represent challenges for the new generation of embedded intelligent manufacturing.

Knowledge management is essential in the globalization framework, where success is effectively based on the cooperation capacity and on creative intelligence.

8. References

Adler, P.S. (1995). Interdepartmental interdependence and coordination: The case of the design/manufacturing interface. *Organization Science*, 6(2): 147-167.

Albus, J.S. (1997) The NIST Real-time Control System (RCS): An approach to Intelligent Systems Research. *Journal of Experimental and Theoretical Artificial Intelligence* 9 pp. 157-174

Albus, J.S. & Meystel, A.M. (2001) *Intelligent Systems: Architecture, Design, Control*, Wiley-Interscience, ISBN-10: 0471193747 ISBN-13: 978-0471193746

Anderson, P. (1999). Complexity Theory and Organization Science. *Organization Science*, 10: 216-232.

Browne, J.; Dubois, D.; Rathmill, K.; Sethi, S.P.& Stecke, K. E. (1984). Classification of Flexible Manufacturing Systems. *The FMS Magazine*, April 1984, p. 114-117.

Burns, T. & Stalker, G. M. (1961). *The management of innovation*. Tavistock, London

Camarinha-Matos L & Afsarmanesh, H. (2005). Collaborative Networks: a new scientific discipline, *Journal of Intelligent Manofacturing* , No.16 , Springer Science, pp 439-452

Carroll, T.N. & Burton R.M. (2000). Organizations and Complexity. *Organization Theory*. 6: 319-337.

Chen, D. & Vernadat, F. (2002). Enterprise Interoperability: A Standardisation View, *Proceedings of the ICEIMT'02 Conference: Enterprise Inter- and Intraorganizational Integration, Building International Consensus* , Ed. K. Kosanke et.al, ISBN 1-4020-7277-5

CIMOSA: Open System Architecture for CIM (1993) Research Reports Esprit / Project 688/5288. AMICE Ed. Springer;, ISBN-10: 3540562567 ISBN-13: 978-3540562566

Davis,J. P.; Eisenhardt K & Bingham B.C. (2007) Complexity Theory, Market Dynamism and the Strategy of Simple Rules, Proceedings of DRUID Summer Conference 2007 on Appropriability, Proximity Routines and Innovation, Copenhagen, CBS, Denmark, June 18 - 20, 2007

Dalkir, K. (2005). Knowledge Management in Theory and Practice. Elsevier, ISBN-13: 978-0-7506-7864-3, ISBN-10: 0-7506-7864-X

Dumitrache, I. (2008) From Model-Based Strategies to Intelligent Control Systems. *WSEAS Transactions on Systems and Control*, No.6, Vol.3, pp.569-575, ISSN 1991-8763

Dumitrache, I. & Caramihai, S.I. (2008) Towards a new generation of intelligent manufacturing systems *Proceedings of the 4th International IEEE Conference on Intelligent Systems*, 2008, vol.I, pp.4-33 - 4-38, IEEE Catalog Number CFP08802-PRT, ISBN 978-1-4244-1740-7

Dumitrache, I.; Caramihai, S.I. & Stanescu A.M. (2009) Knowledge Management in Intelligent Manufacturing Enterprise. *Proceedings of the 8th WSEAS International Conference on Artificial Intelligence, Knowledge Engineering and Data Bases*, pp.453-459, ISBN: 978-960-474-051-2, Cambridge, February 21-23, WSEAS Press

Eisenhardt, K. M. & Mahesh M. B. (2001) Organizational Complexity and Computation. *Companion to Organizations*. A. C. Baum (ed.), Oxford, UK: Blackwell Publishers.

Feigenbaum, E. (1989) - Toward the library of the future. *Long Range Planning*, 22(1):122

Galbraith, J. (1973) *Designing Complex Organizations*. Reading, MA: Addison-Wesley.

Galunic, D. C. & Eisenhardt, K.M. (2001) Architectural Innovation and Modular Corporate Forms. *Academy of Management Journal*, 44: 1229-1250.

Gilbert, C. (2005) Unbundling the Structure of Inertia: Resource vs Routine Rigidity. *Academy of Management Journal*, 48: , 741-763.

Hayes-Roth, F.; Waterman, D. & Lenat, D. (1983) *Building expert systems*. Reading, MA, Addison-Wesley.

Henderson, R. M. & Kim B. C. (1990) Architectural Innovation: The Reconfiguration of Existing Product Technologies and the Failure of Established Firms. *Administrative Science Quarterly*, 35: 9-30

Mehrabi M.G.; Ulsoy A.G. & Koren Y. (2000). Reconfigurable manufacturing systems: key to future manufacturing. *Journal of Intelligent manufacturing*, Vol. 11, 2000, pp. 403-419

Miller, D. & Friesen, P. H. (1980) Momentum and Revolution in Organizational Adaptation. *Academy of Management Journal*, 23: 591-614.

Nof, S.Y.; Filip, F.; Molina A.; Monostori, L. & Pereira, C.E. (2008) Advances in e-Manufacturing, e-Logistics and e-Service Systems – Milestone Report , *Proceedings of the 17th IFAC World Congress*, Seoul, 2008, pp.117-125

Rivkin, J. W. (2000) Imitation of Complex Strategies. *Management Science*, 46: 824-844.

Savage, C. M. (1990) *5th generation management*, Ed. Butterworth-Heinemann, ISBN 0-7506-9701-6

Seppala, P.; Tuominen, E. & Koskinen, P. (1992). Impact of flexible production philosophy and advanced manufacturing technology on organizations and jobs. *The Engineering and Manufacturing*, Prentice Hall, Englewood Cliffs, NJ

Sethi, A. K & Sethi, S. P. (1990). Flexibility in Manufacturing: A Survey. *The International Journal of Flexible Manufacturing Systems*, Vol. 2, 1990, pp. 289-328.

Siggelkow, N. (2001) Change in the Presence of Fit: the Rise, the Fall, and the Renascence of Liz Claiborne. *Academy of Management Journal*, 44: 838-857.

Thoben, K-D Pawar K. & Goncalves R. (Eds.) *Procs. Of the 14th International Conference on Concurrent Enterprising*, June 2008, ISBN 978 0 85358 244 1

Uzzi, B. (1997) Social Structure and Competition in Interfirm Networks: Thc Paradox of Embeddedness. *Administrative Science Quarterly*, 42: 36-67.

Waltz, E. (2003). *Knowledge Management in the Intelligence Enterprise*. Artech House, ISBN 1-58053-494-5

Weick, K. E. & Karlene H. Roberts (1993) Collective Minds in Organizations: Heedful Interrelating on Flight Decks. *Administrative Science Quarterly*, 38: 357-381.

Wooldridge, M. & Jennings N.R. (1995) Intelligent Agents: Theory and Practice. *The Knowledge Engineering Review*, 10(2):115-152

Wooldridge M. (2000). Intelligent Agents. Multiagent Systems: A Modern Approach to Distributed Artificial Intelligence The MIT Press ISBN-10: 0262731312 ISBN-13: 978-0262731317

5

Actor-networking engineering design, project management and education research: a knowledge management approach

José Figueiredo
IST – Technical University of Lisbon
Management and Engineering Department
CEG-IST Engineering and Management Research Centre
Av. Rovisco Pais
1049-001 Lisboa
Portugal
jdf@ist.utl.pt

Abstract

With this research we invest in the integration of four important areas of knowledge interweaved within the sphere of engineering management research: Actor-Network Theory, project management, engineering design and engineering education research. Each of these areas represents a pole of a tetrahedron and they are all equidistant. Our approach has the ability and concern of putting them all at the same distance and with equivalent value, taking advantage of cruising fertilization among them. This entails a research in the frontiers of the engineering and the social where other elements emerge. In fact any technological system is a sociotechnical system and design and development must take this fact into account, which surprisingly enough doesn't seem to be completely accepted. This research is on the integration of knowledge and blurring of frontiers within these four areas. The actor-network embodies the change of settings and facilitates negotiations among heterogeneous actors, translating ideas and meanings and constructing innovations. Actor-Network Theory helps viewing the integration of these different areas as a fruitful integrative process of trade-offs and translations. This integrative process is intended to manage knowledge creation and serve as a context to a reflexive process of organizational learning and engineering academic learning. Narrative is a strategy we intend to use to facilitate the understanding of contexts and the circulation of common and emergent meanings.

Keywords: Knowledge, Actor-network, Design, Project Management, Engineering Education Research

1. Introduction

In this paper we address the four areas of knowledge identified in the title integrated in a space of knowledge management and organizational learning. We also address the use of narratives as an effective strategy to facilitate alignment, learning and decision making.
Actor-Network Theory (ANT) was created within the sociology of sciences (*École de Mines de Paris*, by Latour and Callon, followed by Law, from Lancaster, UK) and was essentially a retrospective approach which followed actors in past settings (Callon, 1986), (Latour, 1987; 1996) and (Law, 1986). ANT analysis focus in a very innovative way on the interpretation of connexions and negotiations among actors (heterogeneous actors like people, teams, organizations, rules, policies, programs, and technological artefacts), but tends to miss the enormous potentialities it offers in the processes of designing the making of technological artefacts. Despite Michel Callon's reference to "designing in the making" in the title of his chapter in the book edited by Bijker, Callon (1987), this approach is generally retrospective and revolves around reflection and explanations on how things could have been different if other actions had been taken. There are some attempts to put ANT into acting in "real time", for example in the information system domain, by Tatnall (1999) and Monteiro (2000), but these attempts are after all and again mainly ex-post. Anyway we can feel that Callon (2002) was himself already alert to some emergent potentialities of ANT. We may also think that Hepso (2001) was looking to more real action. But in fact these attempts were a dead end and our idea is that, more than in action or in the making, we should focus on using ANT in design and development of technological systems (Figueiredo, 2008). So, ANT needs to improve its abilities to be helpful in the making (design and development) of technological systems which entails the construction of sociotechnical systems. Although we used it mainly in requirements analysis and specification of technological artefacts in project management (Gonçalves and Figueiredo, 2008), ANT provides ways of looking into the making of technological systems from a different perspective. That is, ANT can be a new language of design. ANT embeds the social (social actors) and technology (technological artefacts also as actors) into the same network of negotiations and provides a view that can embody the bottom value of technology, integrating new relevant actors, discarding others, crafting specifications and requisites, that is, *purifying* the design of systems (actor-networks). Grabbing new actors and loosing some of the actors previously involved is a *due process* that provides open innovation, dismantling routines and closed specs.
Project management (PM), as a knowledge and research specific area has some internal contradictions. Some of them concern PM autonomy. If we focus on design we address project management in innovation contexts and we need to allow the braking of routines, as some traditional practices doesn't apply. Within engineering design, project management needs to assume new roles and some practices need to be reconstructed. That is why collections (bodies of knowledge) of best practices such as PMBOK (2004), a collection edited by the Project Management Institute, although widely used, are not considered significant enough in these more specialised realms of PM application. Goldratt's Critical Chain (1997), based on the theory of constrains (TOC), promises an alternative approach but it also has limitations and doesn't offer interesting alternatives to this specific problem (design). Also in specific areas of knowledge as for example information systems the world references explore alternative approaches, as James Cadle (2007) and Mark Fuller, Joe Valacich, and Joey George (2007) note. In this important field (information systems), methodologies as Rational Unified Process (RUP) and Agile increase their visibility. There

are also some encouraging signs of new and complementary approaches in risk analysis, maturity studies, project collaborative tools design, project management in services, and system dynamics. We can see some emerging domains, like project management offices (PMOs), project portfolio analysis, multicriteria decision in risk analysis, agile project management (Ambler, 1999), and more. Overall then, we are convinced that addressing the project management in designing technological systems with an ANT approach provides a helpful view that can be applied from the very early stages of the engineering design act, requirement analysis and specifications (Ford and Coulston, 2008), right through its completion (Gonçalves and Figueiredo, 2009), i.e. all along the project life cycle (Figueiredo, 2008b). Project management is a transversal area of knowledge that also needs to integrate technology in its use, that is, needs to adopt a sociotechnical approach. Charles Rosenberg introduced the metaphor of ecology of knowledge that established constructivism as the dominant mode of analysis of science exploring knowledge embedded in material artefacts and skilled practices (Rosenberg, 1997). And the interplaying of the technical and the social is so dramatic in project management that the high rate of failure in project accomplishment is constantly addressed to social failures (communication, stakeholder involvement, team quality, leadership).

Engineering Design in the practitioner domain is at the very kernel of engineering activity. Design is context dependent and user oriented. Design needs specific skills, an inquiry mind able to understand the piece and the system in which it operates, a sociotechnical mind able to understand technology and its uses, an understanding of the organization, communication within the group and with the stakeholders, a hearing ability to understand needs, and permeable borders allowing things going out and others coming in through the borders of the system in design. Design operates in micro and macro mode, travelling through the boundaries of both modes. These two modes need to communicate and act together, with knowledge emerging from the interactivity of this process. Design fructifies in specific informal cultures, so to manage design projects the approaches needs more flexibility. Once again we stress that the actor-network metaphor is refreshing, as actors have freewill and free options resulting from negotiations occurring among them and without any frame limiting or imposing conducts and controlling their behaviour.

Engineering Education Research is for us, academics, a space of reflexion and action with a variety of inputs. What can we learn from practitioners, what can we learn from concepts and how can we apply them out in practice, how can we learn from both sides and how can we teach-learn from the interaction of these approaches. Namely we can address the two distinct modes of knowledge production identified by Gibbons (1994) as Mode 1 and Mode 2 (a context-driven and problem-focussed process more common in the entrepreneurial sphere). Can we act interplaying with both academic and entrepreneurial contexts? Can we engage in observing and playing ourselves around deploying strategies of knowledge production, of knowledge emergence and transference, addressing both Mode 1 (Jorgensen, 2008) and Mode 2, and understanding the tacit and cultural barriers that emerge and dissolve with the evolving of the actor-network, or the networked-actor? Can we take advantages of using the lenses of ANT to understand the mechanisms of knowledge production and knowledge emergence and how they relate with the design *value* and with the organizational learning and students learning?

What do these four areas of knowledge have in common? They all inhabit the as yet under-explored terrain where engineering and technology and the social sciences interplay, share domains and overlap fundaments. They all demand from the researcher more then a pure technological profile as they need a strong perception of the social. Allan Bromley, formerly Yale University dean once said "in the average engineering project, the first 10 per cent of the decisions made / effectively commit between 80 and 90 per cent of all the resources that subsequently flow into the project. Unfortunately, most engineers are ill-equipped to participate in these important initial decisions because they are not purely technical decisions. Although they have important technical dimensions, they also involve economics, ethics, politics, appreciation of local and international affairs and general management considerations. Our current engineering curricula tend to focus on preparing engineers to handle the other 90 percent; the nut-and-bolt decisions that follow after the first 10 per cent have been made. We need more engineers who can tackle the entire range of decisions." We need engineers that can cope with this, which means engineers with a design approach why of thinking and inquiry mind, a sociotechnical mind, communication skills, an understanding of the organization and social value.

This presents a major challenge, a need for researchers and engineers with a strong interdisciplinary sensibility and background, able to understand both the technical and the social. This integrative framework pretends to facilitate the emergence of knowledge in a design context and the management of this knowledge in aligned purposes. This approach also stresses the specific systemic paradigm of integration within a sensibility of border management and the inherent domain overlapping. This integrative approach also intends to explore the peculiarities of an ANT approach to engineering design and knowledge management, and to provide some refreshing considerations on project management and engineering education research.

2. Knowledge construction and learning

There is controversy about the different types of knowledge (tacit, explicit, soft, hard, informal, formal, and others) and how they can be constructed, captured, codified, used and "transferred". The New Production of Knowledge (Gibbons et al, 1994) explored two distinct models of knowledge production (we would say construction), Mode 1 (characterized by the hegemony of theoretical or, at any rate, experimental science; by an internally-driven taxonomy of disciplines; and by the autonomy of scientists and their host institutions, the universities) and Mode 2 (socially distributed, application-oriented, trans-disciplinary, and subject to multiple accountabilities, a context-driven process more common in the entrepreneurial sphere). These two modes are distinct but they are related and they co-exist, sometimes in the same evolving processes. We can say that in a business model mode 1 has only the first part (upstream) of the value chain, away from the market and practice purposes. The differences between these two approaches were recently characterized by Dias de Figueiredo and Rupino da Cunha (2006) as summarized in Table 1:

	Mode 1	Mode 2
Context	academic, scientific, prestige and uniqueness	economic and social applications, utility and profits for the stakeholders are the purposes
Dissemination	linear model, diffusion	problems are set and solved in the context of application, actor-networks
Research	fundamental/applied, exactly what does this mean? Knowledge is mainly for scientific purposes	fundamental and applied melt, theory and practice entangle, multiple sites. Knowledge is built and used in the context
Community	discipline based, homogeneous teams, university based, shared among fellows	transdisciplinarity, integrated teams, networks of heterogeneous actors
Orientation	explanation, incremental	solution focussed
Method	repeatability is important, reuse	repeatability is not vital, sometimes it even impossible
Quality assurance	context and use dependent, peer-review is the most important guarantee, refutability	context dependent: may involve peer-review, customer satisfaction
Definition of success	scientific excellence and academic prestige	efficiency/effectiveness, satisfy multiple stakeholders, commercial success, social value

Table 1. Adapted from Gibbons' Modes 1 and 2 of knowledge production

Sustaining our learning strategies in such differences and inscribing them into the design mind, with a sociotechnical and systemic approach, it is easy to agree that active learning and project-based learning are urgent strategies to adopt in the academia, in the engineering learning field.

"Active learning puts the responsibility of organizing what is to be learned in the hands of the learners themselves, and ideally lends itself to a more diverse range of learning styles....." (Dodge, 1998). Richard Felder and Rebecca Brent are among the most well known apologists of this learn strategy and curiously they mainly address the engineering arena *"Active Learning and engineering education are seen as a natural pair"*, Richard Felder and Rebecca Brent (2003a e 2003b). In a similar approach we can also visit Michael Prince (2004).

Project-based learning is not new, it is a concept that showed up in the twenties namely with the experiences of William Kilpatrick, follower of John Dewey in his reflexive incursion into education systems. This kind of "teaching" is learning oriented as defined by Bolonha and involves students in projects all along its course in school in order they can construct competencies in the specific study domain, see Bess Keller (2007) and Graaff and Kolmos (2007).

To make it simple and picture like, when you are in a car discovering the way to a place you don't know in a quarter where you have never been, if you are driving you learn and probably you can reuse the knowledge you constructed in order to repeat the path, but if you are not driving, if you are just going in the car you can't. The difference in both cases is the way you are situated in the *system*. Similarly in an interesting book by Ivan Illich (1974) there was a citation of José Antonio Viera-Gallo, secretary of Justice of Salvador Allende saying "*El socialismo puede llegar solo en bicicleta*", which is a good metaphor on the same reality. Addressing technology Illich intends that the structure of production devices can irremediably incorporate class prejudice (Ivan Illich - Energy and Equity). Action and knowledge, as technology, are situated and socially constructed.

In organizational terms learning is a survival condition. Learning, knowledge production, organizational contexts, and culture are *things* (actors) we need to network in order to stimulate organizational creativity and innovation. No design activity is possible without the degrees of liberty of a situated context. Double-loop learning (Argyris and Schon, 1978), generative learning (Senge, 1990), adaptive process (Cyert and March, 1963), and the behavioural approaches are just a few among a myriad of topics that consolidated organizational learning as a discipline. Organizational learning focused originally on the practice of four core disciplines, or capacities, *systems thinking* toped as the fifth (Senge, 1990):

• systems thinking
• team learning
• shared vision
• mental models
• personal mastery

The situated context is constructed and often by special leaders that are able to motivate people and engage teams. Leadership is about change. A leader is a constructor of visions, realities, hopes, ways, means, and a flexible planner that plans and re-plans all the time (planning and organizing, doing and re-planning is a constructive practice). True leadership is earned, internally - in the unit, or the organization, or the community. Leadership could be seen as a "distributed leadership," meaning that the role is fluid, shared by various people in a group according to their capabilities as conditions change, (Mintzberg, 1977). Leadership, change, learning, and knowledge management are important topics in engineering design. And we need to understand different cultures. Addressing the cultural problem in a wider way Hofstede defined four/five cultural dimensions (power distance, uncertainty avoidance, individualism, masculinity - femininity, and long versus short term orientation) (Hofstede, 1980). In smaller teams the cultural differences can be addressed as psychological and social types and can be addressed as conditioned competences. And like this we are readdressed to organizational learning as managing competences.

3. Knowledge narratives

As knowledge is socially constructed and depends on interactions and negotiations among the different actors of the group or community, a way to create the appropriate conditions for translation is narrative.

Narrative is an interpretive approach born in the social sciences and gradually gaining recognition in various disciplines outside the social sciences. The approach is intended to enable capture of social representation processes addressing ambiguity, complexity, and dynamism of individual, group, and organisational phenomena. Context plays a crucial role in the social construction of reality and knowledge, especially in engineering design and organizational environments. Narrative can be used to gain insight into organisational change, or can lead to cultural change (Faber, 1998). Storytelling can help in absorbing complex tacit knowledge or can also serve as a source of implicit communication (Ambrosini and Bowman, 2001). Czarniawska (2004) researches on how narrative constructs identity, Abma (2000) on how narrative can aid education, Gabriel (1998) on how stories contribute to sensemaking. Narrative may also provide insight into decision making (O'Connor, 1997) or the processes of knowledge *transfer* (Connell, 2004) and (Darwent, 2000).

Narrative is inherently multidisciplinary and lends itself to a qualitative enquiry in order to capture the rich data within stories. Surveys, questionnaires and quantitative analyses of behaviour are not sufficient to capture the complexity of meaning embodied within stories. Traditional scientific theory adopts a rational and empirical approach to achieve an objective description of the forces in the world, and scientists attempt to position themselves outside the realm of the study to observe. In this way traditional science is kept within a narrow positivist frame, dealing with random samples and statistical analyses. Using the story metaphor, people create order and construct senses and meanings within particular contexts. Narrative analysis takes the story itself as object of inquiry.

In our integrative approach we think that narratives can be used as boundary objects, a notion Susan Leigh Star and James Griesemer (1989) coined. Boundary objects are plastic enough to adapt to local needs and constraints of the several actors using them, and steady enough to keep an identity (commonly accepted) across settings. These objects can be softly structured when in common use and become structured in individual-situated use. Boundary objects are normally explored (in the literature) within a geographic metaphor but they also make sense through temporal boundaries. When we report and explicitly express our lessons learned at the end (closing) of a project we are designing boundary objects to the future, in order we can interplay with them and through them with different communities (project teams) also separated in time.

Exactly as knowledge exists as a spectrum "at one extreme, it is almost completely tacit, that is semiconscious and unconscious knowledge held in peoples' heads and bodies. At the other end of the spectrum, knowledge is almost completely explicit or codified, structured and accessible to people other than the individuals originating it"(Leonard and Sensiper, 1998). Most knowledge of course exists between the extremes. Explicit elements are objective, while tacit elements are subjective empirical and created in real time by doing and questioning options. So does boundary objects, they can be abstract concepts or concrete facts. In this sense taxonomies are boundary objects as they represent an ontological dimension. Systems of classification are part of the building of information environments (Bowker and Star, 1999). Narratives too, they help on this travel of means, where means are common experience in progress. As they both represent means of translation we clearly agree that ANT ca help in the negotiation of these means at the very core of the knowledge construction and learning processes.

4. Knowledge management

The most usual panacea in knowledge management (KM) is about the knowledge to information *translations* that some consider as algorithms to convert knowledge into something transferable, into forms that can be handled, manipulated, stored and even automated. We do not agree with this rationalist - mechanic simplification. We align with the others that having different ideas among themselves simply don't agree with these functionalist and instrumental approaches (Polanyi, Hildreth and Kimble, Hargadon, Vicari et al…) and think that KM can only be addressed from a different paradigm. This paradigm believes technology is not sufficient. In an organizational environment technology is necessary, but not sufficient. But being necessary or sufficient we need to address technology as a sociotechnical thing, embedded in the way it is used, managed, designed and developed. We think that in order to address organizational knowledge and its management we can never separate technology from people and this applies to the full engineering process cycle (requirements analysis, design, development, test, maintenance, and, in terms of knowledge, use and reuse).

The design process should be situated in this full cycle. Organizational knowledge management should address knowledge construction as a socially emergent outcome that results from the *translations* within the actor-networks that includes technology, rules, people, cultures, and organizational communities.

Engineering design has to recognise that if the requirements are not situated in a context of action and use they cannot assure a *valuable* result, that is, the result of the engineering process (full cycle) can be compromised. That is the reason why an earlier stage of the processes needs to be addressed with specific care and a methodological approach. In our approach this early stage is addressed as an emergent actor-network that needs to create the appropriate conditions for translation in an aligned fashion through a process of *problematization, interessement, enrolment* (*inscription*) and *mobilization* (Callon, 1986). This actor-network should encompass not only the initial situational process, but the full engineering process cycle (ANT, Actor-network Theory). This actor-network acts as the tissue where (and within) design and knowledge is constructed and where this construction is nourished and motivated.

In this process our inquiry approach can use convergent thinking (the questioner attempts to converge on and reveal facts) and divergent thinking (the questioner attempts to diverge from facts to the possibilities that can be created from them, which requires the use of surprising alternatives, sometimes *out of the box*, using inductive and abductive types of reasoning) (Dym et al, 2005), so we need to develop qualities that allow us to integrate both thinking types.

In this subject we can understand the importance of divergent thinking in engineering design (Cooperrider, 2008) and Torrence (1988), and visiting Cropley (2006) we can explore the combination and productive interplay among divergent and convergent thinking. In these references we clearly address two domains: the knowledge domain and the concept domain. There is a huge difference between the two as concepts need not to be verifiable, a concept is a concept, but knowledge always does. Recently Hatchuel and Weil (2003) took along this reflexion and explored the creation of a concept dynamic tree, introducing a new theory. Hatchuel and Le Masson (2007), Hatchuel Le Masson and Weil (2006) developed what is called the CK Theory (where C states for Concepts and K for Knowledge). This theory basically explores the idea that organizations have two available sets – a knowledge base (K - knowledge) of disperse things (objects, facts, rules, knowing) and a space of intentional query about things that cannot be answered within the knowledge base (C - concepts). These two spaces, having different structures and logics, are both expandable,

interdependent and they allow negotiations through each other. They are spaces of translation. Within these two sets, concepts leave C and are processed into K where new knowledge emerges, and other processes are sustained in K and move into C to trigger the creation of new concepts and so on. Theory CK "offers a unified model for creative and innovative design", Hatchuel Le Masson and Weil (2006).
We can bridge this with the collaborative design topic explored in Zouari (2007) because in the space of knowledge we have interaction and cooperation among the actors.
We can look at this space of action (knowledge, concepts and application of knowledge in practice) in terms of ANT. In the three views represented in Figure 1 the arrows represent translations from setting to setting. C and K are actor-networks of intangible assets only and A, the space of action and applications, is already a typical actor-network with all kind of heterogeneous actors. ANT can deal with the basic tissue of translation and dynamic capability of the boundaries of these three spaces. In fact, ANT's agnosticism and free association, and the fact that the actors are heterogeneous by nature allow us to tune across different spaces in either micro or macro views. And these travels in meanings represent strong roots for knowledge creation, learning and knowledge management.

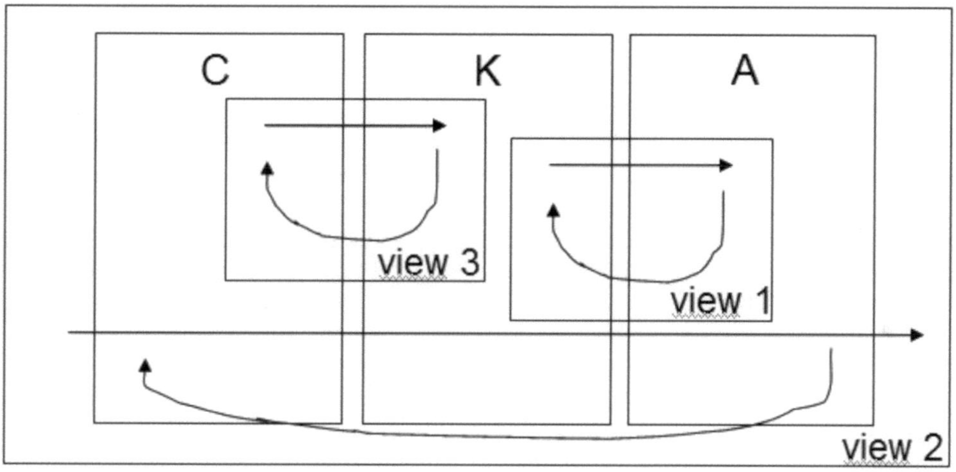

Fig. 1. Theory CK revisited

5. Knowledge, design and learning

In both practice and academia, we long ago passed from a teaching thinking modus into a design paradigm approach. We are mainly doing a choice on the way we think. In this way of thinking we need to construct systems as something that will work and we need to understand why, for what and to whom. In this way of thinking we get enrolled by purposes that are not only technical, they are user dependent, context dependent. We as designers should be concerned with *utility*, the bottom value. The best expected utility value, the best for our design purposes. Metaphors, analogies, divergences, thinking out of the box and serendipity are traditionally recognized ingredients to fuel creative thinking, so they must be considered as *design tools*. Design motivates involvement and learning, it motivates new things happening, it has a purpose of action, so it deals with decisions, knowledge production, a memory system and a learning ability. If you intercept more then one knowledge community then you mix and share motives, fears, problem solutions, analogies, associations and you increase again your own knowledge and both community's collective knowledge. The design approach, inserted in a sociotechnical chain of building artefacts, bridges the gap between the research concept and practice, (Romme, 2003). Design can be a methodology but mainly it is a paradigm (Van Aken, 2004), a way of looking into things understanding their qualities, looking at things in construction within a context. As seen in this loops of conceptual concentration, design is integrative and systemic. We address design in all engineering assertions but mainly in the assertion of "design as a discipline", as defined in Figueiredo and Cunha (2006). This discipline is central in every engineering branch (sometimes addressing one technology only) and particularly in the Engineering and Management domain where it normally involve more than one technologies.

6. Design project management

The mainstream research in project management has been criticised in recent years for its heavy reliance on the functionalist and instrumental view of projects and organisations (Hodgson and Cicmil, 2006). In fact we think projects do not exist as a given reality, ready made and neutral, but they are like networks of actions of interdependent actors through a process of negotiations and translations aligned to evolving shared meanings and goals. The target is moving and the reassemble of goals need to be a process of remaking and not only a steering exercise. In fact the project goal is constructed by the team (with the help of different stakeholders) and not only a cold spot in the horizon of our view.

What we just said is not easily accepted as in fact the mainstream, the project management body of knowledge (PMBOK), has for long emphasised the role of project actors basically as implementers, planning, doing and controlling what was mainly planned and mostly decided in a kind of closed time and defined territory. If we really think that in project management the most important role is the control of time, cost and scope and we think that this is enough, not foreseeing the other important roles actors interplay within the projects, then we are trapped by the classic mechanicists and ultra rational paradigm. So, broadening the scope of the very foundations of the project management discipline to include these new topics, less descriptive and rational, more intangible and more "open than closed", together with a systemic mind (and a sociotechnical mind), represents a new track that is not yet the common track, even if it is of crucial importance, mainly in projects involving innovation and design.

Unveiled in 2001 in Japan, P2P (Project and Program Management) was an attempt to address program conception, design, strategy management, architectures, communities of practice, and integration management of program execution. The major objectives of P2M are solutions to complex issues, accelerated innovation and trying to increase added value. Inscribed in a Japanese strategy, the sustainability of this approach to project and program management needs to be assessed. The Guidebook of Project and Program Management for Enterprise Innovation depicts the philosophy and paradigms behind the initiative.

We have two types of project management: operational and innovation driven. Operational project management pursues efficiency. Project goals and objectives are given by others. The basic concept of operational project management still is to define objectives such as scope, costs, time and quality based on basic architecture design developed by others acquiring desired results in line with the intention of stakeholders while stressing business processes. Innovative program and project management, as addressed in P2M, requires a paradigm shift from predefined project objectives to creative formulation of goals. P2M should address both formulation and complex problem solving while enhancing value through the community.

P2M is an interesting attempt to address creativity in project management but we must admit that some (basic and intangible) elements are and always would be in the centre of project success. Leadership and team building support to creativity and innovation in the operative work of a project management team are some of these elements. That is, the dynamics of creative success emanates from an ambience where generation and implementation of new ideas is stimulated. This ambience needs to be special and socially attractive, and with plain "windows" to the exterior, an exterior that must be invited to come inside whenever it seems possible and rewarding.

7. Conclusion

In an academic world dominated by mechanistic paradigms with positive approaches to the way research has to be conducted, some connections and interactions may seam irrelevant. We intend integration is important and we encourage the investment in systemic thinking, in training design thinking, in developing a sociotechnical mind, and in taking advantage of the actor-network metaphor. These seem to be success factors for today's (pos-industrial) engineering. And are these mainly important to the 10 per cent Allan Bromley referred (see section 1)? We would say no, they are important along all the one hundred per cent of the full engineering cycle and project management cycle. If this is so it must be internalized and some engineering education must take place in newer forms and subjects. And this effort needs to address the mechanics of mind, how it works and how your own values are crafted. Domains like communication, organization of work, psychology of people, organizational forms, an ethical mind, and many more, need to be integrated in the engineering design approach.

As in each day the importance of design in engineering (shorter production cycles, dynamics of technological innovation, reinforcing of competition) and the centrality of project oriented organizations increases (more and more firms are becoming project oriented, or are organizing themselves in a project logic) we need to focus our energies in these two broad domains. We exercised the Actor-Network metaphor in both of the domains, trying to demonstrate the advantages and the robustness of our thinking. Actor-Network is a way of looking into realities as landscapes and as trees, and this micro/macro ability is one of its advantages. But ANT can also address political tensions and power tensions that arise in design and project management situated teams.

The concepts presented in this paper are kind of *work in progress* as we are leading a project on this very subject that aligns the different community's collaboration and integration. Brown and Davis (2004) said the phenomenon of *culture shock*, the tension generated among different cultures, was an essential ingredient for enhancing learning and suggested that this should be directly managed when establishing the community's interaction. We think alike and claim that boundary objects are things to be considered in this creative and learning innovative process.

8. References

Abma, T.A. (2000), Fostering learning-in-organizing through narration: Questioning myths and stimulating multiplicity in two performing arts schools, European Journal of Work and Organizational Psychology, 9(2), 211-231.

Ambrosini, V. and Bowman, C., 2001, Tacit knowledge: Some suggestions for operationalization, Journal of Management Studies, 338(6), 811-829.

Argyris, C. & Schön, D. (1978): Organizational Learning. Reading, MA: Addison-Wesley

Bowker, Geoffrey C. and Susan Leigh Star, 1999, Sorting Things Out Classifications and its consequences, The MIT Press Cambridge, Massachusetts London, England

Brown, A., & Davis, N., 2004, Intercultural learning through digital media. In A. Brown & N. Davis (Eds.), Digital technology communities and education

Cadle, James and Donald Yeates, 2007, Project Management for Information Systems, Prentice Hall; 5 edition

Callon, M., 1986, Some Elements of a Sociology of Translation: Domestication of the Scallops and the Fishermen of St. Brieuc Bay, Power, Action and Belief: A New Sociology of Knowledge, J. Law (ed.), Routledge & Kegan, London

Callon, M., 1987, Society in the Making: The Study of Technology as a Tool for Sociological Analysis, Bijker, W.E. and Hughes, T.P. and Pinch, T.J. (eds.) The Social Construction of Technological Systems, New Directions in the Sociology and History of Technology, MIT Press, Cambridge, MA

Callon, Michel and Méadel, Cécile, Rabeharisoa, Vololona, 2002, The economy of qualities, Economy and Society, Volume 2 May 2002: pag.194-217; Routlege - Taylor & Francis Ltd

Cooperrider, Bryan, 2008, The Importance of Divergent Thinking in Engineering Design, Proceedings of the 2008 American Society for Engineering Education Pacific Southwest Annual Conference

Cropley, A., 2006, In praise of convergent thinking, Creativity Research Journal 18(3): 391-404

Cyert, R.M. & March, J.G. (1963): A Behavioral Theory of the Firm. Englewood Cliffs, NJ

Czarniawska, Barbara, 2004, Narrative in Social Sciences Research, SAGE Publications Ltd.

Darwent, S. (2000), Story telling: An introduction to storytelling, IBM knowledge management.

Dodge, Bernie, 1998, Active Learning on the Web [On Line] Available: http://edweb.sdsu.edu/people/bdodge/ActiveLearning.html

Dym, Clive, Alice Agocino, Ozgur Eris, Daniel Frey, and Larry Leifer, 2005, Engineering design Thinking, Teaching, and Learning, Journal of Engineering education, 94 (1), 103–120

Faber, B. (1998), Toward a rhetoric of change. Journal of Business and Technical Communication, 12(2), 217-243.

Felder, Richard and Rebecca Brent, 2003a, Designing and Teaching Courses to Satisfy the ABET Engineering Criteria, Journal of Engineering Education, 92 (1), 7-25 (2003)

Felder, Richard and Rebecca Brent, 2003b, Learning by Doing, Chemical Engineering Education, 37(4), 282–283 (2003)

Figueiredo, A. D. & Da Cunha P. R., 2006, Action Research and Design in Information Systems, Two faces of a single coin, Chapter 5, Information Systems Action Research: Bridging the Industry-University Technology Gap, Ned Kock (Editor), Springer / Kluwer

Figueiredo, José, 2008, Reviewing the Actor-Network Theory, Encyclopaedia of Networked and Virtual Organizations, Book Chapter, a GI Global Publication edited by Putnik and Cunha, pp 1374 - 1380.

Figueiredo, José, 2008b, Cross-functional Emerging Domains in Engineering: Actor Networks and Collaborative Models, Organizational Learning and Knowledge Management, Proceedings of the IEMC Europe 2008, IEEE International Engineering Management Conference, Estoril, Portugal pp 469 – 473

Ford, Ralph and Chris Coulston, 2008, Design for Electrical and Computer Engineers, McGraw-Hill, Section 1.1

Fuller, Mark, Joe Valacich, Joey George, 2007, Information Systems Project Management: A Process and Team Approach, Prentice Hall

Gabriel, Y. (1998), Same old story or changing stories? Folkloric, modern and postmodern mutations, in D. Grant, T. Keenoy and C. Oswick (eds.), Discourse and Organization, London, Sage, 84-103.

Gibbons, M., Limoges C., Nowotny H., Schwartzman S., Scott, P & Trow M., 1994, The new production of knowledge: The Dynamics of Science and Research in Contemporary Societies, Sage Publications, London

Goldratt, E. M., 1997, Critical Chain, Great Barrington, MA: North River Press

Gonçalves, Abreu and José Figueiredo, 2009, Organizing Competences: Actor-Network Theory in Virtual Settings, International Journal of Networking and Virtual Organisations, Vol. 6, No. 1, 2009, pp 23 – 35.

Gonçalves, Abreu and José Figueiredo, 2008, Constructing scope in project management: an interpretive approach, Proceedings of the IEMC Europe 2008, IEEE International Engineering Management Conference, Estoril, Portugal, pp 485 - 489.

Graaff, Erik de, Anette Kolmos, 2007, Management of Change: Implementation of Problem-Based and Project-Based Learning in Engineering, Sense Publishers

Hargadon, A.B., 1998, Firms as knowledge brokers: lessons in pursuing continuous innovation, California Management Review, 40, (3), 209-227.

Hatchuel A., P. Le Masson and B. Weil, 2002, From knowledge management to design-oriented organisations, International Social Science Journal, Special issue n The Knowledge Society, n°171, UNESCO, pp.25-37

Hatchuel, A and Weil, B, 2003, A new approach of innovative design: an introduction to C-K theory, in ICED'03, Stockholm, 14

Hatchuel, A., Le Masson, P., et Weil, B., 2006, The design of science based-products: an interpretation and modelling with C-K theory, 9th International Design Conference, Dubrovnik, 15th-18th May 2004, D. Marjanovic, 1, 33-44.n

Hatchuel, A., et Le Masson, P., 2007, Shaping the unknown and the emergent: Design theory as a new source of management knowledge, European Academy of Management, Paris, 21

Hepso, V., 2001, The involvement of Human and Non Human Stakeholders, Combining ANT and Action Research, IRIS 23 - 23rd Information Systems Research Seminar in Scandinavia, Doing IT Together, Uddevalla, Sweden

Hildreth, P. and Chris Kimble, 2002, The duality of knowledge, Information Research, Vol. 8 (1), paper n° 142

Hodgson D, Cicmil S (editors), 2006, Making projects critical. Palgrave McMillan Publishing

Hofstede, Geert, 1980, Culture's Consequences: International Differences in Work-related Values, Sage

Illich, Ivan, 1974, Energy and Equity: Ideas in progress, M. Boyars Publishers.

Jesiek, B. K., Newswander, L. K., and Borrego, M., 2009, Engineering Education Research: Discipline, community or field? JEE vol 98, n° 1, pp. 40-41, January 2009.

Jorgensen, U., 2008, Engineering Design in Theory, Teaching, and Practice - The Construction of Design Synthesis and Methods and Contemporary Challenges, submitted manuscripts, Global Perspectives on Engineering, International Network for Engineering Studies Workshop, Lisbon 2008, http://www.inesweb.org/node/202

Keller, B., 2007, September 19, No Easy Project, Education Week, 27(4), 21-23

Le Masson, P., 2001, De la R&D à la RID, modélisation des fonctions de conception et nouvelles organisations de la R&D, thèse de doctorat de L'École des Mines de Paris

Latour, B., 1987, Science in action: how to follow scientists and engineers through society. Oxford: Oxford University Press

Latour, B., 1996, Aramis, or Love of Technology, Harvard University Press, Cambridge, Massachusetts & London, England

Law, J. 1986, On the methods of long distance control: vessels, navigation, and the Portuguese route to India, Power, Action and Belief, A New Sociology of Knowledge, Law, J. (Ed.), Routledge & Kegan Paul, London, Boston and Henley, http://www.comp.lancs.ac.uk/sociology/papers/law-methods-of-long-distance-control.pdf

Lucena, J., Downey, G. Jesiek, B. & Elber, 2008, S. Competencies beyond countries: The Re-Organization of Engineering Education in the United States, Europe, and Latin America. JEE, vol. 97, no.4, pp. 433-447. 2008.

Mintzberg, Henry, 1977, the Nature of Managerial Work, Harper & Row

Monteiro, E., 2000, Actor Network Theory and Information Infrastructure, Claudio Ciborra (Ed.), From Control to Drift, The Dynamics of Corporate Information Infrastructures, Oxford University Press, New York, pp. 71 - 83

O'Connor, E.S., 1997, Telling decisions: The role of narrative in organizational decision-making, in Z. Shapira (ed.), Organizational decision making, New York, Cambridge University Press, 1996, 304-323.

PMBOK Guide, 2004, A Guide to the Project Management Body of Knowledge, Third Edition, Project Management Institut

Polanyi, M., 1967, The tacit dimension, London, Routledge and Kegan Paul

Prince, Michael, 2004, Does Active Learning Work? A Review of the Research, Journal of Engineering Education, July 2004

Romme, A. G., 2003, Making a difference: organization as design, Organization Science: A Journal of the Institute of Management Sciences, 14 (5), 558-573.

Rosenberg, C., Toward an Ecology of Knowledge: On Discipline, Context, and History, No Other Gods: On Science and American Social Thought, revised ed., Johns Hopkins Univ. Press, 1997, pp. 225-239.

Senge, P.M. (1990) The Leader´s New Work: Building Learning Organizations. Sloan Management Review, Fall, 7-23.

Star, Susan Leigh and James Griesemer, 1989, Institutional Ecology, "Translations" and Boundary Objects: amateurs and professional in Berkeley's Museum of Vertebrate Zoology, 1907-39, Social Studies of Science, Vol. 19, pp. 387-420, Sage

Tatnall, A. E Gilding, A., 1999, Actor-Network theory and Information Systems

Torrence, E. P., 1988, The nature of creativity as manifest in its testing, RJ Sternberg (ed), The Nature of Creativity, Cambridge University Press

Van Aken, J. E., 2004, Management research based on the paradigm of the design sciences: The quest for field-tested and grounded technological rules. Journal of Management Studies, 41, 219- 246

Vicari, S., Krogh, G., Roos, J. and Mahnke, V., 1996, Knowledge creation through cooperative experimentation, In: Managing knowledge. Perspectives on cooperation and competition, edited by G. von Krogh and J. Roos, pp. 184-202. Thousand Oaks, CA: Sage.

Zouari, A., M. Tollenaere, H. Ben Bacha, and A.Y. Maalej, 2007, Can C-K theory apply to Knowledge-Based Engineering systems?, International Journal of Product Lifecycle Management (IJPLM), Vol. 2, No. 3, 2007

6

Managing Knowledge in Collaborative Software Maintenance Environment

Mohd Zali Mohd Nor, Rusli Abdullah,
Masrah Azrifah Azmi Murad and Mohd Hasan Selamat
Universiti Putra Malaysia
Malaysia

1. Introduction

In recent years, many organizations consider knowledge management (KM) to be strategically important to their business. KM is envisaged to contribute to the organizations in the following manners (KPMG, 2003):

- Bring synergies among different teams, units or departments
- Accelerate innovation and boosting revenues for market development.
- Improve quality in operational and functional processes
- Reduce costs and exposure to business risks

With the above 'promises', KM is also enticing to software development and maintenance organizations, especially in managing software engineering activities. Within software engineering activities, software maintenance (SM) has yet to receive proper attention (SWEBOK, 2004). It is a costly process, where previous works (Fjeldstad & Hamlen, 1979; Lientz et al., 1981; Pigoski, 1997; Schach et al., 2003) estimated SM costs of between 60% to 90% of total software life cycle costs.

In Software Engineering area, KM have been studied mostly on Software Development environment, but in Software Maintenance (SM) environment, KM has not been widely used nor studied. Therefore, studies on KM in SM shall be beneficial to the SM communities to assist them to perform their daily activities .

The motivation to apply KM in SM in driven by the fact that the SM activities are knowledge-intensive (Rodriguez, 2004a), and depend largely on expertise of the maintainers. Most of the time, maintainers depend on experience and "hunches" when making decisions. Some of these expertise are documented as explicit knowledge, but more are hidden as tacit knowledge due to scarcity of documentation (Viscaino et al., 2003). As SM organizations grow and becoming more distributed, members shall need to collaborate and share these individual knowledge. Various artefacts are 'created' and shared during the SM activities. Among them are:

- Problem reports (PR) (a.k.a. incident report, call tickets) - recorded in helpdesk application, the PR shall remain open and notes are appended until the problem is resolved, or Maintenance Request (MR) is raised.

- MR – A request for maintenance task, either to fix production bug raised via PR, business enhancement, or perfective and preventive maintenance. Normally MR shall be registered in a Software Configuration Management (SCM) application. MR shall be versioned and remain open until the tasks are completed.
- Business Requirement Documents (BRD) (a.k.a. requirement specifications) - For business changes, a BRD is normally required to explain the current application and the intended changes
- Software Requirement Documents (SRD) (a.k.a. software specifications) – In addition to BRD, SRD details out the technical specifications to guide maintainers on the required changes
- Test Plan – a guideline for QA to perform testing on the MR
- Release Notes – a list of changes made for a specific release or version.
- Known Issues – a list of known issues for high-priority MR that could not be completed, with the workarounds, if applicable.

In many SM organizations, the above artefacts are kept in SCM, using various 'containers' such as MS-Word, MS- Excel, pdf and hence making searching difficult. As such, maintainers often have to resort to checking the code to derive the knowledge (Das et al.,2007). Notwithstanding, many other information that are important to maintainers resides somewhere else. For example, the domain knowledge often resides within users community, either explicit in form of best practices, policies and procedures, circulars and others, or implicit, in the mind and experience of the expert users. Are these knowledge important and pertinent to the other parties? In SM, the answer is a resounding yes. As expert users and maintainers leave the organization, the implicit knowledge are gone with them. This is where KM is useful to consolidate all these information together and allow users and maintainers to contribute, share and store knowledge.

In this chapter, we shall present the followings: review the definitions and concepts of KM, KMS and SM collaborative environment; propose a KMS framework for collaborative SM environment; present a Multi Agent System (MAS) tools to support users and maintainers in knowledge sharing; and an combined ontology to structure the required knowledge to be used by the MAS tool

2. Knowledge Management

As an overview, knowledge is defined as *"a fluid mix of framed experience, values, contextual information and expert insight that provides a framework for evaluating and incorporating new experiences and information. It originates and is applied in the mind of knowers. In organizations, it often becomes embedded not only in documents an repositories but also in organizational routines, processes, practices and norms."* (Davenport & Prusak, 2000).

Meanwhile, KM, in technical perspective, is defined as the strategies and processes of identifying, understanding, capturing, sharing, and leveraging knowledge (Abdullah et al., 2006; Alavi & Leidner, 2000; Davenport & Prusak, 2000; Selamat et al., 2006). For individual knowledge creation cycle, Nonaka & Takeuchi SECI framework (Nonaka & Takeuchi, 1995), based on Polanyi's tacit and explicit knowledge, models the knowledge creation stages of socialization, internalization, combination and externalization. This SECI model has been used and synthesized by many others to model the KM for team and organization levels.

The knowledge creation cycle in SM environment and the collaboration technologies used are depicted in the following Fig. 1.

Tacit to tacit knowledge via Socialization SM knowledge are exchanged through experience sharing, brainstorming, observation and practice. *Today technologies*: Collaboration tools - teleconferencing, desktop video conferencing tools, live-meetings, village wells, synchronous collaboration	**Tacit to explicit knowledge via Externalization** Articulate tacit knowledge into explicit via concepts, metaphor, or models. In SM cases, these could be in form of screenshots of errors, shadow sessions, emails, conversations *Today technologies*: Email, terminal sessions, chat
Explicit to tacit knowledge via Internalization Knowledge is documented or verbalized, to help maintainers internalize and transfer knowledge, and also help other maintainers to 're-experience' bug scenarios. *Today technologies*: Helpdesk and SCM applications are used to store bug reports and changes. Visualization tool to read or listen to success stories.	**Explicit to explicit knowledge via Combination** Knowledge are combined, sorted, added , exchanged and categorized, via specifications, SCM entries and error analysis *Today's technologies*: Collaboration tools - E-mail, GroupWare, Homepages, consolidates in SCM. Data mining to sort, and filter information.

Fig. 1. SM Collaboration technologies in Knowledge Creation Cycle- Adapted from Nonaka & Takeuchi SECI Model

2.1 Knowledge Management Framework

KM frameworks for modeling organization knowledge cycles are useful to understand strategies and processes of identifying, understanding, capturing, sharing, and leveraging knowledge within the teams, departmental units and organizations. Among few are frameworks by Szulanski's model of knowledge transfer (Szulanski, 1996), APQC's organizational KM model (Arthur Anderson and APQC, 1996), Choo's model of knowing organization (Choo, 1996), Selamat et al.'s KM framework with feedback loop (Selamat et al., 2006) and Holsapple and Joshi's 3-fold collaborative KM framework (Holsapple & Joshi, 2002). This framework synthesizes the knowledge resources from Leonard-Barton, and Petrach and Sveiby models; KM activities from Nonaka, APQC, Wiig, Van der Spek and Alavi's models, and KM influences from Wiig, APQC, Van der Speck, Szulanski and Leonard-Barton models. The summary of the above frameworks are listed in the following Table 1:

Dimension/ Framework Model	KM Activities		Strategy	Enabler/ Enabling condition
	Activities	Process		
Wiig (1993) 3 pillars of KM	Creation, Manifestation, Use, Transfer	Pillar 1 - Survey and categorize, Analyze knowledge and activities, Elicit, coding and organize Pillar 2 - Appraise and evaluate, Action Pillar 3 - Synthesize, Handle, use and control, Leverage, distribute and automate		
Nonaka & Takeuchi (1995) Knowledge creation	Socialization, Externalization, Combination, Internalization	5-phase model of K-creation process: Sharing tacit knowledge,Concept creation,Concept justification,Archetype building,Cross-levelling		Intention, Autonomy, Creative Chaos, Redundancy, Requisite Variety
Szulanski (1996) Knowledge Transfer model	Knowledge transfer - Initiation, Implementation, Ramp-up, Integration			K-transfer influences - Characteristics of k-transfer, k-sources, recipient, context
APQC (1996) Organizational KM model	Share, Create, Identify, Collect, Adapt, Organize, Apply			Leadership, Culture, Technology, Measurement
Van der Spek & Spijkervet (1997) Four-Cycle KM stage		Conceptualize, Reflect, Act, Retrospect		
Choo (1998) The Knowing Organization	Sense making, K-creation, Decision making			
Davenport & Prusak (2000) Working Knowledge	Knowledge generation-Acquisition, Rental, Dedicated resources, Fusion, Adaptation, Networks Knowledge codification and coordination-Mapping and modeling knowledge, Capturing tacit knowledge, Codifying knowledge		Monopolies, Incompleteness of information, Asymmetry of knowledge, Localness, Artificial scarcity, Trade barriers	Price system - reciprocity, repute, altruism, trust Knowledge market - buyer, seller, brokers
Hansen, Nohvia & Tiernes (1999) KM Strategy			Codification, Personalization	
Australia KM Standards (2001) Integrated KM framework	Knowledge process - Sharing, Acquisition, Creation		Knowledge alignment - Context, Analysis, Planning	Knowledge Foundations - Culture, Technology, Sustaining systems
Holsapple and Joshi (2002) 3-fold collaborative KM framework	Acquiring, Selecting, Internalizing, Using			KM Influences - Resource, Managerial,Enviroment al influences Knowledge Resources - Participants knowledge, Culture,

				Infrastructure, Purpose, Strategies
Handzig & Hasan (2003) Integrated Organizational KM framework				<u>Enablers</u> - Knowledge process, Knowledge stock, External environment <u>Organizational factors</u> - Organizational environment, Technological infrastructure

Table 1. KM Frameworks - Theoretical Construct

2.2 Knowledge Management System Framework

To conceptualize the KM frameworks into a Knowledge Management System (KMS), a KMS framework shall need to be defined for collaborative SM environment. KMS is defined as *"I.T-based system developed to support and augment the organizational process of knowledge creation, storage, retrieval, transfer and application"* (Alavi & Leidner, 2000). In general, a KMS framework consists of influential factors of KMS initiatives and their interdependent relationships and a model of KMS implementation (Foo et al., 2006). However, systems and technology alone does not create knowledge (Davenport & Prusak, 2000), various other social "incentives" and organizational strategy and culture are often required to stimulate use of technology to share knowledge.

In this chapter, we review some of the related KMS frameworks and identified the components that could be synthesized for knowledge-based collaborative SM framework.

Dimension Framework Model	Activities & process	Functionality	Technology	
			Tools	**Architecture**
Meso & Smith (2000) Technical perspective of KMS architecture	Using, finding, creating, packaging Know how, know what, know why, Self-motivated creativity, Personal tacit, Cultural tacit, Organizational tacit, regulatory assets		Computer-mediated collaboration, Electronic task management, Messaging, Video conferencing, GDSS, Web browser, Data Mining, Search and retrieval, Intelligent Agent, Document Management	
Natarajan & Shekar (2000) Dual-KM Framework	Generation, storage, application			Knowledge enterprise - OSI 7-layer model
Hahn & Subramani (2000) Framework of KMS	classifying KMS based on the locus of the knowledge and the a priori structuring of contents		Document repository, Data warehousing, Yellow pages of experts, Electronic discussion forum, collaborative filtering, Intranets & search engine	

Alavi & Leidner (2000) KMS Process framework	Creation, Storage, Retrieval ,Transfer, Application	Coding and sharing best practices, Corporate K-directories, Knowledge network		
Rao (2005) 8'Cs audit framework		Connectivity, content, community, culture, capacity, cooperation, commerce, capital		
Abdullah et al. (2008) Collaborative KMS framework	Acquisition, store, disseminate, use. Soft Components - Awareness, Reward, Motivation, Culture, Strategy, beliefs, values, experience		Portal, EDMS, Workflow, OLAP, Agent	Infrastructure, technology, protocol, repository
Deraman(1998) KMS model for SM	Software knowledge, Change Request knowledge			
Rus and Lindval (2001) KMS framework for SE	3 levels of KM Support in SE - 1st Level: Document mgmt, competence mgmt. 2nd Level: Store organizational memory, design rationale, SCM. 3rd Level: Packaged knowledge			
Dingsoyr & Conradi (2002) Knowledge management "system"	Method to manage tacit knowledge, explicit knowledge		Infrastructure, Software systems, Experience management system	
Rodriguez et al. (2004b) KMS in SM	Collecting, distributing knowledge		Active tools, passive tools	
De Souza et al. (2006) KM framework in global software development	Organizational Focus, Degree of structure, Knowledge repositories in place		Client-server, Peer-to-peer (P2P), Hybrid	

Table 2. KMS Frameworks - Theoretical Construct

3. Collaborative Software Maintenance Environment

As an overview, software maintenance (SM) is defined as "*The totality of activities required to provide cost-effective support to software system. Activities are performed during the pre-delivery stage as well as the post-delivery stage*" (IEEE 14764, 2006; SWEBOK, 2004). SM activities are complex, knowledge-intensive (Rodriguez et al., 2004a), and depend largely on expertise of the maintainers and expert users, as depicted in Fig. 1. Software maintenance processes and activities have been largely standardized. Standard organizations such as ISO, IEEE, and CMMI have detailed the activities to be carried-out by software maintainers (April et al., 2005; IEEE 14764, 2006). At a very minimum, the activities include process implementation, problem and modification analysis, modification implementation, maintenance review and acceptance, migration and software retirements.

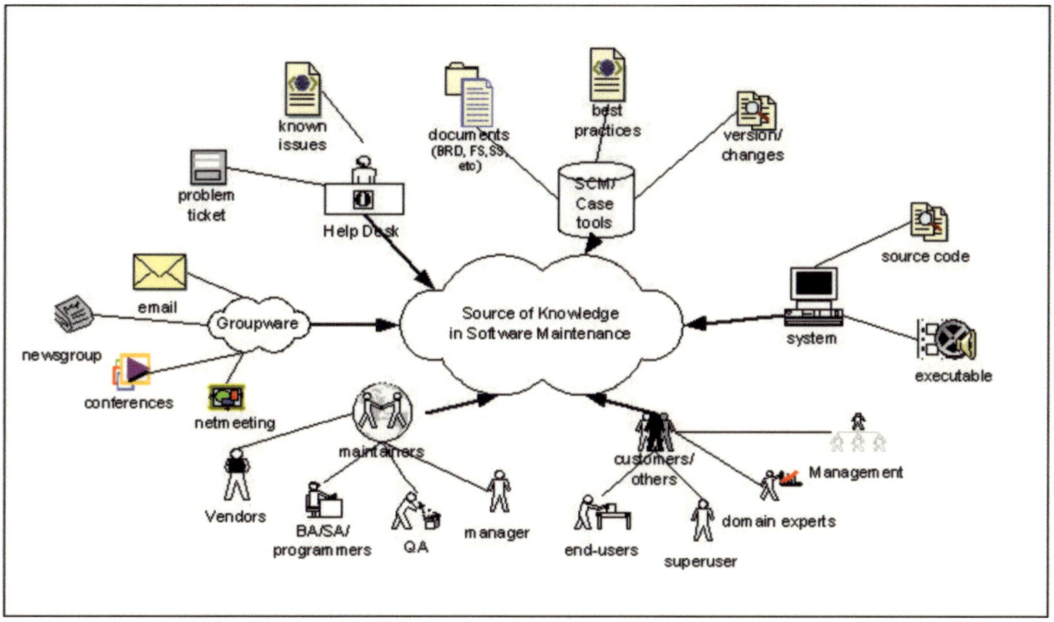

Fig. 2. Sources of Knowledge in SM

However, many software maintenance organizations may have their own best-practice processes and activities to suit the organizational and business practices. Detail activities may vary depending on the following setups:

- Types of maintenance organizations - such as in-house maintenance, vendor or outsourced maintenance, or commercial-of-the-shelf (COTS) application maintenance.
- Team setup - such as similar or separate development and maintenance team.
- Types of software or applications being maintained (Pressman, 2005)
- Maintenance approach or model - For example, those using Waterfall approach may differ from those using Agile approach.

As a broad example, the SM activities are depicted in Fig. 3 below:

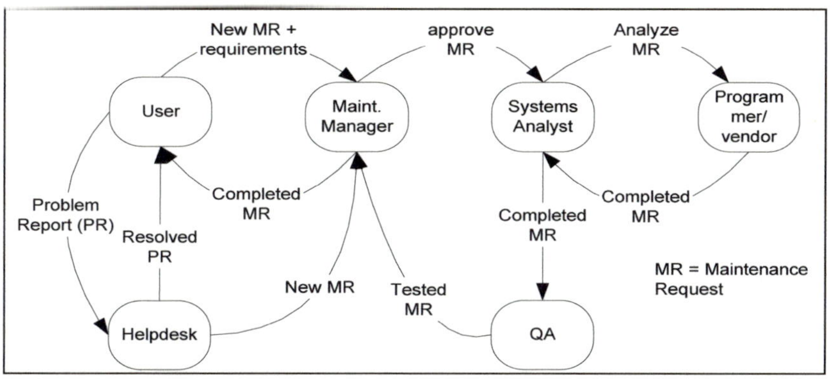

Fig. 3. Sample maintenance activities

Meanwhile, the knowledge needed in SM can be summarized as follows (Ghali, 1993; Rodriguez, 2004a; Rus & Lindvall, 2001):

- Organizational knowledge, such as roles and resources. The parties involved in software maintenance activities consist of various application users and software maintainers. The list may include end-user, superuser, maintenance manager, business analyst, systems analyst, project manager, QA personnel, build manager, implementation personnel and trainer. Attached to these roles are the area of expertise.
- Managerial knowledge - such as resource management, task and project tracking and management.
- Technical knowledge – such as requirement analysis, system analysis, development tools , testing and implementation. Critical to this is also the knowledge on supporting groupware and CASE tools such as Software Configuration Management (SCM), helpdesk and testing tools
- Domain knowledge – knowledge of the products and business processes.
- Knowledge on source of knowledge – where the knowledge resides, such as source codes, documentation, supporting CASE tools and more importantly, the where the experts are.

There are various issues associated with the above knowledge, which makes organizing, storing, sharing and disseminating knowledge difficult. Among the problems are:

- The 'containers' could be in different electronic forms, which sometimes need to be mined and manually extracted. Or worse, in paper form which require more effort to place it in KMS
- Documentation are most of the time not up-to-date. As mentioned earlier, Earlier studies indicates around 50% of efforts are spent on this activity and rely more on source code than any other source of information (Fjeldstad & Hamlen, 1979; Schach et al.,2003)
- Domain knowledge are becoming more important to software maintainers (Santos, 2005). However, this knowledge are often not available within the software maintenance CoP, especially in vendor and distributed environment. Changes to business processes and changes to application affects not only the business users, but also software maintainers
- Human experts hold most of the tacit knowledge that are not readily available to others. are the major source of knowledge. However, there are still reservation toward knowledge sharing. *''If getting promotion, or holding your job, or finding a new one is based on the knowledge you possess - what incentive is there to reveal that knowledge and share it?'* (Wilson, 2002).
- The above problems are further exacerbated in distributed maintenance teams, where members resides in different location and time-zones. As such, face-to-face meetings are seldom and tacit knowledge transfer is difficult.

Managing knowledge in this area is therefore critical to ensure that both users and maintainers can perform SM activities properly and timely, by sharing and obtaining vital knowledge.

3.1 Knowledge-based Framework for Collaborative Software Maintenance

KMS for SM has been studied late 1980s by Jarke and Rose (1988), who introduced a prototype KMS to control database software development and maintenance, mainly to facilitate program comprehension. The KMS is a decision-based approach that facilitates communication across time and among multiple maintainers and users, thus improving maintenance support. However, facilitating program comprehension is not enough as SM is more than just understanding codes and extracting knowledge from codes.

Similarly, Deraman (1998) introduced an KMS model for SM which, albeit very simple, could provide us with the main essence of SM knowledge - the Software Knowledge, Change Request Knowledge and their functional interaction. However, these alone, are not enough for users and maintainers. Newer technologies such as software agents are used to capture SM process knowledge in researches conducted by Viscaino et al.(2004) and Rodriguez et al. (2004b). However, no KMS framework for SM was conceptualized by these studies.

Looking at the wider perspective of software engineering (SE), KMS in SE have been studied by many, including Santos et al. (2005), Rus and Lindval (2001) and Aurum et al.(2003). Rus and Lindval described the three main tasks of SE (individual, team and organization) and identified the three level of KM support for each task. The 1st level includes the core support for SE activities, document management and competence management. Meanwhile, the 2nd level incorporates methods to store organizational memory using method such as design rationale and tools such as source control and SCM. The 3rd KM support level includes packaged knowledge to support Knowledge definition, acquisition and organization. The above should describes the KMS framework for SE. However, this model do not consider the social, physiological and cultural aspects of KM, as identified by the previous other generic KMS frameworks.

In order to propose a suitable KMS framework for SM,, a review of current KMS framework for generic KMS, and related SE/SM KMS are conducted. The theoretical constructs for KM frameworks, KMS frameworks and knowledge components in SM are summarized, and components suitable for SM KMS framework are identified, as follows:

- Required knowledge, such as organizational knowledge, managerial knowledge, technical knowledge, enterprise business domain knowledge and knowledge on source of knowledge, are derived from Ghali (1993), Rus and Lindval (2001) and Rodriguez et al. (2004a)
- KM Activities are derived from Nonaka and Takeuchi (1995), Holsapple and Joshi (1998). This includes Acquiring knowledge, Selecting knowledge, using knowledge, Providing/ Creating knowledge and Storing knowledge.
- SM governance tools are from Rus and Lindval (2001), IEEE 14764 (2006) and Mohd Nor et al.(2008a). To support these flow of SM information, tools such as Helpdesk, Software Configuration Management (SCM), Source Control and Project Management (PM) are crucial to monitor MRs.
- KM Components and Infrastructure are derived from Abdullah et al. (2006), Meso & Smith (2000) and Rus and Lindval (2001) frameworks. The major components includes computer-mediated collaboration, Experience Mgmt System, Document Management, KM portal, EDMS, OLAP, and Middlewares tools.
- Automation and knowledge discovery tools are from Meso and Smith (2000), Abdullah et al. (2006), Rodriguez et al. (2004b) and new internet tools in the

market. Tools such as GDSS, Intelligent Agents, Data mining/warehouse, Expert system and Case-Based Reasoning (CBR). Active tools such as RSS are also useful to get the right knowledge to the right users at the right time.

- KM Influences are derive from Holsapple and Joshi (2002) and Abdullah (2006). Among these are the managerial influences and strategy, and psychological and cultural influences.

To summarize the collaborative SM in perspective of People, Process, Technology and Knowledge Content, the following dimensions are proposed:

Knowledge Dimension		**Relevance to SM**
People	Organization	Routine, rules, culture
		Enterprise Domain knowledge
	Team	Knowledge on roles, expertise and their location
	Individual	Technical skills - requirement analysis, systems analysis, programming, testing and implementation
		Managerial skills - MR management, resource planning
		Domain expertise
Process	Organizational	Best practices, culture, strategy, psychological influences
	Regulatory	Audit, data security
	Best Practices	SM best practices, Software Configuration Management (SCM) process, Versioning process
Technology	SM tools	SCM, Version Control, Source Control, Project Management, Helpdesk tools
	KM tools	KMS portal, Search engine, Data warehouse, EDMS, OLAP, and Middlewares tools
	Collaboration	email, e-group, wikis, SMS, MMS, mobile technologies
	Automation & K- discovery	GDSS, Intelligent Agents, Data mining/warehouse, Expert system, RSS and Case-Based Reasoning (CBR)
Content	Domain knowledge	Products, Business rules
	Knowledge Map	Ontology, yellowpages
	Software artifacts	

Table 3. People, Process, Technology and Content Model for Knowledge-based Collaborative SM

Based on the above, the model for knowledge-based collaborative SM framework is proposed, as per Fig. 4 below:

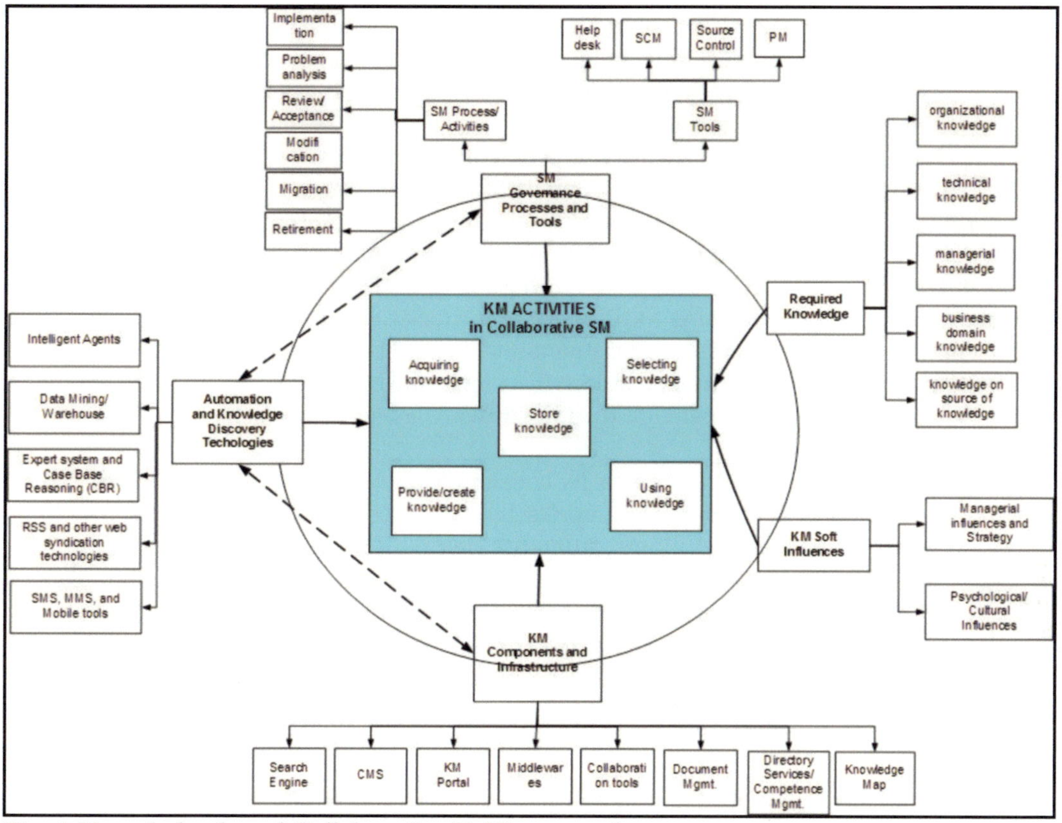

Fig. 4. Knowledge-based Collaborative SM Framework

3.2 Managing Knowledge in Collaborative SM

To provide for all the above components for knowledge-based collaborative SM system is the ultimate goal. However, this will require tremendous efforts and overall revamp of the SM process management tools. In our previous studies, much of the knowledge-based SM tools are siloed and not integrated to allow seamless knowledge combination, which hampers knowledge acquisition and sharing. This was further supported by a survey on managing knowledge of SM process in higher learning institutions (HLI) in Klang Valley, Malaysia, several major issues were identified as follows (Mohd Nor & Abdullah, 2008b):

- 80% of the surveyed SM organization do not use KMS to store knowledge acquired during the maintenance activities. Hence, this could contribute to problems and lateness in getting the information from other experts.
- In various aspects of SM activities (helpdesk, planning and analysis and coding and testing), between 60% to 80% of respondents consider domain knowledge important to assist them in daily SM activities. However, they admit that the knowledge generated from these activities are not stored in KMS or other electronic means, thus making them harder to extract, shared and turned explicit.
- Substantial efforts are spent collaborating with users, experts, SAs, and vendors to ascertain the problems and requirements. In the survey, 41% and 20% of helpdesk time are used to collaborate with maintenance team and users, respectively.

Meanwhile, in the planning and analysis, 22% of the time is spent discussing issues with users, 20% with colleagues and another 20% with developers. Without a systematic approach to these information acquisition and sharing, these efforts shall remain a major issue.

- Overall, in term of the perceived problems, quality of application documentation and inadequate system support remain as major issues.

One good way of solving the above issues is via automation. According to Davenport and Prusak (2001), one of the main goal of a KM system is to automate, as much as possible, the tasks of acquiring, disseminating and storing of knowledge. With all the sources of knowledge located and traversing in different repositories via different tools, keeping track of information useful for both users and maintainers could be a nightmare.

In this chapter, we shall introduce an automation mechanism to allow users and maintainers to acquire, share and use knowledge during software maintenance activities, vis-à-vis the following functionalities:

- Assist users in reporting errors, by checking for previously related reported errors, known issues and related enterprise business domain rules. This would help to reduce unnecessary duplicate errors that Helpdesk personnel need to handle.
- Assist Helpdesk personnel to monitor helpdesk call tickets, create Maintenance Request (MR) and assign it to the respective maintainers
- Assist Maintainers to check for the earlier reported MRs, Domain business rules and the domain experts, as well as monitoring the assigned MRs.
- Store the domain and SM knowledge created during maintenance process onto a repository.

4. Multi-Agent System

The agent-oriented approach is gaining acceptability in supporting maintainers in automating their daily activities (Dam and Winikoff, 2003; Viscaino et al., 2003; Rodriquez et al., 2004b). Intelligent software agent is a computer system capable of flexible autonomous action in some environments. Being flexible means that the agent is reactive (maintains an ongoing interaction with its environment, and responds to changes), proactive (taking initiatives) and social (interact with other agents) (Wooldridge,2002). Hence, a MAS is a system consisting of a number of agents, which interact with each others.

We propose a MAS tool to enable both users and software maintainers to automate some of the SM activities and capture and share the enterprise business domain knowledge and automatically link them to the application and SM process information.

Prometheus methodology was used to design the MAS and based on analyses of goals, data cohesion and agent interaction, the proposed MAS System Overview and architecture are depicted below in Fig. 5 and Fig. 6, respectively (Mohd Nor et al., 2008c).

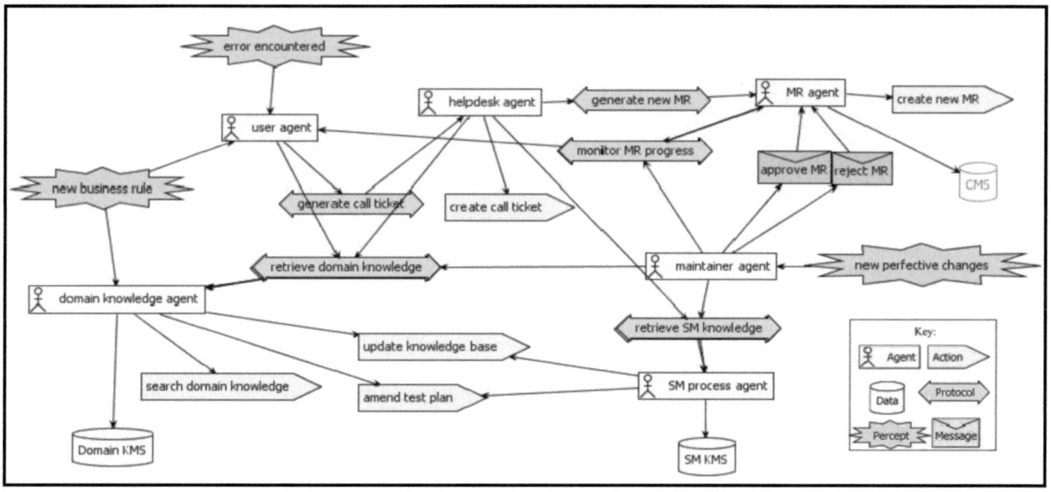

Fig. 5. MAS Systems Overview

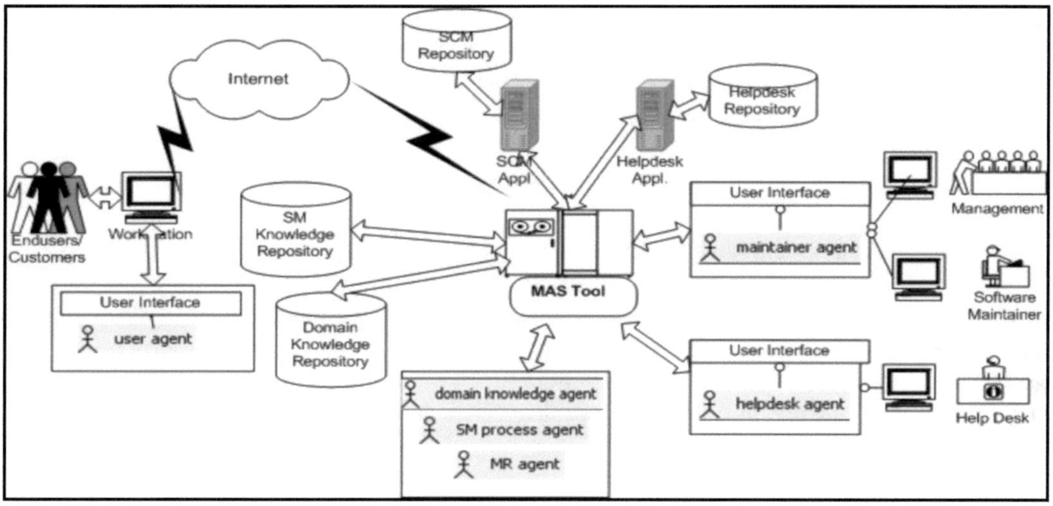

Fig. 6. Multi-Agent Architecture

As a result, six agent types are proposed: User Agent, Helpdesk Agent, Maintenance Request Agent, Maintainer Agent, SM Process Agent and Domain Knowledge Agent, as described below:

- User Agent - represents each user to file complaints, check best practices and application guides, as well as receive MR status from other agents.
- Domain Knowledge Agent - manages the domain knowledge ontology and data. When new knowledge is added, this agent shall inform relevant users and maintainers. When a new version is applied, the domain knowledge is updated with new best practices and old practices are deprecated.
- Helpdesk Agent - represents the role of helpdesk staff, by generating new call tickets based on error reported by User Agent, and assigning them to available

helpdesk personnel. If bugs is valid, Helpdesk Agent shall liaise with MR Agent to create new MR.

- MR Agent - Other than creating new MRs, this agent shall also assist planner to approve/reject MRs, monitor the progress of MRs and assign MRs to maintainers, via Maintainer Agent.
- Maintainer Agent - represents maintainers (analysts, programmers and testers) to monitor MR statuses and assign to maintainer groups for development. This agent also liaise with Domain Knowledge Agent and SM Knowledge Agent to obtain knowledge to assist analysts and tester in their works..
- SM Process Agent - For new artifacts and object changed, SM Knowledge Agent shall update the SM knowledge base, as well as the Domain knowledge. This agent also monitors the releases and versions, and provides maintainers with the information requested.

4.1 Combined Enterprise Domain and SM Ontology

The term ontology, in our context, can be best defined as a formal explicit description of concepts or entities, and their properties, relationships and constraints [Gruninger & Fox, 1995; Noy & McGuinness, 2001). The uses of ontology to support the agent-based tool, development of ontology is critical in the following ways:

- Agents use ontology to share common terms and to communicate to other agents (Wooldridge, 2002).
- Agent must understand the environment in which they operate. When agent retrieves or store the knowledge, it needs to know how the knowledge is structured. These semantics form the ontology of the knowledge (Yusko, 2005).

Critical to the previously identified MAS agents are the ontologies for domain and SM process knowledge. The above agents shall use ontology to make sense of the complex relations between reported errors, MRs, versions and releases, known issues, domain knowledge and users, experts and maintainers profiles.

Henceforth, we outline a combined ontology which links and extends the enterprise business domain to SM process ontology and model the combined ontology using Protégé ontology editor. For SM process ontology, the Ruiz ontology (Ruiz et al., 2004), which was based on Kitchenham et al. (1999) SM ontology, shall be used as the basis, due to similarity of the concepts in author's SM environment. For Domain business ontology, the hierarchical domain ontology proposed by Kabilan (2007), and business process metadata from Ulrich (2002) shall be used as the basis for our enterprise business domain ontology. In summary, the following sub-ontologies are proposed (Mohd Nor et al., 2008d):

- Product subontology - defines the software products that are maintained. These include the various artifacts (components, modules, versions, documents, etc.)
- Process subontology - includes the explicit processes used to carry out different activities. These processes defines the methods for problem reporting, problem identification and various maintenance activities
- Activity subontology - defines the various activities being performed by maintainers, such as support, managerial, maintenance and testing.
- Organization subontology - specifies the organizational units, the roles and the personnel involved.

- Enterprise business domain subontology - which includes:
    - Domain process type - top most layer which includes the generic high-level functionality.
    - Complex process and basic process - describes hierarchical business processes. A complex process may have several basic processes.
    - Process use - how process uses the application.

The redefined schema for the Activity and Product subontologies are drawn using OWL-Vis in Protégé ontology editor and are illustrated in Fig. 7 and Fig. 8, respectively. The linkages between the above SM sub-ontologies and Enterprise business domain sub-ontologies are depicted in Fig. 9.

Compared to other related SM ontologies, The strength of this ontology lies with the much needed details on the links between Domain sub-ontology and the SM sub-ontologies. With this linkage, changes to either Enterprise Domain knowledge or SM artifacts could be traversed and specific actions could be triggered. Also, the agents could relate the current reported errors with the previously reported errors via these ontological links.

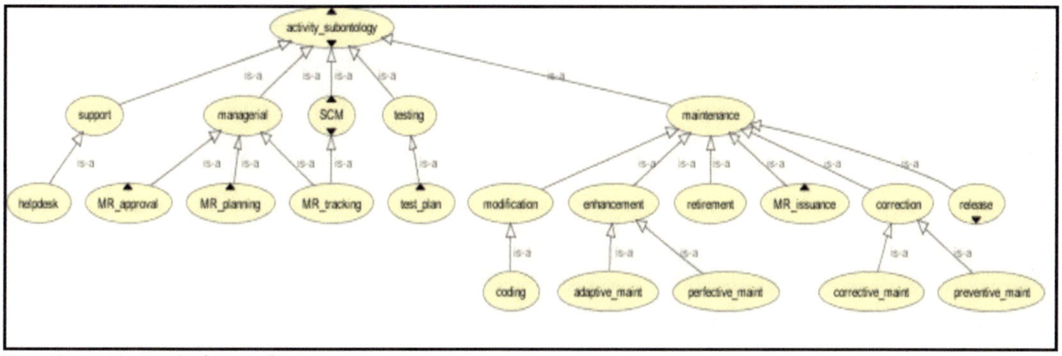

Fig. 7. Activity Subontology

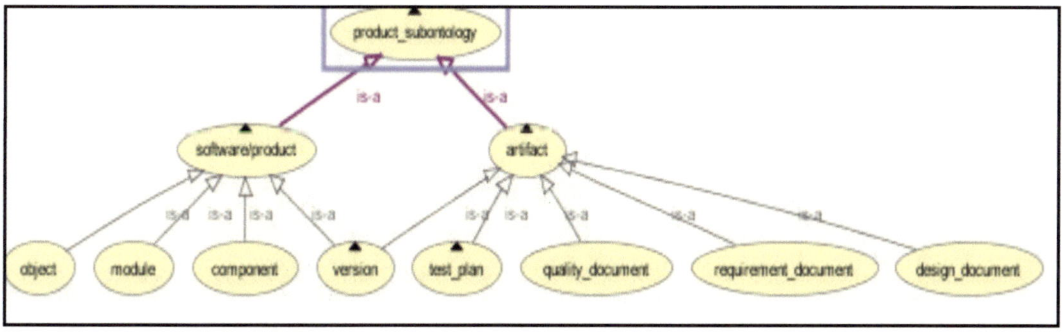

Fig. 8. Product Subontology

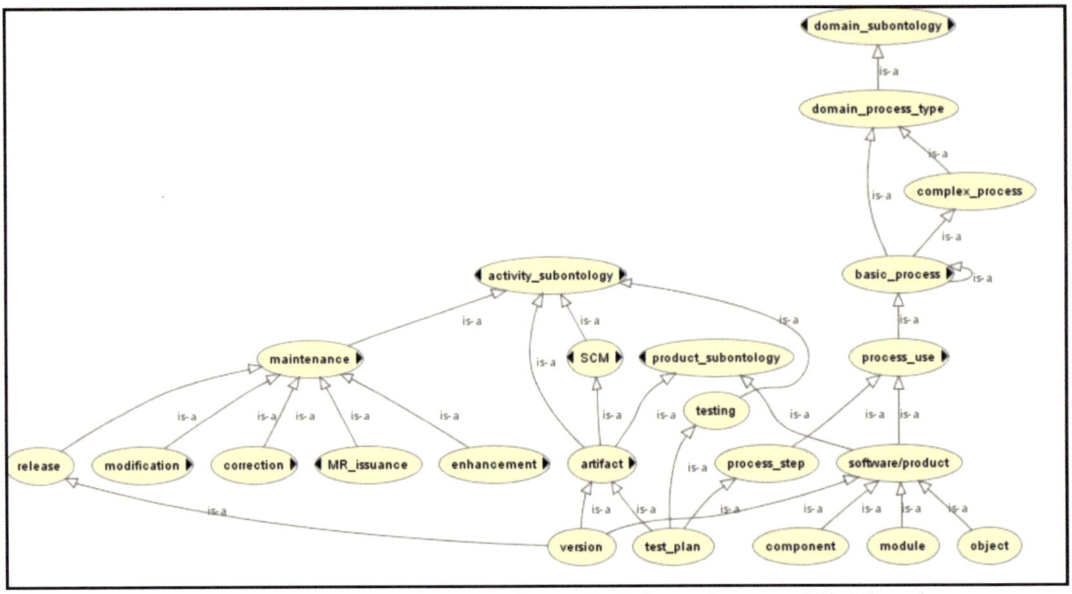

Fig. 9. Relations between Enterprise Business Domain Subontology and SM Ontology

5. Conclusion

In recent years, many organizations consider knowledge management (KM) to be strategically important to their business. In general, Knowledge Sharing (KS), Knowledge Transfer (KT) and Knowledge Management System (KMS) are among the themes to bring synergies among different teams, units or departments, to accelerate innovation, improve quality and reduce costs and exposure to business risks. In Software Engineering area, KM have been studied mostly on Software Development environment, but Software Maintenance (SM) environment are often neglected. SM environment is complex, knowledge-driven and highly collaborative and therefore, KM is critical to SM to provides an environment for creating and sharing knowledge.

One of the major challenges faced by software maintainers is inadequate knowledge to perform daily activities. Maintainers spent considerable efforts checking codes and collaborating with other parties to obtain information. In a survey in selected I.T. departments in higher learning institutions in Malaysia, inadequate enterprise business domain knowledge are deemed important but are seldom stored in KMS or other electronic means. Therefore, resolving these issues should be given high priority.

To overcome the problems associated with lack of knowledge in SM environment, we propose a MAS tool to enable both users and software maintainers to capture and share the enterprise business domain knowledge and automatically link them to the application and SM process information. Prometheus methodology is used to design the MAS and as a result, six agent types are proposed: User Agent, Helpdesk Agent, Maintenance Request Agent, Maintainer Agent, SM Process Agent and Domain Knowledge Agent. Critical to the systematic information organization is the ontology for domain and SM process knowledge, to allow software agents to communicate among each others, and to understand the information structure when retrieving or storing the knowledge. Henceforth, we outline a

combined ontology which links and extends the enterprise business domain to SM process ontology and model the combined ontology using Protégé ontology editor.
With this tool, users and maintainers shall benefits from systematic organization of domain and SM process knowledge, as well as ensuring that changes to either application or domain business knowledge are corroborated and shared among the business users and maintainers. The new tool shall also promote automation and integration of systems or tools to support maintenance processes

6. References

Abdullah, R. (2008). Knowledge Management System in a Collaborative Environment. University Putra Malaysia Press.

Abdullah, R., Sahibuddin, S., Alias, R., & Selamat, M. H. (2006). Knowledge Management System Architecture For Organizational

Alavi, M., & Leidner, D. (2000). Knowledge Management Systems: Issues, Challenges, and Benefits. Communication of AIS, 1.

April, A. (2005). Software Maintenance Maturity Model (SMmm): The Software Maintenance Process Model. Journal of Software Maintenance and Evolution: Research and Practice, 17(3).

Arthur Anderson, & APQC. (1996). The Knowledge Management Assessment Tool: External Benchmarking Version. Arthur Anderson/APQC.

Aurum, A., Jeffery, R., Wohlin, C., & Handzic, M. (2003). Managing Software Engineering Knowledge. Springer.

Choo, C. (1996). An Integrated Information Model of the Organization: The Knowing Organization.

Dam, K. H., & Winikoff, M. (2003). Comparing AgentOriented Methodologies. In 5 th International Workshop on Agent-Oriented Information Systems (AOIS'03).

Das, S., Lutters, W., & Seaman, C. (2007). Understanding Documentation Value in Software Maintenance. In Proceedings of the 2007 Symposium on Computer human interaction for the management of information technology.

Davenport, T., & Prusak, L. (2000). Working Knowledge: How Organization Manage What They Know. Harvard Business School Press.

Deraman, A. (1998). A Framework For Software Maintenance Model Development. Malaysian Journal of Computer Science, 11(2).

Desouza, K. C., Awazu, Y., & Baloh, P. (2006). Managing Knowledge in Global Software Development Efforts: Issues and Practices. Software, IEEE, 23(5), 30-37.

Dingsoyr, T., & Conradi, R. (2002). A Survey Of Case Studies Of The Use Of Knowledge Management In Software Engineering. International Journal of Software Engineering and Knowledge Engineering, 12(4).

Fjeldstad, R., & Hamlen, W. (1998). Application Program Maintenance Study: Report to Our Respondents. In Software Engineering- Theory and Practices. Prentice Hall.

Foo, S., Chua, A., & Sharma, R. (2006). Knowledge management Tools and Techniques. Singapore: Pearson Prentice Hll.

Ghali, N. (1993). Managing Software Development Knowledge: A Conceptually-Oriented Software Engineering Environment, PhD. Thesis. University of Ottawa, Canada.

Handzic, M. and Hasan, H. (2003), "The Search for an Integrated KM Framework", chapter 1 in Hasan H. and Handzic M. (eds.), Australian Studies. in Knowledge Management, UOW Press, Wollongong

Australia KM Standard (2001), Framework. In Australian Studies in Knowledge Management. UOW Press. Retrieved January 14, 2009, from http://www.worldscibooks.com/.

Hahn, J., & Subramani, M. (n.d.). A Framework Of Knowledge Management Systems: Issues And Challenges For Theory And Practice.

Hansen, M., Nohria, N., & Tierney, T. (1999). What's Your Strategy For Managing Knowledge? Harvard Business Review.

Hosapple, C., & Joshi, K. (2002). Understanding KM Solutions: The Evolution of Frameworks in Theory and Practice. In Knowledge Management Systems: Theory and Practice. Thomson Learning.

IEEE 14764 (2006). IEEE 14764-2006, Standard for Software Engineering - Software Life Cycle Process – Maintenance. The Institute of Electrical and Electronics Engineers, Inc.

Jarke, M., & Rose, T. (1988). Managing Knowledge about Information System Evolution. In Proceedings of the 1988 ACM SIGMOD International Conference.

Kabilan, V. (2007). Ontology for InformationSystems (O4IS) Design Methodology: Conceptualizing, Designing and Representing Domain Ontologies. PhD Thesis, The Royal Institute of Technology, Sweden.

Kitchenham, B., Travassos, G., Mayrhauser, A., Niessink, F., Schneidewind, N., Singer, J., et al. (1999). Towards an ontology of software maintenance. Journal of Software Maintenance: Research and Practice, 11(6).

KPMG. (n.d.). KPMG European KM Survey 2003. Retrieved from www.knowledgeboard.com.

KPMG. (n.d.). KPMG Knowledge Management Research Report 2000. Retrieved from www.knowledgeboard.com.

Lientz, B., & Swanson, E. (1981). Characteristics of Application Software Maintenance. Communications of the ACM, 24(11).

Meso, P., & Smith, R. (2000). A Resource-Based View Of Organizational Knowledge Management Systems. Journal of Knowledge Management, 4(3).

Mohd Nor, M. Z., & Abdullah, R. (2008a). A Technical Perspective of Knowledge Management in Collaborative Software Maintenance Environment. In Knowledge Management International Conference (KMICE).

Mohd Nor, M. Z., & Abdullah, R. (2008b). Survey on Software Maintenance Profile and Knowledge Requirement in Public Higher Learning Institutions. In Accepted for 3rd International Symposium on Information Technology Conference (ITSIM) .

Mohd Nor, M. Z., Abdullah, R., Selamat, M. H., & Ghazali, M. (2008c). Agent-based Tool To Support Collaborative KMS In Software Maintenance Process Environment. Proceeding of International Conference on Industrial Engineering and Engineering Management (IEEM) 2008.

Mohd Nor, M. Z., Abdullah, R., Selamat, M. H., & Ghazali, M. (2008d). Combining Business Domain and Software Maintenance Process Ontology, Proceeding of Malaysian Software Engineering Conference (MySEC) 2008.

Natarajan, G., & Shekar, S. (2001). Knowledge Management: Enable Business Growth. McGraw-Hill.
Nonaka, I., & Takeuchi, H. (1995). The Knowledge-Creating Company. New York: Oxford University Press, Inc.
Pigoski, T. (1997). Practical Software Maintenance:Best Practices for Managing your Software Investment. John Wiley & Sons.
Pressman, R. (2005). Software Engineering: A Practical Approach (6th ed.). McGraw Hill.
Rodriquez, O., Martinez, A., Favela, J., Viscaino, A., & Piattini, M. (2004a). Understanding and Supporting Knowledge Flows in a Community of Software Developers. Lecture Notes in Computer Science, 2198.
Rodriquez, O., Martinez, A., Favela, J., Viscaino, A., & Piattini, M. (2004b). How to Manage Knowledge in the Software Maintenance Process. Lecture Notes in Computer Science, 3096.
Ruiz, F., Viscaino, A., Piattini, M., & Garcia, F. (2004). An Ontology for The Management of Software Maintenance Projects. International Journal of Software Engineering and Knowledge Engineering.
Rus, I., & Lindvall, M. (2001). Knowledge Management in Software Engineering. IEEE Software, 19(3).
Santos, G., Vilela, K., Montoni, M., & Rocha, A. (2005). Knowledge Management in a Software Development Environment to Suport Software Process Deployment. Lecture Notes in Computer Science, 3782.
Schach, S., Jin, B., Yu, L., Heller, G., & Offutt, J. (2003). Determining the Distribution of Maintenance Categories: Survey versus Measurement. Journal of Empirical Software Engineering, 8.
Selamat, M., Abdullah, R., & Paul, C. (2006). Knowledge Management System Architecture For Organizational Learning With Collaborative Environment. International Journal of Computer Science and Network Security, 6(8a).
SWEBOK. (2004). Software Maintenance. In Guide to the Software Engineering Body of Knowledge (SWEBOK). The Institute of Electrical and Electronics Engineers, Inc.
Szulanski, G. (1996). Exploring Internal Stickiness: Impediments to the Transfer of Best Practice Within The Firm. Strategic Management Journal, 17.
Ulrich, F. (2002). A Multi-Layer Architecture for Knowledge Management Systems. In Knowledge Management Systems: Theory and Practice (pp. 97-111). Thomson Learning.
Van Der Speck, R., & Spijkervert, A. (1997). Knowledge Management: Dealing Intelligently with Knowledge. In Knowledge Management and its Integrative Elements. CRC Press.
Viscaino, A., Soto, J., & Piattini, M. (2003). Supporting Software Maintenance in Web Repository through a Multi-Agent System. Lecture Notes in Computer Science, 2663.
Vizcaíno, A., Soto, J., & Piattini, M. (2004). Supporting Knowledge Reuse During the Software Maintenance Process through Agents. Proceedings of the 6th International Conference on Enterprise Information Systems (ICEIS).
Wiig, K. (1993). Knowledge Management Foundation. Schema Press.
Wilson, T. (2002). The nonsense of knowledge management. Journal of Information Research, 8(1).

Wooldridge, M. (2002). An Introduction to Multiagent Systems. John Wiley and Sons.
Yusko, J. (2005). The Knowledge Collective: A Multi-Layer, Multi-Agent Framework for Information Management in an Intelligent Knowledge Base. PhD. Thesis, Illinois Institute of Technology.

7

Knowledge Management in Virtual Communities of Practice

Júnio César de Lima[1], Cedric Luiz de Carvalho[2] and Ana Paula Laboissière Ambrósio[2]
[1]Instituto Federal Goiano – Campus Urutaí
[2] Instituto de Informática - Universidade Federal de Goiás
Brazil

1. Introduction

Virtual Communities of Practice (VCoPs) are groups of people who get together to discuss and share their knowledge on a given domain using a virtual environment. Experiences are exchanged within the community. Members use community knowledge to solve their own problems and share the solution with the community. Thus, the more the community helps its members, the more its knowledge grows, and the more it becomes attractive to new members. Key to the concept of VCoPs is the management of knowledge acquired or developed by the community, which must be indexed and stored as to be easily retrieved. This is not an easy task since knowledge is stored in people's mind. It is therefore difficult to capture, to represent and to make persistent so other people can use.

The creation of VCoPs is well aligned with a strong tendency of the modern world, which presents a shift from an industrial society paradigm to that of a knowledge society. In this type of society, where knowledge is the sole really meaningful resource, it is important to have spaces for the representation and sharing of information that reflect the thought of professionals, researchers, teachers, students, etc..

On the other hand, the was designed to support resource sharing at a global level. It has, however, many limitations. The Semantic Web appears as a possible solution for some of these limitations. It represents a revolution in information processing and, consequently, a revolution in the way knowledge is organized. The Semantic Web requires all available resources to have enough expressiveness so machines and/or software agents are able to "understand" the real meaning of data. The use of these Semantic Web technologies can be very useful in the construction of tools to support VCoPs.

The central idea of this chapter is to structure the concepts of knowledge representation and retrieval, as well as to characterize how semantics can contribute in the management of knowledge within a virtual community of practice.

The first part of the chapter is an introduction to knowledge management. It describes some basic domain concepts, showing the relation between data, information and knowledge.

The second part, discusses Virtual Communities of Practice and the role of knowledge in this environment. Since the domain of a VCoP characterizes a shared interest, each member

of the community is expected to have a minimum degree of domain knowledge. This common understanding can be used to the advantage of knowledge management. The use of ontology to represent the domain associated to Semantic Web technologies can contribute in the communication process, helping users to store, access and visualize information in a more transparent, democratic and intuitive way.
The third part of the chapter discusses how semantics can be used to help in the representation and retrieval of knowledge. Usually, when semantics is attributed to data or information, it facilitates their automatic processing. There are several tools that help in the retrieval of information in shared environments, but they still present problems, mainly linked to the lack of semantic treatment in documents and queries. This is due to imprecision and ambiguities inherent to the communication process. Meaning (semantics) is in the mind of people and not in graphic signs.
The fourth part discusses how the use of well-defined contexts may help reduce this problem. Ontology is being widely used to represent information context in shared environments, as they can be used to define domains, generating a set of words that identify it. Ontology therefore allows a common and shared comprehension of a domain, playing an important role in knowledge exchange by introducing a semantic structure for the data belonging to that domain.
The chapter concludes discussing in sections 5 the aspects that must be tackled by VCoP Environments to help manage the documents generated within the community, facilitating storage, indexation and retrieval. It discusses how these environments may contribute to the generation of new knowledge, encompassing the four modes of knowledge conversion represented in Nonaka and Takeuchi's spiral model, introducing Semantic Web Technologies. Section 6 concludes the chapter.

2. Knowledge Management: an overview

The term "Knowledge Management" appeared in the mid 90's and is the meeting point of the Information Technology and Administration domains. Landini and Damiani (2001) define knowledge management as a systematic process for connecting people to other people and to knowledge they need to act efficiently and create new knowledge. Its main objective is to enhance an enterprise's performance and that of its workers, not simply by sharing knowledge, even though this is a valuable sub product of the process, but through the identification, capture, validation and knowledge transference. Knowledge management has also been defined as a necessary process to capture, code and transfer knowledge so an enterprise can fully attain its objectives (Archer, 2006).
Initially, knowledge management was seen as an innovative manner of solving several organizational problems, creating what was referenced by Peter Druker (2006) as "Knowledge Society". The global importance of knowledge management has only recently been recognized, being treated as a critical resource for the success of enterprises.
However, knowledge management is still in its infancy. If, on one hand, technology and the development of information networks foster knowledge dissemination, on the other hand it facilitates direct publication by the author. This leads to a lack of patterns in the documents/information made available in the Internet, making search and retrieval more difficult. Thus, information technology is faced with the increasing challenge of offering this "new society" knowledge that is reliable, precise, on time and relevant.

In addition to the lack of patterns, information processing to generate knowledge is, on its own right, a complex activity, since information, depending on the context and knowledge domain, may have several meanings. A term may represent different concepts with different conceptual relations depending on the situation.
Despite the evolution in the communication processes, enterprises have encountered difficulties in defining processes that minimize or solve the problems related to knowledge management, maintaining themselves competitive in face of the numerous innovation needs (Davenport & Prusak, 1998). To fulfill this objective, it is necessary to create mechanisms and processes that facilitate knowledge manipulation. This implies understanding what is "knowledge", as well as the distinction between knowledge, information and data.

2.1 Data

According to Setzer (2006), data are mathematical entities and therefore purely syntactic. This means data can be fully described through formal structural representations. He suggests that information may be mentally characterized, but not physically defined, declaring that it is not possible to process information directly in a computer without it being reduced to data. Data processing in a computer is limited exclusively to their structural manipulation. He ends by arguing that knowledge is an internal, personal abstraction of something that was experienced by someone. In this argument, knowledge cannot be totally described, but may be conceptualized in terms of information.
Mizzaro (1997) arguments that, from a computational point of view, data is everything that is given as input to be processed, while information is everything that this process returns as output. Thus, there is no distinction, in computational processes, between data, information and knowledge, where all, assuming an input role, would be named data.
A more formal definition of data can be found in Davenport and Prusak (1998), where "Data are sets of distinct and objective facts related to an event". As proposed by Peter Drucker, cited in (Davenport & Prusak, 1998), information is "data covered of small relevance". Thus it is necessary to aggregate value to this data so information can be obtained. This can be done through methods specified in Davenport and Prusak (1998):

- Contextualization: the purpose for which the data has been collected is known.
- Categorization: the data's essential analysis units or components are known.
- Calculus: data can be mathematically or statistically analyzed.
- Correction: errors are eliminated from the data.
- Condensation: data can be summarized into a more concise form.

2.2 Information

Information, according to Claude Shannon (2005), is "something that adds to a representation[...] We receive information when what we know is modified. Information is that which logically justifies the change or reinforcement of a representation or state of things. Representations may be explicit as in a map or proposition, or implicit as in the state of an activity oriented to the receptor".
In this approach, the concept of information is seen as something the receptor agent receives, through a message, from an emitting agent in a communication process. Its representation measure or importance is given by the Entropy, that defines the measure of importance of a word in the context of a given domain (Hotho et al., 2005).

In opposition to Claude Shannon`s model, Dretske referenced in (Nonaka & Takeuchi, 1995), arguments that a genuine information theory is a theory about message contents, and not a theory about the model in which this content is incorporated. Information is a flow of messages, while knowledge is created by that same message flow, anchored in the beliefs and commitments of its beholder. Thus knowledge is related to the human action (Nonaka & Takeuchi, 1995).

According to Setzer (2006), information is an informal abstraction that is in the mind of a person, representing something meaningful to her, and cannot be formalized through a mathematical or logic theory. The information contained in a data depends on what a person knows about a theme and, in general, that can vary from person to person. Thus, what constitutes information for a person may not be more than data for others.

A fundamental distinction between data and information is that the first is purely syntactic and the second necessarily contains semantics. It is interesting to note that it is very hard to introduce and process semantics in a computer because the machine is purely syntactic (Setzer 2006). Today, there are several on going researches in this sense, being the Semantic Web (Berners-Lee et al., 2001) one of them. Its objective is to provide semantics to resources scattered in the web, making them processable by computers.

2.3 Knowledge

Knowledge is the object of Knowledge Management and Knowledge Engineering that aim to capture it, even though comprehension of its meaning is still controversial.

Knowledge, defined in Davenport and Prusak (1998), "is a fluid mixture of condensed experience, values, context information and experimental insight, that offers a structure for evaluation and incorporation of new experiences and information. It has an origin and is applied in the mind of experts. In organizations it is often embedded not only in documents and repositories, but also in routines, processes and organizational norms. "

Knowledge, in (Goble et. al., 2004), is described as information put into use to execute a goal or to fulfill an intention, being knowledge the result of the familiarity obtained by experience or association with some other knowledge.

According to Fischler and Firschein, referenced in (Haykin, 1998), knowledge refers to stored information or to models used by a person or machine to interpret, predict and respond appropriately to the exterior world. In a comparison between knowledge and data, knowledge is a complex symbolic representation of some aspect of the universe of discourse while data is a simple symbolic representation.

Knowledge can exist in two forms: tacit and explicit. "Explicit knowledge" is the knowledge that can be easily collected, organized and transferred through digital means while "tacit knowledge" is knowledge that is personal, in a specific context and hard to formalize and communicate.

Explicit knowledge is the knowledge that exists in documents, books, software and other means. Knowledge expressed in the explicit form may be easily reproduced and distributed at low cost, or no cost, but for that same reason is harder to guarantee its unauthorized use.

Tacit knowledge is knowledge a person acquires during her life and is in her head. It may be the most valuable knowledge of a person or organization. Usually it is hard to be formalized and explained to another person, since it is highly localized, subjective and inherent to a person's abilities and requires, for its transfer, a direct involvement of the sources and users and an active teaching and learning process (Bolisani et. al., 2006).

For Nonaka and Takeuchi (1995), knowledge is created through a cyclic process where tacit knowledge is converted into formalisms, symbols and becomes publicly available as explicit knowledge and vice-versa. To transform tacit knowledge into explicit knowledge, making it reusable by other people, is not an easy task. As described before, tacit knowledge is personal and hard to be articulated in a formal language as it involves several factors (emotional, psychological and others).

For knowledge transformation to occur, and thus its expansion, a social interaction is necessary between tacit and explicit knowledge. From there, the accumulated individual knowledge will need to be again socialized as to generate new concepts when applied to new needs. The conversion process from tacit into explicit and vice-versa may occur in four ways (Nonaka & Takeuchi, 1995):

- Socialization: conversion from tacit to tacit. Is the experience sharing process between individuals in a group and usually occurs due to observation, imitation and practice. In this manner it is possible to transfer tacit knowledge between individuals and the association of a given type of knowledge to different individual contexts;
- Externalization: conversion from tacit into explicit. Is the organization process that transforms tacit knowledge into explicit knowledge through the use of metaphors, analogies, concepts, hypothesis and models, permitting the creation of new and explicit concepts based on the tacit knowledge;
- Combination: conversion from explicit into explicit. Is the concept systematization process in a knowledge system. It involves the combination of a set of explicit knowledge (such as classification, summarization, research and information categorization) using database technology and may lead to the creation of new knowledge;
- Internalization: conversion from explicit into tacit. Is the process through which explicit knowledge becomes a learning tool through the use of manuals and documents, and assumes again an abstract and subjective context for each member of the organization.

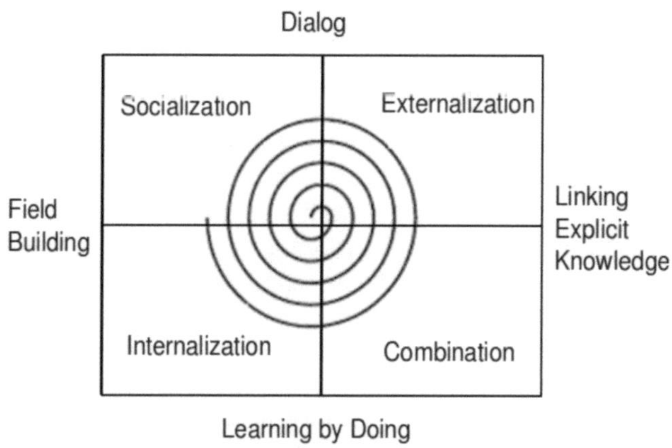

Fig. 1. SECI Model (Nonaka & Takeuchi, 1995).

These four types of knowledge conversion: socialization (shared knowledge), externalization (conceptual knowledge), combination (systemic knowledge) and internalization (operational knowledge) in time form a Knowledge Spiral (Figure 1) (Nonaka & Takeuchi, 1995). Tacit knowledge constitutes the base of organizational knowledge since it is in the minds of the organization's members and can be transmitted to the other members. In this case, these clusters can be modeled through Communities of Practice (CoPs).

3. Communities

The term "community" according to Koch and Lacher (2000), is defined as a group of people that share the same interest or are inserted in the same context. Generally speaking, a community can be defined as a group of people that share the same purposes as to permit and/or contribute to a problem's solution. That is, groups of people and/or professionals with similar interests and/or work. Therefore, the basic elements that form any community are the individuals, the way they relate and the context or domain in which these individuals are inserted.

A community can be seen as the identity of a group of people. There are several examples of communities such as all the students in a university program, the people that live in a neighborhood or the persons interested in a given subject such as football or films. These groups may gather to exchange knowledge, that may be collected and stored for future reference and retrieval, helping people that are looking for help in different situations.

3.1 Overview of Communities of Practice

There are several types of communities with different characteristics. One of these are the Communities of Practice (CoPs). The term "Community of Practice" was first used in the beginning of the 90's by Jean Lave and Etienne Wenger to designate the learning that occurred through working practice, even though, in fact, these type of communities already existed, as when company workers learned in their working environment.

Lave and Wenger, in 1991, proposed a knowledge acquisition model as a social process where persons could participate in the common learning at different levels, according to authority and antiquity in the group. Thus a member would start with a peripheral participation, acquiring for example, the community's domain knowledge, moving on to an insertion in the knowledge acquisition context associated to specific community working practices that would became more complex as learning progresses, elevating the member's level of authority.

The key factor that distinguishes CoPs from other types of communities are its objectives, emphasizing knowledge sharing within the group of practitioners through activities such as brainstorming and exchange of reading materials such as articles, news, and experiences. Thus, what links members of a CoP are the interest relations they have in common.

These groups are organized so professionals from given domains may exchange relevant information about their day-to-day, i.e., their best practices and the way they structure their processes, in addition to sharing solutions to their most common problems. CoPs can be seen as environments that existed in the past, where young apprentices learned from their masters, and when they become masters passed on their acquired knowledge to new apprentices. In this environment there is an exchange of knowledge, and in some cases, apprentices may also pass knowledge to their masters.

A key characteristic of CoPs is that each community must center on a given knowledge domain (context), and each member must have a minimum level of domain knowledge to be able to participate in the community. A shared context is essential to the development of a community as it gives sense and direction to the discussions that occur and may help members decide the direction the community will take. The context may include purpose, content, history, and values and make explicit the shared domain knowledge, being decisive for the success or failure of a CoP.

Another important aspect of a CoP is the community itself, i.e., the way members are kept engaged in joint activities, discussions, mutual help and information sharing.

Interaction is another key requirement for members to belong to this type of community. The functioning of CoPs starts in the way people become members. Persons belong to a CoP when they start to share their best practices. They are linked to each other through the mutual involvement in common activities. This is the coupling that links CoP members as a social entity (Wenger et. al., 2002).

The production of practices by the CoP members is also very important for its definition. It is concentrated in the shared repositories that represent the material traits of the community. Examples of products include: written archives, proceedings, experiences, documents, policies, rituals, specific idioms, blogs, wikis, forums and chats.

Furthermore, the community members must have the same set of goals and purposes. Such purpose set is centered on knowledge sharing between practitioner groups and, for this reason, efficient CoPs are structured mainly around activities of knowledge sharing (for example: video conferences, forums, reading and writing material, meetings, brainstorming, relations and exchange of reading material). A well consolidated community develops its own language and offers its members better communication.

In the literature there are several CoP classifications. Vestal (2003) suggests there are four types of communities:

- Innovation communities: to elaborate new solutions using the existing knowledge;
- Help communities: to solve problems;
- Best Practice communities: searching, validating and disseminating information;
- Knowledge-Stewarding: connecting people, collecting and organizing information and knowledge in organizations.

Each one of these types of CoPs will demand different efforts, levels of functionality and support. Another classification is given by Archer (2006) that identifies four classifications for CoPs:

- Internal Communities of Practice: Communities internal to an organization. They add value to the organization in several ways such as: help conduct strategies, start of new business lines, rapid solution of problems, transference of best practices, development of professional abilities and recruiting and retention of company talents.
- Communities of Practice in Network Organizations: a network organization is a relation between independent organizations. These networks have grown rapidly in number and extension in the last years, and most enterprises belong to at least one network. A supply chain, for example, is a network organization. Organization members in a network work in strait and continuous cooperation in projects and

processes that involve partnership, common products and/or services. Reasons to build these networks include rapid market insertion, capacity to concentrate in essential competencies, increase of competency due to the network partners, as well as the need to guarantee the availability of resources and materials.

- Formal Networks of Practice: are formal networks that include organizations but are not part of other formal relations. They have a composition that is controlled by taxes and/or acceptance by some central authority that also helps in the organization, facilitating and supporting the members in their communication, events and discussions.
- Self-Organizing Networks of Practice: are networks of individuals with *ad-hoc* relations and without formal ties. It is an informal network, loosely organized, that has no central administration authority or responsible person, where joining is voluntary and there is almost no explicit compromise. The members may choose to join or leave the community when they want. Most of these networks are virtual, thus the communication strategy is based essentially on knowledge codification.

3.2 Virtual Communities of Practice (VCoP)

The Internet, as an agile, flexible and low cost communication mean, was the propulsion factor for the adoption, in large scale, of virtual communities. VCoP can be seen as an environment where people with common interests exchange information through an on-line network, such as the Internet. Through these information exchanges, the participants develop links with other community members and with the community as a whole. Furthermore, the members tend to be physically distant, geographically in different locations.

VCoPs are organized using e-mail, chats, forums, wikis and website technologies for communication, and offer an environment where professionals from given domains can exchange relevant information about their best practices (such as experiences, history, tools, etc.) and the way they structure their processes, as well as share solutions for their most common problems.

An important VCoP characteristic is asynchronous communication, i.e., it is not limited to having all parts interacting at the same time. With this, using the Internet, a disperse group of people can talk asynchronously according to their convenience, during a long period of time, facilitating exchanges that simply could not happen physically. This tends to augment the communication intensity between its members and provide for their basic needs.

Another important VCoP aspect is scalability since the number of members in a virtual community tends to be bigger than in other types of communities, with members being able to enter and leave the community in a more rapid and intense fashion. However, for any VCoP to have success it must be able to increase the number of participants without loosing the "sense of community", i.e., all the individuals in the community must continue to have the same objectives.

A problem found in VCoP is establishing a confidence relation between members. As the members will possibly never meet in person, it may be hard to trust entirely another member's practice. Thus, an important aspect in VCoP are the security issues related to its members and practices. VCoPs must implement safety measures to allow entrance of new members and their practice sharing within the community.

Cothrel and William (2000) have studied Virtual Communities to determine the best way to establish and/or maintain them. They have developed a model that identifies the main activities that must be available to obtain success in the creation of a virtual community. They are:

- Member Development: is the need to promote the growth of the community and substitute the members that leave. It is necessary to clearly define the objectives and member demography as to promote the community.
- Content Management: is related to information content, alliances and infrastructure. Content management must create the members' profile, divide them in sub-communities according to specific topics, capture, disseminate knowledge and create processes that facilitate member involvement.
- Relations Management: must be developed based on explicit general rules that help members solve conflicts that often arise, on their own or with the help of moderators.

According to Kimble and Hildreth (2006), in their work related to CoPs, Wenger identified two fundamental processes that form a duality: participation and reification. Participation is "a social experience of living in the world in terms of joining (adhering) social communities and of active participation in the organizations' social life. Reification is the "process of giving form to our experience, producing objects that solidify that experience". Still according to Wenger, participation and reification are analytically separable, but in fact inseparable. Participation is the process through which people become active participants in the community's practice and reification gives concrete form to the community's experience to produce artifacts.

In VCoPs the participation process is harder to be sustained as the members are dispersed and are not obliged to participate. Reification, at this point, has a more important role in VCoPs. Reification maintains a VCoP feasible. It is therefore necessary a reification process that allows members to formalize their experiences so they can be transmitted to others.

4. Semantics in the Representation and Retrieval of Knowledge

Once knowledge becomes the organization's main strategic asset, their success depends on their ability to gather, produce, maintain and disseminate knowledge. The development of procedures and routines to optimize creation, retrieval and sharing of knowledge and information is crucial. This implies in creating knowledge management procedures that are machine processable, since there are enormous amounts of information scattered throughout an organization.

One of the main difficulties in knowledge management is information representation, as a given information may have several different semantic relations at the same time, such as, for example, the homonym semantic relation, the synonym relation and the subclass relation. Thus, to treat knowledge one must have in hands the information obtained from data.

According to Geisler (2008), the relation between data, information and knowledge can be summarized as follows: for data to be considered information it is necessary some type of analysis, a consensus of adopted terms as to their meaning is expected, and to have knowledge, it is necessary to be in synthony with the target public so it can execute an information related action.

Thus, knowledge comes from the interpretation of data within a context, i.e., from information. Librelotto et. al. (2005) define interpretation as the mapping between a set of structured data and a model of some set of objects in a domain with respect to the desired meaning for these objects and the relations between them. Thus interpretation can be seen as a mapping between notations. For example, the sequence of binary codes (for pictures) or characters in an alphabet (for texts) and what these notations pretend to signify in a given domain.

It can be said that notations are symbols without meaning unless they are given an interpretation. For notations to have meaning they must be mapped to an object in a model. Thus one can conclude that to interpret is to apply the desired semantics to the notation.

The knowledge generation process arises from a process in which given information is compared with many others and combined with people's values and experiences, being these combinations subjected to laws universally accepted. When speaking of knowledge, some hypothesis and delimitations are necessary.

Thus knowledge cannot be described; what is described is information. Also, knowledge does not depend only on personal interpretation, as information, since it requires an experience of the knowledge object. Thus knowledge is in the purely subjective sphere.

In this sense, when humans interpret (understand) something, they symbolically represent the domain objects in some model, as well as the relations between these objects. Humans have the semantics of a domain in their minds, which is well structured and interpreted. However, as humans are not capable of manipulating the complexity of the whole, they need to find models (reduced/partial) to understand and work reality.

When a person reads a poetry book, for example, he reads notations in the pages and interprets them according to his mental model. He interprets giving them semantics. If one wishes to spread knowledge contained in a text, it must be made available to other persons, expecting them to furnish a semantic interpretation using his mental models. Therefore there will be knowledge in that text only if there is interpretation.

The objective of knowledge representation research is that computers may help in the spreading of knowledge. For this to be possible, it is necessary to partially automate the interpretation process, which means that it is necessary to build and represent in a computer usable format some portion of human's mental models.

4.1 Structuring Knowledge

To automate the knowledge management process, it is necessary to structure the existing domain knowledge in such a manner that a computer can process and make decisions based on that knowledge. This means passing from the information level to the knowledge level.

Knowledge Representation is something that substitutes the object or real phenomenon as to permit an entity to determine the consequences of an act through thought instead of realization (Davis et al., 1993). Knowledge representation is thus a way of structuring and codifying what is known about a domain.

There are several ways of organizing knowledge that can be differentiated between the logic adequacy, that observes if the formalism being used is capable of expressing the knowledge that one wishes to represent, and the notation convenience, that verifies the representation language conventions. The ways of structuring knowledge can be divided in (Librelotto et. al., 2005):

- Universal type for internal representation of information:

    - Feature Structures.
- Systems based on lists of terms: normally this type of list has a simple structure for knowledge representation. Their main representatives are:
    - Dictionaries;
    - Indexes.
- Systems based on graphs: determine associations between the terms through a set of semantic relations. The best known examples are:
    - Taxonomies;
    - Thesaurus;
    - Ontology.

Feature Structures, when used to describe information, puts them in compartments that associate the name of an attribute to a value. This value may be an atomic value or another feature structure.

A dictionary is a set of language vocabulary or terms proper to a science or art, usually organized in alphabetical order with their respective meaning, or its version in another language. May also be seen as a mapping of terms to its description or definition. The main characteristics of a dictionary, according to (Librelotto et. al., 2005), are:

- Is a simple document for the definition of terms that require clearing, with the objective of enhancing communication and reducing the risk of ambiguity;
- Is continually evaluated and, as new terms are found, the dictionary evolves with the addition of these new terms;
- Is made in parallel to the requirements specification.

An index is a detailed list of terms, subjects, people's names, geographical names, happenings, etc., usually in alphabetical order, with an indication of its location in the repository or publication in which they are defined or in which they appear.

For example, a remissive index in a book is an index in alphabetical order containing the different subjects treated in the book, with an indication of the page, chapter, etc. in which they appear. Thus, while an index points to all the occurrences of a concept, facilitating retrieval, a dictionary only gives a concept's definition.

Taxonomy is a classification science. It is a classification system that describes the hierarchical relationship between concepts, identifying members in classes and subclasses. According to (Librelotto et. al., 2005), a good taxonomy must present only one dimension, the categories must be mutually exclusive, a concept must be found in one place only, and it must be exhaustive, with all possibilities included.

Thesaurus is an instrument that gathers terms chosen from a conceptual structure previously established, for indexing and retrieval of documents and information in a given domain. If compared to a taxonomy, a thesaurus may be seen as an extension of a taxonomy, more complete for the description of a domain, allowing other types of relations between terms, in addition to a simple hierarchy. For example, given a term, the thesaurus indicates the terms that have the same meaning, its super class, its subclasses, etc.

Thus, a thesaurus is the vocabulary of a controlled indexation language, formally organized, in such a way that the relations between the concepts are made explicit. Situated between an ontology and a taxonomy, the thesaurus describes relations of synonymy and hierarchies.

As for ontologies, there are today different definitions and characterizations. An often referenced definition is that given by Gruber (1995) that states that and ontology is an explicit and formal specification of a shared conceptualization. This means that an ontology conceptualizes an abstract model of some world phenomenon into some consensual knowledge, shared by all. Furthermore, the concepts, properties, functions, axioms must be explicitly specified and be computer manipulated. In this sense, an ontology is an extension of a thesaurus.

Ontologies do not always have the same structure, but some characteristics and components may be found in most of them. For Gruber (1995) the basic ontology components are its classes, relations, that represent the interactions between concepts, axioms and instances, that represent data. For Uschold and Jasper (1999), an ontology may have a variety of forms, but necessarily includes a vocabulary of terms and some specification of their meaning. This includes definitions and an indication of how the concepts are inter related, collectively imposing a structure to the domain and restricting the possible interpretations of the terms.

Therefore there is a strong connection between the means of expressing knowledge seen above. Ontology, thesaurus, taxonomy, index and dictionary are similar in the following aspects:

- They are approaches to structure, classify, model and represent concepts and relations belonging to a domain;
- Allows a community to adopt and use the same set of terms in a clear and non ambiguous manner;
- The meaning of each term is specified in some way in a certain level of detail.

However, the concepts and their relations are described and defined in different manners among these types of knowledge representation. Furthermore, different aspects of the knowledge structure are implemented in each one of them. Among them, the one considered more adequate for knowledge representation in communities are the ontologies as they offer the following advantages: concept reuse in different domains, domain structuring in an unambiguous manner, sharing and interoperability of knowledge between different domains.

5. Knowledge Management in VCoPs

According to Drucker (1994), knowledge combined with new technologies, and with the talent of the workers involved in the processes may boost and add value to products and services. Nonaka and Takeuchi (1995) identified that organization's knowledge assets are better mobilized and shared in spaces or places they call 'ba', where the tacit knowledge held by individuals is converted and amplified by the spiral of knowledge.

In this context, conversation management influences significantly the knowledge creation process (Von krogh, Ichijo and Nonaka, 2000). Conversation is an excellent way of exchanging ideas, experiences, opinions and personal belief, making it a fundamental human activity for augmenting organizational knowledge. As they foster group discussion and induce the sharing of new insights, conversations, if well managed, help in the efficiency of relationships and solicitude among collaborators.

Environments must provide services that offer an efficient support and promote the four modes of knowledge transformation and innovation described in Nonaka and Takeuchi (1995), creating the "ba" atmosphere, allowing the creation of solid relations and efficient collaboration. These spaces may be physical (meeting room) or virtual (computer network). In the environments, tools must allow knowledge to be created at an individual level to be then transformed into group knowledge and finally into organizational knowledge. Even though these levels are independent, they are constantly Interacting, leading to Innovation.

According to Nonaka and Takeuchi (1995), when organizations innovate, they not only process information outside-in, aiming to solve existing problems and adapting to an environment in transformation. They create new knowledge and information, inside-out, aiming to redefine the problems as well as the solutions, and in this process recreate the environment. In this theory, the key to the creation of knowledge is to mobilize and convert tacit knowledge. In this dynamic model, knowledge creation is anchored in the premise that human knowledge is created and expanded through the social interaction between tacit and explicit knowledge.

Independent of the knowledge creation phase, good relationships eliminate fear and distrust, demolishing personal and organizational barriers. Efficient conversations provide a greater level of creativity; stimulate sharing of tacit knowledge and the creation and justification of concepts; are essential to the development of powerful prototypes and lubricate the flow of knowledge through the different organizational levels (von Krogh, Ichijo and Nonaka, 2000).

VCoPs should represent this "ba" space, vouching for its members, promoting socialization between them, creating trust, through mechanisms that guarantee the quality of information, offering solutions for the access, categorization and sharing of knowledge, offering an environment that facilitates the creation, exchange, retention and reuse of knowledge. These environments introduce a new dimension to relations, allowing members to work as a team, collaboratively, increasing their individual and collective knowledge.

Most VCoPs offer resources that facilitate and promote social interaction and information sharing. Socialization, Externalization, Combination and Internalization are supported by the use of social software and knowledge management technology. Social software commonly used in VCoPs include: Email, Instant Messaging, Chats, Forums, Blogs, Wikis, Video Conferencing, Virtual Worlds, etc. In addition, VCoPs also offer users the option to upload data and media.

All these processes generate different types of information that must be managed by the community. Knowledge made available by VCoP members, explicitly or implicitly (through different communication methods or by the upload of documents), must be formalized, captured and stored in information repositories. To organize and allow retrieval, knowledge management techniques may be used.

In a study undertaken by Choo et al. (2000), a diagram of the main resources found in the internet and how they contribute to the four modes of knowledge transformation (Figure 2) is presented.

Although these environments have been useful in establishing new communities and contributed to their success, the task of knowledge conversion has been left on the hands of the community members. Users are responsible for deciding what information to load into the community, help solving other member's problems, etc. The environment offers the communication means and facilitates knowledge transformation. However, the environment is not capable of participating in the process.

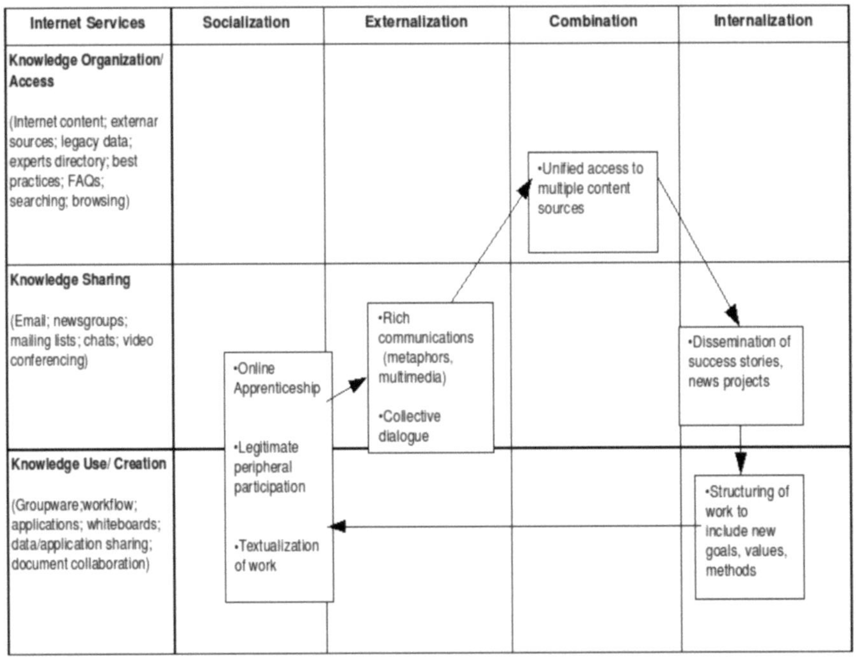

Fig. 2. Intranet Support for Nonaka & Takeuchi's Knowledge Processes (Choo et al., 2000).

With the introduction of new "intelligent" technology the tendency is that these tasks, that are currently being undertaken by members, be transferred to the environment, that should be capable of interfering in the knowledge transformation process.

This can be achieved by introducing Semantic Web concepts into VCoPs. The Semantic Web project aims the performance of more complex tasks in the information retrieval process. It proposes the existence of collections of structured information and inference rules that will lead to automatic reasoning. For this, techniques associate semantics to the information stored in the web as to make it "understandable" to the computer that is then capable of processing them. According to Berners-Lee (2001), if the Semantic Web is adequately projected it may promote the evolution of human knowledge as a whole.

The Semantic Web principles are implemented in technology layers and patterns (Figure 3). The *Unicode* layer handles character formatting. The *URI (Uniform Resource Identifier)* layer allows semantic binding between identifiable resources in the Semantic Web. The XML layer, with the definition of *namespaces* and *schema* establish that Semantic Web definitions may be integrated with other patterns based on XML. The *RDF (Resource Description Framework)* and *RDF Schema* layers define metadata structure that ensures structural interoperability and allows machine-understood information resource sharing. The *Ontology* layer provides additional vocabulary to help understand terms found in the Internet. It supports vocabulary evolution and defines relations between concepts. The *Digital Signature* layer detects modifications in documents. The *Logic* layer permits rule definition. The *Proof* layer executes these rules and evaluates, in conjunction with the *Trust* layer, the mechanisms that allow applications to trust or not the proofs undertaken.

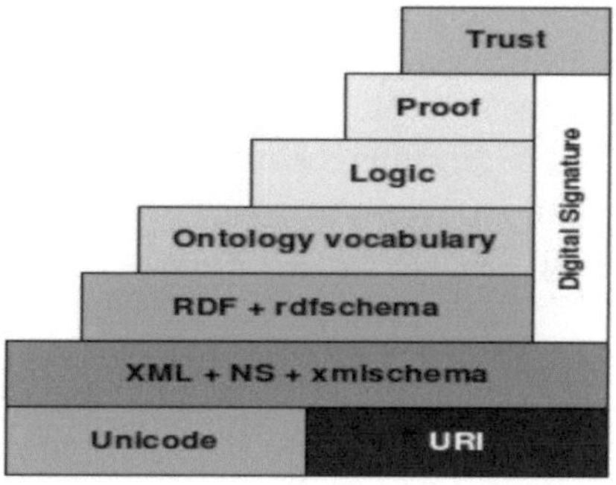

Fig. 3. Semantic Web Layers.

The use of ontology within a community brings several advantages. It helps define the domain of interest of the community, establishing a common vocabulary for better communication between its members, and serves as an indexing structure for the community content, facilitating recovery.

Inference rules can be defined to promote Knowledge extraction. Resources within a community may come in many different formats and types such as images, videos, binary files, as well as text documents that include not only traditional documents as books and papers, but also email messages, forum discussions, wikis, etc.

Text information resources may be classified in two groups. The first includes reports, papers, manual, books, etc. A common characteristic to all these elements is that their authors have made explicit the knowledge they wish to share with the community. Knowledge may be extracted from them "manually", simply by reading. If an analysis of a great volume of documents is necessary to obtain the knowledge for a given activity, the knowledge extraction process may be automated, or semi-automated, using text mining techniques (Feldman & Sanger, 2006). By integrating knowledge extraction and inference techniques available in the Logic, Proof and Trust layer of the Semantic Web, it is possible to transform explicit knowledge into more explicit knowledge contributing to the Combination phase.

A second group of text information includes email messages, forum discussions, annotations in a Wiki page, etc. In this second group the main characteristic is that the community members do not purposefully explicit their knowledge. They appear in the form of answers to questions, tips to solve a problem, metaphors, analogies, concepts, hypothesis and models. These exchanges between members help them to articulate tacit knowledge that would otherwise be difficult to transmit. It is important for the environment to be able to treat this information, contributing to the Externalization process. Once more, the use of Semantic Web concepts may facilitate the process, helping to transform tacit knowledge into explicit knowledge.

As an example of what can be done, suppose a forum for the discussion of hardware installation. If a member has problems installing any hardware, he may post a message explaining his problem, and other members may give him solution ideas. He may test these ideas and give feedback to the forum, saying what worked and what didn't. If the problem is not solved, other iterations occur. The process continues until the user is satisfied. Eventually there may be problems that continue unsolved even after a long discussion.

A big challenge is to capture the implicit knowledge contained in these communication processes. The procedure to solve the original problem may be inferred from the sequence of messages exchanged in that specific topic of the forum. If this is possible, the problem and its solution may be stored in the community's knowledge base, making it accessible. If other members have the same or similar problems, they will be able to use this knowledge without having to post a new message to the forum and pass through the same process as the first user. As in forums, messages sent by email or Wiki annotations may also contain embedded knowledge.

6. Conclusions

Using an infinity of tools and the web's ease of communication, VCoPs gain space and are today an important domain of research and application, allowing the development of more complete and useful environments for the management of knowledge, i.e., the sharing of their best practices by the community members.

For an effective knowledge transfer between community members it is necessary a high level of confidence between the members and a strong cooperation and collaboration culture. This confidence is developed through work practices that promote and allow members to work together in projects and problems. With this, the members tend to cooperate and collaborate within the community implementing an effective management of the knowledge that circulates through the VCoPs.

VCoPs need computer-based tools that facilitate communication between its members to survive. These tools must provide an efficient management of its information resources. Most environments that support VCoPs offer support for conversation and sharing between group members, as well as repository technology for managing documents. They provide community members with mechanisms to support them when they want to formalize and persist their knowledge and they offer support to the communication processes.

However, these environments only facilitate but do not interfere in the knowledge transformation process. This is done solely be the community members. The adoption of Web Semantic technology in the context of VCoPs presents an interesting option for knowledge management in these communities. The possibility of automatically "reasoning" about the information contained in the repositories may contribute to the knowledge transformation process. In this case, the environment will no longer be only a support tool, but an active member of the community.

Its main contribution would be in the Externalization phase of Knowledge transformation, sometimes considered the key to knowledge creation as it creates new and explicit knowledge from tacit knowledge contained in people's minds. Furthermore, with the use of Semantic Web technologies, VCoP management tends to be easier, since, it is expected it will ameliorate the relations between community members as these members, due to the facility of insertion and knowledge search, tend to make available more of their knowledge, synergistically enriching the community.

7. References

Ahmad, K. & Al-Sayed R. (2006). Community of Practice and the Special Language "Ground", In: *Encyclopedia of communities of practice in information and knowledge management,* Elayne Coakes and Steve Clarke, eds., 77-88, Idea Group Reference, ISBN 1591405564, Hershey.

Archer, N. (2006). A Classification Communities of Practice, In: *Encyclopedia of communities of practice in information and knowledge management,* Elayne Coakes and Steve Clarke, eds., 21-29, Idea Group Reference, ISBN 1591405564, Hershey.

Bolisani, E.; Scarso, E. & Di Biagi, M. (2006). Economic Issues of Online Professional Communities, In: *Encyclopedia of communities of practice in information and knowledge management,* Elayne Coakes and Steve Clarke, eds., 148-156, Idea Group Reference, ISBN 1591405564, Hershey.

Berners-Lee, T.; Hendler, J. & Lassila, O. (2001).The Semantic Web. *Scientific American*, May, 2001.

Cothrel, J. & Williams, R. (2000). Four Smart Ways to Run Online Communities. *Sloan Management Review*, p.81-91, USA.

Choo, C. W; Detlor, B. & Turnbull, D. (2000) .Web Work: information seeking and knowledge work on the World Wide Web. Boston: Kluwer Academic Publishers.

Davenport, T. & Prusak, L. (1998). *Working Knowledge*. Harvard Business School Press. ISBN 1578513014. USA.

Davis, R.; Shrobe, H. & Szolovits, P. (1993). *What is a Knowledge representation?*. AI Magazine. p. 17-33.

Drucker, P. (2006). *Classic Drucker*. Harvard Business. School Press. ISBN 1422101681. USA.

Geisler, E. (2008) *Knowledge and Knowledge Systems – Learning from the Wonders of the Mind*. IGI Publishing. Illinois Institute of Technology, Hershey, New York, USA.

Goble, C.; Roure, D.; Shadbolt, N. & Fernandes, A. (2004). Enhancing Services and Applications with Knowledge and Semantics, In: *The grid : blueprint for a new computing infrastructure,* Foster I. and Kesselman C., eds., 431-458, Morgan-Kaufmann.

Gruber, T. (1995). Toward Principles for the Design of Ontologies Used for Knowledge Sharing. *International Journal Human-Computer Studies*. p.907-928

Haghirian, P. (2006). International Knowledge Transfer as a Challenge for Communities of Practice, In: *Encyclopedia of communities of practice in information and knowledge management,* Elayne Coakes and Steve Clarke, eds., 234-238, Idea Group Reference, ISBN 1591405564, Hershey.

Herman, I. (2007). *Web Ontology Language (OWL)*. http://www.w3.org/2004/OWL/, accessed in April 2009.

Haykin, S. (1998). *Neural Networks: A Comprehensive Foundations*. Prentice Hall. ISBN 0132733501.

Hotho, A.; Nürnberger, A. & Paab, G. (2005). A Brief Survey of Text Mining. *GLDV-Journal for Computational Linguistics and Language Technology*, 16-92, May.

Kimble, C. & Hildreth, P. (2006). The Limits of Communities of Practice, In: *Encyclopedia of communities of practice in information and knowledge management,* Elayne Coakes and Steve Clarke, eds., 327-334, Idea Group Reference, ISBN 1-59140-556-4, Hershey.

Koch, M. & Lacher, M. (2000). Integrating Community services: A Common Infrastructure Proposal. *Knowledge-Based Intelligent Engineering Systems and Allied Technologies.* Proceedings. Fourth International Conference on. p.56-59. ISBN 0780364007.

Lave, J. & Wenger, E. (1991). *Situated Learning: Legitimate Peripheral Participation.* Cambridge University Press: NewYork, NY. USA.

Landini, M. & Damiani, J. (2001). Knowledge Management: An Exploratory Study in the Brazilian Aerospace Program. *Proceedings PICMET´01.* ISBN 1890843067. Portland, OR, USA.

Librelotto, G.; Ramalho J. & Henriques, P. (2005). Representação de Conhecimento na Semantic Web. *XXV Congresso da Sociedade Brasileira de Computação: XXIV Jornadas de Atualização em Informática.* p. 1210-1261. São Leopoldo, RS. Brasil. (in Portuguese).

Mizzaro, S. (1997). Relevance: The Whole History. *Journal of the American Society for Information Science,* v.48, n.9, p. 810-832.

Nonaka, I. & Takeuchi, H. (1995). *The Knowledge-Creating Company: How Japanese Companies Create the Dynamics of Innovation.* Oxford University Press. ISBN 0195092694. New York.

Russell, S. &; Norving, P. (2004). *Artificial Intelligence. A Modern Approach.* Prentice-Hall. ISBN 013080302

Setzer, V. (2006). Data, Information, Knowledge and Competence. *Proceedings of the 3rd International Conference on Information Systems and Technology Management.* p. 1676-1695. São Paulo.

Shannon, C. (1948). A Mathematical Theory of Communication. *The Bell System Technical Journal,* p. 379–423,623–656, 1948.

Uschold, M. (1996). Building Ontologies: Towards a Unified Methodology. *In: 16th Annual Conference of the British Computer Society Specialist Group on Expert Systems,* Cambridge, UK.

Uschold, M. & Gruninger. M. (1996). Ontologies: principles, methods and applications. *Knowledge Engineering Review,* p.93-155.

Uschold, M. & Jasper, R. (1999). A Framework for Understanding and Classifying Ontology Applications. *Proceedings of the IJCAI-99 workshop on Ontologies and Problem-Solving Methods (KRR5).* Stockholm, Sweden.

Vestal, W. (2003). Ten Traits for a Successful Community of Practice. *Knowledge Management Review,* 5(6), 6.

von Krogh, G., Ichijo, K. & Nonaka, I. (2000) Enabling Knowledge Creation: How to Unlock the Mystery of Tacit Knowledge and Release the Power of Innovation, Oxford University Press.

Wenger, E.; McDermott, R & Snyder, W. (2002). *Cultivating Communities of Practice: A Guide to Managing Knowledge.* Harvard Business School Press. ISBN 1578513308.

Linkage Knowledge Management and Data Mining in E-business: Case study

Ming-Chang Lee
Department of Information Management, Fooyin University, Taiwan, R. O. C.
Department of Business Administration, National Kaohsiung University of applied Sciences, Taiwan

Abstract
E-business has changed the face of most business functions in competitive enterprises. E-business functions are enterprise resource planning (ERP) and related systems such as supply chain management (SCM) and customer relationship management (CRM), are incorporating decision support tools and technologies. Data mining has matured as a field of basic and applied research in e-business. Effective knowledge management (KM) enhances products, improves operational efficiency, speeds deployment, increases sales and profits, and creates customer satisfaction. The aim of this study is to make an association with e-business, KM and data mining. Therefore, firstly, it will brief review the existing on knowledge management, e-business, and data mining, decision support system. We then present on linkages or supplementary relationships between the knowledge management and e-business with data mining. Secondly, knowledge, knowledge management and knowledge process is defined, and point out the need for integration with e-business. Thirdly, it introduces data mining and examined data mining in data warehouse environment. Fourth, the e-business is defined. Using this definition, it can drive e-business application architecture and knowledge process frameworks with business process. Finally, Integrating Intelligent Decision Support System and knowledge management with data mining model is discussed. It presents the proposed KM architecture and discusses how decision support system and data mining can enhance KM. In this study some suggestions are made to get knowledge with data mining, which will help, for the improvement of e-business. Chinese Motor Corporation's knowledge and Sequent Computer's knowledge are discussed.
Keywords: E-business; knowledge management; data mining; decision support system

1. Introduction

E-business is defined as Internet-mediated integration of business, applications, and information systems (Kalakota and Robinson, 1999). E-business is considered as a new business model that emerging in the Web-driven environment and has descended across the corporate world. Joyce and Winch (2005) draws upon the emergent knowledge of e-business model together with traditional strategy theory to provide a simple integrating

framework for the evaluation and assessment of business models for e-business. Timmers (1998) proposed a business mode, it elements of a business model are (1) the business architecture for product, service and information flows (2) description of potential benefits (3) description of the sources of revenues. Business model are defined as summary of the value creation logic of an organization or a business network including assumptions about its partners, competitors and customers. Wald and Stammers (2001) proposed a model for e-businesses based on the separation between standard processes and e-processes.
Business, when properly linked with knowledge process and aligned with an organization's culture, aids a firm's strategic growth. The implementation of their e-business application also can benefit from experience acquired from their knowledge management practices. For example, Plessis and Boon (2004) studied e-business in South Africa and found that knowledge management is a prerequisite for e-business and its increasing customer-centric focus and is an integral part of both customer relationship management and e-business. Bose and Sugumaran (2003) found a U.S. application of KM technology in customer relationship management, particularly for creating, structuring, disseminating, and applying knowledge. The development of e-business, focus knowledge organizations is needed to enhance customer relationship management, supply management, and product development (Fahey et al., 2001).
DSS is a computer-based system that aids the process of decision-making (Finlay, 1994). DSS are interactive computer-based systems that help decision makers utilize data and models to solve unstructured problems. DSS can also enhance the tacit to explicit knowledge conversion by eliciting one or more what-if cases (i. e., model instances) that the knowledge worker wants to explore. That is, as the knowledge worker changes one or more model coefficients or right hand side values to explore its effect on the modeled solution. That is, the knowledge worker is converting the tacit knowledge that can be shared with other workers and leveraged to enhance decision. DSSs which perform selected cognitive decision-making functions and are based on artificial intelligence or intelligent agent's technologies are called Intelligent Decision Support Systems (IDSS) (Gadomaski, et al., 2001). IDSS was applied to solve problems faced by rice framers desiring to achieve maximum yields in choosing the proper enterprise management strategies. IDSS is needed and is economically feasible for generic problems that require repetitive decisions. Dhar and Stein (2000) use term to characterize the degree of intelligence provided by a decision support tool. It describes intelligence density as representing the amount of useful decision support information that a decision maker gets from using the output from some analytic system for a certain amount of time (2000).
Data mining is a decision-making functions (decision support tool). Data mining (DM) has as its dominant goal, the generation of no-obvious yet useful information for decision makers from very large data warehouse (DW). DM is the technique by which relationship and patterns in data are identified in large database (Fayyadand and Uthurusamy, 1995). Data Warehouse, an integral part of the process, provides an infrastructure that enables businesses to extract, cleanse, and store vast amount of corporate data from operational systems for efficient and accurate responses to user queries. DW empowers the knowledge workers with information that allows them to make decisions based on a solid foundation of fact (Devlin, 1997). In DW environment, DM techniques can be used to discover untapped pattern of data that enable the creation of new information. DM and DW are potentially critical technologies to enable the knowledge creation and management process (Berson and

Smit, 1997). The DW is to provide the decision-maker with an intelligent analysis platform that enhances all phase of the knowledge management process. DSS or IDSS and DM can be used to enhance knowledge management and its three associated processes: i.e., tacit to explicit knowledge conversion, explicit knowledge leveraging, and explicit knowledge conversion (Lau et al., 2004). . The purpose of this study is to proposed KM architecture and discusses how to working DSS and data mining can enhance KM.
A firm can integrate an ERP (e- business) system with an IDSS in integrate existing DSS that currently sit on top of a firms' ERP system across multiple firms. Dharand Stein (2000). describes six steps of processing to transform data into knowledge. Figure 1 is showed as a framework of e-business and IDSS. The integration of ERP and IDSS can extend to include the collaboration of multiple enterprises. Firms need to share information with their supplier-facing partners. Firm need to gather information from their customer-facing partners (i.e. retailers, customers). Firm need to increase intelligent density through the various IDSS tools and technologies integrated with their respective e-business system. In multi- enterprise collaboration, it develop relationship with its partners through systems such as CRM, SCM, Business-to-Business (B2B), data warehouse, firms are able to provide their decision makers with analytical capabilities (i. e. OLAP, Data Mining, MOLAP). From Figure 1, the integrated of e-business and IDSS included ERP system, Enterprise Application integration and IDSS system.

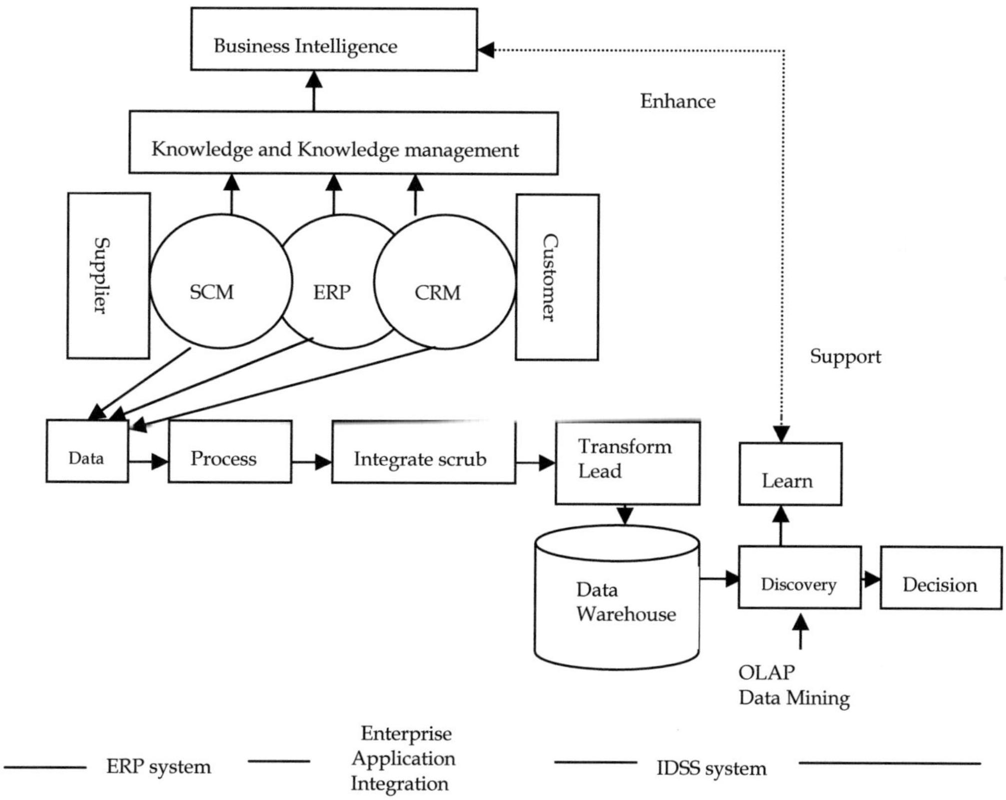

Fig. 1. Framework of e-business, knowledge management, data mining and IDSS, Source from: Lee and Cheng (2007)

2. Knowledge Management

2.1 Knowledge and Knowledge Management

We define KM to be the process of selectively applying knowledge from previous experiences of decision making to current and future decision making activities with the manifestations of the same process only in different organizations. Knowledge management is the process established to capture and use knowledge in an organization for the purpose of improving organization performance (Marakas, 1999). Knowledge management is emerging as the new discipline that provides the mechanisms for systematically managing the knowledge that evolves with enterprise. Most large organizations have been experimenting with knowledge management with a view to improving profits, being competitively innovative, or simply to survive (Davenport and Prusak, 1998; Hendriks and Virens, 1999; Kalakota and Robinson, 1999; Loucopoulos and Kavakli, 1999). Knowledge management systems refer to a class of information systems applied to managing organization knowledge, which is an IT-based system developed to support the Organizational knowledge management behavior: acquisition, generation, codification, storage, transfer, retrieval (Alavi and Leidner, 2001). In face of the volatility and rate of change in business environment, globalization of marketing and labor pools, effective management of knowledge of organization is undoubtedly recognized as, perhaps, the most significant in determining organizational success, and has become an increasingly critical issue for technology implementation and management. In other words, KMS are meant to support knowledge processes. Knowledge management systems are the tools for managing knowledge, helping organizations in problem-solving activities and facilitating to making of decisions. Such systems have been used in the areas of medicine, engineering, product design, finance, construction and so on (Apostolou and Mentzas, 1999; Chau et al., 2002; Davenport and Prusak, 1998; Hendriks and Virens, 1999).

Knowledge assets are the knowledge of markets, products, technologies and organizations, that a business owns or needs to own and which enable its business process to generate profits, and value, etc. KM is not only managing these knowledge assets, but managing the processes that act upon the assets. These processes include: developing knowledge, preserving knowledge, using knowledge, and sharing knowledge. From an organizational point of view, Barclay and Murray (1997) consider knowledge management as a business activity with two primary aspects. (1) Treating the knowledge component of business activities as explicit concern of business reflected in strategy, policy, and practice at all levels of the organization. (2) Making a direct connection between an organization's intellectual assets - both explicit and tacit - and positive business results.

The key elements of knowledge management are collaboration, content management and information sharing (Duffy, 2001). Collaboration refers to colleagues exchanging ideas and generating new knowledge. Common terms used to describe collaboration include knowledge creation, generation, production, development, use and organizational learning (Duffy, 2001). Content management refers to the management of an organization's internal and external knowledge using information skills and information technology tools. Terms associated with content management include information classification, codification, storage and access, organization and coordination (Alavi and Leidner, 2001; Davenport and Prusak, 1998; Denning, 1999). Information sharing refers

to ways and means to distribute information and encourage colleagues to share and reuse knowledge in the firm. These activities mat be described as knowledge distribution, transfer or sharing (Alavi and Leidner, 2001; Davenport and Prusak, 1998; Duffy, 1999).
Nonaka and Takeuchi (1995) view implicit knowledge and explicit knowledge as complementary entities. There contend that there are four modes (Socialization, Externalization, Combination, and Internalization) in which organizational knowledge is created through the interaction and conversion between implicit and explicit knowledge. Figure 2 is denoted as conversion of tacit to explicit knowledge and voice versa (or a cyclical conversion of tacit to explicit knowledge).

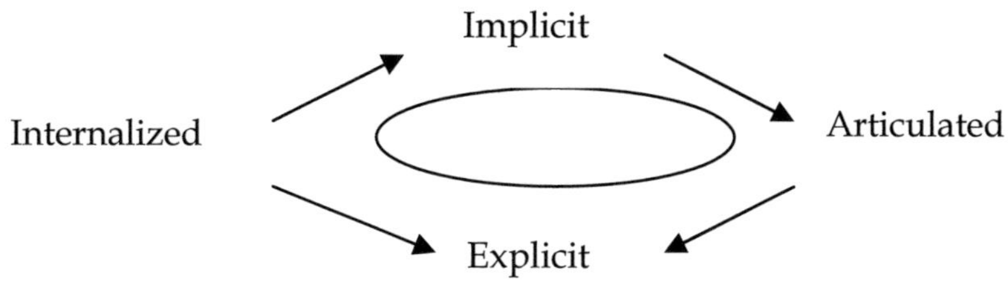

Fig. 2. A cyclical conversion of tacit to explicit knowledge

2.2 Knowledge process

Common knowledge management practices include: (1) Creating and improving explicit knowledge artifacts and repositories (developing better databases, representations, and visualizations, improving the real-time access to data, information, and knowledge; delivering the right knowledge to the right persons at the right time). (2) Capturing and structuring tacit knowledge as explicit knowledge (creating knowledge communities and networks with electronic tools to capture knowledge and convert tacit knowledge to explicit knowledge). (3) Improving knowledge creation and knowledge flows (developing and improving organizational learning mechanisms; facilitating innovation strategies and processes; facilitating and enhancing knowledge creating conversations/dialogues). (4) Enhancing knowledge management culture and infrastructure (improving participation, motivation, recognition, and rewards to promote knowledge sharing and idea generation; developing knowledge management enabling tools and technologies). (5) Managing knowledge as an asset (identifying, documenting, measuring and assessing intellectual assets; identifying, prioritizing, and evaluating knowledge development and knowledge management efforts; document and more effectively levering intellectual property). (6) Improving competitive intelligence and data mining strategies and technologies.
This process focuses on tacit to tacit knowledge linking. Tacit knowledge goes beyond the boundary and new knowledge is created by using the process of interactions, observing, discussing, analyzing, spending time together or living in same environment. The socialization is also known as converting new knowledge through shared experiences. Organizations gain new knowledge from outside its boundary also like interacting with customers, suppliers and stack holders. By internalization explicit knowledge is created using tacit knowledge and is shared across the organization. When this tacit knowledge is read or practiced by individuals then it broadens the learning spiral of knowledge creation. Organization tries to innovate or learn when this new knowledge is shared in

socialization process. Organizations provide training programs for its employees at different stages of their working with the company. By reading these training manuals and documents employees internalize the tacit knowledge and try to create new knowledge after the internalization process. Therefore, integration organizational elements through a knowledge management system created organizational information technology infrastructure and organizational cluster (see Figure 3).

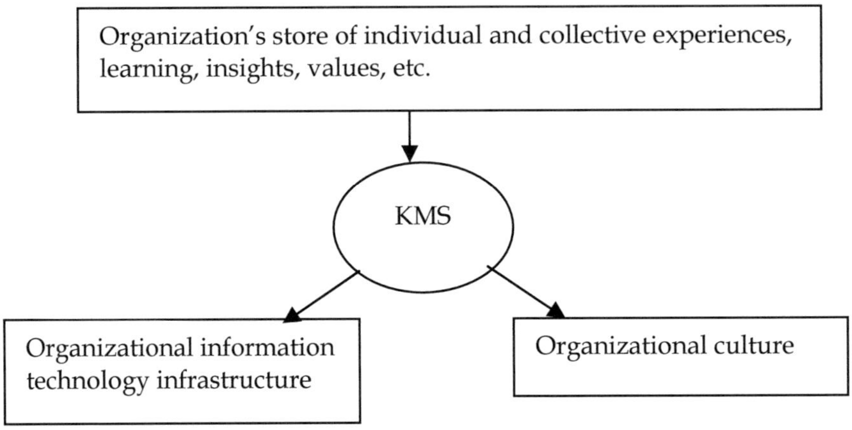

Fig. 3. Integration organizational elements through a knowledge management system

2.3 SECI process and knowledge creation flow

Nonaka (1994) proposes the SCEI model, which asserts that knowledge creation is a spiral process of interactions between explicit and tacit knowledge. Socialization is a process of creating tacit knowledge through share experience. Externalization is a process of conversion of tacit knowledge into explicit knowledge supported by metaphors and analogies. Combination involves the conversion of explicit knowledge into more complex sets of explicit knowledge by combining different bodies of explicit knowledge held by individuals through communication and diffusion processes and the systemization of knowledge. Internalization is the conversion of explicit knowledge into tacit knowledge. The four models of knowledge creation allow us to conceptualize the actualization of knowledge with social institutions through a series of self-transcendental processes. An organization itself will not be capable of creating knowledge without individuals, but knowledge spiral will not occur if knowledge is not shared with others or does not spread out the organization. Thus, organizational knowledge creation can be viewed as an upward spiral process, starting at the individual level moving up to the collective (group) level, and then to the organization al level, sometimes reaching out to the inter-organizational level. Figure 4 illustrates the spiral SECI model across individual, group, organization, and inter-organization granularities.

The core behavioral assumption in the model is that knowledge creating companies continually encourage the flow of knowledge between individuals and staff groups to improve both tacit and explicit knowledge stocks. The critical knowledge management assumption of the SECI process is the knowledge is created and improved as it flows through different levels of the organization and between individuals and groups. Thus knowledge value is created through synergies between knowledge holders (both individual and group) within a supportive and developmental organization context. The core competencies of organization are linkage to explicit and tacit knowledge (see Figure 5). Figure 6 is denoted as the key elements of the SECI model.

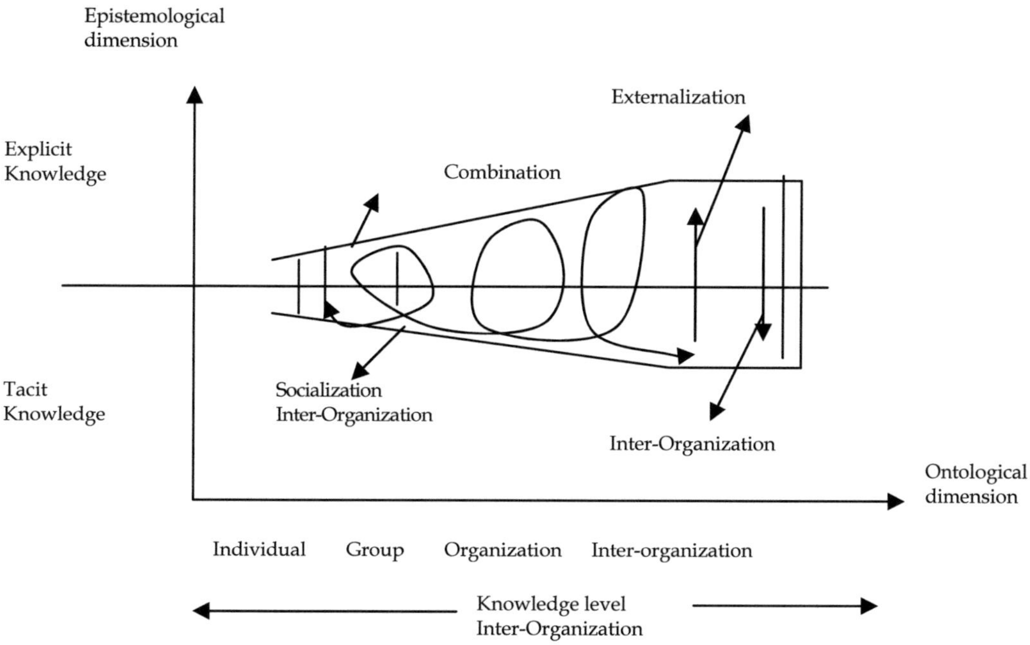

Fig. 4. Spiral of Organization Knowledge Creation (Nonaka, 1994)

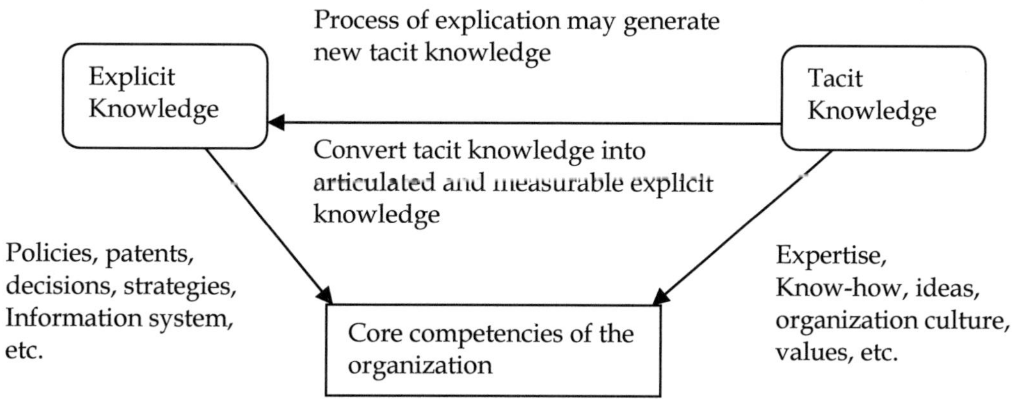

Fig. 5. the core competency of the organization

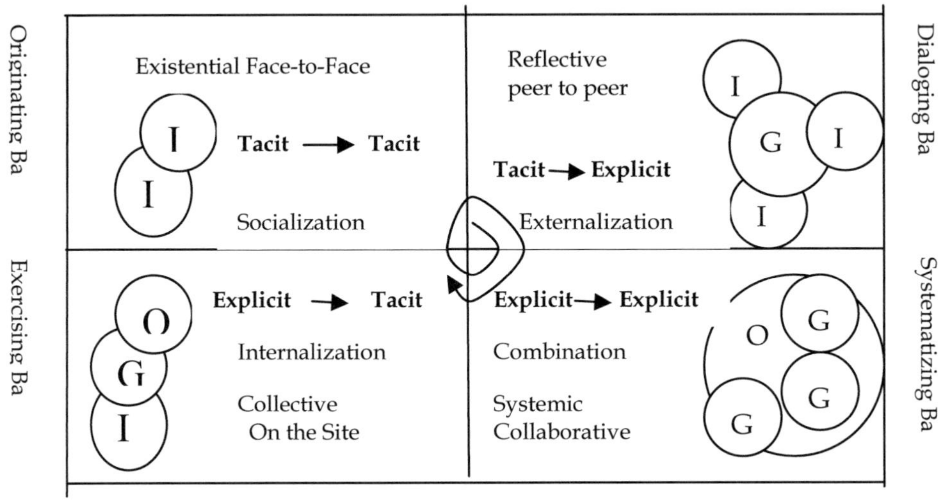

Fig. 6. The key elements of the SECI model (Nonaka, et al., 2000; Nonaka, et all., 2001)

In Figure 6, I, G, O symbols represent individuals, group and organization aggregates. Four different notions of Ba are defined in relation to each of the gour quadrants of the SECI model which make up the knowledge spiral. These are as follows:

1. The Originating Ba: a local where individuals can share feelings, emotions, experiences and perceptual models.
2. The Dialoguing Ba: a space where tacit knowledge is transferred and documented to explicit form. Two key methods factors are through dialogues and metaphor creation.
3. The Systematizing Ba: a vitual space, where information technology facilitates the recombination of existing explicit knowledge to form new explicit knowledge.
4. The Exercising Ba: a space where explicit knowledge is converted into tacit knowledge.

3. Data mining methods

Data mining is a process that uses statistical, mathematical, artificial intelligence, and machine learning techniques to extract and identify useful information and subsequent knowledge from large databases (Nemati and Barko, 2001). The various mechanism of this generation includes abstractions, aggregations, summarizations, and characterizations of data (Chau, et al., 2002). If you are a marketing manager for an auto manufacturer, this somewhat surprising pattern might be quite valuable. DM uses well-established statistical and machine learning techniques to build models that predict customer behavior. Today, technology automates the mining process, integrates it with commercial data warehouses, and presents it in a relevant way for business users.

Data mining includes tasks such as knowledge extraction, data archaeology, data exploration, data pattern processing, data dredging, and information harvesting. The following are the major characteristics and objectives of data mining:

. Data are often buried deep within very large databases, which sometimes contain data from several years. In many cases, the data are cleansed and consolidated in a data warehouse.

. The data mining environment is usually client/server architecture or a web-based architecture.

. Data mining tools are readily combined with spreadsheets and other software development tools. Thus, the mined data can be analyzed and processed quickly and easily.

. Striking it rich often involves finding an unexpected result and requires end users to think creatively.

. Because of the large amounts of data and massive search efforts, it is sometimes necessary to used parallel processing for data mining.

3.1 Data mining in data warehouse environment

The data warehouse is a valuable and easily available data source for data mining operations. Data extractions the data mining tools work on come from the data warehouse. Figure 7 illustrates how data mining fits in the data warehouse environment. Notice how the data warehouse environment supports data mining.

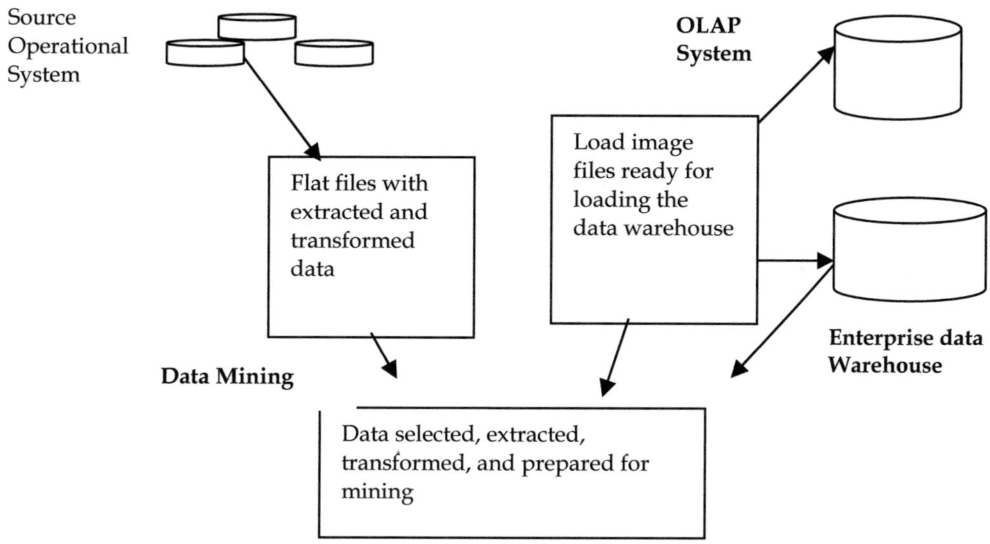

Fig. 7. Data mining in data warehouse environment

3.2 Decision support progress to data mining

Business analytics (BA), DSS, and KM apparatus enable both active and passive delivery of information from large scale DW, providing enterprises and managers with timely answers to mission-critical questions. The objective of these apps is to turn the enormous amounts of available data into knowledge companies can used. The growth of this class of apps has been driven by the demand for more competitive business intelligence and increases in electronic data capture and storage. In addition, the emergence of the Internet

and other communications technologies has enabled cost-effective access to and delivery of information to remote users throughout the world. Due to these factors, the overall for BA, KM, and DSS is projected to grow substantially.
Link all decision support systems, data mining delivers information. Please refer to Figure 8 showing the progression of decision support.

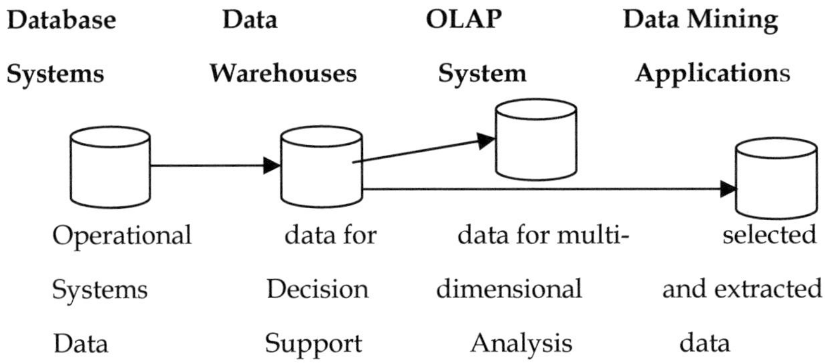

Fig. 8. Decision support progresses to data mining

Progressive organizations gather enterprise data from the source operational systems, move the data through a transformation and cleansing process, and store the data in data warehouse in a form suitable for multidimensional analysis.

3.3 Integration of knowledge management and data warehouse

3.3.1 Data warehouse and Knowledge management

Knowledge management system (KMS) is a systematic process for capturing, integrating, organizing, and communicating knowledge accumulated by employees. It is a vehicle to share corporate knowledge so that the employees may be more effective and be productive in their work. Knowledge management system must store all such knowledge in knowledge repository, sometimes called a knowledge warehouse. If a data warehouse contains structured information, a knowledge warehouse holds unstructured information. Therefore, a knowledge framework must have tools for searching and retrieving unstructured information. Figure 9 is integration of KM and data warehouse.

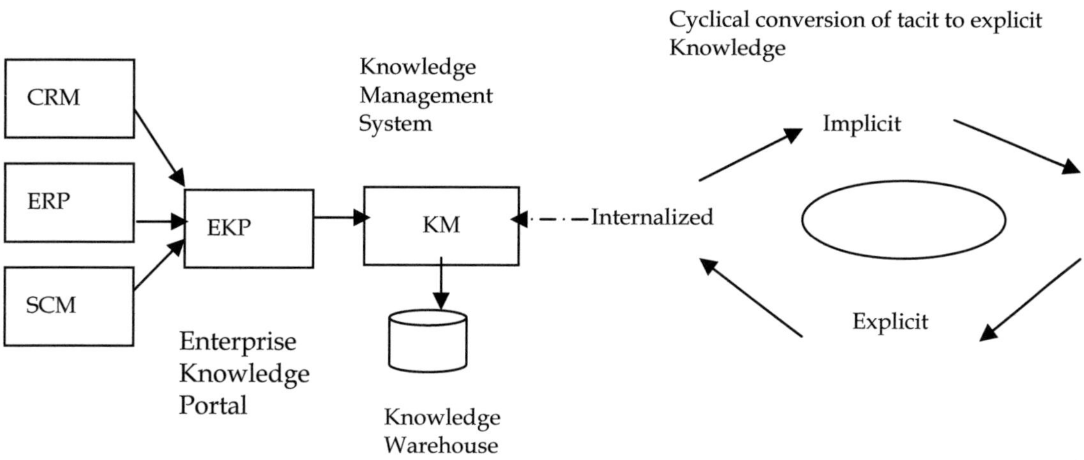

Fig. 9. Integration of KM and data warehouse

3.3.2 Knowledge discovery in data warehouse

Knowledge discovery Databases (KDD) in DW is a process used to search for and extract useful information from volumes of document and data. It include task such as knowledge extraction, data archaeology, data exploration, data pattern processing, data dredging and information harvesting. All these activities are conduct automatically and allow quick discovery, even by nonprogrammers. AI methods are useful data mining tools that include automated knowledge elicitation from other sources. Data mining tools find patterns in data and may even infer rules from them. Pattern and rules can be used to guide decision making and forecast the effects of decision. KDD can be used to identify the meaning of data or text, using knowledge management tools that scan documents and e-mail to build an expertise profile of a firm's employees.

Extending the role of data mining and knowledge discovery techniques for knowledge externalization, Bolloju et al. (1997) proposed a framework for integrating knowledge management into enterprise environment for next-generation decision support system. The knowledge track knowledge center offers integrated business to business functions and can scale from Dot-COM to large enterprise sitting on top, the way most intranet portals do. The knowledge center integrates with external data houses, including enterprise resource planning (ERP), online analytical process (OLAP), and customer relationship management (CRM) systems.

3.3.3 Integrating DSS and Knowledge

While DSS and knowledge management are independent activities in many organizations, they are interrelated in many others. Herschel and Jones (2005) discuss of knowledge management, business intelligence (BI) and their integration. Bolloju et al. (2002) proposed a framework for integrating decision support and knowledge management processes, using knowledge-discovery techniques. The decision maker is using applications fed by a data warehouse and data marts and is also using other sources of knowledge. The DSS information and the knowledge are integrated in a system, and the knowledge can stored in the model base. The framework is based on the relationship shown in Figure 10. Framework for Integrating DSS and KMS

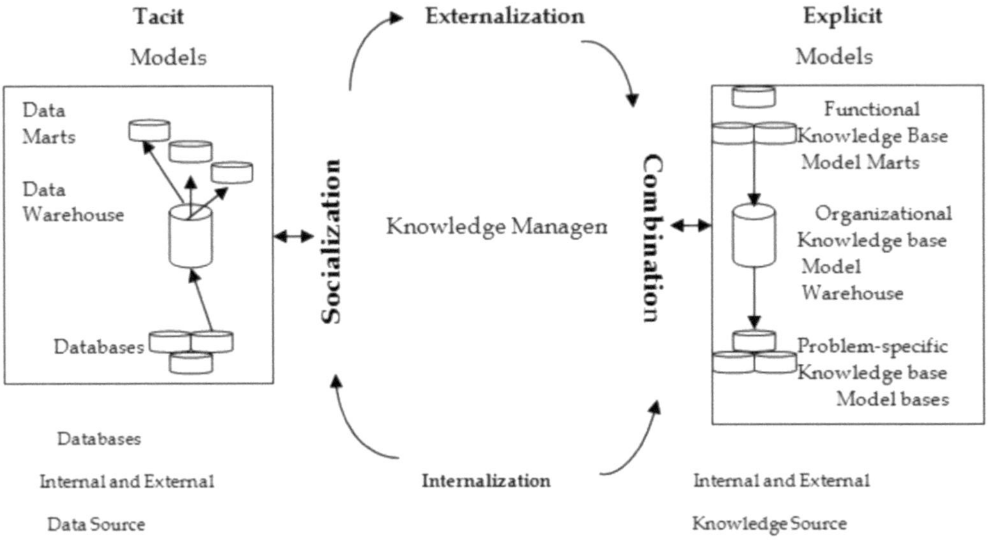

Fig. 10. Framework for Integrating DSS and KMS Source from :Bolloju and Turban (2002)

4. E-business

4.1 E-business application architecture

E-business is a broader term that encompasses electronically buying, selling, service customers, and interacting with business partner and intermediaries over the Internet. E-business describes a marketplace where businesses are using web-based and other network computing-based technologies to transform their internal business processes and their external business relationships. So e-business opportunities are simply a subset of the larger universe of opportunities that corporate investment boards consider everyday. Joyce and Winch (2005) draws upon the emergent knowledge of e-business model together with traditional strategy theory to provide a simple integrating framework for the evaluation and assessment of business models for e-business.

Enterprise resource planning (ERP) is a method of using computer technology to link various functions—such as accounting, inventory control, and human resources—across an entire company. ERP system supports most of the business system that maintains in a single database the data needed for a variety of business functions such as Manufacturing, supply chain management (SCM), financials, projects, human resources and customer relationship management (CRM). ERP systems developed by the Business Process Reengineering (BPR) vendors such that SAP was expected to provide lockstep regimented sharing the data across various business functions.

These systems were based on a top-down model of information strategy implementation and execution, and focused primarily on the coordination of companies' internal functions. The BPR vendors such that SAP are still evolving to develop better external information flow linkages in terms of CRM and SCM. The ERP functionality, with its internal focus, complements the external focus of CRM and SCM to provide a based for creating E-business applications.

Figure 11 shows how all the various application clusters are integrated to form the future model of the organization. The blueprint is useful because it assists managers in identifying near-term and long-term integration opportunities. Figure 11 also illustrates the underlying premise of e-business design. Companies run on interdependent application clusters. If one application cluster of the company does not function well, the entire customer value delivery system is affected

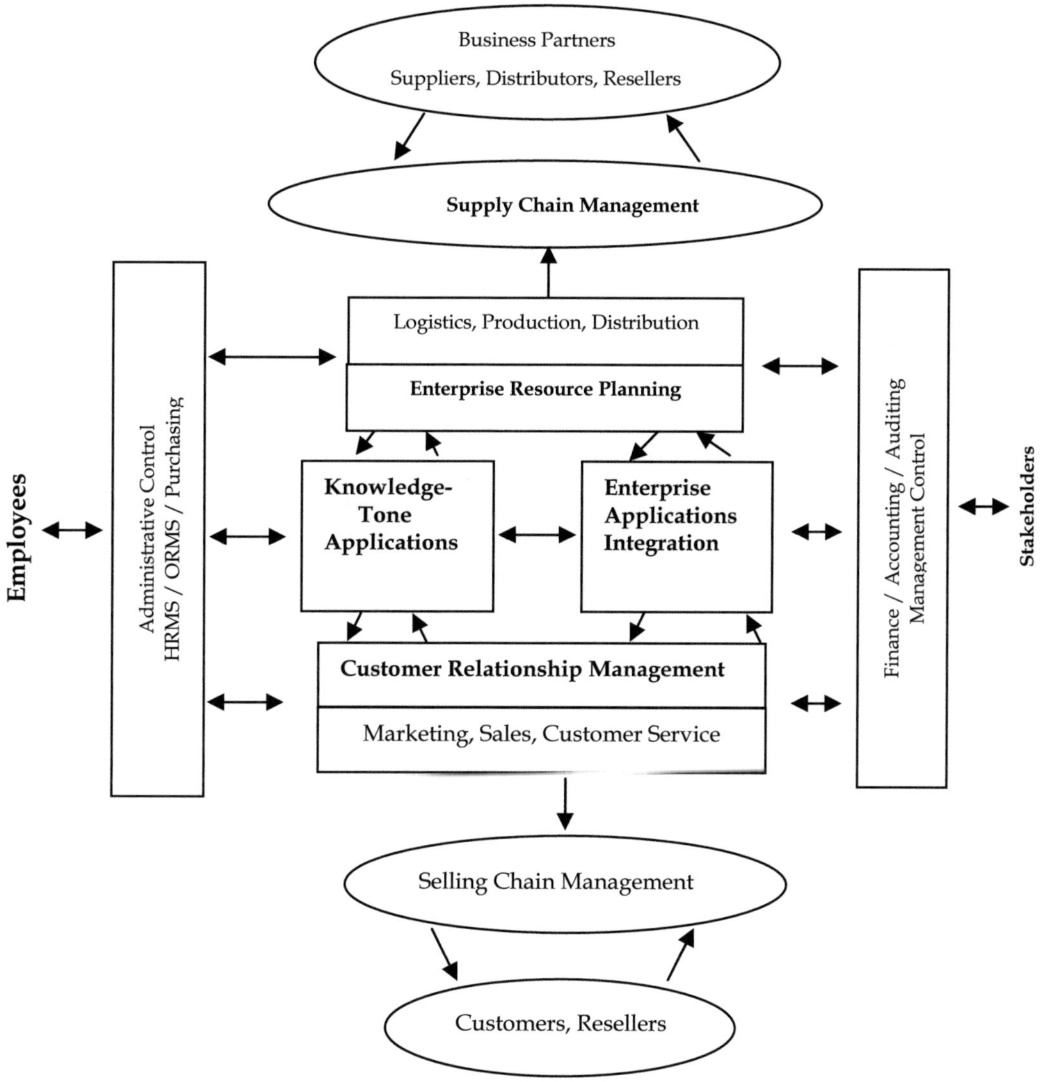

Fig. 11. E-business Application Architecture

4.2 Knowledge process framework with business

A business process is defined as a set of logically related tasks performance to achieve a defined business outcome (Davenport and Robinson, 1999). The knowledge process through facilitating the transfer or creation of knowledge serves the business process. E-business is defined as Internet-mediated integration of business, applications, and information systems (Kalakota and Robinson, 1999). E-business is considered as a new business model that emerging in the Web-driven environment and has descended across the corporate world. Business, when properly linked with knowledge process and aligned with an organization's culture, aids a firm's strategic growth. The implementation of their e-business application also can benefit from experience acquired from their KM practices. For example, Plessis and Boon (2004) studied e-business in South Africa and found that knowledge management is a prerequisite foe e-business and its increasing customer-centric focus and is an integral part of both customer relationship management and e-business. Bose and Sugumaran (2003) found a U.S. application of KM technology in customer relationship management, particularly for creating, structuring, disseminating, and applying knowledge. The development of e-business, focus knowledge organizations is needed to enhance customer relationship management, supply management, and product development (Fahey, et al., 2001).

The Enterprise Resource Planning (ERP) systems developed by the Business Process Reengineering (BPR) vendors such that SAP was expected to provide lockstep regimented sharing the data across various business functions. These systems were based on a top-down model of information strategy implementation and execution, and focused primarily on the coordination of companies' internal functions. The BPR vendors such that SAP are still evolving to develop better external information flow linkages in terms of customer relationship management (CRM) and supply chain management (SCM). The ERP functionality, with its internal focus, complements the external focus of CRM and SCM to provide a based for creating E-business applications. The continue challenge remains in terms of ensuring the adaptability and flexibility of information interfaces and information flows. The more recent development of E-business architectures based on software components self-contained packages of functionality that can be snapped together to create complete business applications (Malhotra, 2000). Knowledge management and e-business would seem to supplement each other (Bose and Sugumaran, 2003). According the above argument, we have Framework of knowledge process with business process, and are shown as Figure 12.

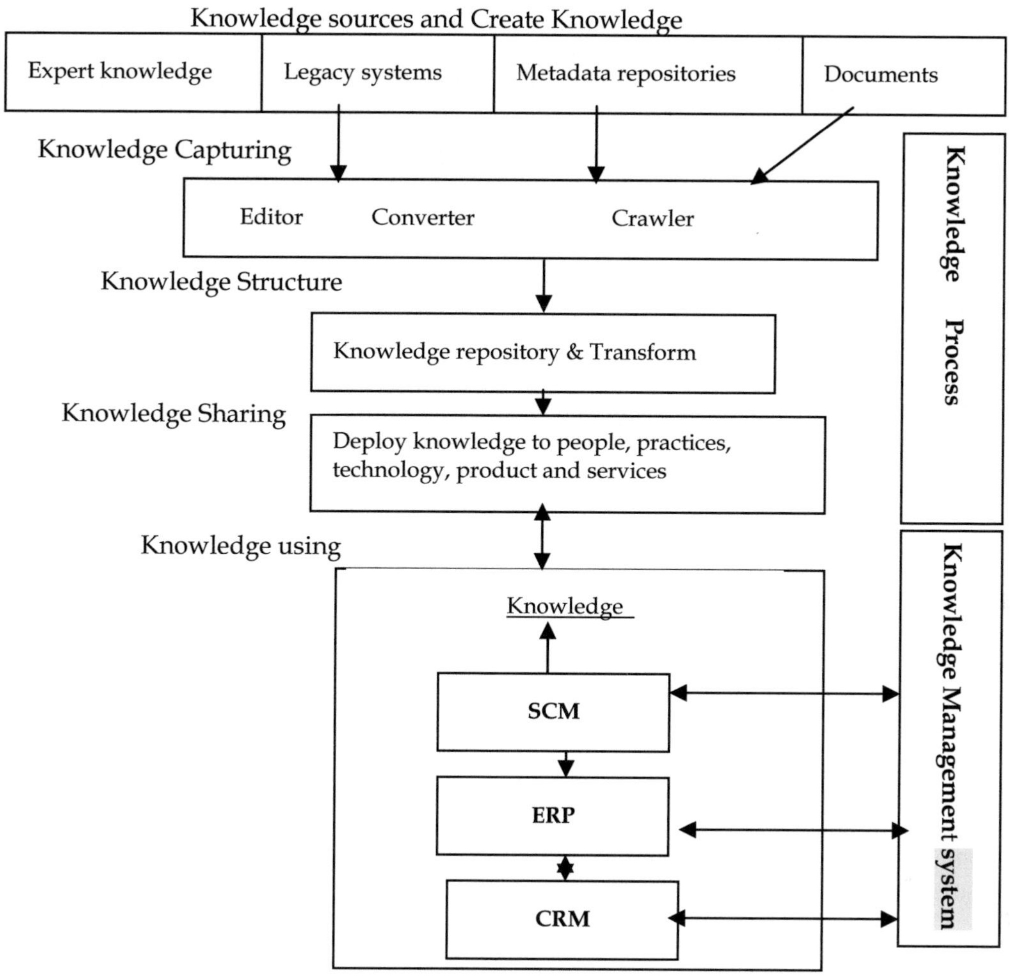

Fig. 12. knowledge Process frameworks with business process Source from: (Lee, 2008)

4.3 Integration DSS and Knowledge management with data mining

Knowledge management and e-business would seem to supplement each other (Bose and Sugumaran, 2003). The knowledge process through facilitating the transfer or creation of knowledge serves the business process. Business, when properly linked with knowledge process and aligned with an organization's culture, aids a firm's strategic growth. The implementation of their e-business application also can benefit from experience acquired from their KM practices. For example, Plessis and Boon [38] studied e-business in South Africa and found that knowledge management is a prerequisite foe e-business and its increasing customer-centric focus and is an integral part of both customer relationship management and e-business. The development of e-business, focus knowledge organizations is needed to enhance customer relationship management, supply management, and product development (Fahey, 2001). Knowledge management and

e-business would seem to supplement each other (Bose and Sugumaran, 2003).
Enterprise develop relationship with their partners through system such as CRM, SCM, Business to Business (B2B) procurement, and Online Stores (Data Warehouse), firms are able to provide their decision makers with analytical capabilities. According to Power (2002), academics and practitioners have discussed building DSS in terms of four major components: (a) the user interface (b) the database, (c) the model and analytical tools, and (d) the IDSS architecture and network. Marakas (1999) proposes a generalized architecture made of five distinct parts: (a) the data management system, (b) the model management system, (c) the knowledge engine, (d) the user interface, and (e) the user(s).
To collaborate at a multi-enterprise level, the firm connects with its partners through EAI technology, processes, and information with all their partners along their extended value chains. These partners in turn may also integrate their respective technologies, process, and information, thus creating a network like multi-enterprise collaborative structure. The implementation of multi-enterprise collaboration architecture is showed as Figure 13.
In Figure 13, during the planning process, data and models are manipulated through DBMS, knowledge management system (KMS) and model base management systems (MBMS), respectively. Instructions for data modifications and model executions may come from the ES interface directly. The MBMS obtains the relevant input data for model executions from the MBMS and, in return, results generated from model executions are sent back to DBMS for storage. The data base also provides facts for ES as part of the Knowledge base. Using these facts together with the predefined rules, the interface ending on the ES performs model validations and planning evaluations, according to what a domain expert is support to do. In Data Warehouse, firms are able to provide their decision makers through with analytical capabilities and Data mining.
Many data mining practitioners seem to agree on a set of data mining functions that can be used in specific application areas. Various data mining techniques are applicable to each type of function. Table 1 is showed as the application areas, examples of mining functions, mining process, and mining techniques.

Application area	Examples of Mining functions	Mining Process	Mining Techniques
Fraud Detection	Credit card frauds Internal audits Warehouse pilferage	Determination of variations	Data Visualization Memory-based Reasoning
Risk Assessment	Credit card upgrade Mortgage Loans Customer Retention Credit Ratings	Detection and analysis of link	Decision Trees Memory-based Reasoning
Market Analysis	Market basket analysis Target marketing Cross selling Customer Relationship Marketing	Predictive Modeling Database segmentation	Cluster Detection Decision Trees Link Analysis Genetic Algorithm

Table 1. Data mining functions and application areas

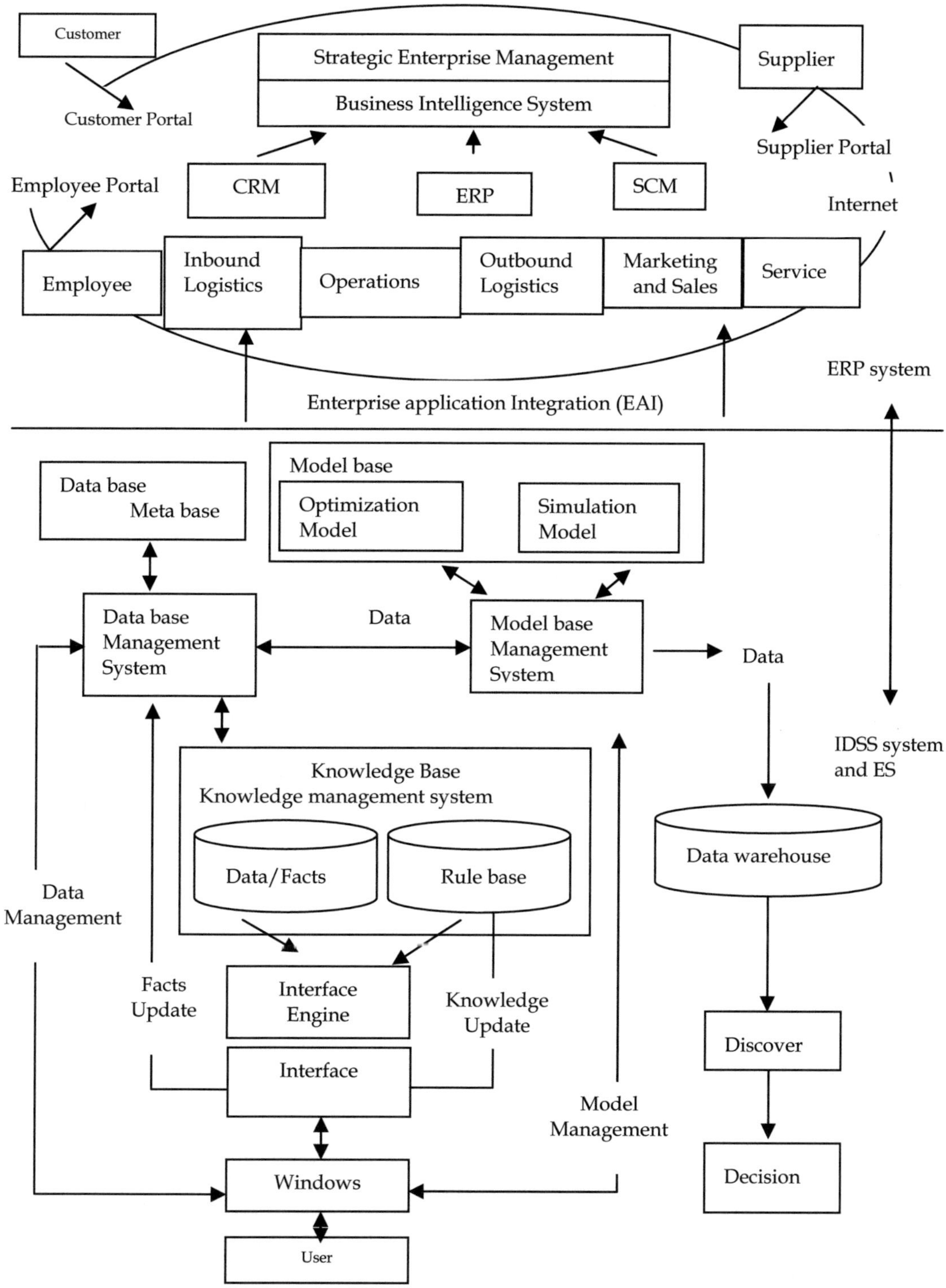

Fig. 13. The implementation of multi-enterprise collaboration architecture Source from: modified Cheung et al. (2005)

5. Case Study

5.1 Chinese Motor Corporation's knowledge

5.1.1 Company Overview

CMC (Chinese Motor Corporation) was founded in June of 1969 and signed a technical collaboration with Mitsubishi Motors Corporation the following year. The Tang-Mei plant was completed at the end of 1973, establishing the manufacturing base for CMC's future growth. The company has been listed on Taiwan Stock Exchange (TSE) since March 1991.

Beginning with producing commercial vehicles, CMC is the leader of Taiwan's commercial vehicles manufactures. While the company's Yang-Mei plant produced less than 3000 vehicles per month through 1975, by the year 1983, total output had surpassed the 100, 000 unit mark. This was, in part, made possible by our most advanced painting facility in Taiwan. This was as well a prelude to the rapid growth that accompanied Taiwan's emergence as an industrial and economic power. Since 1987, CMC's revenues began an extended run of double-digit growth, gaining accolades as one of Taiwan's best-managed companies.

In 1993, the company garnered both ISO 9002 certification and the National Quality Award of Taiwan. In 1997, the company also obtained ISO 14001 environment Management certification. The company has invested in china's South East Motor Corporation (SEM) since 1995 our investment in China gives us access to one of the world's fastest-growing economies, while increased production capacity enables us to develop new models and penetrate foreign markets.

CMC is adept at taking advantage of market opportunities, and promoting fiscal transparency along with a merit-based personnel system that has molded its employees into a cohesive unit. Meanwhile, a cooperative, win-win purchasing system involving the enterprise and its suppliers has enhanced flexibility and improved quality. Thorough implementation of strategic policy has allowed the company to accurately access markets, and manufacture the right vehicle, at the right time

5.1.2 Enterprise Operation

CMC's business operations are guided by the principles expressed in the acronym HIT, which stands for Harmony, Innovation, and Top.

Harmony --True harmony allows the amicable resolution of problems and issues in a spirit of cooperation, creating a win-win situation. This is much like the interplay of instruments in any fine symphony orchestra. CMC's management strives to conduct its affairs to the benefit of all its constituencies: customers, employees, the government, society, shareowners, and suppliers. This creates a harmonious environment that offers mutual rewards.

Innovation --Innovation is the active process of invention, discovery, and improvement. It can also view as a continuous process of renewal providing a vision and wisdom that transcends transient condition. CMC is forever striving to enhance its existing competitive advantage through conceptual innovation in its product, technology, manufacturing process, management, and services.

Top-- Top is the litmus test for quality, much like the athlete who sets his sights on the ultimate goal. CMC expects Top performance in all phases of enterprise operations, strategic planning implementation, and long-term vision. Overall, the top concept benefits Taiwan's whole society.

Under enterprise operation, CMC build the knowledge management objective and organization. The strategic of building knowledge management are: higher-level manager support, plastic a sharing business culture, to plant one's feet on solid ground, to praise knowledge management contribution and application, to establish a platform of knowledge management.

E-Business model design and implementation in Supply-Chain Management based on DySco Framework. It has five stages: data-base, virtual communities, training center, intellectual capital and systematical knowledge. In data-base, it contains product knowledge, manufacturing knowledge, R & D knowledge, and management knowledge and sale management. CMC knowledge management flow and structure are shown on figure 14.

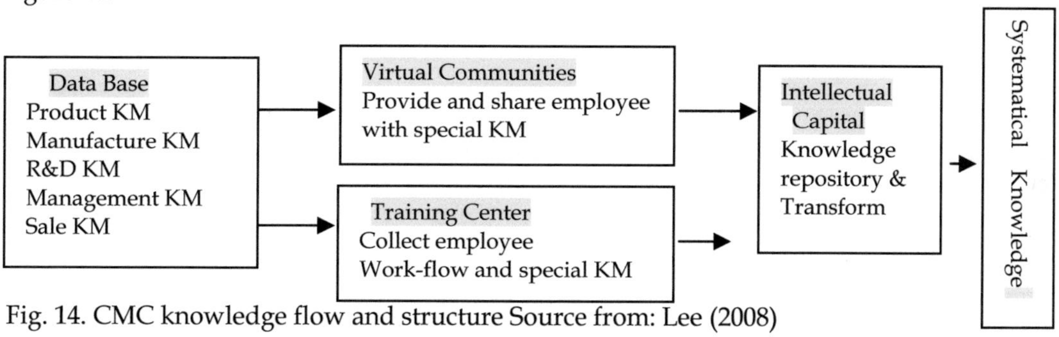

Fig. 14. CMC knowledge flow and structure Source from: Lee (2008)

The China Motor Training Center is a professional training center. It has top quality space layout and all-inclusive design. It can be used for educational training, conferences, seminars, audio video reports, and product exhibition. CMC center is contains the following five features:

Convenient Location -- The China Motor Training Center is located next to the You Shi exit on the Zhong Shan Expressway. It is only a ten-minute drive from the Pu Shin Train Station and the Yang Mei Train Station. The location and transportation are convenient.

Complete Function -- A unique space designed specifically for training and conferences. A learning environment is in place with facilities that serve every function including quiet, interruption free classrooms, dining rooms, guest rooms, and recreation facilities.

Professional Facility -- Advanced audio/video equipment and teaching aids assure a high quality of learning and conferences. Guest rooms are decorated elegantly and warmly and are furnished in wood.

Training Consultation--Professional educators and trainers provide consultation on course teaching, training program design, instructor engagement, and location arrangement.

Total Service -- Complete coordination with businesses for various customs ordered accessories for special events, such as billboard advertisement placement, banners, flowers, etc. Provide free service for event decoration, and there is professional staff to provide

5.1.3 CMC business process and profit

(1) Division Profile

Setting up a joint venture in Mainland China, known as South East Auto Industry LTD, which is one of the fast-growing auto-manufacturer in Mainland China. The capacity by two shifts is 160,000 units in 2004, and projected to expand up to 300,000 units in next stage. It participates in Mitsubishi's component complementary system. In the Mitsubishi Asian Car-Freeca (KZ) project, CMC is supplying 25% and 98% of parts to Mitsubishi's affiliate in the Philippines and Vietnam.

(2) One-Stop-Shopping purchasing center of auto-parts

CMC provides all kinds of exterior/interior and electrical parts, which can be easily applied to your vehicle to enhance your competitiveness in your local market. Being familiar with all parts suppliers in every category, total about 115 QS-9000-certificated suppliers in our parts supplying system, CMC is able to easily search for the right manufacturers that make products according to your drawings and engineering specifications. With our strong engineer teams in products-development division and quality-assurance division, CMC and its suppliers can work together for your products, especially in system integration, to provide a quick-responses and in-time delivery service. Now, we have been supplying our parts to United State, Southeast Asia, Japan and India. As a result, CMC is the best choice of regional agent for OEM/ODM parts in your out-sourcing program. Please check the below parts category, and find out what you need.

5.1.4 CMC implements steps for driving knowledge management

CMC is the leader of Taiwan commercial vehicles manufacturers. On driving e-business and knowledge management, CMC is a benchmark of learning in Taiwan companies. CMC implements steps for driving knowledge management are:

1. Communication and common view

Owing to the change of enterprise environment, CMC has more and more clear and definite knowledge requirement. For example, CMC's technical department has straight knowledge requirement. It thinks to keep a successful experiment and technology. Therefore, CMC studies the possibility of entering knowledge management. In 2000 the former year, CMC the Internet part went deep into studying and a common view. The latter year, CMC investigated and visited some knowledge management successful companies. Knowledge management is long-term driving work; CMC stipulates and develops a knowledge view. IT becomes "big Chinese nation knowledge style enterprise benchmark". This benchmark is a guideline for employee communication and motion knowledge. CMC has four strategies: developing core knowledge, building knowledge platform, making sharing culture, and creating community network. It creates CMC knowledge development system, so CMC has changed from traditional business knowledge system.

2. Interior popularization

Three steps on CMC's knowledge interior popularization are: guide period, horizontal popularize, and basic level popularize. There are 42 discussion platforms in group discuss area. In improved area, there are 2700 articles of "knowledge" which employees afford.

3. Select suitable software technical company

Eland technical company (Taiwan) provided mellow knowledge management system. It provided Java solution, Web solution and good platform equipment. The product of Eland technical company for example, Work-flow can easily integrate other company.

5.2 Sequent Computer's Knowledge

5.2.1 Background

Sequent Computers is a virtual "David-holding-a-slingshot" unlike its major competitors HP, IBM, DEC and Sun Microsystems in the UNIX systems industry. Based in Beaverton, Oregon, it employs only 2,700 in 53 field locations in the US, Europe and Asia. As small as the company is, it is valued for providing multi-million dollar solutions to many industries. As such, the expertise of employees has become critical to its success.

Aware that customers value its knowledgeable sales force, Sequent began to manage knowledge like an asset in 1993. It began by analyzing its business model by identifying and targeting its knowledge-sensitive points where improvement will yield the best results. The analysis revealed that the company would do best by focusing on its direct sales channel that is in close contact to its customers. The goal then was to make knowledge available to everyone so that each front-line employee in direct contact with the customers would be able to respond to them with the collective intelligence of the organization.

5.2.2 The Sequent Corporate Electronic Library (SCEL)

Sequent started KM by building the necessary technology infrastructure. SCEL or Sequent Corporate Electronic Library, an intranet site that contains corporate and individual knowledge domains focused on market and sales support to help employees do their jobs better.

IT and KM are two separate functions critical to SCEL. IT provides the technology, and human and financial resources to support KM programs. KM is responsible for the company's patent portfolio and the corporate library. A cross-functional SCEL team consists of librarians, a Web master, programmers, a SCEL architect, a SCEL evangelist, and other members linked to other parts of the organization.

SCEL includes a combination of database management systems, full text retrieval engines, file system storage, and complex structure of programs, all of which are integrated to Sequin's worldwide internal Web and accessible to all employees through Web browsers.

SCEL works on a publisher/consumer relationship. Every employee is a publisher/consumer if they use SCEL. Publishers put knowledge into the system and consumers use that knowledge. Applying a laissez faire capitalist approach to knowledge, content is not controlled centrally. However, the influx of useful information as determined by the users is regulated by the SCEL team. User feedback is encouraged within the system. Outstanding presentations, strategy and script for sales calls and design documents are readily available. SCEL's other features are metadata capture, hyper-mail and a soon-to-be-developed partner library.

Sequent fosters a laissez-faire KM philosophy - the company's approach to practice and content is decidedly hands-off. Knowledge that comes to the system is not dictated by management but controlled by its direct users - whether information is helpful and meets their knowledge quality standards.

5.2.3 Results

The KM efforts of Sequent have yielded good results. According to the company's KM leaders, SCEL has helped Sequent raise project average selling price, and reduce delivery and response time at all stages in the sales and post sales process. It has also increased the customer-specific and generic knowledge captured by its employees and customers. SCEL has focused the sales teams more effectively on proper targets and has made the assimilation process for new employees more efficient. Finally, the company has increased the customer-perceived value of its offerings, in hard (financial) and soft (loyalty) ways.

5.2.4 Key Learning

Based on Sequent's experience with SCEL, Swanson offers the following key leanings:

- *Look for the business linkage.* Think how knowledge can influence the world of its customers: for instance, sales folks are motivated by faster close cycles.
- *Business means not just revenue generation,* but also improving efficiency internally through best practice in operational processes.
- *Technology is important.* However, since more and more applications are being developed with the Web technology in mind, KM managers need not be preoccupied with the migration and development of new KM/ IT tools.
- *Culture is very important.* But do not wait for the culture to change to start implementing knowledge networks.
- *Start small and don't worry about imperfections.*

6. SUMMARY AND CONCLUSION

In this paper we have proposed a framework for integrating DSS and KMS as an extension to data warehouse model. The data warehouse and data mining will not only facilitate the capturing and coding of knowledge but will also enhance the retrieval and sharing of knowledge across the enterprise. The primary goal of the framework is to provide the decision marker with an intelligent analysis platform that enhances all phases of knowledge. In order to accomplish these goals, the DW used to search for and extract useful information from volumes of document and data. DSS can enhance the tacit to explicit knowledge conversion through the specification models. Specifically, in the model building process the knowledge worker is asked to explicitly specify the goal or objective of the model, the decision variables, and perhaps the relative importance of the decision variables. The knowledge warehouse will include a feedback loop to enhance its own knowledge base with the passage of time, as the tested and approved of knowledge analysis is fed back into the knowledge warehouse as additional source of knowledge.
A case study of China Motor Corporation is showing the process of knowledge used on e-business. It introduces CMC Enterprise Operation, CMC knowledge flow and structure, CMC implements steps for driving knowledge management, and CMC business process and profit. It is a guideline for enterprise entering knowledge process. This is an important issue as the system of future, including knowledge systems are designed to work together with applications that are developed on various platforms.
A case study of Sequent Computer is started KM by building the necessary technology infrastructure. SCEL or Sequent Corporate Electronic Library, an intranet site that

contains corporate and individual knowledge domains focused on market and sales support to help employees do their jobs better.

7. References

Alavi, M. and Leidner, D. R. (2001), 'Review: Knowledge Management and Knowledge Management Systems: Conceptual Foundations and Research Issues', MIS Quarterly, Vol. 25, No. 1, pp. 107-136

Apostolou , D. and Mentzas, G., "Managing Corporate Knowledge: Comparative Analysis of Experiences in Consulting Firms", Knowledge and Process Management, Vol. 6,3, 1999, pp. 129-138.

Barclay, R. O. and Murray, P. C., What is Knowledge Management, A Knowledge Praxis, USA,1997.

Berson, A. and Smith, S., Data Warehouse, Data Mining, and OLAP, New York, McGraw-Hill, 1997.

Bolloju , N. M. and Turban, E., "Integrating Knowledge Management into Enterprise Environments for Next Generation of Decision Support", Decision Support Systems, Vol. 13, . 2002.

Bose, R. and Sugumaran, V., "Application of knowledge management technology in customer relationship management", Knowledge and Process Management, Vol. 10, 1, pp. 3-17, 2003.

Carbone, P. L., "Expanding the meaning of and applications for data mining", IEEE int. Conf. on System Man and Cybernetics, pp. 1872-1873, 2000.

Chau, L. W., Chuntian, C. and Li, C. W., (2002), 'Knowledge management systems on flow and water quality modeling', Expert System with Application, Vol. 22, pp. 321-330.

Cheung, W., Leung, L. C., and Tam, P. C.F.,(2005), An intelligent decision support system for service network planning, Decision Support System, 39, pp. 415-428

Davenport , T. and Prusak, L., (2000), "Working Knowledge: how organizations manage what they know", Harvard Business School Press, Boston

Davenport, T. and Prusak, L., Working Knowledge: how organizations manage what they know, Harvard Business School Press, 1998.

Davenport, T. H. and Short, L. (1990), 'The new Industrial Engineering: Information Technology and Business Process Redesign, MIT Sloan Management Review, Vol. 41, No. 4, pp. 11-27Gao et al., 2002

Denning, S., "The knowledge Perspective: A New Strategic Vision", The Knowledge Advantage, pp.143-161, 1999.

Devlin, B., Data warehouse: From Architecture to implementation, Addison Wesley Longman, Inc., Menlo Park, CA, 1997.

Dhar, V. and Stein, R., (2000), Intelligent Decision Support Methods: The Science of Knowledge Work, Prentice Hall, Upper Saddle River, N J., U.S.A.

Duffy, J., Knowledge management finally becomes mainstream, Information Management Journal, Vol. 35, 4, pp. 62-65, 2001.

Fahey, L., Srivastava, R., Sharon, J. S., and Smith, D. E., (2001), Linkage e-business and operating process: The role of knowledge management, IBM Systems Journal, 40(4), pp.889-907.

Fayyad, U. M. and Uthurusamy, R., "First International Conference on Knowledge Discovery and Data Mining", AAAI Press, 1995.

Finlay, P. N. Introduction decision support systems, Oxford, UK Cambridge, Mass., NCC Blackwell; Blackwell Publishers. 1994.

Gadomaski, A. M. et al., "An approach to the Intelligent Decision Advisor (IDA) for Emergency Managers", International Journal Risk Assessment and Management, Vol. 2, 3 2001.

Hendriks, P. and Virens, D. (1999),'Knowledge -based systems and knowledge management: Friends or Foes?, Information & Management, Vol. 30, pp. 113-125

Herschel, R. T. and Jones, N. E., "Knowledge Management and Blithe Importance of Integration", Journal of Knowledge Management, Vol. 9, 4, 2005.

Holsapple,C. W. and Sena, M., "ERP plans and decision Support Benefits", Decision Support System, Vol. 38, 4, 2005.

Joyce, P. and Winch, G. W., An e-business design and evaluation framework based on entrepreneurial, technical and operational considerations, International Journal of electronic Business, Vol. 2, 2005, pp. 198-214.

Kalakota, R. and Robinson, M., (1999), 'e-business: Roadmap for success', Reading, MA: Addison Wesley.

Lau, H. C. W. , Choy, W.L., Law, P. K. H., Tsui, W. T. T., and Choy, L. C., "An intelligent Logistics Support System for Enhancing the Airfreight Forwarding Business", Expert Systems, Vol. 21, 5, 2004.

Loucopoulos, P. and Kavakli, V. (1999),'Enterprise Knowledge Management and Conceptual Modeling', Lecture Notes in Computer Science, Vol. 1565, pp. 123-143

M. C. Lee and T. Chang, Linkage knowledge management and innovation management in e-business, International Innovation and learning, 4(2), 2007, pp. 145-159.

M. C. Lee, and J. F., Cheng, Development multi-Enterprise Collaborative Enterprise intelligent decision support system, Journal of Convergence Information Technology, 2(2), 2007 pp. 2-6.

M. C., Lee, Linkage Knowledge process and Business Process: A case study in China Motor Corporation, 2008 International Conference on Convergence and Hybrid Information Technology, 2008, pp.407-412

Malhotra, Y., (2000), 'Knowledge Management for E-Business Performance: Advancing Information Strategy to "Internet Time"', Information Strategy, The Executive's Journal, Vol.16, No. 4, pp. 5-16.

Marakas, G. M. (1999). Decision support systems in the twenty-first century. Upper Saddle River, N.J., Prentice Hall.

Nemati, H. R. and Barko, K. W., "Issues in Organizational Data Mining: A Survey of Current Practices", Journal of Data Warehousing, Vol. 6, 2, 2001(winter).

Nonaka, I. and Takeuchi, H., "The knowledge-creating company", Oxford University Press, NY, 1955.

Nonaka, I., A dynamic theory theory of organizational knowledge creation, Organization Sciences, 5(1), pp. 14-37, 1994.

Nonaka, I., Toyama, R. and Konno, N.,SECI, Ba and Leadership: a Unified Model of Dynamic Knowledge Creation, Managing Industrial Knowledge: Creation, Transfer and Utilization, Sage, London, 2001, pp. 1-43.

Nonaka, T., Toyama, R. and Konno, N., (2000), 'SECI, and leadership: a. unified model of dynamic knowledge creation', Long Range Planning, Vol.33, No. 1, pp. 5-34

Plessis, M. and Boon, J. A., (2004),'Knowledge management in e-business and customer relationship management: South Africa case study finding,' International Journal of Information Management, 24 (10), pp. 73-85

Power, D. J. (2002). Decision support systems: concepts and resources for managers. Westport, Conn., Quorum Books.

Timmers, P., "Business models for Electronic Markets", EM-Electronic Markets Vol. 8, 2, pp. 3-8, 1998).

Tiwana, A. and Ramesh, B. (2001),'A design knowledge management system to support collaborative information product evolution', Decision Support Systems, Vol. 31, pp. 241-262

Wald, E. and Stammers, E., "Out of the alligator pool: a service-oriented approach to development", EAI Journal, March, pp. 26-30, 2001

Malaysian Business Community Social Network Mapping on the Web Based on Improved Genetic Algorithm

Siti Nurkhadijah Aishah Ibrahim, Ali Selamat and Mohd Hafiz Selamat
Universiti Teknologi Malaysia
Malaysia

1. Introduction

The issues of community social network mapping on the web have been intensively studied in recent years. Basically, we found that social networking among communities has become a popular issue within the virtual sphere. It relates to the practice of interacting with others online via blogsphere, forums, social media sites and other outlets. Surprisingly, Internet has caused great changes to the way people do business. In this chapter, we are focusing on the networks of business in the Internet since it has become an important way of spreading the information of a business via online. Business networking is a marketing method by which business opportunities are created through networks of like-minded business people. There are several popular businesses networking organization that create models of networking activity that, when followed, allow the business person to build new business relationship and generate business opportunities at the same time. Business that increased using the business social networks as a means of growing their circle of business contacts and promoting themselves online and at the same time develop such a "territory" in several regions in the country. Since businesses are expanding globally, social networks make it easier to keep in touch with other contacts around the world.

Currently, searching and finding the relevant information become a high demand from the users. However, due to the rapid expansion of web pages available in the Internet lately, searching the relevant and up-to-date information has become an important issue especially for the industrial and business firms. Conventional search engines use heuristics to decide which web pages are the best match for the keyword. Results are retrieved from the repository which located at their local server to provide fast searched. As we know, search engine is an important component in searching information worldwide. However, the user is often facing an enormous result that inaccurate or not up-to-date. Sometimes, the conventional search engine typically returned the long lists of results that saddle the user to find the most relevant information needs. Google, Yahoo! and AltaVista are the examples of available search engine used by the users. However, the results obtain from the search engines sometimes misrelated to the users query. Moreover, 68% of the search engine users will click a search result within the first page of results and 92% of them will click a result within the first three pages of search results (iProspect, 2008). This statistic concluded that the users need to view page by pages to get the relevant result. Thus, this will consume the time to go through all the result provides by search engine. From our experienced, the relevant result also will not always promise found even after looking at page 5 and above. Internet also can create the abundance problem such as; limited coverage of the Web (hidden Web sources), limited query interface: keyword-oriented search and also a limited customisation to individual users. Thus, the result must be organized so that them looks more in effective and adapted way. In previous research, we present the model to evaluate the searched results using genetic algorithm (GA). In GA, we considered the user profiles and keywords of the web pages accessed by the crawler agents. Then we used the information in GA for retrieving the best web pages related to the business communities to invest at the Iskandar Malaysia in various sectors such as education, entertainment, medical healthcare etc.

The main objective of this chapter is to provide the user with a searching interface that enabling them to quickly find the relevant information. In addition, we are using the crawler agent to make a fast crawling process and retrieve the web documents as many as it can and scalable. In the previous paper, we also using genetic algorithm (GA) to optimize the result search by the crawlers to overcome the problem mention above. We further improve the GA with relevance feedback to enhance the capabilities of the search system and to find more relevant results. From the experiments, we have found that a feedback mechanism will give the search system the user's suggestions about the found documents, which leads to a new query using the proposed GA. In the new search stage, more relevant documents are retrieved by the agents to be judged by the user._From the experiments, the improved GA (IGA) has given a significant improvement in finding the related business communities to potentially invest at Iskandar Malaysia in comparison with the traditional GA model.

This chapter is organized as follows. Section 2 defined the problem that related to this chapter. Section 3 is details on improved genetic algorithm and section 4 are the results and discussion. Section 5 explains the results and discussion of this chapter and Section 6 presented the case study. Finally, section 7 describes the conclusion.

2. Problem Definition

In this chapter, we define the business networks as βD whereby it will be represent as a graph G= (V, E) where V is a set of vertices (URL or nodes) and E is a set of links (URLs) that link two elements of V. Fig. 1 shows the networks that represent as a graph. As explained in (Pizutti, 2008), a networks of community is a group of vertices that have a high density of edges among them but have lower density of edges between groups. The problem with the community network is when the total of group, g is unknown how can the related g' can be found? Basically, adjacency matrix is used to find the connection between g. For instance, if the networks consist of V nodes then the networks can be represented as $N \times N$ adjacency matrix (Pizutti, 2008). Nevertheless, we used the binary coding [0, 1] to represent the occurrence of terms in the network or each web page so that we can find the related networks. In the results section, we will show how the searching technique using genetic algorithm and improved genetic algorithm works in order to get the most related information to the V.

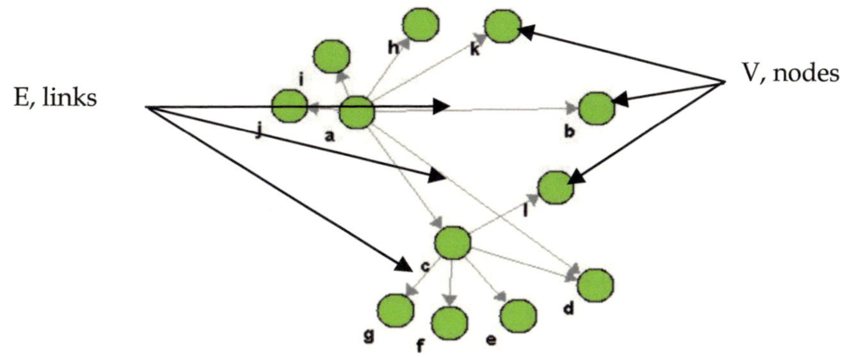

Fig. 1. Networks that represent as a graph

3. Improved Genetic Algorithm

As claim by Zhu (Zhu et al., 2007), a traditional and very important technique in evolutionary computing (EC) is genetic algorithm (GA). GA are not particularly a learning algorithms but they offer a powerful and domain-independent search capability that can be used in many learning tasks, since learning and self-organization can be considered as optimization problems in many cases. Nowadays, GA have been applied to various domain, including timetable, scheduling, robot control, signature verification, image processing, packing, routing (Selamat, 2005), pipeline control systems, machine learning (Bies, 2006) (Goldberg, 1989) and information retrieval (Zhu, 2007) (Selamat, 2005) (Koorangi).

Genetic algorithms (GA) are not new to information retrieval. So, it is not surprising that there have recently appeared many applications of GA's to IR. Genetic algorithm (GA) is an evolutionary algorithm that used for many functions such as optimization and evolves the problem solutions (Luger, 2002). GA used fitness function to evaluate each solution to decide whether it will contribute to the next generation of solutions. Then, through operations analogous to gene transfer in sexual reproduction, the algorithm creates a new population of candidate solutions (Luger, 2002). Figure 2 shows the basic flow of genetic algorithm process.

Fitness function evaluates the feature of an individual. It should be designed to provide assessment of the performance of an individual in the current population. In the application of a genetic algorithm to information retrieval, one has to provide an evaluation or fitness function for each problem to be solved. The fitness function must be suited to the problem at hand because its choice is crucial for the genetic algorithm to function well.

Jaccard coefficient is used in this research to measure the fitness of a given representation. The total fitness for a given representation is computed as the average of the similarity coefficient for each of the training queries against a given document representation (David, 1998). Document representation evolves as described above by genetic operators (e.g. crossover and mutation). Basically, the average similarity coefficient of all queries and all document representations should increase.

Text-based search system is used for constructing root set about user query. However, the root set from text-based search system does not contain all authoritative and hub sources about user query (Kim, 2007). In order to optimize the result, we are using the genetic algorithm that works as a keyword expansion whereby it expends the initial keywords to certain appropriate threshold.

```
Input: N, size of population;
Pc, Pm: ratio of crossover and mutation.
Output: an optimization solution

Procedure:
Begin
Initialize with population of size N at generation t=0;

Repeat while (|Pop (t+1)|<N)
Select two parent solutions from Pop (t) by fitness function
Copy the selected parents into child solutions (Cloning process)
Randomly generated a number, r, 0≤r≤1

If(r<Pc)
        Carry out crossover operation on the child solution
        Randomly generated a number, r, 0≤r≤1
If(r<Pm) // in this process mutation are set to 0 to prevent changes, Pm=0;
        Carry out mutation operation on the child solution
        Place the child solution in the new population, denoted by Pop (t+1)
End While

Until termination conditions are satisfied return the best solution in Population
End.
```

Fig. 3. Improved genetic algorithm pseudocode

3.1 Process in Improved Genetic Algorithm (IGA)

The main difference between GA and IGA is how to generate new individuals in the next population. We combine two mechanisms to generate new individuals. IGA used the Jaccard coefficient (formula 1) since the vector space model (VSM) has been used in this research.

$$\frac{1}{n} \bullet \sum_{k=1}^{n} \frac{|d_j \cap d_q|}{|d_j \cup d_q|} \qquad (1)$$

Then, we implement the elitism process to the selected best chromosomes (parents) and clone them into the appropriate size of population. The main purpose of using the elitism is to maintain the best parents and keep the population in the best solution until the end of the optimization process.

We proceed to the cloning process to keep the child as same as the best parents. After that, we used two point crossover and mutation to prevent the solution stuck at the local optimum. The process is repeated until the stopping conditional is fulfilled.

In addition, relevance feedback is used because it is one of the techniques for improving retrieval effectiveness. The user first identifies some relevant (D_r) and irrelevant documents (D_{ir}) in the initial list of retrieved documents and then the system expands the query, q by extracting some additional terms from the sample relevant and irrelevant documents to produce q_e.

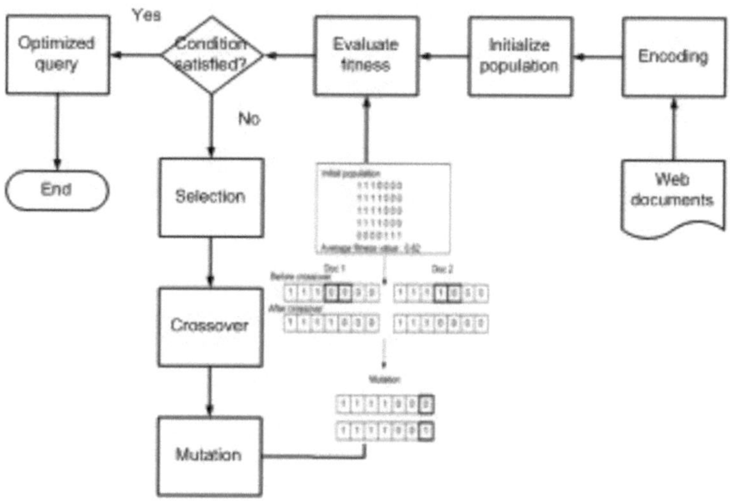

Fig. 4. Improved genetic algorithm flow chart design

4. Experimental Setup

We retrieved the web pages of business networks that related to Iskandar Malaysia (Table 1). The seed URLs are retrieved from the website and several URLs need to be retrieved from each of the URL. The related web pages can be defined in many categories such as ICT or computers, government, bank and etc. There are several processes involve in this research such as initialization, web crawling, optimization and visualization. Below are the details about the processes:

4.1 Initialization

Crawling process start with defines the initial seed URLs to explore the related business web pages from the Internet. The list of URLs is obtained from the Iskandar Malaysia website. The business web pages can be defined in many categories such as ICT or computers, government, universities, bank and etc. Table 1 shows some examples of related URLs from Iskandar Malaysia's web pages.

No	Categories	URLs
1	ICT/ computer / information technology	http://www.msc.com.my
2	Government/ business areas	http://www.iskandarjohoropen.com http://www.khazanah.com.my http://www.epu.jpm.my http://www.kpdnhep.gov.my http://www.mida.gov.my http://www.kpkt.gov.my http://www.imi.gov.my http://www.customs.gov.my http://www.jpj.gov.my http://www.jkr.gov.my http://www.marine.gov.my http://www.rmp.gov.my http://www.nusajayacity.com http://www.ptp.com.my http://www.iskandarinvestment.com http://www.cyberport.my http://www.royaljohorcountryclub.com
3	Bank	http://www.bnm.gov.my
4	Tourism	http://www.tourismjohor.com http://www.dangabay.com

Table 1. Related URLs from Iskandar Malaysia's web pages

4.2 Web crawling

Crawler will take place on retrieved the related business web pages after initialized the seed URLs. The crawler will use the breadth-first search technique.

4.3 Optimization

Optimization is the process of making something better. The advantages of optimization are to save the building time and memory. In this phase, GA is used to select the best result in the searching process whereby the keyword entered by the user will be expanded to produce the new keyword. In the improved genetic algorithm we set the parameter slightly different from the conventional genetic algorithm. Table 2 is details on paramater setting for improved genetic algorithm compared to previous genetic algorithm and Table 3 shows some example of user queries.

Techniques	Population	Generation	Crossover rate, Pc	Mutation rate, Pm	Elitism
GA	5	5	0.4	0.005	No
IGA	16	100	0	0	Yes

Table 2. Setting paramaters for improved genetic algorithm

Queries	Information	Expanded queries
Q1	iskandar malaysia development	IRDA
Q2	iskandar	IRDA, Malaysia, johor
Q3	iskandar malaysia	IRDA, development
Q4	iskandar johor open	Johor, Iskandar
Q5	IRDA iskandar johor	IRDA

Table 3. Example of user queries and expanded queries found by the system

The detail processes in the system are as below:

1. User enter query into the system.
2. Match the user query with list of keywords in the database.
3. Results without GA are represented to the users.
4. Used user profiles when selecting the relevant results found by the system.
5. Encode the documents retrieved by user selected query to chromosomes (initial population).
6. Population feed into genetic operator process such as selection, crossover and mutation.
7. Repeat Step 5 until maximum generation is reached. Then, get an optimize query chromosome for document retrieval.
8. Decode optimize query chromosome to query and retrieve new document (with GA process) from database.

Most of the information in the Internet is in the form of web texts. How to express this semi-structured and unstructured information of Web texts is the basic preparatory work of web mining (Song, 2007). Vector space model (VSM) is one of the most widely used model in the application of GAs to information retrieval. In this research, VSM has been chosen as a model to describe documents and queries in the test collections. We collect the data from the (Iskandar Malaysia, 2009) to retrieve the related web pages link to it.

4.5 Term Vectorization and Document Representation

Before any process can be done, we first implement the pre-processing to the retrieve data. To determine the documents terms, we used procedure as shows in Fig. 4. Vector space model (VSM) is one of the most widely used models in the application of GAs into information retrieval. Thus, VSM has been chosen as a model to describe documents and queries in the test collections. Let say, we have a dictionary, D;

$$D = (t_1, t_2, \ldots, t_i) \tag{2}$$

where i is the number of distinguished keywords in the dictionary. Each document in the collection is described as i-dimensional weight vector;

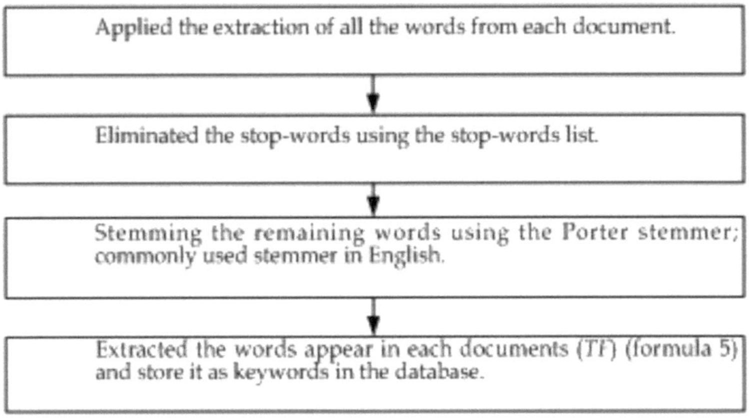

Fig. 4. Pre-processing procedure

$$d = (w_1, w_2, .., w_i) \tag{3}$$

where w_j represents the weight of the jth keyword t_j for $j = 1,2,...i$ and is calculated by the Term Frequency Inverse Document Frequency (TF.IDF) method. Each query in the collection is also described as a weight vector, *q*;

$$q = (u_1, u_2, .., u_i) \tag{4}$$

where u_j represents the weight of the jth keyword t_j for $j = 1,2,...i$ and is calculated by the Term Frequency (TF) method.

$$tf_{ij} = \frac{f_{ij}}{\max\{f_1, f_2, .., f_{|v|j}\}} \tag{5}$$

Based on natural selection in environments and natural genetics in biology, the GA is evolved according to the principle of survival of the fittest and is mostly applied in many optimization problems. When applying the binary GA to the document classification, most research uses gene positions in the chromosome to represent candidate keywords. In this paper, we used GA as an optimization method to expanding the keywords to form new queries. Basically, genetic algorithm is the heuristics search that previously applied in data mining (Chou et al., 2008). Each term is represented as a vector. Given a collection of documents *D*,

$$let V = \{t_1, t_2, .., t|V|\}; V = terms \tag{6}$$

be the set of distinctive words/terms in the collection. A weight w_{ij} > 0 is associated with each term t_i of a document d_j ∈ D. For a term that does not appear in document

$$d_j, w_{ij} = 0; d_j = \left(w_{1j}, w_{2j}, .., w|V|_j\right) \tag{7}$$

Then, the terms are encoded as chromosome such as:

Doc1 = 0000001000001000

Doc2 = 0110000110100000

Doc3 = 1000001000000100

Doc4 = 0001100011010111

Doc5 = 0000011000000100

These chromosomes are called the initial population that will be feed into genetic operator process. The length of chromosome depends on number of keywords of documents retrieved from user query. From our example the length of each chromosome is 16. We used fitness function to evaluate how good the solution will be. After evaluated the population's fitness, the next step is the chromosome selection. Satisfied fitness chromosomes are selected for reproduction. Poor chromosomes or lower fitness chromosomes may be selected a few or not at all.

4. Results and discussion

From Table 4, we can see how slightly the results between the conventional GA and IGA. This is because of the small improvement made to the conventional GA. 0.85% of the precision average increase and 0.37% of the recall average increase from the conventional GA to IGA. However Q2 and Q5 do not shows any improvement. These results shows that the IGA can perform better than conventional GA even the results are slightly different. From the results also, we can detected the community of the Iskandar Malaysia since the results can be expanded to many other terms that related to Iskandar Malaysia.

Queries	GA			IGA		
	P	R	F1	P	R	F1
Q1	98.01	49.50	65.78	99.34	50.17	66.67
Q2	100.00	100.00	100.00	100.00	100.00	100.00
Q3	95.86	50.00	65.72	96.05	50.15	65.89
Q4	51.22	33.87	40.78	53.95	34.91	42.39
Q5	100.00	100.00	100.00	100.00	100.00	100.00

Table 4. Results on conventional genetic algorithm and improved genetic algorithm

5. Case Study: Iskandar Malaysia

Iskandar Malaysia (formerly known as Wilayah Pembangunan Iskandar) is one of the well-known community company that closely related to social communities in Malaysia. There are five existing clusters within Iskandar Malaysia that are mostly not fully developed. The most developed is the electrical and electronics (E&E) cluster which as noted, is actually an integral part of the Singapore E&E cluster, though the part within Iskandar Malaysia occupies the lower end of the value chain.

Fig. 5 shows an example of the main networks of Iskandar Malaysia whereby this network will brings many advantages to the country in order to improve the quality of the social networking in business matter.

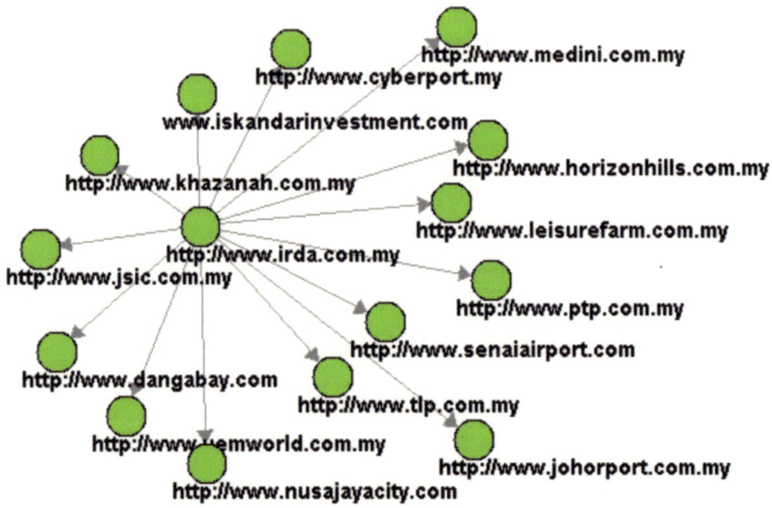

Fig. 5. Business networks of Iskandar Malaysia

Table 1 shows several numbers of related URLs for Iskandar Malaysia. Most of the URLs are connected to the governments and business areas web pages. So, logically we found that the business networks can be spreading into several fields that can attract investors to come and invest in Malaysia. As stated before, our main objective is to show the related industries or links connected to this web page so that we can see the total or statistics of the investors and profits of the business areas.

From the results, we can see the expansion of the related web pages from the first URL. In Fig. 6 we show that the networks can be spreading into many categories and influence the business industries improvement. This result clearly explained that the objective to see the related industries can be achieved by using the mention technique.

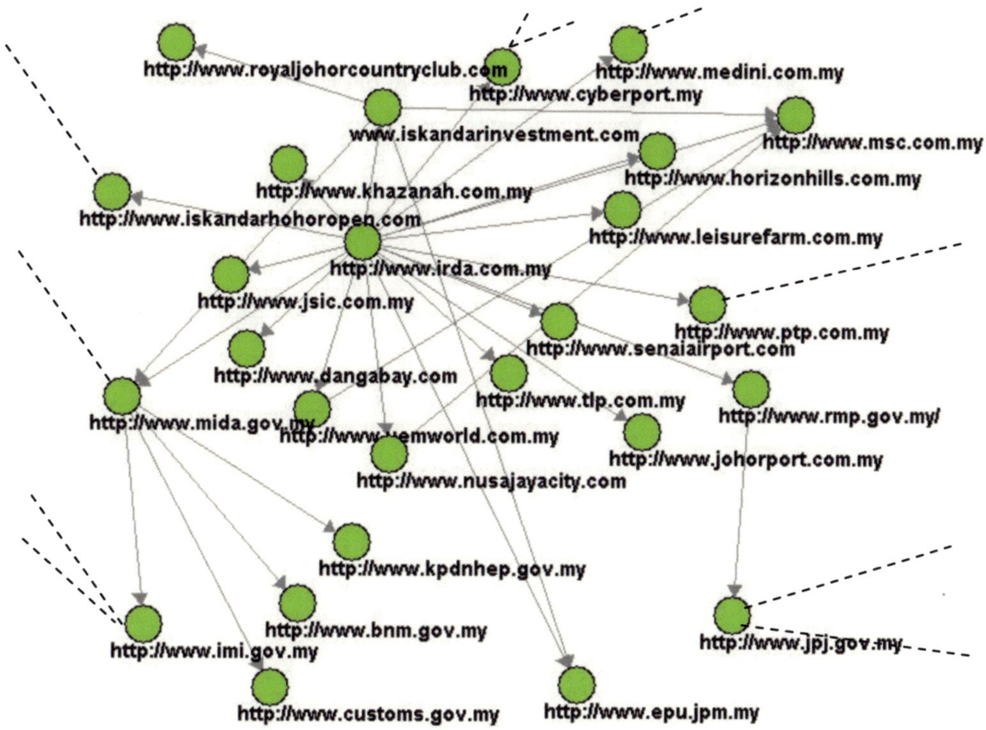

Fig. 6. Expansion of business networks of Iskandar Malaysia

6. Conclusion

In this chapter, we have shown how an evolutionary algorithm can help to reformulate a user query to improve the results of the corresponding search. The evolutionary algorithm is in charge of selecting the appropriate combination of terms for the new query. To do this, the algorithm uses fitness function a measure of the proximity between the query terms selected in the considered individual. Then, the top ranked documents are retrieved using these terms. We have carried out some experiments to have an idea of the possible improvement that the IGA can achieve. In these experiments, we have used the precision obtained from the user relevance judgments as fitness function. Results have shown that in this case, the IGA achieve a slight improvement compared to the conventional GA. However, we want to emphasize that this feedback mechanism improves the search system by considering users suggestions concerning the found documents, which leads to a new query using IGA. In the new search stage, more relevant documents are given to the user. As a conclusion, the conventional genetic algorithm model was improved. In the future, we hope that the system can be improved further and the results can achieve higher accuracy rate in solving the data mining problems.

7. References

Bies, Robert R; Muldoon, Matthew F; Pollock, Bruce G; Manuck, Steven; Smith, Gwenn and Sale, Mark E (2006). A Genetic Algorithm-Based, Hybrid Machine Learning Approach to Model Selection. *Journal of Pharmacokinetics and Pharmacodynamics*: 196-221. Netherlands: Springer.

Chih-Hsun Chou , Chang-Hsing Lee , and Ya-Hui Chen (2008). GA-Based Keyword Selection for the Design of an Intelligent Web Document Search System. The Computer Journal Advance Access published on October 14.

David A. Grossman, Ophir Frieder (1998). Information Retrieval: Algorithms and Heuristics. *Springer*.

iProspect.http://www.midiaclick.com.br/wp-content/uploads/2008/10/researchstudy_apr2008_blendedsearchresults.pdf. Accessed on October 2008.

Goldberg, David E (1989), *Genetic Algorithms in Search, Optimization and Machine Learning*, Kluwer Academic Publishers, Boston, MA.

Iskandar Malaysia Development. *www.idr.com.my*. Accessed on January 2009.

Kim, K. and Cho, S. (2007). Personalized mining of web documents using link structures and fuzzy concept networks. *Appl. Soft Comput.* 7, 1 (Jan. 2007), 398-410.

Luger, F. G. (2002). Artificial Intelligent Structures and Strategies for Complex Problem Solving. 4th Ed. Edinburgh Gate, England: Eddison Wesley.

M. Koorangi, K. Zamanifar, A distributed agent based web search using a genetic algorithm, IJCSNS, *International journal of computer science*

Pizzuti, C. (2008). GA-Net: A Genetic Algorithm for Community Detection in Social Networks. *Springer*, 2008, 5199, 1081-1090.

Selamat, A. and Selamat, M. H. (2005). Analysis on the performance of mobile agents for query retrieval. *Inf. Sci. Inf. Comput. Sci.* 172, 3-4 (Jun. 2005), 281-307.

Song Liangtu, Zhang Xiaoming (2007). Web Text Feature Extraction with Particle Swarm Optimization. *IJCSNS International Journal of Computer Science and Network Security*, Vol. 7 No. 6 pp. 132-136.

Zhengyu Zhu, Xinghuan Chen, Qingsheng Zhu, Qihong Xie (2007): A GA-based query optimization method for web information retrieval. *Applied Mathematics and Computation* 185(2): 919-930.

10

An Ontological Framework for Knowledge Management in Systems Engineering Processes

Olfa CHOURABI, Yann POLLET, Mohamed BEN AHMED
CNAM, CEDRIC- SEMPIA laboratory, PARIS
RIADI laboratory, TUNISIA)

1. Introduction

Systems Engineering (SE) processes comprise highly creative and knowledge-intensive tasks that involve extensive problem-solving and decision-making activities among interdisciplinary teams (Meinadier, 2002). SE projects involve the definition of multiple artifacts that present different formalization degrees, such as requirements specification, system architecture, and hardware/ software components. Transitions between the project phases stem from decision making processes supported both by generally available domain knowledge and engineering experience.
We argue that Knowledge about engineering processes constitutes one of the most valuable assets for SE organizations. Most often, this knowledge is only known implicitly, relying heavily on the personal experience background of system engineers. To fully exploit this intellectual capital, it must be made explicit and shared among project teams. Consistent and comprehensive knowledge management methods need to be applied to capture and integrate the individual knowledge items emerging in the course of a system engineering project.
Knowledge management (KM) is a scientific discipline that stems from management theory and concentrates on the systematic creation, leverage, sharing and reuse of knowledge resources in a company (Awas el al, 2003). Knowledge management approaches are generally divided into personalization approaches that focus on human resources and communication, and codification approaches that emphasize the collection and organization of knowledge (McMahon et al. 2004).
In this work, we consider the latter approach for KM. Special focus is put on the comprehensive modeling of system engineering project knowledge. This knowledge partly resides in the product itself, while a lot of different types of knowledge are generated during the engineering processes. The background information such as why engineers came up with the final shape or geometry, what constraints were to be considered in engineering processes, and so on, can not be found either (Chan-Hong.P et al.2007). In other words, most of design rationale either disappear or exist partially in the form of engineering documents.
The analysis of current engineering practices and supporting software tools reveals that they adequately support project information exchange and traceability, but lack essential capabilities for knowledge management and reuse.(C. Brandt et al., 2007)

The recent keen interest in ontological engineering has renewed interest in building systematic, consistent, reusable and interoperable knowledge models (Mizoguchi et al. 2000)(Kitamura, 2006).
Aiming at representing engineering knowledge explicitly and formally for sharing it among multidisciplinary engineering teams, our work builds upon ontological engineering as a foundation for capturing implicit knowledge and as a basis of knowledge systematization.
In this chapter we present our vision about the main building blocks of a semantic framework for knowledge capitalization and sharing in Systems Engineering domain. The key idea behind our proposal is a flexible ontology-based schema with formally defined semantics to enable the capture and reuse of system engineering experiences.
The main contributions of this work can be summurized as follows:

- A generic ontological framework for System Engineering Knowledge systematization :. The framework sets the fundamental concepts for a holistic System Engineering knowledge model involving explicit relationships between process, products, actors and domain concepts.
- A Knowledge capitalization model: we focus on problem resolution records during project execution. We address this problem through the use of the formal framework for capturing and sharing significant know-how, situated in projects context. we introduce the concept of Situated Explicit Engineering Knowledge (SEEK) as a formal structure for capturing problem resolution records and design rationale in SE projects.
- A Knowledge sharing model: we propose a semantic activation of potential relevant SEEK(s) in an engineering situation.

The chapter is structured as folowing: the next section discusses key background information about System Engineering processes and knowledge management issues in SE setting. Section 3 discusses roles and representative examples of ontological engineering in SE. In section 4, we detail the ontological framework for system engineering knowledge modelling. Section 5, presents a formal approach for Situated Explicit Engineering Knowledge capitalization and sharing. Section 6, illustrates our proposal in a transport system engineering process. Section 7, discusses relevant related work.

2. Problem statement

2.1 System Engineering

System Engineering (SE) is an interdisciplinary approach to enable the realization of successful systems. It is defined as an iterative problem solving process aiming at transforming user's requirements into a solution satisfying the constraints of: functionality, cost, time and quality (Meinadier, 2002). This process is usually comprised of the following seven tasks: State the problem, Investigate alternatives, Model the system, Integrate, Launch the system, Assess performance, and Re-evaluate. These tasks can be summarized with the acronym SIMILAR: State, Investigate, Model, Integrate, Launch, Assess and Re-evaluate. (Bahill et al. 1998). This Systems Engineering Process is shown in Figure 1.

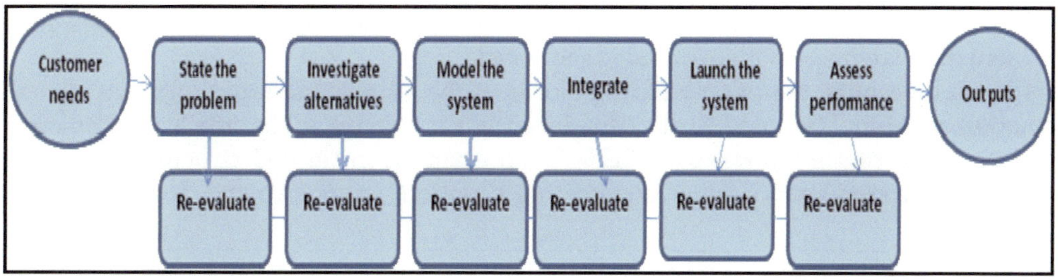

Fig. 1. SIMILAR Process

It is important to note that the Systems Engineering Process is not sequential. The tasks are performed in a parallel and iterative manner. At each step a comprehensive set of possible engineering models arises which are progressively combined and refined to define the target system.

Because of its inherent creative nature, it is a special case of business process. It is poorly structured and, as a rule, it evolves in an unpredictable manner. In such highly dynamic settings with continuously changing requirements, the overwhelming majority of the engineering ways of working are not properly formalized, but are heavily based on the experience knowledge of the human performers.

As a consequence, engineering support environments have further to deal with the systematic collection of experience from previous project cycles and its dissemination and utilization from analogous problem solving contexts in the future. (Miatidis& Jarke, 2005). in section 4, we present a knowledge modeling framework that acts as a backend for what we expect to be a "Next generation of engineering support environment" i.e.: "knowledge centric" rather than "data centric".

2.2 Knowledge Management issues in SE

The Above-delineated characteristics of SE processes show that a significant amount of knowledge is involved to solve a mix of ill- and well-defined problems. System engineers require topic knowledge (learned from text books and courses) and episodic knowledge (experience with the knowledge) (Robillard, 1991).

One of the main problems in SE processes is the lack of capture and access to knowledge underpinning the design decisions and the processes leading to those decisions (Ali-Babar et al., 2005).

System Engineers spend large portions of their time searching through vast amounts of corporate legacy data and catalogs searching for existing solutions which can be modified to solve new problems or to be assembled into a new device. This requires utilizing databases or online listings of text, images, and computer aided design (CAD) data. Browsing and navigating such collections are based on manually-constructed categorizations which are error prone, difficult to maintain, and often based on an insufficiently dense hierarchy. Search functionality is limited to inadequate keyword matching on overly simplistic attributes; it lacks the formal framework to support automated reasoning. (Miatidis& Jarke, 2005)

In this work, we focus firstly on the knowledge modeling issue which is often considered as the first step in developing Knowledge-Based Systems (KBS). The aim of this process is to understand the types of data structures and relationships within which knowledge can be held, and reasoned with. We use ontologies to describe the knowledge model in a formal representation language with expressive semantics.

In order to determine the basic building blocks of the knowledge repository, we introduce the notion of "SEEK" Situated Explicit Engineering Knowledge as the smallest granularity in the system experience knowledge. "SEEK", represent an integrated structure that capture product and process knowledge in engineering situations in conformance to a set of layered ontologies.

3. Background: Ontological Engineering

Ontologies are now in widespread use as a means formalizing domain knowledge in a way that makes it accessible, shareable and reusable (Darlington, 2008). In this section, we review relevant ontological propositions for supporting engineering processes.

In the knowledge engineering community, a definition by Gruber is widely accepted; that is, "explicit specification of conceptualization" (Gruber, 1993), where conceptualization is "a set of objects which an observer thinks exist in the world of interest and relations between them". Gruber emphasizes that ontology is used as agreement to use a shared vocabulary (ontological commitment).

The main purpose of ontology is, however, not to specify the vocabulary relating to an area of interest but to capture the underlying conceptualizations.(Gruber, 1993)

Uschold (Uschold& Gruninger, 1996) identifies the following general roles for ontologies:

- Communication between and among people and organizations.
- Inter-operability among systems.
- System Engineering Benefits: ontologies also assist in the process of building and maintaining systems, both knowledge-based and otherwise. In particular,
  - Re-Usability: the ontology, when represented in a formal language can be (or become so by automatic translation) a re-usable and/or shared component in a software system.
  - Reliability: a formal representation facilitates automatic consistency checking.
  - Specification: the ontology can assist the process of identifying a specification for an IT system.

One of the deep necessities of ontologies in SE domain is, we believe, the lack of explicit description of background knowledge of modeling. There are multiple options for capturing such knowledge; we present a selection of representative efforts to capture engineering knowledge in ontologies.

(Lin et al., 1996) propose an ontology for describing products. The main decomposition is into parts, features, and parameters. Parts are defined as a component of the artifact being designed". Features are associated with parts, and can be either geometrical or functional (among others). Examples of geometrical features include holes, slots, channels, grooves, bosses, pads, etc. A functional feature describes the purpose of another feature or part. Parameters are properties of features or parts, for example: weight, color, material. Classes of parts and features are organized into an inheritance hierarchy. Instances of parts and features are connected with properties component of, feature of, and sub-feature of.

(Saaema et al,, 2005) propose a method of indexing design knowledge that is based upon an empirical research study. The fundamental finding of their methodology is a comprehensive set of root concepts required to index knowledge in design engineering domain, including four dimensions:

- The process description i.e. description of different tasks at each stage of the design process.
- The physical product to be produced, i.e. the product, components, sub-assemblies and assemblies.
- The functions that must be fulfilled by a particular component or assembly.
- The issues with regards to non functional requirement such as thrust, power, cost etc.

(Kitamura& Mizoguchy, 2004) has developed a meta-data schema for systematically representing functionality of a product based on Semantic Web technology for the management of the information content of engineering design documents.
An ontology that supports higher-level semantics is function-behaviour-structure (FBS) ontology (gero et al, 2006) . Its original focus was on representing objects specifically design artifacts. It was recently applied to represent design processes.
For ontology reusability, hierarchies are commonly established; (Borst et al, 1997) propose the PhysSys ontology as a sophisticated lattice of ontologies for engineering domain which supports multiple viewpoints on a physical system
Notwithstanding the promising results reported from existing research on SE ontologies, the reported ontological models don't provide a holistic view of the system engineering domain. They are either too generic or only focus on specific aspects of system representation.
As development of ontologies is motivated by, amongst other things, the idea of knowledge reuse and share ability, we have considered a coherent reuse of significant ontological engineering work as complementary interrelated ontologies corresponding to the multiple facets of system engineering processes.

4. Ontological framework for knowledge modeling in System Engineering projects

In this section, our framework for knowledge modeling in system engineering projects is described. It structures the traces of engineering in the form of semantic descriptions based on a system engineering ontology. Section 4.1 introduces the so-called "SE general Ontology", Section 4.2. Describes the modeling layers considered for semantic knowledge capture and section 4.3 presents an engineering illustrative example.

4.1 SE general Ontology

We focus here on the knowledge modeling issue that is often considered as the first step in developing a knowledge management system. The aim of this process is to understand the types of data structures and relationships within which knowledge can be held and reasoned with. We use ontologies to describe the knowledge model by a formal representation language with expressive semantics.
In order to determine the basic building blocks of the knowledge model, we introduce the notion of Situated Explicit Engineeing Knowledge "SEEK" as the smallest granularity in the system experience knowledge. The systems engineering project assets represent an integrated structure that captures product and process knowledge in engineering situations

as an instance of loosely connected ontology modules that are held together by a general ontology for systems engineering.
This general ontology is developed in domain, product, and process modules. The three levels are required to provide a comprehensive semantic model for the systems engineering project asset through an integrated representation of its semantic content, its structural content, and its design rationale.
By instantiating these ontological concepts, concrete "SEEK" could be stored in a system engineering repository for future reuse. Furthermore, the ontology itself can serve as a communication base about the products and processes e.g. for exploring domain knowledge for system engineers.
-Domain facet: The domain ontology defines the specific domain concepts, attributes, constraints, and rules. It aims to capture formally a target system according to its different abstraction levels; in other words, for each engineering domain, the ontology defines a consensual semantic network to represent domain-specific requirements, functions, behavior and physical components, as well as their structural relationships (such as "is a" "part of") and their semantic relationships (such as "allocation"). For example, domain ontology for electric circuits might define, among other things, generic types of electric components such as transistor, connection relation among components, physical laws among physical quantities, functions of components, and allocation relations between components and functions.
Figure 3 presents a high level description of a typical domain facet.

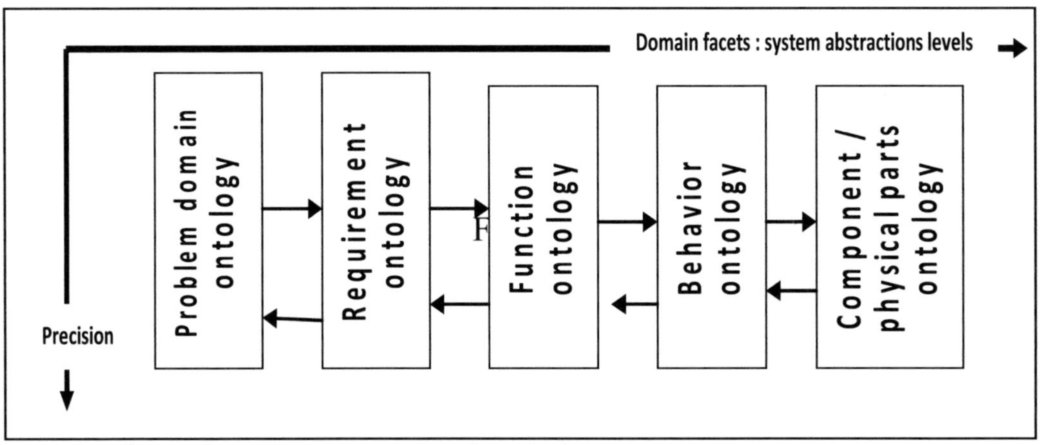

Fig. 2. Ontologies for system engineering domain facets

-Product facet: The product ontology contains concepts and relations that represent artifact types such as requirement documents, functional models, or conceptual schema. The product ontology provides logical structure and basic modeling constructs to describe engineering artifacts. This means that data can be extracted from domain ontology and packaged into an ontological constructed conceptual model or an engineering document. By formally relating modeling elements to domain concepts we could provide a systematic and semantic description of an engineering solution.
-Process facet: The process ontology contains concepts and relations that formally describe engineering activities, tasks, actors, and design rationales concepts (goals, alternatives,

arguments, and justifications for engineering decisions). Both the process and the product facets act as a formal logical structure for the systems engineering project asset. The domain facet provides semantic content for this structure.
Both the process and the product facets act as a formal structure for the SEEK. The domain facet provides semantic domain values for characterizing this structure.
Figure 4, illustrates the relationships and the complementarily of our three modeling facets for comprehensively representing system engineering knowledge.

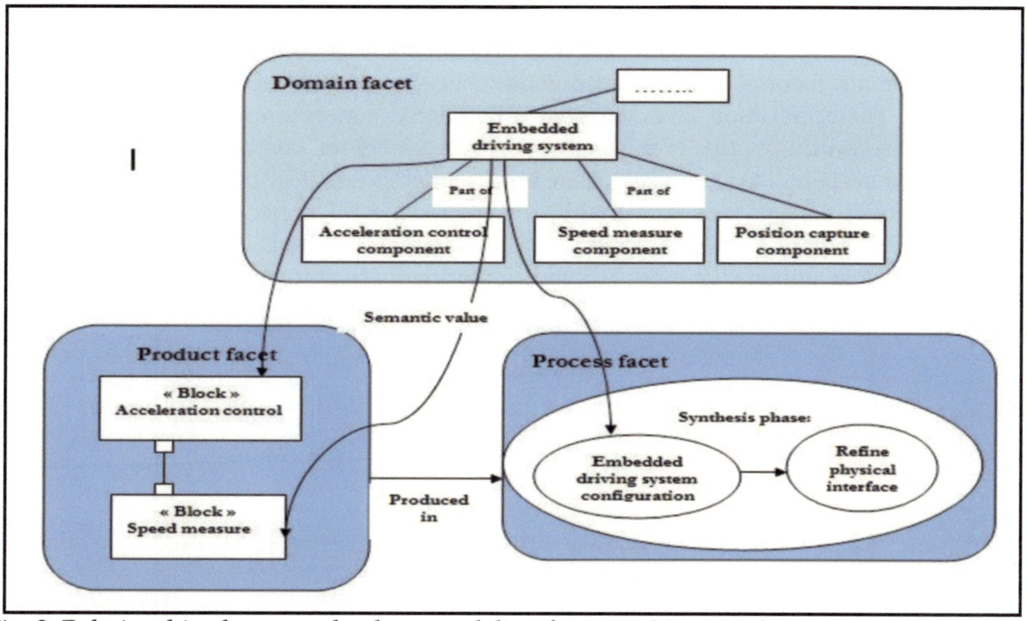

Fig. 3. Relationships between the three modeling facets in SE general ontology.

4.2 Multi-layered ontologies for SE knowledge modeling

While the ontological modules for domain, product, and process introduce general-level concepts that describe a systems engineering project asset, they need to be specialized and refined in order to provide an operational knowledge model for systems engineering projects. To this end, we introduce a layered organization of these ontological modules: a general ontology for system engineering, a specialized ontology for an engineering domain (such as automotive or information systems), and an application-specific ontology. Layers subdivide the ontology into several levels of abstraction, thus separating general knowledge from knowledge about particular domains, organizations, and projects. This allows all the engineering assets to be based on generic concepts while at the same time providing a mechanism to enable different stakeholders to define their own specific terminology and concept interpretation. By instantiating the most specific ontological concepts, concrete information items can be stored in a centralized project repository. Ontological concepts act as a semantic index for engineering artifacts.
Each layer is defined along the two axes of abstraction and semantic links. Abstraction allows modeling a gradual specification of models that are more and more concrete, that is, from abstract system requirement to concrete system components. The semantic links define

how the concepts within and between an ontology module are related to each other. Typical semantic links are subsumption relations, "part of" relations and traceability relations. For example, in an ontological module for a domain, the "part of" relation could be defined on physical components assemblies and a traceability relation (allocation) could be defined to map system functions onto physical components.
Basically, knowledge in a certain layer is described in terms of the concepts in the lower layer. Figure 5 shows a hierarchy of ontologies built on top of SE general ontology.
The first layer aims to describe super-concepts that are the same across all domains, it corresponds to the SE General ontology. The domain layer defines specializing concepts and semantic relations for a system engineering domain such as aeronautics. It integrates for examples domain theories and typical domain concepts that are shared in an engineering community. The application layer, presents specialized concepts used by specific system engineering organization, this is the most specialized level for knowledge characterization and acts as a systematized representation for annotating engineering knowledge projects. The fourth layer corresponds to semantic annotation on SE project assets defined using conceptual vocabulary from the application layer. In this way, all SE project assets are captured as formal knowledge models, by instantiating these ontological concepts.

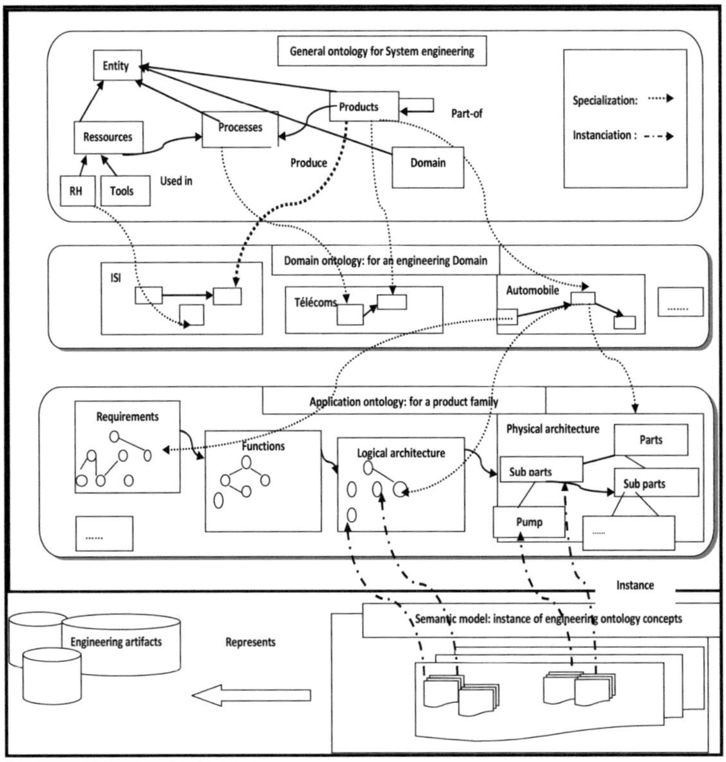

Fig. 4. Layered ontologies for systems engineering knowledge modeling

4.3 Illustrative example:

We describe a knowledge modeling scenario in the domain of aeronautics engines construction. As a single scenario cannot cover all the application possibilities, we focus in this example on the formal modeling of an engineering artifact as an instance of a domain facet excerpt.

The association of a formal knowledge description to the engineering artifact in the figure 6, allows to retrieve it by a semantic search. This artifact is modeled as instances of the concepts "aircraft engine driven pump", "jet engine" and "hydraulic pump".

A query formulated with the concept "pump" allows to retrieve this engineering artifact by reasoning on the subsuming relation between "pump" and "hydraulic pump".

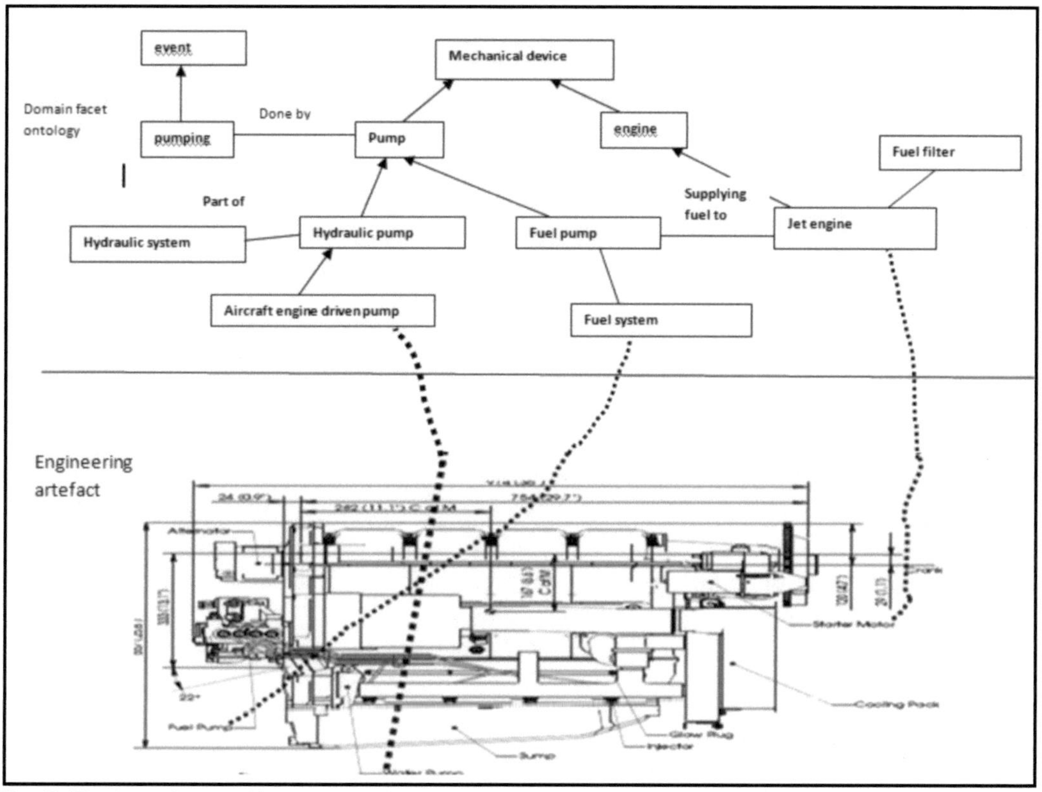

Fig. 5. Engineering artifact semantic annotation

5. Situated Explicit Engineering Knowledge capitalization and sharing

In this section we further detail the experience management module of the framework. We address the dynamic aspect of engineering process with the aim to capture implicit knowledge, decision and argumentation over the proposed ontological based support for SE. We Concentrate on providing knowledge items relevant to assist the human expert in solving knowledge-intensive tasks.

Our proposal relies on an explicit modeling of the relation between engineering situation, engineering goals, engineering alternatives and solutions.

The core of the model is denoted "SEEK": Situated Explicit Engineering Knowledge a formal pattern for representing knowledge in context. SEEK (s) are defined by instantiating the ontologies of the application layer.

5.1 Formal definitions

Before defining the Situated Explicit Engineering Knowledge, let us formalize the ontologies modules mentioned in section 4: we consider here two complementary ontologies : the system oriented ontology that corresponds to the domain facet and the context oriented ontology that corresponds to the product and the process facet.

We are representing formally ontology as:

$O = (\mathbf{C}, \leq_C, \mathbf{R}, \leq_R, \mathbf{A})$ consisting of a set of concepts C organized in a hierarchy with a subsumption relation ≤C, a set of semantic relations organized with ≤R, and a set of axioms stating restrictions on the conceptualization such as cardinalities, transitivity and constraints.

Definition 1: System oriented ontology (OS)

$\mathbf{O^S = (C^S, \leq_C, R^S, \leq_R, A^S)}$ contains the background (domain) knowledge required to engineer a system. It systematizes domain knowledge according to different system abstraction levels.

System ontology is organized as a network of modular sub-ontologies representing domain-specific requirements, functions and physical components, as well as their structural relationships (such as "is a" "part of") and their semantic relationships (such as "allocation").

$\mathbf{O^S := (O_{REQUIREMENT}, O_{FUNCTION}, O_{STRUCTURE}, R_{REQUIREMENT\text{-}FUNCTION}, R_{FUNCTION\text{-}STRUCTURE}, R_{STRUCTURE\text{-}REQUIREMENT})}$

Definition 2: Context oriented ontology (OC)

$\mathbf{O^C = (C^C, \leq_C, R^C, \leq_R, A^C)}$ contains knowledge required to express the circumstances under which system knowledge will be used. It consists of concepts and relations that formally describe engineering activities, roles, tools and artifacts models. Context ontology is organized as a network of modular sub-ontologies

$\mathbf{O^C := (O_{PROCESS}, O_{TOOLS}, O_{ROLE}, O_{PRODUCTS}, R_{PROCESS\text{-}TOOLS}, R_{PROCESSUS\text{-}ROLE}, R_{PROCESSUS\text{-}PRODUCT})}$

Definition 3: Semantic Annotation (Annot)

Annot :=(Ca, Ra, I), where:

- Ca is a set of ontological concepts.
- Ra is a set of ontological relations.
- I is a set of tuple (c,r), with : c□ Ca and r□ Ra.

A semantic annotation is defined as a set of ontological concepts and semantic relations instances. We use semantic annotation to express a particular modeling choice or a particular engineering situation. Figure 7, shows an example of semantic annotation defined over a system ontology fragment.

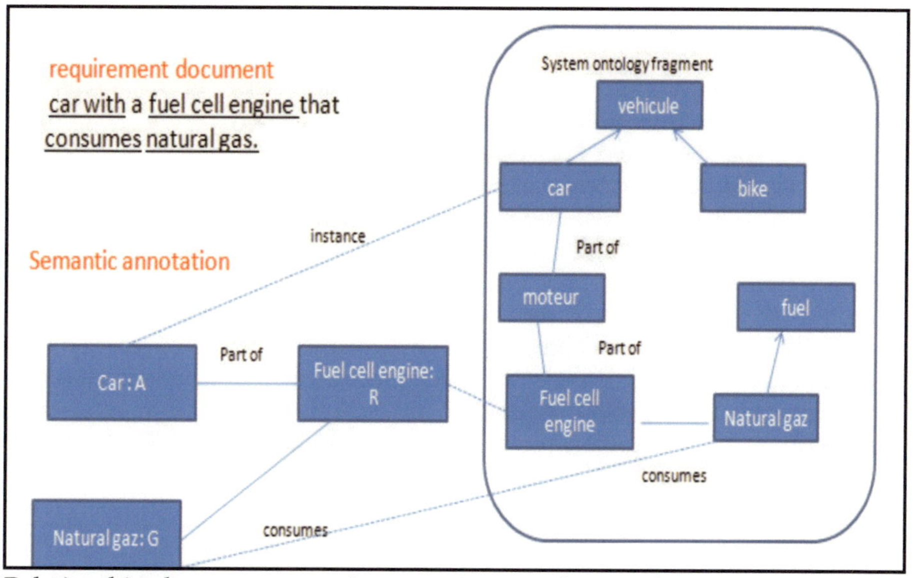

Fig. 6. Relationships between semantic annotation, ontology and engineering product.

The association of a formal knowledge description to the engineering artifact (requirement document) in the figure 7, allows to retrieve it by a semantic search. Semantic search retrieves information based on the types of the information items and the relations between them, instead of using simple String comparaisons (Brandt et al, 2007)

Definition 4: Situated Engineering Explicated Knowledge (SEEK)

Let OS and OC be, respectively, the system ontology and the context ontology, AnnotS and AnnotC be respectively semantic annotations over OS and OC.

A SEEK is a formal pattern for capitalizing experience knowledge.

SEEK = (EST, EG, AS, ES, REST-EG, REG-AS,RAS-ES, RES-EST) where :

- EST : Engineering Situation :=((annotS, annotC))
- EG: engineering goal :=((annotS,annotC))
- AS: alternative solutions (annotC)
- ES: engineering solution (annotC)
- REST-EG: an engineering situation have an engineering goal
- REG-AS: an engineering goal generates alternative solutions
- RAS-ES: engineering solution choice
- Rs-p: justification against engineering situation

5.2 Knowledge representation model

SEEK's operationalization requires an appropriate representation language, with clear and well-defined semantics.

We choose conceptual graphs (sowa, 1984) as a representation language. The attractive features of conceptual graphs have been noted previously by other knowledge engineering researchers who are using them in several applications (chein et al, 2005), (Dieng et al., 2006) (corby et al., 2006) Conceptual graphs are considered as a compromise representation

between a formal language and a graphical language because it is visual and has a sound reasoning model.
In the conceptual graph (CG) formalism, the ontological knowledge is encoded in a support. The factual knowledge is encoded in simple conceptual graphs. An extension of the original formalism (Baget, 2002) denoted "nested graphs" allows assigning to a concept node a partial internal representation in terms of simple conceptual graphs.
To represent SEEK (s) in conceptual graph formalism we use this mapping:

- The context ontology and the system ontology are represented in a conceptual graph support.
- Each semantic annotation is represented as a simple conceptual graph.
- A SEEK is a nested conceptual graph, where the concepts engineering situation, engineering goal, alternative solution, engineering solution are described by means of nested CG. This generic model has to be instantiated each time an engineering decision occurs in a project process. Figure 8 describes a SEEK model as a nested conceptual graph.

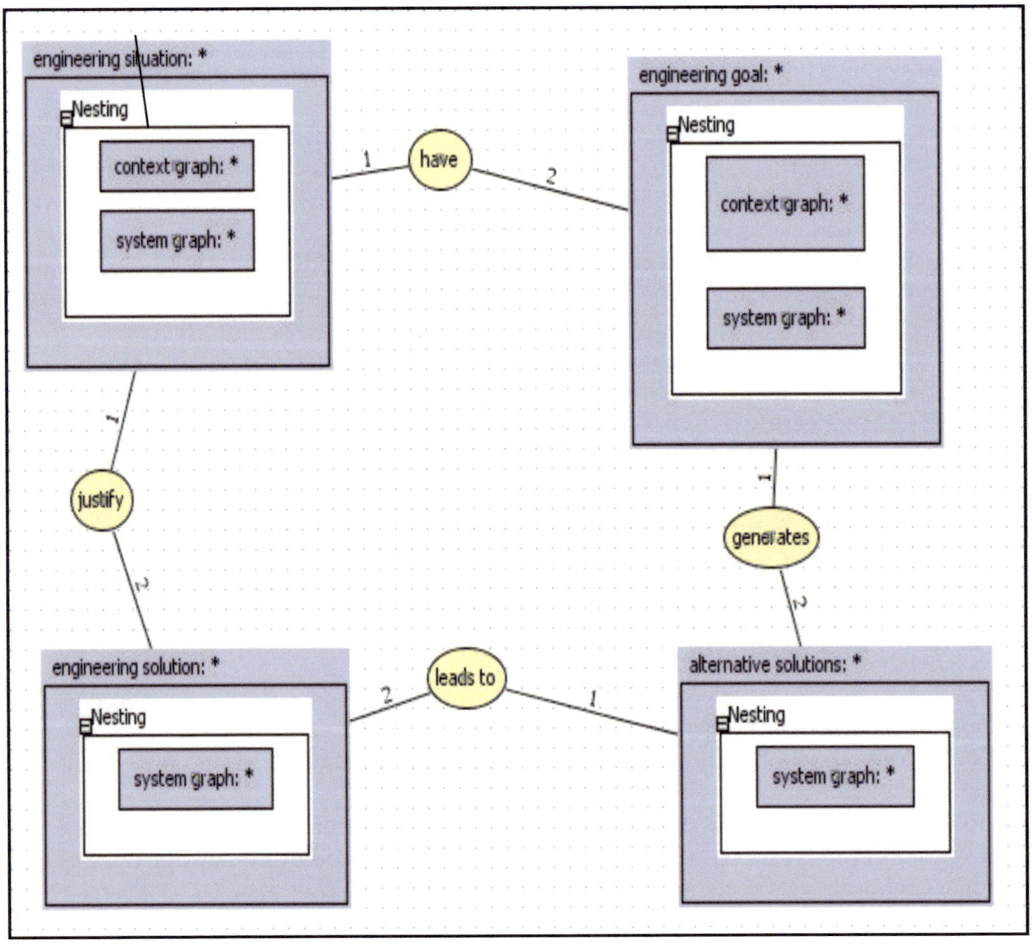

Fig. 7. SEEK as a nested conceptual graph

5.2 Knowledge sharing model

We aim to provide a proactive support for knowledge reuse. In such approaches (Abecker et al., 1998) queries are derived from the current Work context of application tools, thus providing reusable product or process knowledge that matches the current engineering situation.

Finding a matching between an ongoing engineering situation and goal and a set of capitalized SEEK(s) relies on a standard reasoning mechanism in conceptual graphs: the projection. Let's remind the projection operation as defined by (Mugnier &Chein, 1992)

Mugnier and Chein Projection (Mugnier &Chein, 1992)

Given two simple conceptual graphs G and H, a projection from G to H is an ordered pair of mappings from (RG, CG) to (RH, CH), such that:

- For all edges rc of G with label i, Π(r) Π(c) is an edge of H with label i.
- ∀r ∈ RG, type (Π(r)) <= type(r); ∀c ∈ CG, type (Π(c)) <= type(c).

There is a projection from G to H if and only if H can be derived from G by elementary specialization rules

Using the projection, the reasoning system is able to find not only descriptions of experiences that are annotated by exact concepts and relationships but also those annotated by subtypes of these concepts. Besides, to search with imprecise and/or incomplete experiences or to answer a vague query, approximate projections can be used.

We also work on an extension to conceptual graphs projection in order to take into account partial (part-of) engineering situation matching.

Our ultimate goal consist in defining an approximate situation matching, having as result a partial ordering on the SEEK (s) according to their relevance for the current engineering situation.

6. Case study: automated transport sub system.

This section presents a case study of ontology based modeling for situated engineering experience. The application domain is automatic transport sub system: an automated wagon. As an example, we consider a typical component allocation process of this sub systeme.

We assume that the sub system's functional view is represented by the data flow diagram (DFD) depicted in figure 9. The main functions considered are: capture speed, capture position, control movement, propel, break, and contain travelers. The DFD is a result of structured functional decomposition of the initial requirement: "to transport travelers from one point to another". The design know-how including such functional knowledge used in the conceptual design phase is usually left implicit because each designer possesses it. In complex engineering domains, this implicit knowledge could play a crucial role for systematizing conceptual design. As multidisciplinary teams (mechanical, electrical, software developer..) often work concurrently on a single system, it would be beneficial to have an agreement about functional concepts describing a family of system in a unambiguous and explicit manner.

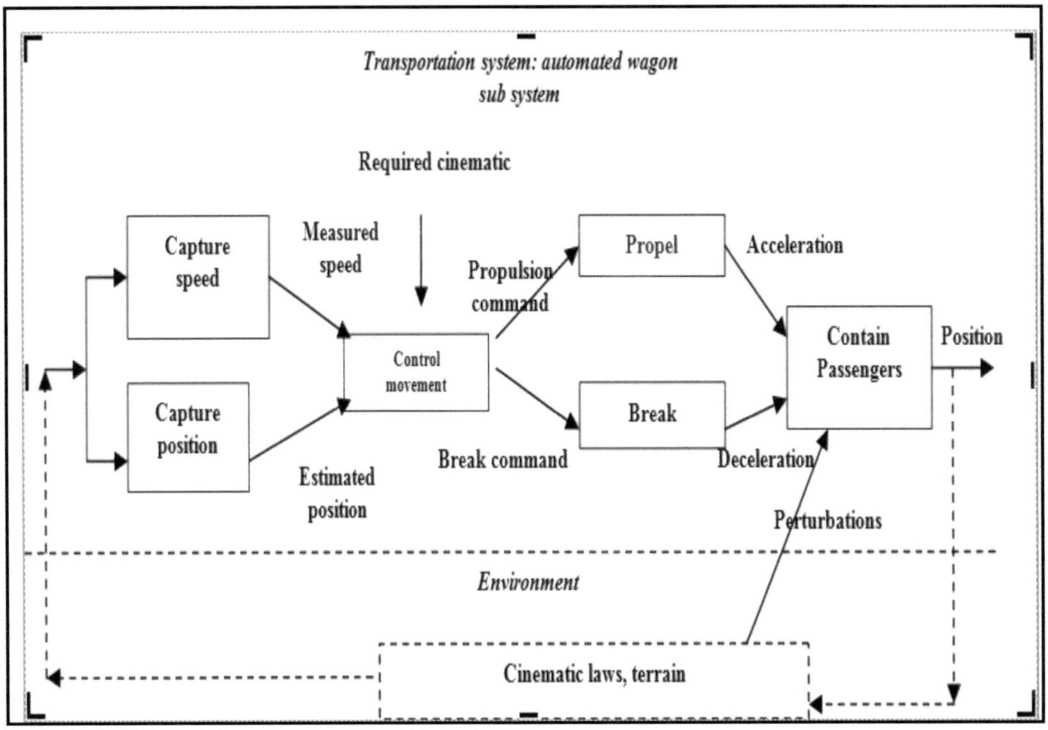

Fig. 8. Data flow diagram for an automated wagon sbsystem

The system functions should be mapped to the physical components. Functions mapping to physical components can be one to one or many to one. In addition Physical solution is constrained with non functional requirements (or soft goals) such as: system performance with attributes of travel duration, facility, acceleration limitation, comfort, and reliability.

Each physical solution choice raises a set of possible engineering alternatives. The global requirements are traded-off to find the preferred alternatives. An intricate interplay usually exists among alternatives. For example, the functions speed capture and position estimation choosing inertial station that delivers the speed as well as the position, for implementing the function speed capture would restrict the engineering choices to exclude specific transducers.

Given a specific function set, it would be helpful for novices' engineers to find the corresponding physical components as well as the constraints about function allocation choices.

Like in the functions decomposition context, this knowledge is scattered in a huge mass of engineering documents, and thus not explicitly modeled. We argue that an explicit representation of the links between components and functions could improve the quality of the allocation process.

Furthermore, designers usually wish to reuse captured design knowledge to adapt past solutions and apply these to current problems, and novice designers may wish to understand lessons from previous experiences. In this case, a machine readable representation of engineering decision trace during projects should enable effective reuse of previous decisions. To address these issues, we draw upon ontological engineering for providing a systematic basis for domain engineering knowledge and using it as a foundation for describing engineering choices and tradeoffs emanating from previous projects.

To illustrate the use of the proposed ontological framework to define a Situated Engineering Knowledge, we use the ontologies excerpts depicted in figure 10 and 11 .

- The OS fragment captures the functional and the structural facet
- The OC fragment captures the process and the product facet. In this example, we adopt a recommended process (leblanc, 2008) for SE with SysML modeling language.

Using these sub ontologies we can describe the SEEK for a design decision of a speed and position capture sub system of an automated wagon, subject to a particular non functional requirement of reliability. The SEEK model is shown in figure 12.

If we consider a new engineering situation, described by the same contextual ontology, and aiming at allocating the function "move" for an automated wagon. The capitalized SEEK is matched with this engineering situation by taking the specialization relation between ontological concepts into account.

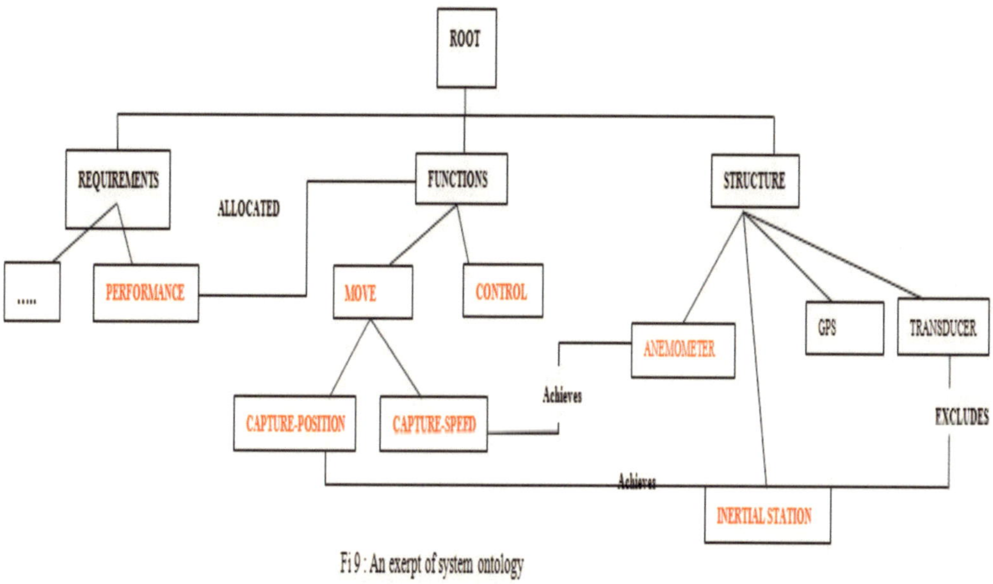

Fig. 9. a exerpt of system ontology

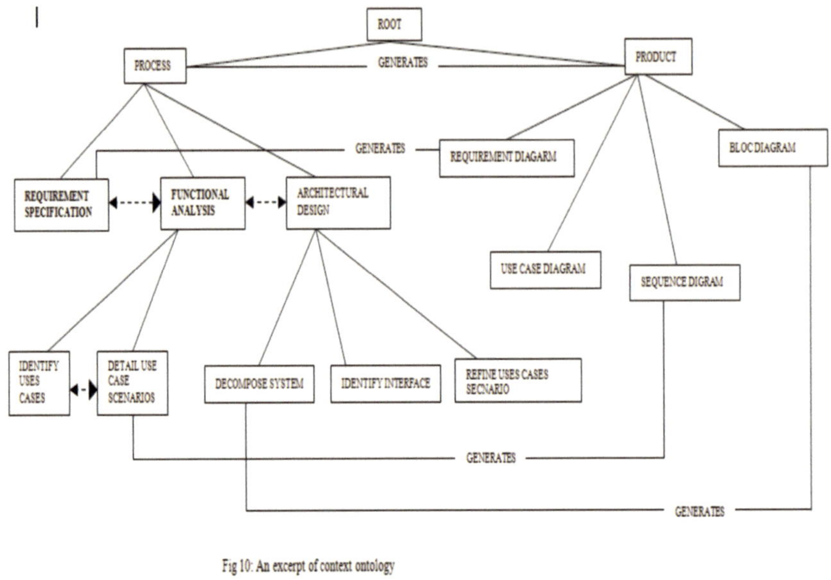

Fig. 10. an excerpt of context ontology

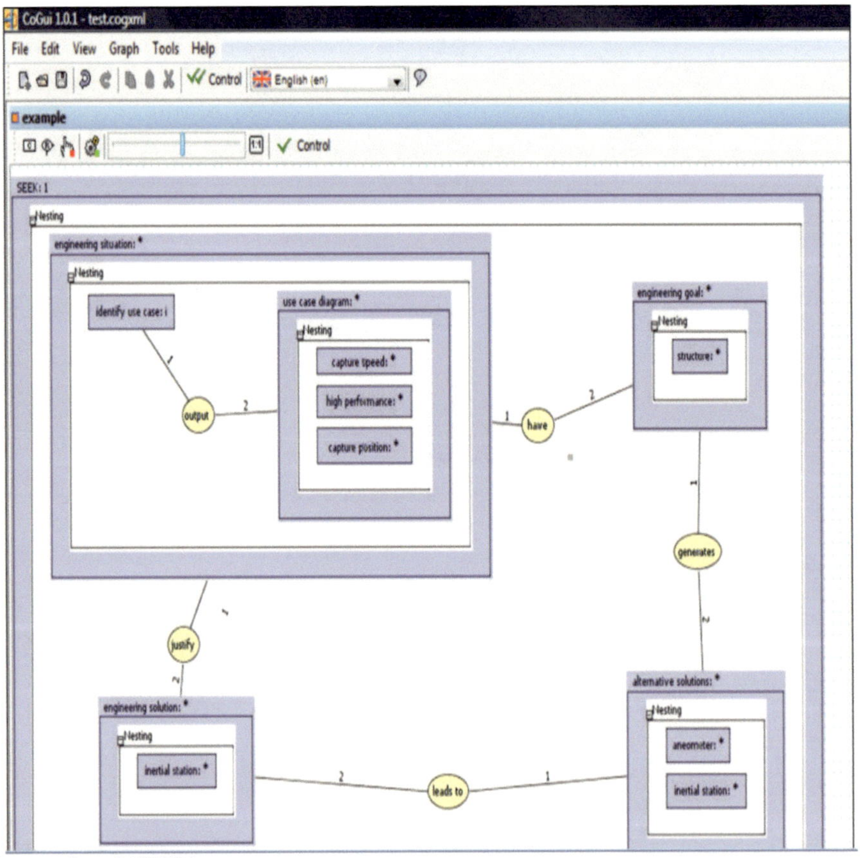

Fig. 11. Instantiated SEEK

7. Related work

Most of the existing SE tools still lack essential aspects needed for supporting knowledge capitalization and reuse during projects processes. Some recent research projects try to address this issue in specific engineering domains. To our knowledge, there is no generic framework for knowledge management in SE domain. We discuss, here some related works to our researches. As system engineering domain provides a generic methodological scheme to several engineering domain, we discuss some approaches from the software engineering and design engineering (sub)-domains.

In the software engineering domain Efforts such as, REMAP (Ramesh et al., 1992), REFSENO (Tautz et al., 1998) and BORE (Henninger, 1998) can be regarded as the main research stream that contributes to software knowledge management. However, the knowledge models employed by these approaches vary. REMAP and REFSENO are the closest efforts to our approach. REMAP also installs argumentations as an embedded component similar to our knowledge model, but our model extends REMAPS characterization of what is considered to be a system engineering knowledge asset.

In the design engineering domain, (Kim et al., 2001) have integrated concepts of artificial intelligence into commercial PDM systems. The software is based on a dynamic and flexible workflow model, as opposed to the deterministic workflows seen in most commercial PDM applications. A built-in workflow management system enables the integrated management of task processes and information flows. The system can be searched by means of a semantic query and manipulation language. However, the system relies on prescriptive process definitions which require relatively well-understood and well-documented processes. As this does not apply to conceptual process engineering, this approach must be extended to ill structured processes.

(gao et al, 2003) Describes an integration of a PDM system with ontological methods and tools. The Protégé ontology editor is combined with a commercial PDM system to provide knowledge management capabilities for the conceptual design stage. In an associated research project, a graphical interface for user-friendly knowledge acquisition has been developed. In contrast to our approach experience knowledge is not recorded. Again, this approach relies on a domain where the processes are better understood than in system engineering

(Kopena & Regli, 2003) Have designed ontology for the representation of product knowledge. A Core Ontology defines the basic structure to describe products from a functional view. Vocabulary extensions describe the domain of electromechanical devices. The model representation is based on a Description Logic (DL) system with low expressivity to achieve good computability and scalability. In this work, only product description facet is addressed.

An ontological architecture for knowledge management that resembles to our proposed framework has been proposed by (Brandt et al. 2007) and illustrated in the context of chemical engineering processes. The application and the extension of their ontological concepts to system engineering domain were among our initial research investigation.

This survey is not exhaustive, we have discussed the important projects that guides our modeling choices, there are several recent research approaches pointing in this direction; that is exploiting ontological engineering and semantic web technologies to improve engineering processes.

8. Conclusion

System engineering processes implies the management of information and knowledge and could be considered as a knowledge production process. The main objective of this chapter is to present our ongoing work concerning the validation of our ontological based framework for experience capitalization and reuse. A principal strand of future research is the application of this modeling framework in the context of an engineering organization to trigger further improvement. We plan also to use the same framework for capturing "best practices" knowledge. The problem of providing a knowledge management interface integrated to existing system engineering support tools is also under investigation.

9. References

J.Meinadier (2002). Le métier d'intégration de systèmes. Hermes Science Publications.

Awad, E. M., & Ghaziri, H. M..(2003) Knowledge management. Prentice Hall.

McMahon, C., Lowe, A., & Culley, S. J. (2004). Knowledge management in engineering design, personalisation and codification. Journal of Engineering. Design, 15(4), 307–325

Chan-Hong park, M.Kang, J.Ahn, (2007).A knowledge representation framework in design repositories. Solid state phenomena Vol 120 , pp.235-240.

Sebastian C. Brandt, Jan Morbach, Michalis Miatidis ,Manfred Theißen, Matthias Jarke , Wolfgang Marquardt. (2007). An ontology-based approach to knowledge management in design processes. Computers and Chemical Engineering

Riichiro Mizoguchi, Yoshinobu Kitamura.(2000) "Foundation of Knowledge Systematization: Role of Ontological Engineering". The Institute of Scientific and Industrial Research, Osaka University, 8-1, Mihogaoka, Ibaraki, Osaka, 567-0047, Japan.

Yoshinobu Kitamura. (2006) "Roles Of Ontologies Of Engineering Artifacts For Design Knowledge Modeling". In Proc. of the 5th International Seminar and Workshop Engineering Design in Integrated Product Development. (EDIProD 2006), 21-23 September 2006, Gronów, Poland, pp. 59-69.

T. Bahill and B. Gissing (1998).Re-evaluating systems engineering concepts using systems thinking, IEEE Transaction on Systems, Man and Cybernetics, Part C: Applications and Reviews, 28 (4), 516-527.

Michalis Miatidis, Matthias Jarke. (2005) "Toward Improvement-Oriented Reuse of Experience in Engineering Design Processes". R. Khosla et al. (Eds.): KES 2005, LNAI 3684, pp. 228–234.

Robillard, P.N.(1991) The role of knolwedge in software development. Communications of the ACM,.42(1): p. 87-92.

Ali-Babar, M., I. Gorton, and B. Kitchenham,(2005). A Framework for Supporting Architecture Knowledge and Rationale Management, in Rationale Management in Software Engineering, A.H. Dutoit, et al., Editors.

Darlington, M. & Culley, S. (2008). Investigating Ontology Development for Engineering Design Support. Advanced Engineering Informatics, 22(1): 112-134.

GRUBER, T. R.(1993). A translation approach to portable ontology specifications. Knowledge Acquisition, 5 (2): 199-220.

M. Uschold, M. Gruninger, (1996). Ontologies: principles, methods and applications, Knowledge Engineering Review 11 (2) , June.

J. Lin, M.S. Fox, T. Bilgic,(1996). A Requirement Ontology for Engineering Design, in: Proceedings of the Third International Conference on Concurrent Engineering, pp. 343–351.

Ahmed, S., Kim, S., Wallace, K. M., (2005). A Methodology for Creating Ontologies for Engineering Design, In Proc. Of ASME DTM, 2005, DETC2005-84729.

Yoshinobu Kitamura, Riichiro Mizoguchi,(2004) Ontology-Based Functional-Knowledge Modeling Methodology and Its Deployment. EKAW : 99-115.

John s gero and Udo kannengiesser. (2006) A function-behaviour-structure ontology of processes. Design Computing and Cognition '06. Part 6,407-422.

Borst, P. Akkermans, H., and Top, J, (1997). Engineering Ontologies, Human-Computer Studies, 46(2/3), pp. 365-406.

J.F. Sowa,(1984). Conceptual Structures: Information Processing in Mind and Machine, Addison-Wesley Publishing Company, Reading, MA.

D. Genest, M. Chein, (2005).A Content-search Information Retrieval Process Based on Conceptual Graphs. Knowledge And Information Systems, vol. 8, no. 3, Springer, pp. 292–309.

R. Dieng-Kuntz, D. Minier, M. Ruzicka, F. Corby,O. Corby, L. Alamarguy, (2006) .Building and using a medical ontology for knowledge management and cooperative work in a health care network, Computers in Biology and Medicine 36 (7–8) 871–892.

O. Corby, R. Dieng-Kuntz, C. Faron-Zucker, F. Gandon,((2006) . Searching the Semantic Web: approximate query processing based on ontologies, IEEE Intelligent Systems Journal 21 (1) 20–27.

J.F. Baget, M.-L. Mugnier, (2002). Extensions of simple conceptual graphs: the complexity of rules and constraints, Journal of Artificial Intelligence Research (JAIR) 16 , 425–465.

Abecker, A., Bernardi, A., Hinkelmann, K., K¨uhn, O., & Sintek, M. (1998). Toward a technology for organizational memories. IEEE Intelligent Systems, 13(3), 40–48.

CHEIN M. & MUGNIER M.-L. (1992). Conceptual Graphs : Fundamental Notions. Revue d'Intelligence Artificielle, 6(4), 365–406.

Philippe Leblanc, (2008) Telelogic. Modélisation SysML par l'Exemple. Revue de génie logiciel. ISSN 1265-1397 , no 83.

Ramesh, B., and Dhar, V. (1992), "Supporting Systems Development by Capturing Deliberations during Requirements Engineering", IEEE Transactions on Software Engineering,Vol. 18, No 6, pp. 498-510.

Tautz, C.;Wangenheim, C.G.V. (1998), "REFSENO REpresentaion Formalism for Software Engenieing Ontologies", IESE-Report NO. o15.98/E, Version 1.1.

Henninger, S. (1998), "An Environment for Reusing Software Process", In Proc. of the 5th IEEE International Conference on Software Reuse (ICSR5), Victoria, BC, Canada.

Kim,Y., Kang, S., Lee, S.,&Yoo, S. (2001).A distributed, open, intelligent product data management system. International Journal of Computer Integrated Manufacturing, 14, 224–235.

Gao, J. X., Aziz, F. L., Maropoulos, P. G., & Cheung, W. M. (2003). Application of product data management technologies for enterprise integration. International Journal of Computer Integrated Manufacturing, 16(7–8), 491–500.

Kopena, J., & Regli,W. C. (2003). Functional modeling of engineering designs for the semantic web. IEEE Data Engineering Bulletin, 26(4), 55–61.

Ontological Knowledge Representation for Resolving Semantic Heterogeneity in Software Requirements Traceability

Namfon Assawamekin[1], Thanwadee Sunetnanta[2,3] and Charnyote Pluempitiwiriyawej[2,3]
[1]*School of Science, University of the Thai Chamber of Commerce*
[2]*Department of Computer Science, Faculty of Science, Mahidol University*
[3]*Faculty of Information and Communication Technology, Mahidol University*
THAILAND

1. Introduction

Heterogeneity in software requirements has regularly been discussed as a challenging problem, especially in the areas of requirements traceability. In practice, requirements are fundamentally expressed by customers in terms of natural language which inevitably inherits ambiguity. Pieces of requirements may be expressed in such a way that is best suited the view of an individual. Vocabularies and terminologies used in requirements expression therefore can be varied, habitually depending on customer roles, their background knowledge, perspectives and levels of understanding on system problems. Often, system analysts may capture requirements expressed by using different vocabularies or terminologies, yet conveying similar meaning.

Taking account of diversity of how software requirements can be expressed and who expresses the requirements, system analysts may use different techniques to elicit the requirements from customers. Requirements elicitation techniques range from typical ones like introspection, questionnaires, interviews, focus group and protocol analysis (Goguen & Linde, 1993) to modern one like scrum and agile requirements modeling (Paetsch et al., 2003). No matter which elicitation techniques are deployed, requirements from different customers often overlap, possibly are intertwined and inconsistent. As systems become more complex it becomes increasingly difficult for system analysts to resolve heterogeneity in software requirements so that the requirements can be verified and validated easily and effectively.

The impact of heterogeneity is even more crucial in distributed and collaborative software development environment since the heterogeneity is an inherent characteristic in such environment. With the advents of outsourcing and offshoring software development, software specifications can be collaboratively constructed by a team of developers in multiple sites, possibly with various development methods and tools. It is therefore important that system analysts must understand and be able to resolve the analogy and

poly-forms to requirements expression and representation to better communicate, check consistency and trace between pieces of requirements in a distributed manner.
In view of that, we propose to deploy ontology as a knowledge representation to intervene mutual "understanding" in requirements tracing process. By "ontological knowledge representation", we provide a basis modeling view for system analysts to express "a domain of discourse" for software requirements elicitation as well as the basic categories of requirements elements and their relationships. With our ontological knowledge representation, ontology matching is applied as a reasoning mechanism in automatically generating traceability relationships without restricting the freedom in expressing requirements differently. The relationships are identified by deriving semantic analogy of ontology concepts representing requirements elements. We will exemplify our ontological knowledge representation for software requirements traceability and compare our work to the applicability of other knowledge representations for the same purpose. Section 2 contains our literature reviews that lead to the development of ontological knowledge representation in this work. Section 3 presents our main idea of ontological knowledge representation for expressing software requirements. Section 4 elaborates how we can automate requirements traceability through ontology matching process. Section 5 concludes our contributions and further directions of our work.

2. Managing Semantic Heterogeneity in Software Development Life Cycle with Knowledge Representation

Software development is the processing of knowledge in a very focused way (Robillard, 1999). Knowledge acquisition is underlying cognitive process of software requirements gathering and elicitation to obtain information required to solve problems. Software models are forms of knowledge representation resulting from transitory construction of knowledge built up for presenting software solutions in software analysis process. Likewise, application programs are also forms of knowledge representation of software solutions that can be interpreted and processed by computer processors. Knowledge representation is therefore a key vehicle for organizing and structuring information in software development life cycle so that the information can be easily understood, systematically verified and validated by system developers and by the end users.
To manage semantic heterogeneity in software development, it is important to select knowledge representation that has sufficient expressive power as follows. Firstly, it is required that such knowledge representation should be able to recognize semantic differences in requirements expression and various software models. Secondly, it should preserve the meaning of the expression and the models, without restricting how the requirements are stated and the choices of software models that system developers want to use. In view of that, the basic constructs of the knowledge representation should be able to recognize type and instance definitions in requirements elements so that it can differentiate the meaning of requirements from its syntactic forms. Lastly, the knowledge representation should naturally support reasoning and inferences to resolve semantic heterogeneity arising in software development process.
There currently exists a collection of knowledge representations that are application to software development. Notable works are *RML*-the object-based knowledge representation for requirements specifications in (Borgida et al., 1985), *Cake*-the knowledge representation

and inference engine based on logics and plan calculus for software development in (Rich & Feldman, 1992) and *Telos*-the object-based knowledge representation with integrity constraints and deduction rules in (Mylopoulos et al., 1990). These works provide a solid proof on the application of knowledge representation to software development. However, each of these knowledge representations do not emphasize on their resolution in managing semantic heterogeneity that may arise. Although a certain degree of semantic inference may be derived from structuring mechanisms such as generalization, aggregation and classification as in Telos, the consistency of knowledge entered are verified through the an explicit constraint rules.

In our view, semantic heterogeneity can be both implicit and explicit in requirements expression. By semantic heterogeneity the meaning of words and understanding of concepts may differ or be interpreted differently from one community to another, regardless of syntax which refers to the structure or the schema by which the words or the concepts are represented. In view of that, it is not possible to explicitly define constraint rules or relationships that can be completely resolved semantic heterogeneity. Most of the times, semantic heterogeneity is implicit and is not known to the person who expresses such semantics of words or concepts.

Towards that view, we further explore the principle of ontology as explicit and formalized specifications of conceptualizations to extract and formalize the semantics. In the field of software engineering, there are many works that have applied and used ontology to different processes or phases in software development life cycle, starting from software requirements analysis (Kaiya & Saeki, 2005), cost estimation in project planning (Hamdan & Khatib, 2006) to re-engineering (Yang et al., 1999). There is also a particular set of work related to using ontology for multi-site distributed software development (Wongthongtham et al., 2005; Wongthongtham et al., 2008). From the literature, these works focus on using a single ontology to share a common understanding, manual construction of ontology and applying the ontology to specific application domains. In contrast to the above relevant works, our approach is concerned with ontology interoperability that does not force many stakeholders into a single ontology, but supports multiple ontologies for expressing multiperspective requirements artifacts. To be more precise, we aim to give various stakeholders with the freedom to communicate among each other based on their own defined ontologies. Additionally, our approach provides an automatic construction of multiple ontologies that is applicable to represent multiperspective requirements artifacts of any specific application domains. Next section will further describe ontology application in our work.

3. Ontological Approach to Knowledge Representation for Software Requirements

An ontology is an explicit formal specification of a shared conceptualization (Gruber, 1993; Borst, 1997; Studer et al., 1998). The ontology captures consensual knowledge, which is described in the terms of a formal model. In the ontology, a set of concept types and a set of formal axioms are explicitly defined with both human-readable and machine-readable text. Ontologies provide a common vocabulary of an area and define – with different levels of formality – the meaning of the terms and relations between them. Generally speaking, knowledge in the ontologies is formalized using five kinds of components: classes, relations, functions, axioms and instances (Gruber, 1993). Classes in the ontology are usually organized in the taxonomies.

The ontology is widely used as an important component in many areas, such as knowledge management (Jurisica et al., 2004), electronic commerce (Hepp et al., 2007), distributed systems (Haase et al., 2008), information retrieval systems (Jung, 2009) and in new emerging fields like the Semantic Web. Ontology can prove very useful for a community as a way of structuring and defining the meaning of the metadata terms that are currently being collected and standardized. Using ontologies, tomorrow's applications can be "intelligent", in the sense that they can more accurately work at the human conceptual level.

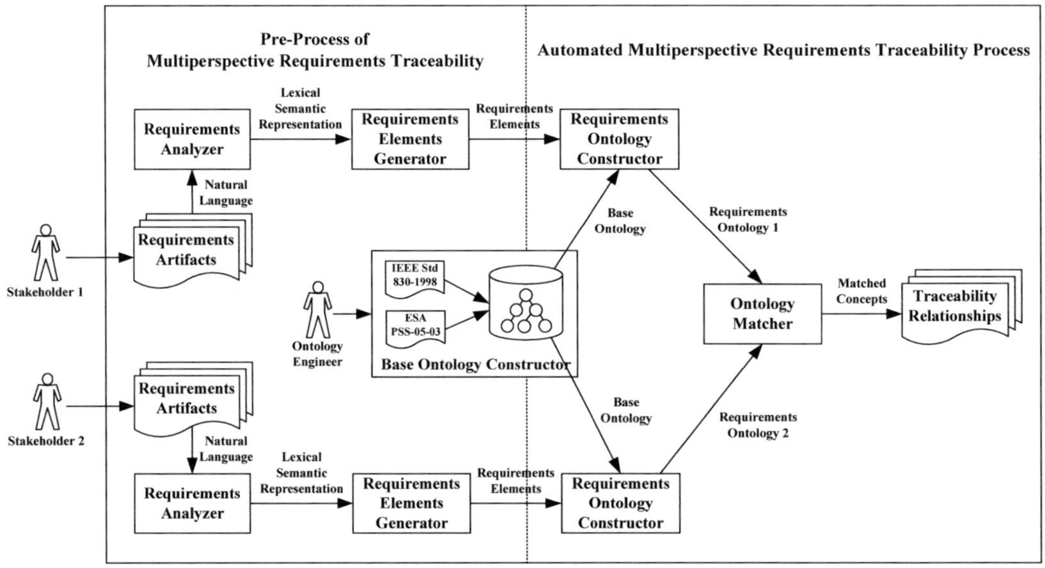

Fig. 1. Multiperspective requirements traceability (MUPRET) framework

We apply ontology concept to our multipersepctive requirements traceability (MUPRET) framework which merges the natural language processing (NLP) techniques, rule-based approaches and ontology concepts in order to resolve the heterogeneity in multiperspective requirements artifacts. Figure 1 illustrates our MUPRET framework containing five main modules: requirements analyzer (RA), requirements elements generator (REG), base ontology constructor (BOC), requirements ontology constructor (ROC) and ontology matcher (OM). The details of all modules deployed in the MUPRET framework are presented in depth elsewhere in our previous papers (Assawamekin et al., 2008a; Assawamekin et al., 2008b). The five main modules can be briefly explained as follows:

1. The RA module obtains a set of requirements artifacts represented in terms of natural language or plain English text. It uses the NLP techniques to syntactically analyze these artifacts and generate lexical semantic representation as the output.
2. The REG module utilizes rule-based approaches to automatically extract requirements elements from requirements artifacts.
3. The BOC module constructs a base ontology to classify requirements types of requirements artifacts in the domain of software requirements.

4. The ROC module attaches requirements elements into the base ontology to automatically construct requirements ontology of each stakeholder as a common representation for knowledge interchange purposes.
5. The OM module applies ontology matching technique in order to automatically generate traceability relationships when a match is found in the requirements ontologies.

In summary, we propose our MUPRET framework which deploys *ontology* as a knowledge management mechanism to intervene mutual "understanding" without restricting the freedom in expressing requirements differently. *Ontology matching* is applied as a reasoning mechanism in automatically generating traceability relationships. The relationships are identified by deriving semantic analogy of ontology concepts representing requirements elements.

4. Matching Ontologies for Requirements Traceability

As briefly discussed in the introductory part, large-scaled software development inevitably involves a group of stakeholders, each of which may express their requirements differently in their own terminology and representation depending on their perspectives or perceptions of their shared problems. Such requirements result in *multiperspective requirements artifacts*. These artifacts may be enormous, complicated, ambiguous, incomplete, redundant and inconsistent. However, they must be traced, verified and merged in order to achieve a common goal of the development. Moreover, requirements artifacts are frequently subject to changes. Planning, controlling and implementation of requirements changes can be tedious, time-consuming and cost-intensive. Determining of effects caused by requirements changes on software systems is based on *requirements traceability* (Gotel & Finkelstein, 1994).

The traceability of multiperspective requirements artifacts has regularly been discussed as a challenging problem, particularly in the requirements change management (Grunbacher et al., 2004). The heterogeneity of multiperspective requirements artifacts makes it difficult to perform tracing, verification and merging of the requirements. More specifically, it can be very problematic when multiperspective requirements artifacts are expressed with synonyms (i.e. different terminologies representing the same concept) and homonyms (i.e. the same term representing different concepts) and various stakeholders want to share these artifacts to each other. In this situation, ontology can play an essential role in communication among diverse stakeholders in the course of an integrating system.

To be able to achieve our goal, this section presents ontology matching process executed in the following four steps to reason on traceability that arises between requirements.

Step 1: Compute concepts of labels, which denote the set of concepts that one would classify under a *label* it encodes.

Step 2: Compute concepts of nodes, which denote the set of concepts that one would classify under a node, given that it has a certain *label* and *position* in the graph. For object concepts, the logical formula for a concept at node is defined as a conjunction of concepts of labels located in the path from the given node to the root. For relationship concepts, the concept at node is identified as a conjunction of domain, range and relationship concepts. For process concepts, the concept at node is defined as a conjunction of actor, input, output and process concepts.

Step 3: Compute the relations between concepts of labels, called *element matching*. In this work, we contribute *a base ontology* to define the types of concepts. If two concepts have different types, the relation between two concepts is mismatch. We also use external resources (i.e., domain knowledge and WordNet (Miller, 1990; Miller, 1995)) and string matching techniques (i.e., prefix, suffix, edit distance and n-gram) with threshold 0.85. Lexical relations provided by WordNet are converted into semantic relations according to the rules as shown in Table 1.

Step 4: Compute the relations between concepts of nodes, called *concept matching*. Each concept is converted into a propositional validity problem. Semantic relations are translated into propositional connectives using the rules described in Table 1.

Lexical relations	Semantic relations	Propositional logic	Translation of formula into conjunctive normal form
Synonym	$a = b$	$a \leftrightarrow b$	$axioms \wedge \forall(context_1 \wedge \neg context_2)$ $axioms \wedge \forall(\neg context_1 \wedge context_2)$
Hyponym or meronym	$a \subseteq b$	$a \rightarrow b$	$axioms \wedge \forall(context_1 \wedge \neg context_2)$
Hypernym or holonym	$a \supseteq b$	$b \rightarrow a$	$axioms \wedge \forall(\neg context_1 \wedge context_2)$
Antonym	$a \perp b$	$\neg(a \wedge b)$	$axioms \wedge \forall(context_1 \wedge context_2)$
	$a \cap b$	$(a \wedge b) \vee (a \wedge \neg b) \vee (\neg a \wedge b)$	$axioms \wedge \exists(\neg context_1 \vee \neg context_2) \wedge \exists(\neg context_1 \vee context_2) \wedge \exists(context_1 \vee \neg context_2)$

Table 1. The relationships among lexical relations, semantic relations and propositional formula

The criterion for determining whether a relation holds between concepts is the fact that it is entailed by the premises. Thus, we have to prove that this formula *(axioms)* → *rel(context₁, context₂)* is valid. A propositional formula is valid iff its negation is unsatisfiable. A SAT solver (Berre, 2006) run on the formula fails.

We use types of overlap relations defined in (Spanoudakis et al., 1999) to generate traceability relationships in our work. The traceability relationships can be generated when a match is found in the requirements ontologies. Thus, the semantic relations will be mapped to traceability relationships as shown in Table 2.

Semantic relations	Traceability relationships
Equivalence (=)	overlapTotally (=)
More or less general ($\supseteq$, $\subseteq$)	overlapInclusively ($\supseteq$, $\subseteq$)
Mismatch ($\perp$)	noOverlap ($\perp$)
Overlapping ($\cap$)	overlapPartially ($\cap$)

Table 2. Conversion of semantic relations into traceability relationships

The distinction and implication among different types of traceability relationships is important not only because these relationships have different impact on the requirements traceability status of two requirements artifacts but also because the corrections of requirements changes occurring due to each of these types of traceability relationships might not be the same. In our work, we order traceability relationships as they have been listed, according to their binding strength, from the strongest to the weakest. The more general and less general have the same binding strength. Hence, *overlapTotally* is the strongest relationship since the sets of source concept have exactly the same as the sets of target concept. The source and target concepts are *overlapInclusively* if one of the designated sets is proper subset of the other. Both source and target concepts are *overlapPartially* if their designated sets have both concepts in common and non-common concepts. More importantly, we discard *noOverlap* relationship which is the weakest relationship in this work because there is no effect on multiperspective requirements artifacts changes.

As a prototype of the processes in the MUPRET framework, we have developed the MUPRET tool which is a Java-based tool with Prolog and WordNet-based semantic inference engine. This tool aims to support our framework and to demonstrate its feasibility for distributed, collaborative and multiperspective software development environment. The details of MUPRET tool are presented in depth elsewhere in our paper (Assawamekin et al., 2009). This tool runs on PCs running MS-Windows as a standalone environment. Our design of the MUPRET tool primarily focuses on demonstrating "proof-of-concept" rather than on optimizing technique used in the framework. The aim of our approach is to build a generic support environment for the MUPRET framework. This approach is constructed with specialized tools and techniques that either demonstrate the feasibility of the approach or address a particular requirements traceability issue.

The MUPRET tool facilitates the automatic extraction and construction of requirements elements of an individual stakeholder into a so-called requirements ontology. As a result, multiperspective requirements artifacts of different stakeholders are captured in a common taxonomy imposed by the sharing base of requirements ontology. The tool then automatically generates traceability links by matching requirements ontologies.

To demonstrate how to use the MUPRET tool, we will illustrate how to generate traceability relationships via two different requirements artifacts with respect to two different perspectives. These two requirements artifacts describe parts of a hospital information system. More specifically, they describe a doctor investigation system (DIS) and an in-patient registration system (IPRS). These requirements artifacts are written in format of plain English text as follows.

Requirements 1: (DIS perspective)

Each patient has a unique hospital number (HN) and a name. A patient is admitted by a doctor. Nurses and doctors are considered as staffs. A nurse has a name. The nurse's name consists of a first name, an initial and a last name. A doctor is identified by an identification number and a name.

Requirements 2: (IPRS perspective)

Physicians and nurses are staffs. Staffs have an ID, a name and an address. A surgeon is a physician.

Both requirements are presented as a source (DIS) and a target (IPRS) in our *MUPRET browser*. After both requirements are passed to the RA and REG modules, the ROC module will attach requirements elements into the base ontology. Accordingly, the DIS and IPRS requirements ontology are automatically constructed as depicted in Figures 2 and 3 respectively.

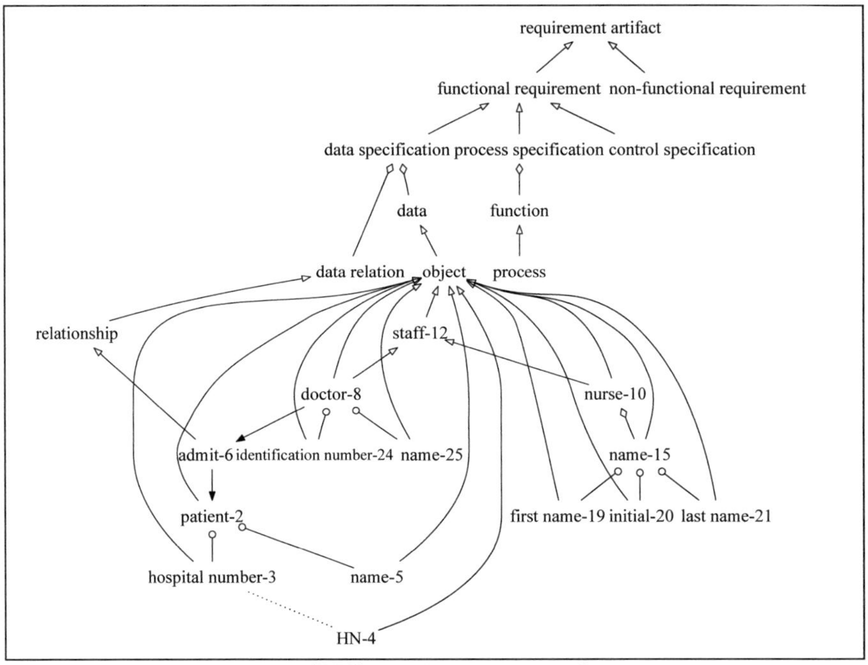

Fig. 2. Doctor investigation system (DIS) requirements ontology

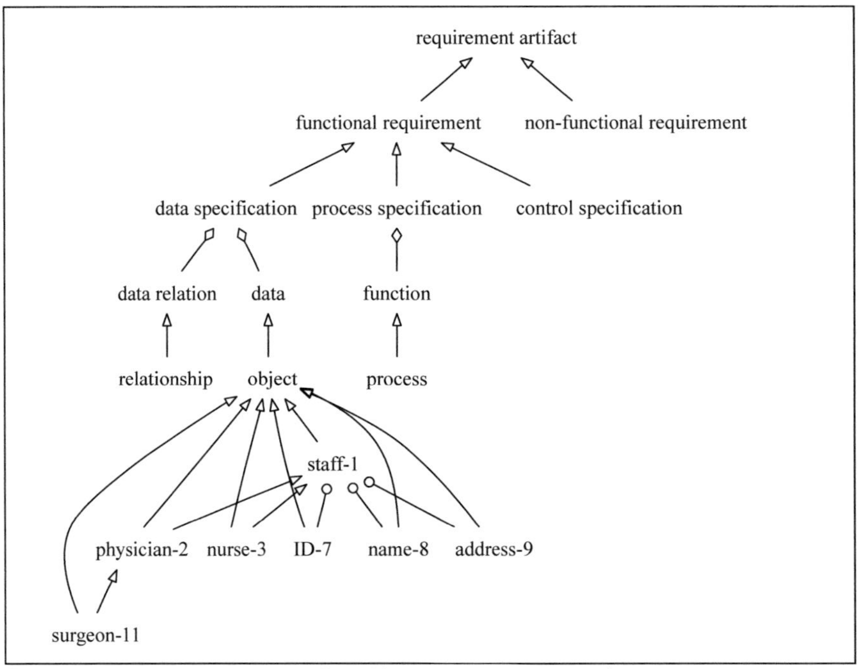

Fig. 3. In-patient registration system (IPRS) requirements ontology

A part of traceability relationships between DIS and IPRS requirements artifacts can be expressed in the first-order logic (FOL) or predicate terms for machine-readable text as shown below.

overlapTotally(Requirements 1/S2T7, S3T3, S6T2/doctor | Requirements 2/S1T1, S3T5/physician)
overlapInclusively(Requirements 2/S2T4/ID | Requirements 1/S2T7, S3T3, S6T2/doctor)
overlapInclusively(Requirements 2/S2T7/name | Requirements 1/S2T7, S3T3, S6T2/doctor)
overlapInclusively(Requirements 2/S2T10/address | Requirements 1/S2T7, S3T3, S6T2/doctor)
overlapInclusively(Requirements 2/S3T2/surgeon | Requirements 1/S2T7, S3T3, S6T2/doctor)
overlapInclusively(Requirements 1/S3T1, S4T2, S5T2/nurse | Requirements 2/S1T5, S2T1/staff)
overlapPartially(Requirements 1/S2T7, S3T3, S6T2/doctor | Requirements 2/S1T3/nurse)

From the example, overlapTotally(Requirements 1/S2T7, S3T3, S6T2/doctor | Requirements 2/S1T1, S3T5/physician) means that *doctor* of sentence 2 token 7, sentence 3 token 3 and sentence 6 token 2 in the Requirements 1 (DIS requirements artifacts) overlaps totally with *physician* of sentence 1 token 1 and sentence 3 token 5 in the Requirements 2 (IPRS requirements artifacts). Using the Figures 2 and 3, trying to prove that $doctor_1$ in DIS requirements ontology is less general than $physician_2$ in IPRS requirements ontology, requires constructing the following formula.

$$((staff_1 \leftrightarrow staff_2) \wedge (doctor_1 \leftrightarrow physician_2)) \wedge (staff_1 \wedge doctor_1) \wedge \neg(staff_2 \wedge physician_2)$$

The above formula turns out to be unsatisfiable, and therefore, the less general relation holds. It is noticeable that if we test for the more general relation between the same pair of concepts, the corresponding formula would be also unsatisfiable. As a result, the final relation for the given pair of concepts is the equivalence.
Equally, an example screen of traceability relationships can be depicted in Figure 4 for human-readable text and user-friendly. The totally, (superset or subset) inclusively and partially overlapped target can be represented with green, red, cyan and yellow color respectively while the grey color means the source of requirements. As seen as an example in this figure, *doctor* in the Requirements 1 (DIS requirements artifacts) overlaps totally with *physician*, overlaps inclusively (superset) with *ID*, *name*, *address* and *surgeon*, overlaps inclusively (subset) with *staff* as well as overlaps partially with *nurse* in the Requirements 2 (IPRS requirements artifacts).

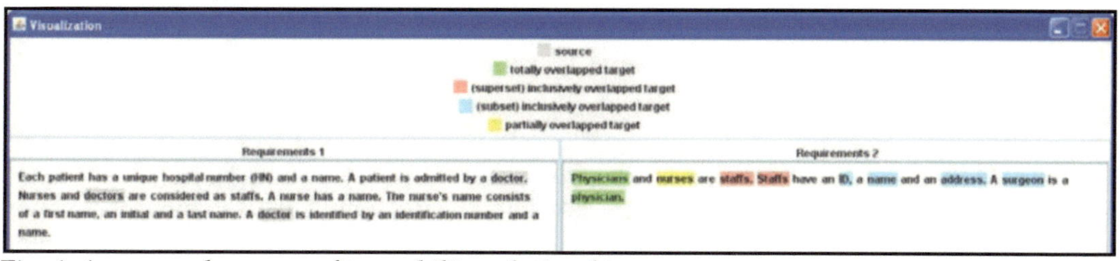

Fig. 4. An example screen of traceability relationships

Let us consider again the example of Figure 4, the overlap between *doctor* in the Requirements 1 and *physician* in the Requirements 2 is total. In the view of traceability, if *doctor* in the Requirements 1 is changed then the modification of *physician* in the

Requirements 2 must be needed. On the other hand, if *doctor* in the Requirements 1 is changed then *staff* in the Requirements 2 may be modified since *doctor* in the Requirements 1 overlaps inclusively (subset) with *staff* in the Requirements 2. Additionally, if *doctor* in the Requirements 1 is modified then the modification of *nurse* in the Requirements 2 may be needed with respect to overlap partially relationship. In contrast, if *patient* in the Requirements 1 is changed then there is no modification needed for *physician* in the Requirements 2 due to no overlap relationship.
To sum up, the MUPRET tool automatically constructs requirements ontologies from multiperspective requirements artifacts with the aim of generating traceability relationships. The ontology matching technique is executed without any user interaction in order to achieve this goal. Suppose that the relations between element matching are correct, the relations between concept matching can generate the precise semantic relations. In view of that, traceability relationships are also accurate.

5. Conclusions and Ongoing Work

This chapter points out the semantic heterogeneity problems found in multiperspective requirements artifacts and introduces the ontological knowledge representation to help resolve such problems. The resolution is described via our MUPRET framework and tool. Our MUPRET framework merges the NLP techniques, rule-based approaches and ontology concepts to automatically generate traceability relationships of multiperspective requirements artifacts, which can be applied to any software requirements domain. In MUPRET, the base ontology representing the fundamental concepts is defined and used to classify requirements types of requirements artifacts. Regarding the base ontology, multiple requirements ontologies can be developed and virtually integrated through ontology matching process. The result of the ontology matching is a set of traceability relationships of software requirements.
Although the current stage of the MUPRET framework and tool emphasizes on tracing multiperspectives in requirements analysis phase and focuses on requirements that are expressed in terms of natural language or plain English text. It is possible to extend MUPRET to cover multiperspective software artifacts expressed in terms of typical analysis models. This can be done by adding semantics of those model elements to the base of the MUPRET's requirements ontology. In addition, we also aim at exploring further how to apply our MUPRET to support traceability throughout a complete software development process.

6. References

Assawamekin, N.; Sunetnanta, T. & Pluempitiwiriyawej, C. (2008a). Automated Multiperspective Requirements Traceability Using Ontology Matching Technique, *Proceedings of the Twentieth International Conference on Software Engineering and Knowledge Engineering (SEKE 2008)*, pp. 460-465, Hotel Sofitel, Redwood City, San Francisco Bay, C.A., U.S.A., July 1-3, 2008

Assawamekin, N.; Sunetnanta, T. & Pluempitiwiriyawej, C. (2008b). Resolving Multiperspective Requirements Traceability Through Ontology Integration, *Proceedings of the Second IEEE International Conference on Semantic Computing (ICSC 2008)*, pp. 362-369, Santa Clara Marriot Hotel, Santa Clara, C.A., U.S.A., August 4-7, 2008

Assawamekin, N.; Sunetnanta, T. & Pluempitiwiriyawej, C. (2009). MUPRET: An Ontology-Driven Traceability Tool for Multiperspective Requirements Artifacts, *Proceedings of the 8th IEEE/ACIS International Conference on Computer and Information Science (ICIS 2009)*, pp. 943-948, Pine City Hotel, Shanghai, China, June 1-3, 2009

Berre, D.L. (2006). A Satisfiability Library for Java. Available at http://www.sat4j.org, June 15, 2006

Borgida, A.; Greenspan, S. & Mylopoulos, J. (1985). Knowledge Representation as the Basis for Requirements Specifications. *IEEE Computer*, Vol. 18, No. 4, pp. 82-91

Borst, W.N. (1997). *Construction of Engineering Ontologies for Knowledge Sharing and Reuse*, Doctoral Dissertation, Enschede, NL-Centre for Telematics and Information Technology, University of Tweenty

Goguen, J.A. & Linde, C. (1993). Techniques for Requirements Elicitation, *Proceedings of IEEE International Symposium on Requirements Engineering*, pp. 152-164, January 4-6, 1993

Gotel, O.C.Z. & Finkelstein, A.C.W. (1994). An Analysis of the Requirements Traceability Problem, *Proceedings of the 1st International Conference on Requirements Engineering (ICRE 1994)*, pp. 94-101, Colorado Springs, Colorado, U.S.A., April 18-22, 1994

Gruber, T.R. (1993). A Translation Approach to Portable Ontology Specifications. *Knowledge Acquisition*, Vol. 5, No. 2, pp. 199-220

Grunbacher, P.; Egyed, A. & Medvidovic, N. (2004). Reconciling Software Requirements and Architectures with Intermediate Models. *Journal for Software and System Modeling (SoSyM)*, Vol. 3, No. 3, pp. 235-253

Haase, P.; Siebes, R. & Harmelen, F.v. (2008). Expertise-Based Peer Selection in Peer-to-Peer Networks. *Knowledge and Information Systems*, Vol. 15, No. 1, pp. 75-107

Hamdan, K. & Khatib, H.E. (2006). A Software Cost Ontology System for Assisting Estimation of Software Project Effort for Use with Case-Based Reasoning, *Innovations in Information Technology*, pp. 1-5

Hepp, M.; Leukel, J. & Schmitz, V. (2007). A Quantitative Analysis of Product Categorization Standards: Content, Coverage, and Maintenance of eCl@ss, UNSPSC, eOTD, and the RosettaNet Technical Dictionary. *Knowledge and Information Systems*, Vol. 13, No. 1, pp. 77-114

Jung, J.J. (2009). Consensus-Based Evaluation framework for Distributed Information Retrieval Systems. *Knowledge and Information Systems*, Vol. 18, No. 2, pp. 199-211

Jurisica, I.; Mylopoulos, J. & Yu, E. (2004). Ontologies for Knowledge Management: An Information Systems Perspective. *Knowledge and Information Systems*, Vol. 6, No. 4, pp. 380-401

Kaiya, H. & Saeki, M. (2005). Ontology Based Requirements Analysis: Lightweight Semantic Processing Approach, *Proceedings of the Fifth International Conference on Quality Software (QSIC 2005)*, pp. 223-230

Miller, G.A. (1990). WordNet: An On-line Lexical Database. *International Journal of Lexicography*, Vol. 3, No. 4, pp. 235-312

Miller, G.A. (1995). WordNet: A Lexical Database for English. *Communications of the ACM*, Vol. 38, No. 11, pp. 39-41

Mylopoulos, J.; Borgida, A.; Jarke, M. & Koubarakis, M. (1990). Telos: Representing Knowledge about Information Systems. *ACM Transactions on Information Systems (TOIS)*, Vol. 8, No. 4, pp. 325-362

Paetsch, F.; Eberlein, A. & Maurer, F. (2003). Requirements Engineering and Agile Software Development, *Proceedings of the Twelfth IEEE International Workshops on Enabling Technologies: Infrastructure for Collaborative Enterprises (WET ICE 2003)*, pp. 308–313, June 9-11, 2003

Rich, C. & Feldman, Y.A. (1992). Seven Layers of Knowledge Representation and Reasoning in Support of Software Development. *IEEE Transactions on Software Engineering*, Vol. 18, No. 6, pp. 451-469

Robillard, P.N. (1999). The Role of Knowledge in Software Development. *Communications of the ACM*, Vol. 42, No. 1, pp. 87-92

Spanoudakis, G.; Finkelstein, A. & Till, D. (1999). Overlaps in Requirements Engineering. *Automated Software Engineering*, Vol. 6, No. 2, pp. 171-198

Studer, R.; Benjamins, V.R. & Fensel, D. (1998). Knowledge Engineering: Principles and Methods. *Data and Knowledge Engineering*, Vol. 25, pp. 161-197

Wongthongtham, P.; Chang, E. & Cheah, C. (2005). Software Engineering Sub-Ontology for Specific Software Development, *Proceedings of the 2005 29th Annual IEEE/NASA Software Engineering Workshop (SEW 2005)*, pp. 27-33

Wongthongtham, P.; Kasisopha, N.; Chang, E. & Dillon, T. (2008). A Software Engineering Ontology as Software Engineering Knowledge Representation, *Proceedings of the Third International Conference on Convergence and Hybrid Information Technology (ICCIT 2008)*, pp. 668-675, November 11-13, 2008

Yang, H.; Cui, Z. & O'Brien, P. (1999). Extracting Ontologies from Legacy Systems for Understanding and Re-Engineering, *Proceedings of the Twenty-Third Annual International Conference on Computer Software and Applications*, pp. 21-26

12

Classifying Expertise in a Special Interest Group Knowledge Portal Using a Point-Based Semi-Automatic Expertise (PBASE) Method

Aisyah Ismail[1], Shahida Sulaiman[1], Maziani Sabudin[1],
Rosni Abdullah[1] and Sarina Sulaiman[2]
Universiti Sains Malaysia[1], Universiti Teknologi Malaysia[2]
Malaysia

1. Introduction

Knowledge is information and skills acquired through experience or education. We live in the knowledge era where knowledge is available almost everywhere in abundance. Therefore, knowledge should not be neglected; it needs to be shared and exchanged. Based on Newman and Conrad (1999), knowledge management is a discipline that seeks to improve the performance of individuals and organizations by maintaining and leveraging the present and future value of knowledge assets.

Knowledge portal is an enhancement of the ordinary web portal. While the web portal focuses on offering users a broad array of resources and services, the knowledge portal does not only offer the resources and services, it also acts as a knowledge repository where it will extract and analyze knowledge submitted among its community members. According to Niwa (1990), a knowledge sharing paradigm perceives knowledge supplier as the same set of system users who use the knowledge base system. Hence, knowledge portal is one of the means for knowledge sharing.

Based on Giarratano and Riley (1998), there are three ways to represent knowledge: rules, frames and semantic nets. Rules are the most common type of knowledge representation. Rules are easy to implement due to its straightforward structure. However, ordering of the rules is important. Frames represent related knowledge about an object. Frames are easy to understand and they allow unrestrained alteration or cancellation of slots. Frames are suitable to describe a mechanical device. Semantic nets are simple, economical and relatively intuitive representation form. The structure of semantic nets is denoted by nodes and arcs as shown in Fig. 1. This research will use semantic nets to represent its knowledge because it is easy to be implemented and manipulated due to its flexibility to cluster related knowledge in our problem domain.

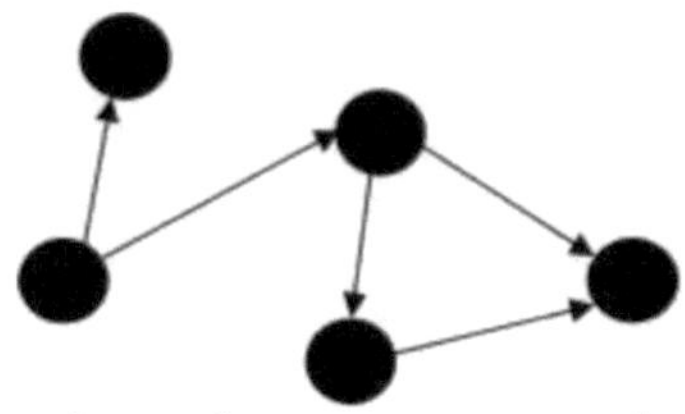

Fig. 1. Semantic nets consist of nodes and arcs to represent knowledge

In a Special Interest Group (SIG) knowledge portal, people from various backgrounds gather for several reasons. For instance, students join a SIG to derive some guidance from people who are already in the industry. They can also be experts in certain fields who are willing to answer questions from anyone and share their expertise. On the other hand, there are also some people who join the portal simply to make new friends with others who have the same interest. Likewise, these people posses knowledge and they are willing and eager to share their knowledge with each other through this online community.
Having people with various backgrounds in the community, we find the need to classify the users' expertise. Knowledge can be organized by classifying expertise of the user. In other words, users' expertise is the knowledge in the portal. When users join the portal for the first time, they may want to find other users' who share the same interests and problems. They may also want to seek help with their problems by looking for someone in the portal who is an expert in a certain field. Classification of the users' expertise is a very crucial task. Hence, we anticipate the expertise classification of the SIG knowledge portal will ensure the convenience of the members to exchange their knowledge and seek help among various expertise levels.
In Section 2 we will discuss the related work and the problems that motivate this study. Section 3 will describe the proposed method, followed by Section 4 that which explains will explain the implementation of the proposed solution. Section 5 will explain the qualitative evaluation of the proposed method. Finally, we will conclude our work in Section 6.

2. The Motivation

Online communities are not much different from other real world communities. Both communities consist of people who are tied together by their interests. In an online community, a group of people from different backgrounds are strangers to each other and this makes them become keen to get some information about the people in their community. Knowing one's level of expertise will make knowledge sharing and discussion more meaningful. Usually, the portal will state users' level of expertise for all community members to view. This section will discuss the existing classification methods in Web portals and the related work in classifying expertise in SIG portals.

2.1 Existing SIG portals

Both ITTutor.net (2009) and Computer Forum (2009) is popular web portals with registered users more than 40,000 and the number of members keep increasing. The portals rank users based on the number of posts they make in the portal in which the more forums posted, the higher users' rank will be. By doing so, even when users post query on a certain topic or post something irrelevant to the topic, users' rank will increase. Given a scenario where *A*,

who is a total beginner, posts a lot of queries in the forum without really contributing anything. Then there is *B*, who on contrary answers other users query in the forum. However, the number of *A*'s posts are larger than *B*'s posts. Based on the existing ranking approach, *A* will be ranked higher than *B*, which is inappropriate and misleading.
In ITTutor.net (2009), there are three ways to identify users' position in the portal (See Fig. 2). They are users' status, military-based ranks and rating from other users in the portal. Users' status will be assigned *Core, Ahli Biasa* (Normal Member), *Pengendali* (Administrator), *Ahli Professional* (Professional Member) or *Ahli* (Member). However, the users' status is not used to classify the users' expertise.

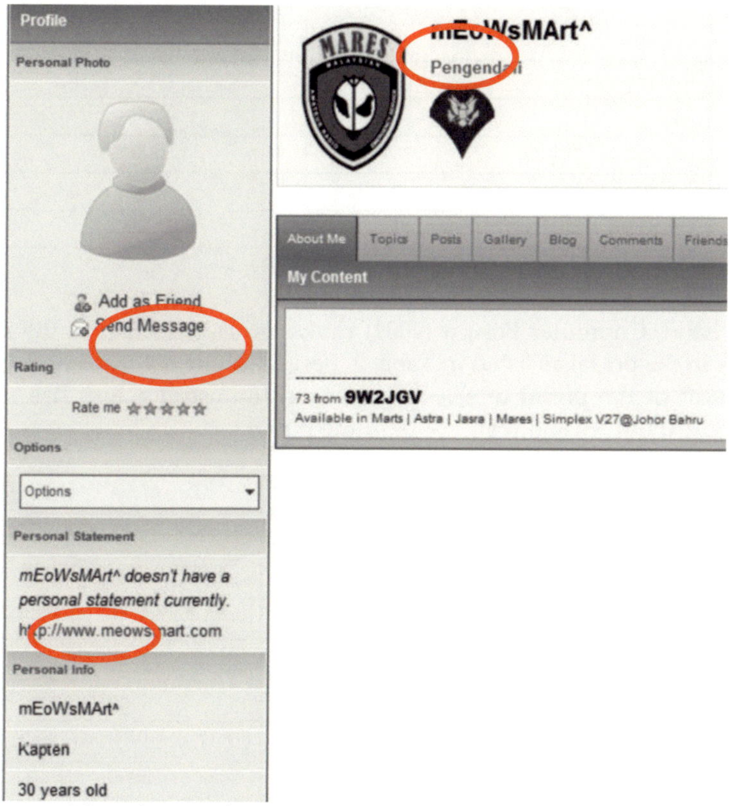

Fig. 2. Three ways to identify users' position in ITTutor.net (2009)

Instead military-based ranks as listed in Table 1 are used to rank the users in the portal. Users are ranked based on points they collected in the portal. The rating function will collect points given by other users in the portal and will be presented using 5-star rating. The three ways (users' status, military-based ranks and rating from other users in the portal) to identify users' position in the portal, will lead to users' confusion of the actual users' level of expertise.

Rank	Minimum Points
Kadet	0
Korporal	50
Sarjan	100
Staf Sarjan	150
Sarjan Mejar	200
Pegawai Waran 1	300
Pegawai Waran 2	400
Leftenan Muda	500
Leftenan	1000
Kapten	1500
Mejar	2500
Leftenan Kolonel	3000
Kolonel	3500
Certified ITTutor Professional	10000

Table 1. Military-based rank used in ITTutor.net (2009)

On the other hand, Computer Forum (2009) ranks its users based on the minimum posts made by users in the portal as listed in Table 2. Besides, there are also special ranks given by the administrator of the portal to selected users. Administrator also has the right to ban users who violate the rules and regulations of the portal.

Rank	Minimum Posts
New Member	0
Bronze Member	25
Silver Member	100
Gold Member	250
Platinum Member	500
Diamond Member	1000
Unspecified by computerforum.com	2000
Unspecified by computerforum.com	4000
Unspecified by computerforum.com	6000
Unspecified by computerforum.com	8000
Unspecified by computerforum.com	10000

Table 2. Ranks in Computer Forum (2009)

2.2 Expertise classification methods

The existing methods include that of Zhang *et al.* (2007) who proposed z-score measures, and ExpertiseRank that was based on PageRank algorithm proposed by Page *et al.* (1998). In the work of Zhang *et al.* (2007), the proposed algorithms were compared with Hypertext

Induced Topic Selection (HITS) of Kleinberg (1999) and simple statistical measures in a Java forum of an e-community to analyze the relative expertise of different users. The evaluation showed that both ExpertiseRank and z-score performed the best in e-community with different characteristics.

The z-score measures (Zhang *et al.*, 2007) combine both the asking and replying patterns. For example if users ask the same number of queries and answers, the z-score will be close to 0. If they answer more than asking questions, the z-score will be positive otherwise it will be negative. In addition, ExpertiseRank (Zhang *et al.*, 2007) increases expertise scores using question-answer network. For instance if *A* is able to answer *B*'s questions, and *C* is able to answer *B*'s questions, then *C*'s expertise rank should be promoted because *C* is able to answer *B*'s question where *B* also happens to be someone who has some expertise. Nevertheless, the measures produced are still questionable, as the quality of the answers is not considered in the measures.

On the other hand, HITS (Kleinberg, 1999) rate e-community users based on their authority and hub values in the community network nodes. Authority value is the sum of the scaled hubs values that point to the user and hub value is the sum of the scaled authority values of the user. Users with the highest authority score are experts in the community whilst users with the highest hub values are beginners who have good contact with the experts. Yet the setting of values for authority and hub could be affected if the actual contents of network nodes are of low quality that cause the increased number of authority and hub values when more unnecessary communication occurs.

Another work by Löser and Tempich (2005) suggested three semantic overlay layers to give scores to e-community peers using peer monitor based on the frequency to answer a query either as responses to information requests, asking similar questions, providing related documents and asking questions of diverse topics in the past. Peer monitor is a good way that needs users' intervention to rank the peers. However the peers may give unjustified scores that cause discrepancies in the peer monitor.

Hence, this research proposes a point-based semi-automatic expertise classification that employs z-score of Zhang *et al.* (2007). The score is mapped to a 5-scale point with the combination of a manual classification towards the answers given by the members of a SIG e-community.

3. Point-Based Semi-Automatic Expertise (PBASE) classification method

The proposed work is called Point-Based Semi-Automatic Expertise (PBASE) classification method. This is a two-way classification method in which the knowledge portal will automatically classify users' expertise level based on users' interaction in the portal and users' rating. PBASE method consists of two parts; automatic classification using z-score measures of Zhang *et al.* (2007) and manual classification using users' rating. PBASE method takes the average of the two parts as the users' level of expertise. Users are classified as beginner, intermediate and expert based on the accumulated points.

There are two types of post in the portal. They are 'query' and 'answer' posts. The 'query' post is made by a user to ask questions under a certain topic. On the other hand, 'answer' post is a post that answers questions to the 'query' post. Logically, users who make more 'answer' posts are experts and users who make more 'query' posts are beginners in the portal. This research will be using the z-score measures as introduced by Zhang *et al.* (2007) to classify users in the portal.

$$\sum_{i=1}^{n} Z_i = \frac{a_i - q_i}{\sqrt{a_i + q_i}} \tag{1}$$

Let Z_i be the z-score for user *i*, *i* =1 until *n* where *n* is the number of users, *a* is the number of 'answer' post made by a user and *q* is the number of 'query' post made by a user.
Once the z-score for all users are calculated, the value will be sorted in ascending order and will be mapped to an appropriate point as illustrated in Fig. 3. The top 20% of the users will be given 5 points. The last 20% of the users will be given 1 point. The other users will be given points as shown in Fig. 3. The top 20% of the users (based on an ascending order of calculated z-score) are the active contributors in the portal and will be given 5 points each.
The rationale behind this mapping system is that the experts are always the active contributors of the portal. This means, even when a user is an expert but if the user stops contributing to the portal, the user's level of expertise may drop if there are other users who contribute more. If there is a tie for the highest contributor, both users will be given 5 points.

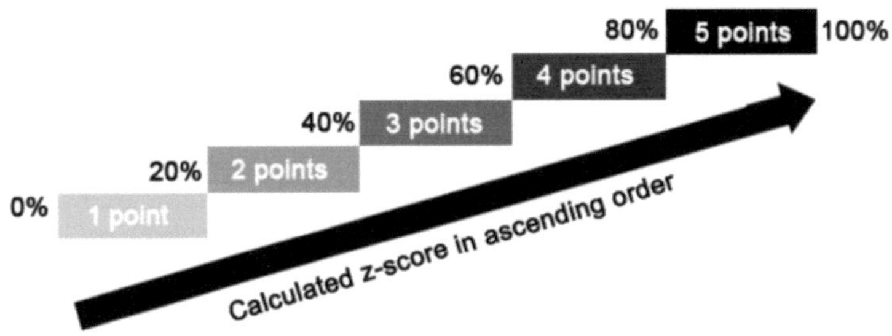

Fig. 3. Mapping of the z-score measures into a five-point scale

Table 3 shows an example of mapping the z-score measures. Let U_i be the users, *i* = 1 until *n* where *n* is the number of users, *q* is the number of queries posted, *a* is the number of answers posted, *Z* is the z-score measures (Zhang *et al.*, 2007) and *M* is the mapped z-score.
When users view 'answer' posts in the portal, they are required to rate by the scales: 0 (Unacceptable), 1 (Poor), 2 (Fair), 3 (Average), 4 (Very Good) or 5 (Excellent). By doing so, the sender of the post will receive points given by the other users. We treat all post equally, thus the user rating points, *R* is calculated by dividing the total points collected for each user, *T* with the numbers of users who make the rating, *N*. The purpose of user rating, *R* is to counter check the automatic classification using z-score measure (Zhang *et al.*, 2007).

$$\sum_{i=1}^{n} R_i = \frac{T_i}{N_i} \tag{2}$$

The final points (for each user); F is the average of the sum of mapped z-score, M and users' rating, R. The mapping of the final points, F to the expertise level, L is: expert E (4 or 5 points), intermediate I (2 or 3 points) and beginner B (0 or 1 points).

$$\sum_{i=1}^{n} F_i = \frac{M_i + R_i}{2} \tag{3}$$

				Z-score in ascending order		
U_i	q	a	Z	U_i	Z	M
U_0	0	0	0	U_0	0	0
U_1	5	0	-2.24	U_6	-7.07	1
U_2	0	5	2.24	U_9	-4.08	1
U_3	5	5	0	U_1	-2.24	2
U_4	10	5	-1.29	U_4	-1.29	2
U_5	5	10	1.29	U_3	0	3
U_6	50	0	-7.07	U_8	0	3
U_7	0	50	7.07	U_5	1.29	4
U_8	50	50	0	U_2	2.24	4
U_9	100	50	-4.08	U_{10}	4.08	5
U_{10}	50	100	4.08	U_7	7.07	5

Table 3. An example of mapping the z-score values to a five-point scale

Fig. 4 illustrates an overview of PBASE. Let U_i be the users, i = 1 until n where n is the total number of users, q is the number of queries posted, a is the number of answers posted, Z is the z-score measures (Zhang *et al.*, 2007), M is the mapped z-score, R is the users' rating, F is the final points and L is the level of expertise {B: Beginner, I: Intermediate, E: Expert}.

An example of classification using PBASE is shown in Table 4. Based on PBASE method, the user rating, R played an important role in classifying the users' expertise level. In the case of U_9, although the mapped z-score is the lowest (1 point), the users' expertise can still be promoted through the rating. For U_1 and U_6, the user rating, R will be automatically set to zero since the users do not make any 'answer' post and U_0 is an example of users who do not contribute anything in the SIG.

In addition, users are also allowed to flag posts if they find it inappropriate to the topic. After users flags certain posts, the administrator of the portal will be notified to take further action. Through the rating and flagging process, the users of the community are also contributing in giving point to users. As a result, members of the community also contribute to classify users' level of expertise in the portal.

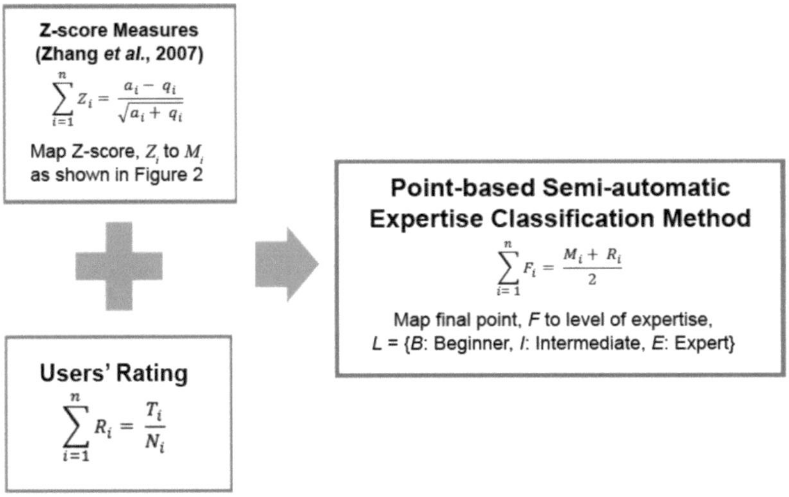

Fig. 4. Measures by PBASE method

4. Implementation and results

This research will use software engineering as the domain problem. We find that software engineering is an interesting domain as it concerns the creation and maintenance of software application by applying technologies and practices from computer sciences, project management, engineering, application domains, and other fields. The proposed PBASE method is applied in an existing web portal for software engineers in Malaysia called Malaysian Software Engineering Interest Group (MySEIG). The online interest group was founded in mid 2005 to provide a platform for software engineers to share knowledge, ideas and experience related to software engineering issues (MySEIG, 2009).

4.1 Knowledge representation

The field topics in MySEIG are based on Software Engineering Body of Knowledge or SWEBOK (Abran *et al.*, 2004) as listed in Table 5. For the convenience of MySEIG users to discuss common knowledge without specific software engineering topic, a general field named 'Others' is added.

Users are allowed to choose one or more field of interest from the listed topic. This means each user have a different set of field of interest. Example of users' set of field of interest includes: User A {Software Design, Software Testing, Software Maintenance, Others}, User B {Software Engineering Process, Software Quality, Others}, and User C {Software Requirement, Others}.

As mentioned previously, users' level of expertise reflects the knowledge in such SIG portals which the knowledge can be presented using a semantic net. Fig. 5 illustrates how semantic net represents users' level of expertise in MySEIG knowledge portal.

U_i	q	a	Z	M	R	F	L
U_0	0	0	0	0	0	0	*B*
U_1	8	0	-2.83	2	0	1	*B*
U_2	0	5	2.24	4	0	2	*I*
					1	2.5	*I*
					2	3	*I*
					3	3.5	*E*
					4	4	*E*
					5	4.5	*E*
U_3	7	7	0	3	0	1.5	*I*
					1	2	*I*
					2	2.5	*I*
					3	3	*I*
					4	3.5	*E*
					5	4	*E*
U_4	20	10	-1.83	2	0	1	*B*
					1	1.5	*I*
					2	2	*I*
					3	2.5	*I*
					4	3	*I*
					5	3.5	*E*
U_5	5	10	1.29	4	0	2	*I*
					1	2.5	*I*
					2	3	*I*
					3	3.5	*E*
					4	4	*E*
					5	4.5	*E*
U_6	40	0	-6.32	1	0	0.5	*B*
U_7	0	60	7.75	5	0	2.5	*I*
					1	3	*I*
					2	3.5	*E*
					3	4	*E*
					4	4.5	*E*
					5	5	*E*
U_8	30	30	0	3	0	1.5	*I*
					1	2	*I*
					2	2.5	*I*
					3	3	*I*
					4	3.5	*E*
					5	4	*E*
U_9	110	40	-5.72	1	0	0.5	*B*
					1	1	*B*
					2	1.5	*I*
					3	2	*I*
					4	2.5	*I*
					5	3	*I*
U_{10}	60	150	6.21	5	0	2.5	*I*
					1	3	*I*
					2	3.5	*E*
					3	4	*E*
					4	4.5	*E*
					5	5	*E*

Table 4. An example of classification

No	Topic
1	Software Configuration Management
2	Software Construction
3	Software Design
4	Software Engineering Management
5	Software Engineering Process
6	Software Engineering Tools and Methods
7	Software Maintenance
8	Software Quality
9	Software Requirement
10	Software Testing
11	Others

Table 5. Field of interest in MySEIG based on SWEBOK (Abran *et al.,* 2004)

4.2 Classification Process Using PBASE

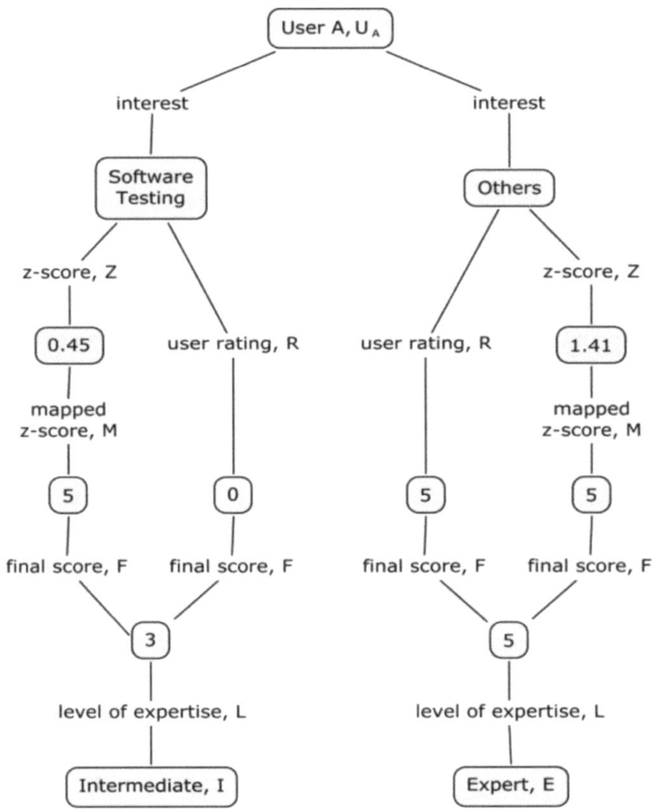

Fig. 5. Example of knowledge representation using semantic net

The first step of PBASE method in MySEIG knowledge portal is to calculate the z-score of each user. In order to calculate the z-score, we have to identify the type of posts or forums created. When users create a new post, they are required to choose the type of post from the dropdown list topic as illustrated in Fig. 6.
There are six types of post the users can choose from. The six types can be categorized into two; 'query' post and 'answer' post. The 'query' post include 'request', 'announcement' and 'question' while 'answer' post could be either 'opinion', 'information' or 'answer'. The default post is 'request'.
Then we can calculate z-score measures (Zhang *et al.*, 2007). After z-score values are calculated for every user under a certain field, we can map the z-score values to the five-point scale as shown in Fig. 3.
PBASE is a two-way classification method where its users also take part in the classification process. When users view 'answer' post, they are required to rate by the scales: 0 (Unacceptable), 1 (Poor), 2 (Fair), 3 (Average), 4 (Very Good) or 5 (Excellent) as shown in Fig. 7. Users also can contribute in the classification process by flagging post that they find inappropriate to the topic as in Fig. 7.

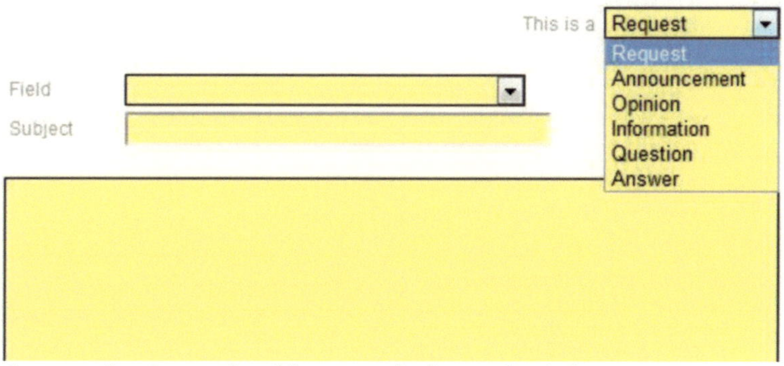

Fig. 6. Types of post to be determined by users before submitting a post

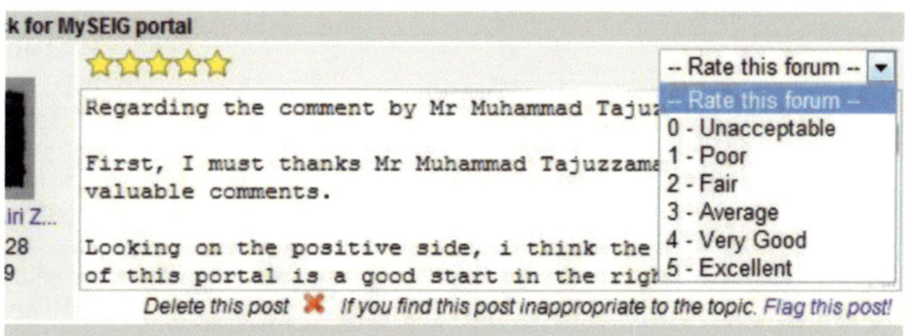

Fig. 7. Users' post that can be rated by other members in MySEIG knowledge portal

The z-score mapping in MySEIG by default will be as in Fig. 3 but the admin can change the z-score mapping as shown in Fig. 8. Admin also can reset the z-score mapping to a default value and the classification for each user will be recalculated.

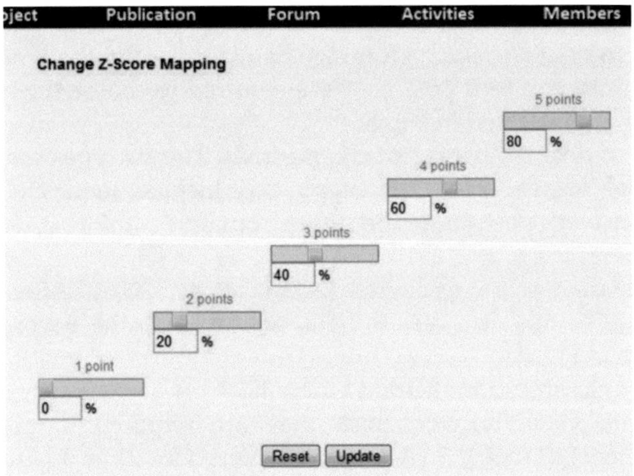

Fig. 8. Administrator can change the percentage of the five-point scale in z-score mapping

5. Qualitative evaluation

Characteristic	ITTutor.net (2009)	Computer Forum (2009)	PBASE
Direction of classification	One-way classification method where the users are not involved in the classification process	One-way classification approach. The users are not involved in the classification process but the administrator has the privilege in awarding selected users.	two-way classification method where users are involved in the classification process
Basis of classification	Classify its users based on the number of posts they created in the forum (See Table 1 and Table 2)		
Differences in type of post	No. All post treated equally and will be included in the classification process		Yes. The z-score measures will calculate the distribution of the questions and answers of each user
Competitiveness to be an expert	Not available because the expertise level of the user will not dropped.	Not available because the expertise level of the user will not dropped but users can be banned by the administrator if they are found violating the rules and regulation of the portal.	Yes because the expertise level of the user can dropped if the user stop contributing in the portal. Experts in the portal are always the current active contributors in the portal.

Table 6. Comparison of classification approaches

Comparison of PBASE with existing expertise classification method used in ITTutor.net (2009) and Computer Forum (2009) is listed in the following aspects:

(a) Direction of classification
(b) Basis of classification
(c) Differences in type of posts
(d) Competitiveness to be an expert

6. Conclusions and future works

Instead of using the conventional way to classify users based on the number of posts, this research proposes a two-way classification method called Point-Based Semi-automatic Expertise (PBASE). By proposing the PBASE method, we hope to maximize the capability of SIG knowledge portal for the convenience of its community members to seek help among the members.

Furthermore, we have identified that there is a limitation in identifying the type of posts. Based on the current approach, users are required to state the type of post. Thus as part of the future work, we plan to integrate Natural Language Processing (NLP) technique with PBASE. Hence, users will no longer need to state the type of post since NLP will automatically analyze and identify the type of posts.

Other future work include that the system should suggest automatically to other members list of people who in the same area or expert. In other word it involves either expert system or decision support system concept.

7. Acknowledgements

This research is partially supported by research university grant of Universiti Sains Malaysia, 1001/PKOMP/817002.

8. Reference

Abran, A. *et al.* (eds.), *Guide to Software Engineering Body of Knowledge SWEBOK: 2004 Version*, USA, IEEE Computer Society Press, 2004.

Computer Forum, Jelsoft Enterprises Ltd., 2009, http://www.computerforum.com.

Giarratano, J. and Riley, G., *Expert Systems Principles and Programming: 3rd Edition*, PWS Publishing Co., London, 1998.

ITTutor.net, 2009, http://ittutor.net.

Kleinberg, J. M., "Hubs, Authorities, and Communities", *ACM Computing Surveys*, Volume 31, Article No. 5, 1999.

Löser, A. and Tempich, C., "On Ranking Peers in Semantic Overlay Networks", 2005.

MySEIG, 2009, http://www.myseig.org.

Newman, B. (Bo), and Conrad, K. W., "A Framework for Characterizing Knowledge Management Methods, Practices, and Technologies", *The Knowledge Management Forum*, 1999.

Niwa, K., "Towards Successful Implementation of Knowledge-Based Systems: Expert Systems vs. Knowledge Sharing Systems", *IEEE Transactions on Engineering Management*, 37(4), November 1990.

Page, L., Brin, S., Motwani, R. and Winograd, T., "The PageRank Citation Ranking: Bringing Order to the Web", *Stanford Digital Library Technologies Project*, 1998.

Zhang, J., Ackerman, M. S., and Adamic, L., "Expertise Networks in Online Communities: Structure and Algorithms", *Proceedings of the International World Wide Web Conference WWW 2007*, ACM Press, 2007, pp. 221-230.

13

Towards the Optimization of Client Transport Services: Negotiating by Ontology Mapping Approach between Mobile Agents

Sawsan Saad, Hayfa Zgaya and Slim Hammadi
LAGIS UMR 8146, Central School of Lille
France

1. Introduction

This work belongs to the national French project VIATIC.MOBILITE from the industrial cluster I-trans*, which is an initiative bringing together major French players in rail technology and innovative transport systems. In fact, Transport users require relevant, interactive and instantaneous information during their travels. A Transport Multimodal Information System (TMIS) can offer a support tool to response and help network customers to make good decisions when they are travelling providing them all needed information in any existent and chosen format (text, multimedia…), in addition, through different handheld wireless devices such as PDAs, laptops, cell phones, etc. So in a previous work (Zgaya, 2007a), we proposed a Multi Information System (MIS) based on a special kind of software agent called Mobile Agent (MA) (Carzaniga et al., 1997).The realization was successful, thanks to a two-level optimization approach (Zgaya et al., 2007b), where the system optimizes the selection of nodes to answer the different requests. Our customer is satisfied if he obtains rapidly a response to his request, with a suitable cost.
But in the case of network errors, the MAs begin the negotiation process which allows new assignments to cancelled services to available network nodes. For this purpose, we designed a negotiation protocol intended for the transport area which permits to the agents to negotiate when perturbations may exist (Zgaya et al., 2007c). Our protocol uses messages to exchange the information. Those messages are exchanged between initiators and the participants in the negotiation process. Indeed, this protocol has studied before only the cases of the simple messages without using ontology and did not include the solutions when the participant agents did not understand the messages sent from the initiators agent. Thus, we propose an approach that will improve the negotiation protocol through the multi-agent systems by adding ontology in the negotiation process. Our solution bases on the knowledge management system to facilitate automatically the management of the

* http://www.i-trans.org

negotiation messages and to solve the semantic heterogeneity. In our proposal, we incorporate architecture for negotiation process with that uses an Ontology-based Knowledge Management System (NOKMS) (Saad et al., 2008c). The architecture consists of three layers: (Negotiation Layer (NL), Semantic Layer (SEL) and Knowledge Management System Layer (KMSL)). But in this work we talked about only (NL and SEL) that describes the negotiation process as well as illustrates the different messages types by using the different ontologies. Our proposed NOKMS improves the communications between heterogeneous negotiation mobile agents and the the quality of service (QoS) response time with the best cost in order to satisfy the transport customers
This paper is organized in six parts, as follow: in the second section, we discuss some related work. Then, we illustrate the ontology mapping idea. We present in section 4 the global system architecture describing its general functioning. In section 5, we illustrate our negotiation protocol with using the ontology approach. A case study will discuss in (Section 6). Finally, conclusion and prospects are mentioned in last section.

2. Related Work

Negotiation is a process by which two or more parties make a joint decision (Zhang et al., 2005). Negotiation has been done by different research works; (Bravo et al. 2005) presented a semantic proposition for manipulating the lack of understanding messages between the seller and buyer agents during the exchange of messages in a negotiation process. Otherwise, (Zgaya et al., 2007c) provided a negotiation protocol for the transport area to facilitate the communications between the agents. A generic negotiation model for multi-agent systems has been proposed by (Verrons et al., 2004), built on three levels: a communication level, a negotiation level and a strategic level and the later is the only level reserved for the application. In addition, they have illustrated their negotiation protocol which based on a contract which in turn based on negotiation too. Negotiations can be used to resolve conflicts in a wide variety of multi-agent domains. In (Jennings et al., 2000), an application include conflicts illustrated the usage of joint resources or task assignments, conflicts concerning document allocation in multi-server environments and conflicts between a buyer and a seller in electronic commerce.
For ontology approach, it has an important role in the multi-agent systems. In fact, there are many of definitions of the ontology according to the different domains where we use it. Firstly, Ontology is the branch of philosophy which considers the nature and essence of things. From the point of view of Artificial intelligence, it deals with reasoning about models of the world. A commonly agreed definition of ontology is: '*ontology is an explicit and formal specification of a conceptualization of a domain of interest*' (Gruber, 1993). In this definition, a *conceptualization* refers to an abstract model of some phenomenon in the world which identifies the concepts that are relevant to the phenomenon; *explicit* means that the type of concepts used, and that the constraints on their use are explicitly defined; *formal* refers to the fact that an ontology should be machine-readable, and *shared* reflects the notion that an ontology captures consensual knowledge, that is, it is not private to some individual, but not accepted by a group(Studer et al., 1998), (Obitko et al., 2004).
Within a multi-agent system, agents are characterized by different views of the world that are explicitly defined by ontologies, that is views of what the agent recognizes to be the concepts describing the application domain which is associated with the agent together with

their relationships and constraints (Falasconi et al., 1996). Interoperability between agents is achieved through the reconciliation of these views of the world by a commitment to common ontologies that permit agents to interoperate and cooperate while maintaining their autonomy. In open systems, agents are associated with knowledge sources which are diverse in nature and have been developed for different purposes. Knowledge sources embedded in a dynamic

3. Ontology Mapping

Ontology mapping process aims to define a mapping between terms of source ontology and terms of target ontology. The mapping result can be used for ontology merging, agent communication, query answering, or for navigation on the Semantic Web.
The approach for ontology mapping varies from lexical to semantic and structural levels. Moreover, the mapping process can be grouped into data layer, ontology structure, or context layer. The process of ontology mapping has five steps: information ontology, obtaining similarity, semantic mapping execution and mapping post-processing (Maedche and Motik, 2003). The most important step of ontology mapping is the computation of conceptual similarity. First define similarity:
Sim: w1 w2 o1 o2 → [0, 1], the similar value from 0 to1.
Sim (A, B) denote the similarity of A and B. w1 and w2 are two term sets. O1 and O2 are two ontologies.
Sim (e, f) =1: denote concept e and concept f are completely sameness.
Sim (e, f) =0: denote concept e and concept f are completely dissimilar.

4. The Proposal Architecture

4.1 General System

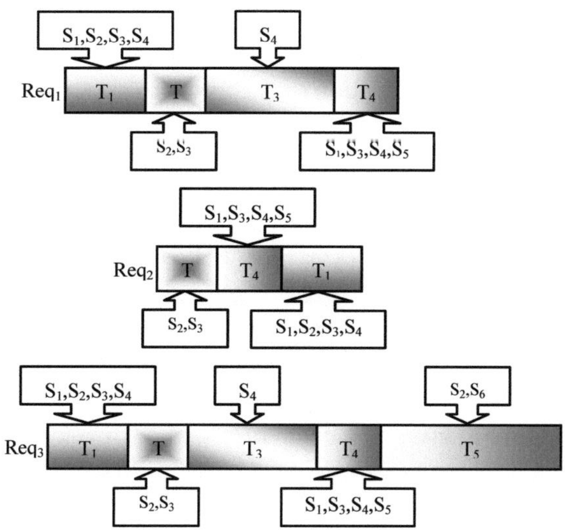

Fig. 1. Nodes identification

Firstly, we will illustrate the problem by which our TMIS bases. From general point of view, our system has a two-step assignment problem: firstly the assignments of network nodes to MAs to build their initial Workplans and then, a sub-set of these nodes are selected to assign tasks. A task is an independent sub-request which belongs to one or several requests formulated simultaneously by different customers. So, information providers which propose services corresponding to identify tasks are recognized (figure 1). Consequently, nodes must be assigned to tasks in order to satisfy all connected users and respecting delays of responses and minimizing their cost (QoS).
To resolve the described problem, we have proposed a system based on the coordination of five kinds of software agents (Zgaya et al., 2007b, 2007c) (figure 2):

1) **Interface Agents (IA):** These agents interact with system users, allowing them to choose appropriate form of responses to their demands so IA agents manage requests and then display results. When a multimodal network (MN) customer access to the MIS, an agent IA deals with the formulation of his request and then sends it to an available identifier agent. This one relates to the same platform to which several users can be simultaneously connected, thus it can receive several requests formulated at the same time.
2) **Identifier agents (IdA):** This agent manages the decomposition of the requests which were formulated through a same short period of time ε* (ε-simultaneous requests). The decomposition process generates a set of sub-requests corresponding, for example, to sub-routes or to well-known geographical zones. Sub-requests are elementary independent tasks to be performed by the available set of distributed nodes (information providers) through the Transport Multimodal Network (ETMN). Each node must login to the system registering all proposed services. A service corresponds to the response to a defined task with fixed cost, processing time and data size. Therefore, an agent IdA decomposes the set of existing simultaneous requests into a set of independent tasks, recognizing possible similarities in order to avoid a redundant search. The decomposition process occurs during the identification of the information providers. Finally, the agent IdA transmits cyclically all generated data to available scheduler agents. These ones must optimize the selection of providers, taking into account some system constraints
3) **Scheduler Agents (SA):** Several nodes may propose the same service with different cost and processing time and data size. The agent SA has to assign nodes to tasks minimizing total cost and processing time in order to respect due dates (data constraint). Selected set of nodes corresponds to the sequence of nodes building Workplans (routes) of the data collector agents. The agent SA has firstly to find an effective number of collector agents then he has to optimize the assignments of nodes to different tasks. This behaviour will be developed later.
4) **Intelligent Collector agents (ICA):** An agent ICA is a mobile software agent which can move from a node to another through a network in order to collect needed

* Fixed by the programmer

data. This special kind of agent is composed of data, code and a state. Collected data should not exceed a capacity threshold in order to avoid overloading the MA. Therefore, the agent SA must take into account this aspect when assigning nodes to tasks. When they come back to the system, the agents ICA must transmit collected data to available fusion agents.

5) ***Fusion Agents (FA)*:** These agents have to fusion correctly collected data in order to compose responses to simultaneous requests. The fusion procedure progresses according to the collected data availability. Each new answer component must be complementary to the already merged ones. Providers are already selected and tasks are supposed independent. Therefore, there is no possible conflict. A response to a request may be complete if a full answer is ready because all concerned components are available. It can be partial if at least a task composing the request was not treated, for example, because of an unavailable service. Finally, a response can be null if no component is available. If an answer is partial, the correspondent result is transmitted to the concerned user through the agent IA which deals with request reformulation, with or without the intervention of the user.

To respond the tasks, needed data is available through the ETMN and their collect corresponds to the jobs of ICA agents. Then, it must search the optimizing solution to solve the problem of the assignment process. This optimization is the topic of the SA behaviour explicit in the next section.

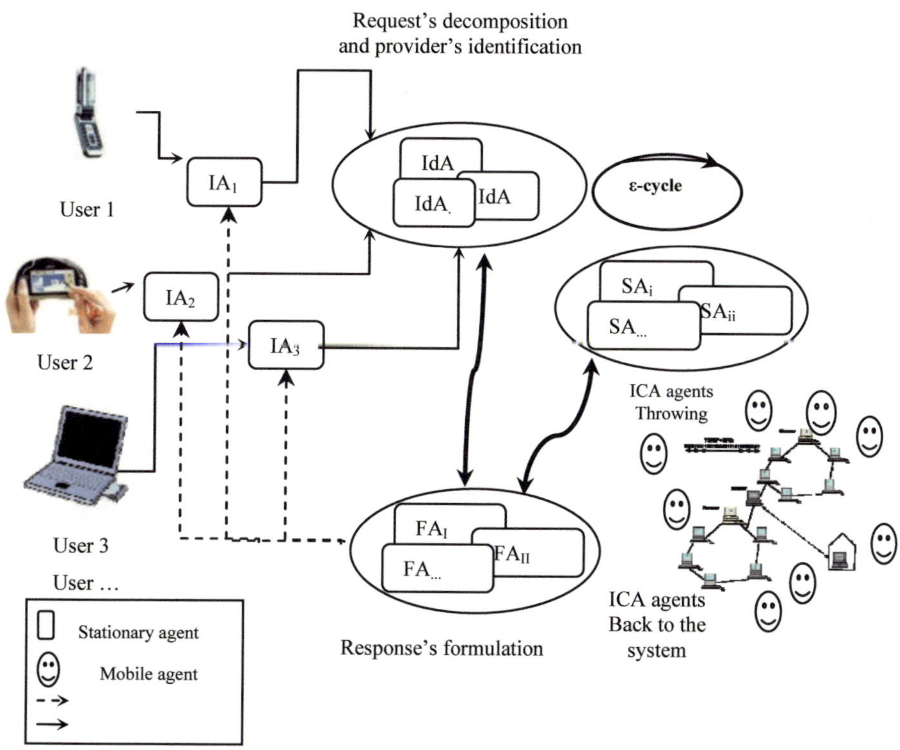

Fig. 2. Multi-Agent Approach

3.2 The Optimizing Solution by Scheduler Agents SA Behavior

Since his creation, the SA agent calculates an actual number of ICA agents that created at the same time, and then he gives everyone an Initial Workplan (IWp) which updates whenever the network status varies considerably. When the IdA agent, from the same society (we call agents IdA, SA, FA and ICA created at the instant t the agents society), gives him a number of tasks thus the SA agent has to begin the optimization process (Figure 3).

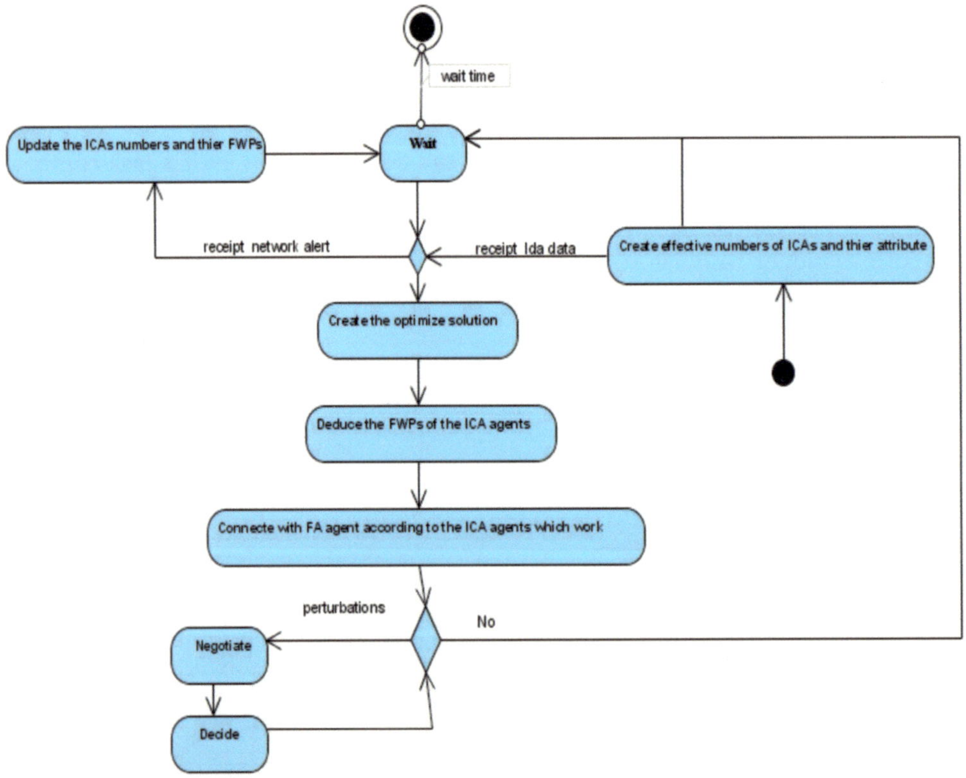

Fig. 3. SA Behaviour

The SA agent has to optimize the assignments of nodes to the exiting tasks, by minimizing total cost and processing time to respect due dates. To solve this assignment problem, we proposed a two level optimization solution, expressing the complex behaviour of an agent SA, which was already studied and implemented in previous works (Zgaya et al., 2007b, 2007c). The first level aims to find an effective number of ICA agents, building their initial Workplans in order to explore the ETMN completely (Zgaya et al., 2007b). The second level represents the data flow optimization corresponding to the nodes selection in order to increase the number of satisfied users (Zgaya et al., 2007c).This last step deduces final Workplans of ICA agents from initial ones, by using Evolutionary Algorithms (EA). So we have designed an efficient coding for a chromosome (the solution) respecting the problem constraints (Zgaya, 2007a). A possible solution is an instance of a flexible representation of the chromosome, called Flexible Tasks Assignment Representation (FeTAR). The chromosome is a matrix CH(I′×J′) where rows represent independent identified tasks (services), composing globally simultaneous requests and columns represent recognized distributed nodes (providers). Each element of the matrix specifies the assignment of a node S_j to the task T_i as follows:

$$CH[i,j] = \begin{cases} 1: \text{if } S_j \text{ is assigned to } T_i \ ; 1 \leq i \leq I' \text{ and } 1 \leq j \leq J' \\ *: \text{if } S_j \text{ may be assigned to } T_i \\ X: \text{if } S_j \text{ cannot be assigned to } T_i \end{cases}$$

We notice that each task must be assigned, so we assume that each task must be performed at least by a node, selected from a set of nodes proposing the service which corresponds to a response to the concerned task where this is the first selection step. After that, we apply the second selection step which is one of the most important aspects of all EA. It determines which individuals in the population will have all or some of its genetic material passed on the next generations. We have used random technique, to give chance to weak individuals to survey: parents are selected randomly from current population to crossover with some probability p_c ($0<p_c<1$).

In our case, we use the fitness function where a chromosome is firstly evaluated according to the number of responses which respect due dates, namely responses minimizing correspondent ending dates and respecting correspondent due dates. Then a solution is evaluated according to its cost. Therefore, a chromosome has to express ending responses date and the information cost. As we mentioned, a request req_w is decomposed into $I_{t,w}$ tasks. Therefore, the total processing time $EndReq_w$ for each req_w is computed by the means of the algorithm *fitness_1* below. This time includes only the effective processing time on the MN. We assume that, the ending date D_w corresponding to the total execution time of a request req_w, includes also the average navigation time of ICA agents. This is expressed by:

$$\gamma = \delta - \frac{\sum_{j=1}^{J} CT''_j}{J} \quad (1)$$

$$\Rightarrow \forall\ 1 \leq w \leq R,\ D_w = EndReq_w + \gamma \quad (2)$$

_Fitness_1_ algorithm

Step 1:

m' is the ICA agents number so

$\forall\ k$ with $1 \leq k \leq m'$, initialize :

- The set of tasks U_{ck} to Ø
- Total time $EndU_{ck}$ to perform U_{ck} to 0

Step 2:

Look for the set of tasks U_{ck} performed by each ICA_{ck} and their processing time *EndUk* as follows:

```
for k := 1 to m'
  for j := 1 to J'
    for i := 1 to I'
        if S_cj belongs to the Workplan of ICA_ck and S_cj is assigned to T_ci
          {
           U_ck := U_ck ∪ {T_ci};
           EndU[ck] :=EndU[ck]+P_cicj;
          }
```

Step 3:

Compute processing time of each request require the identification of ICA agents which perform tasks composing the request. Total processing time of a request is the maximum processing times of all ICA agents which perform tasks composing this request. This is calculated as follow:

```
for w := 1 to R
{
  for k := 1 to m'
    treatedAC[ck] := false;

        EndReq[w] := 0;

        i := 1;
    while i ≤ I' and ∃ k1/1 ≤ k1 ≤ m' and
        treatedAC[ck1]=false
    {
        if T_ci ∈ req_w
      {
        ck := 1;
      while k ≤ m' and T_i ∉ U_k
        ck := ck+1;//end while
       if ¬ TreatedAC[ck]
        {
        EndReq[w] := max(EndReq[w], EndU[ck]);

        TreatedAC[ck] := true;
```

```
            }//end if
        }//end if
      } //end while
    }//end outer for-loop
```

Form the other side, total cost of a request req_w is *CostReq[w]* expressed by C_w, is given by the mean of the algorithm below:

_Fitness_2_ algorithm

```
Repeat steps 1 and 2 for each request req_w (1 ≤ w ≤ R)
Step 1:
    CostReq[w] := 0
Step 2:
    for i :=1 to I'
      {
        if T_ci ∈ req_w {
          find the node S_cj (1 ≤ j ≤ J') assigned to T_ci
           in FeTAR instance
           CostRe[w] := CostRe[w] + Co_cicj
        }//end if
    }// end for
```

Knowing that by using expression (1), we can deduce ending date from fitness_1 algorithm, the new FeTAR representation of the chromosome express for each request reqw $1 \le w \le R$, its ending date and its cost.

An example of a generated FeTAR instance with I'=8 and J'=10, where the evaluation of this chromosome is illustrated by a evaluation vector which explicit: for each reqw, its total cost (Cw) and the total time required for his response (Dw). The average cost of all requests and the response time can be deducted from generated vector, can be illustrated as follows:

w	d_w	C_w	D_w
1	10	5	6
2	5	1	1
3	10	4	2
4	5	3	2
4	3	2	1
6	5	3	2

CH	S_1	S_{13}	S_{24}	S_{55}	S_{68}	S_{70}	S_{71}	S_{78}	S_{79}	S_{93}
T_8	*	*	*	*	1	*	*	*	*	*
T_{12}	*	*	*	*	x	*	*	1	*	*

T_{18}	*	1	*	*	x	*	*	*	*	*
T_{22}	*	*	*	*	x	*	1	*	*	*
T_{35}	x	*	1	x	x	x	*	*	x	x
T_{51}	x	x	*	*	x	x	x	1	*	*
T_{52}	*	*	*	1	x	x	x	x	*	*
T_{58}	*	*	*	1	x	x	*	*	*	*

Table. 1. Example of a FeTAR instance

In this work, we are interested into the interaction between SA agents and ICA agents, especially in case of some network disturbances. In that case, these two kinds of agents have to negotiate the reassignment of tasks which still need providers. We will illustrate that in the rest.

4. The Negotiation Ontology Protocol

4.1 Problem Description

Some perturbations can occur during the mobile agents moving through the distant network nodes (bottleneck, failure, crash…). In this case, the ICA agents have to avoid the unavailable nodes in their remained final Workplans. In addition, they have to change their itineraries in order to take into account the cancelled tasks which still need assignment because of the conflicts. Therefore, a new assignment process has to occur to find suitable new available providers (Saad et al., 2008a) To do this, we have to benefit of active ICA agents who are still travelling through the network and to exploit new ones otherwise. So ICA agents have to interact with SA agents in order to find suitable solution to the current situation. Thus, in (Zgaya et al., 2007c) we proposed a negotiation process inspired from the well-known contract net protocol (CNP) between the ICA agents who represent the participants of the negotiation and SA agents who are the initiators.
This protocol has studied before only the cases of the simple messages and it proposed ontology without illustrating it, and this later didn't illustrate the problem which will take place when the participants don't understand the communication messages, or when the new agent wants to participate in a negotiation process Thus agent must to understand the protocol and the communication language messages, in this case the agents need an interoperable language between themselves for understanding each other. But as we know in open and dynamic environments (such as the Web and its extension the Semantic Web) are by nature distributed and heterogeneous. In these environments ontologies are expected to complement agreed communication protocols in order to facilitate mutual understanding and interactive behaviour between such agents. Thus, agents may differ in their view of the world, creation, representation and exploration of domain ontologies they commit to. Because, for each common domain ontology; people may store their data in different structures (structural heterogeneity) (Malucelli and Oliveira, 2004). And they use different terms to represent the same concept (semantic heterogeneity). Moreover there is no formal mapping between ontologies.

4.2 Initiators

An initiator of a negotiation is a SA agent who never knows the exact position of each travelling ICA agent. However, he knows all initial Workplans schemes and the final assignments of the servers (final effective Workplans). SA agent does not need to wait for all answers to make a decision, since he can accept a subset of responses to make pressing sub-decisions; urgent actions must be made according to the current positions of ICA agents. Consequently, SA agent can make decisions every short period of time. In that case, he must update the set of services which need to be reassigned by providers through the confirmation step. After that, he has to propose a new contract according to the updated services set and to the different capabilities of the participants of the negotiation. We suppose that errors on the network are identified before that an ICA agent leaves one functioning node towards a crashed one.

4.3 Participants

For a given task, the participants may respond with a proposal or a refusal to negotiate. In our protocol we have two types of participants in negotiation process according to the SA agent propose.

4.3.1 Intelligent Collector Agents (ICAs)

A participant of a negotiation is Intelligent Collector Agents ICAs who never knows anything about the other participants of the same negotiation process. Obviously, he knows his own initial Workplan scheme and his final assignments of servers (final effective Workplan). In addition, each ICA agent has his own priorities, preferences and constraints which are dynamic, depending on the network state and on his current position in the already defined final Workplan. He has own ontology too.

- *Constraints* of an ICA agent express the tasks which he can't perform or the servers which he can't visit because they cause problems (overloading, time consuming, high latency…).
- *Priorities* express servers where the ICA agent prefers visit because they are already programmed in his remained final Workplan.
- *Preferences* express servers which are already programmed in the remained initial Workplan but not in the final one.
- *Ontology,* if we expect that all agents share same ontology which is General Ontology. The later uses the Communication vocabularies (Cv). Cv defined as the set of concepts to be used in communication and is specified as an ontology (Ocv) which is shared by agents (Diggelen et al., 2005). General Ontology defines the Cv with which queries and assertions are exchange between agents. But one of the big problems to communication-based agents is that each one uses different terms with the same meaning or the same term for different meanings. Once we took this problem as a challenge, representing these differences in a common ontology becomes essential. The ontology includes the entire domain's knowledge, which is made available to all the components active in an information system. The use of a common ontology guarantees the consistency (an expression has the same meaning for all the agents) and the compatibility (a concept is designed, for the same expression, for any agent) of the information present in the system. However, it is

not sure that all the agents will use a common ontology. Usually, each agent has its heterogeneous private ontology and it cannot fully understand other agent's ontology. In our system, each time an ICA agent receives a new contract; it analyzes it to make a decision (refusal or total/partial acceptance) according to its ontology.

4.3.2 Translation Agents (TAs)

Another participant of a negotiation is a Translation Agents TAs. TA responsible for providing the translation services that support the negotiation agents (i.e. SA agents and ICT agents).Thus, it helps solving the interoperability problems. TA uses a dictionary (or a lexical database, in our system, we use EuroWordNet) to obtain the set of synonyms terms of each term from the source ontology. The task of TA consists of applying methodology to detect semantic similarities between two concepts in the conversion between different ontologies. Once the TA has established the similarity between a pair of terms from different ontologies, this knowledge is stored in Knowledge Management System Layer (KMSL) (Saad et al., 2008b) in order to be available for future negotiation rounds. The intelligent of this system is improved occurs with time, because the matched terms is memorized. When the number of negotiations rounds increases; we aim that our system by using TA provides the following services:

- *Mapping Terms Service (MTS):* where in common domain ontology, people may store their data in different terms to represent the same concept (semantic heterogeneity).for example if we use English Transport Ontology where we defines the "Concept" (e.g., "destination"). There is the possibility when we do the negotiation process the receiver of the message don't understand this concept because it is not listed in its ontology. The correspondent concept is defined as (e.g., "arrived-City") in its private English Transport Ontology.

- *Translation Services (TS):* here we discuss the translating ontologies in the context of Multilingual Ontology Mapping. We exemplified the negotiation between two transport systems that use two different ontologies (English and French) languages, respectively. We represent as the terms "Destination" in the source ontology is mapped to the term "Arrivée" in the target ontology. These terms represent the destination areas related to client travel.

4.4 Negotiation Ontology based on Knowledge Management Systems Model (NOKMS)

Our general architecture tries to improve the work of the negotiation protocol to facilitate the communication through the agents and to solve the semantic heterogeneity by adding the Semantic Layer (SEL) and Knowledge Management Systems Layer (KMSL). Based on these changes, (Figure 4) presents the new system architecture for negotiation process which uses ontology-based knowledge management system (Saad et al., 2008c) .

We organized our architecture as follow: the first layer contains the Negotiation Layer (NL) where the SA agent sends the first massage to the ICA agents to start the negotiation process.

The second layer represents the Semantic Layer (SEL); our purpose is to find a solution especially in the case of misunderstanding of the negotiation messages among the agents.

The SEL uses a translator semantic which is Translator Agent (TA) in order to help it to translate automatically the various types of exchanges between the agents. In SEL, the translator semantic examines the level of transibility among the ontologies by sending a word to the KMSL layer which resends the set of semantically equivalences words.

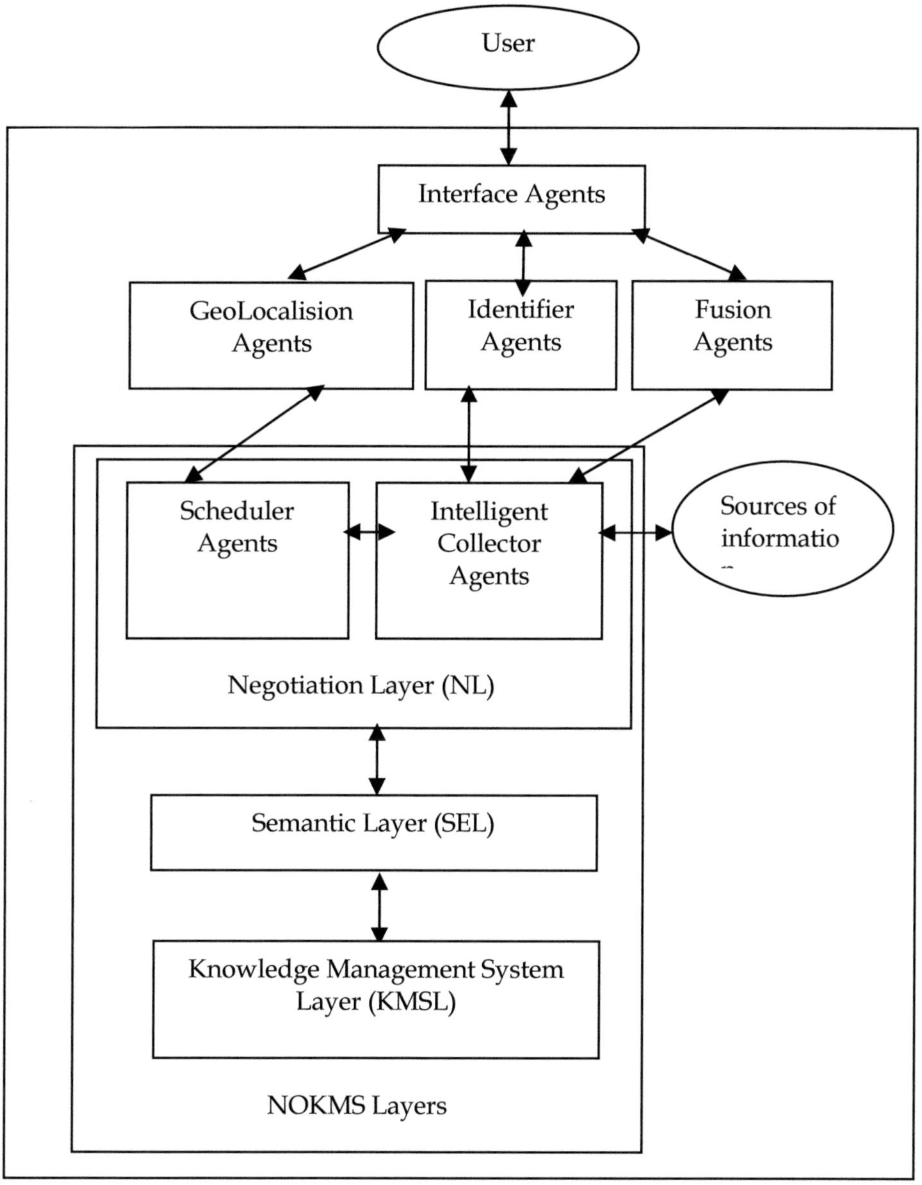

Fig. 4. Multi-agents Structure

The third one is the Knowledge Management Systems Layer (KMSL): this layer uses ontology in purpose of automatic classifying and using of the news ontologies and meta-ontologies. The architecture in this layer consists of:

1) *Domain Ontology(DOnto):* DOnto contains the list of application domains in which the ontology is applicable. By using this domain, the agents communicate with each other through common domain knowledge, in other words as mention in (Diggelen et al., 2005): a common ontology can serve as a knowledge-level specification of the ontological commitments of a set of participating agents.

2) *Ontology Services (OntoSV):* The task of OntoSV is to define the semantics of ontologies (actions, predicates used in the content of the conversation with the Agents Ontologies (AOs)) which the agents use to interact with each other and support the knowledge acquisition operations (Creation, Translation, Retrieval). OntoSV adopts Open Knowledge Base Connectivity (OKBC) knowledge model as fipa-meta-ontology (an ontology used to access the AOs).Where ,Open Knowledge Base Connectivity (OKBC) is an application programming interface (API) for knowledge representation system (KRSs) that has been developed to address the problem of KB tools reusability. The name OKBC was chosen to be analogous to ODBC (Open Database Connectivity), as used in the database community (Geiger, 1995).

3) *Knowledge Acquisitions*: are a very important part in the ontology process and it applies different operations like (Knowledge Creation, Knowledge Translation, Knowledge Retrieval), we have illustrated how we can apply those operations on the shared ontologies (languages) in (Saad et al., 2008b).

4) *Intelligent Knowledge Base (IKB):* each agent of Multi-Agent System (MAS) holds a KB which based on the domain ontology. In our IKB uses the OKBC, which in turn, connects to a wide verity of IKBs servers where these IKBs are applied the Knowledge Acquisitions.

4.5 Ontology Negotiation Process

Negotiation defines as a process whose transitions and states are described by the negotiation mechanism. From the ontology point of view, this means that modelling domain factual knowledge, that is, knowledge concerning the objective realities in the domain of interest (Chandrasekaran et al., 1998). The implementation of our negotiation process combines the Ontology Negotiation Protocol (ONP) which will interact with an additional protocol called Ontology Mapping Protocol (OMP). We will explain the two protocols later. We adopt the formula of the Agent Communication Language **ACL** messages is as follow (FIPA0081):

<Sender, Receiver, Services, Performative, Contents, Language, Ontology, Protocol>

- **Sender:** the identity of the sender of the message.
- **Receiver:** the identity of the intended recipients of the message.
- **Services:** the "yellow pages" proposed by the recipient of the message
- **Performative:** the type of the communicative act of the ACL message. The performative parameter is a required parameter of all ACL messages.

Performative = {Propose, Agree (total, Partial), Confirm, Cancel, Call for Proposal, Not Understood…}

- **Content:** the content of the message. The meaning of the content of any ACL message is intended to be interpreted by the receiver of the message.
- **Language:** the language in which the content parameter is expressed.
- **Ontology:** the ontology(s) is used to give a meaning to the symbols in the content expression (vocabulary, terms, relations…).
- **Protocol:** the protocol which is used to described by the negotiation mechanism

The usage of this formula is very easy when the agents interact by exchanging the messages which contain the same ontology. But the semantic interoperability problems take place when the sharing information and knowledge use different ontologies, or when there are multiple ontologies which resemble a universal ontology. How can we use the message formula? We well illustrate that in the rest of paper.

4.5.1 Ontology Negotiation Protocol (ONP)

The fist protocol is Ontology Negotiation Protocol (ONP) represents the general scenario of agents where the SAs agents start the negotiation process by sending the messages to the ICAs agents. As we illustrated previously, we search to find the solution when there are some network errors and the agents search to find suitable new available providers for new assignment process. Here, the ICA agents participate in the negotiation by using their languages for formulating negotiation messages in order to interact and to take the decision.
Our Ontology Negotiation protocol (ONP) (figure 5) is characterized by successive messages exchanges between SA agents and ICA agents. We designed our protocol so that a negotiation process can occur between several initiators and participants, it can be, for example, the case of simultaneous requests overlapping, but it is not the purpose of this paper. Here, we describe the ONP between a unique initiator and several participants. In our ONP, we allowed a partial agreement of the proposed contract from each ICA agent, to be confirmed partially or totally by the initiator of the negotiation (SA agent).
A renegotiation process is necessary while there are still tasks which need to be reassigned. The purpose of this solution is to allow the ICA agents to cooperate and coordinate their actions in order to find globally near-optimal robust schedules according to their priorities, preference, constraints and ontologies which depend on their current positions in their correspondent Workplans. Through the negotiation process tours, SA agents must assure reasonable total cost and time. We will detail the different exchanged messages between initiators and participants in next paragraph.

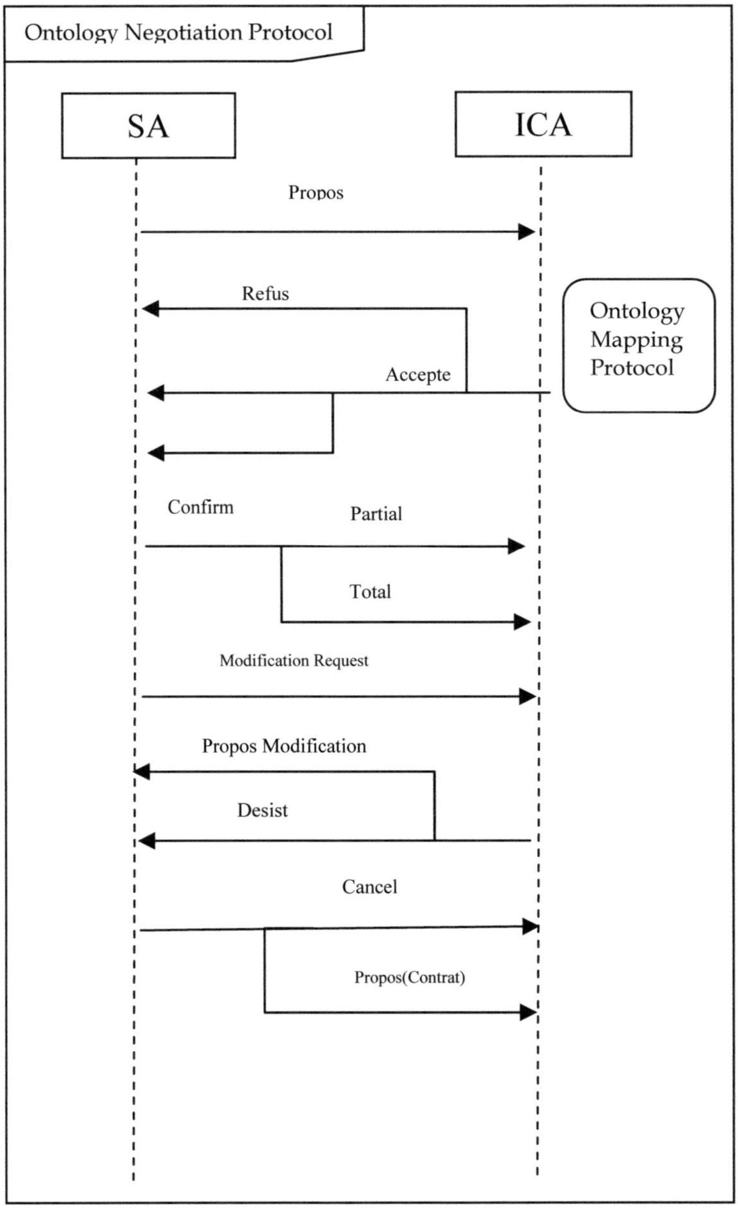

Fig. 5. ONP

4.5.3 Ontology Mapping Protocol (OMP)

As we mentioned previously that another problem may take place when the participants don't understand the communication messages, or when the new agent wants to participate in a negotiation process then he has to understand the protocol and the communication language messages.

For implements the message flow which is necessary for solving the problems of interoperability, including the interaction of SA and ICA agents when requesting/receiving a service. We designed the Ontology Mapping Protocol (OMP) with the purpose of facilitating the interaction between the agents and services. (figure 6)

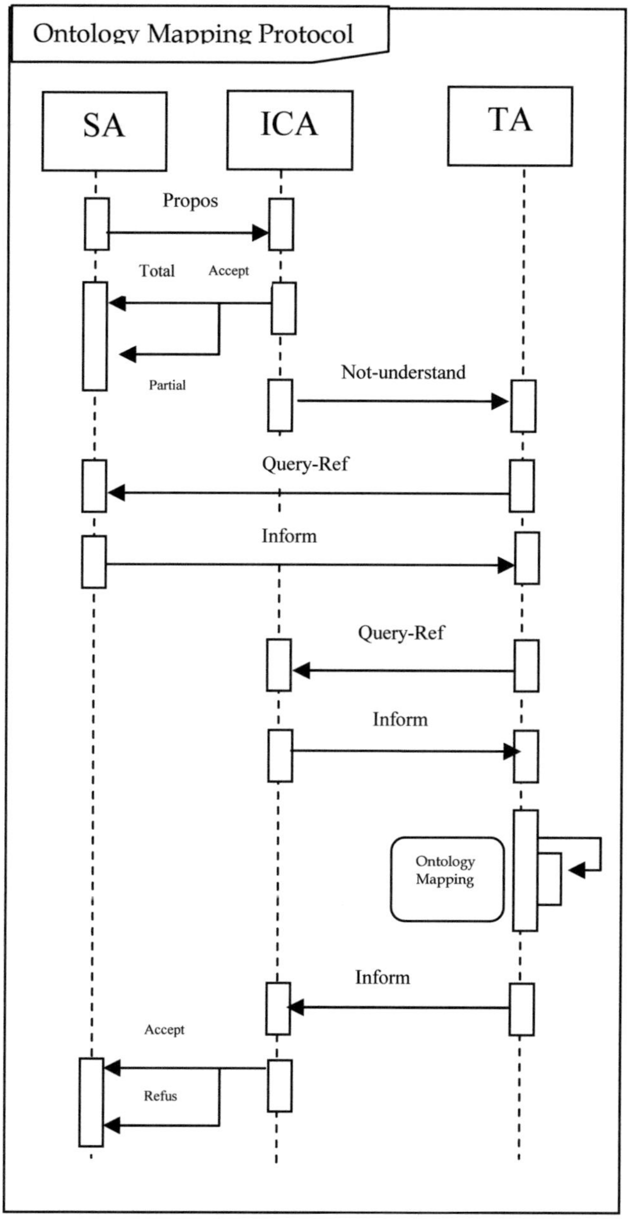

Fig. 6. OMP

After having received an ONP and not being able to interpret the requested service, the ICA sends a message with the performative NOT_UNDERSTOOD to the TA ask him who sent

the ONP and the name of the unknown service. The TA sends the name of the service which it has just received to the SA in order to get further information about it. The SA will analyze that request and send back attributes of the concept, i.e. all the information about this service.
After having received the answer from SA, the TA knows the description, of the demanded service under negotiation and sends it to the ICA. The later selects among all service the ones whose time value is near of the received value. After the selection, the ICA answers with a list containing names of potential correspondent concepts.
After receiving all the information about the service under negotiation and a list of possible corresponding services, the TA is able to apply methods in order to match the services. In the previous work (Saad et al., 2008a); we have applied the Quick Ontology Mapping (QOM) method where this method aims to detecting semantic similarity of terms. Every term of the proposed, potential correspondent service is compared to the requested term. By using QOM method, we apply the first task of our OMP which is the Mapping Terms Service (MTS). For the second service which is Translation Services (TS), it is not in the domain of this paper.
In final step, the TA informs the ICA about the result of the comparisons delivered from the ontology mapping methods. The ICA is then able to respond to the SA, either with a ACCEPT or with a REFUS that is part of our ONP.

4.5 The Agent Messages

As we have seen in the previous section, we proposed a structure for our ONP and OMP protocols. In what follows, we detail the different exchanged messages between initiator and participants.

4.5.1 Proposition of the contract:

The contract message is a proposition of a new organization (the first contract) or reorganization of final Workplans to achieve tasks. If the execution of some services was cancelled because of some network perturbations, it is indeed the case of reorganization. This will be done by reassigning one more time servers to these tasks which represent the set of the Dynamic Reassigned Tasks (DRT) (Saad et al., 2008a). The initiator sends an individual contract to each active ICA_k agent who proposes the contract-reception service:

<SA_i, ICA_k, contract-reception, propose, ∂, fipa-sl, Ontology, protocol>

With ∂ =∂1 if it acts of the first contract and ∂ =∂2 otherwise:

$\partial_1 \equiv$ Workplan (	$\partial_2 \equiv$ FinalWk (
Owner : ICA_k	Owner : ICA_k
Initial : $i_1,\ldots,i_{k_i}$	Final : $f_1,\ldots,f_{k_f}$
Final : $f_1,\ldots,f_{k_f}$)	)

With $i_1,\ldots,i_{k_i}$ represent references of nodes which belong to the initial Workplan of the ICA agent k (ICAk) and $f_1,\ldots,f_{k_f}$ represent references of nodes which belong to the final Workplan of the same agent. Thus we have $ki \leq kf$.

4.5.2 Response to the contract:

When a participant receives the proposed contract, he studies it and answers by:

- ***Total Acceptance*** : if he agrees to coordinate all tasks chosen by the initiator, included in his remaining trip (remained final Workplan), according to his current position,

  <ICA_k, SA_i, Ø, accept-proposal, ∂, fipa-sl, ontology, protocol>

- ***Partial Acceptance***: if he agrees to coordinate a subset of the tasks selected by the initiator, included in his remaining trip (remained final Workplan) or if he doesn't understand the received message sending by the initiator. Then, according to his current position, the partial-accept-proposal message content expresses the references of cancelled tasks and those of unavailable servers (the reason of the non total-acceptance):

  <ICA_k, SA_i, Ø, partial-accept-proposal, ∂, fipa-sl, ontology, protocol >
  With $\partial \equiv$ (tasks: $t_1,\ldots,t_n$ nodes : $s_1,\ldots,s_m$)

- ***Refusal:*** if he does not agree with any task in the proposed contract (i.e. he uses the ONP for check the services only) or if he doesn't understand the received message sending by the initiator (i.e. he didn't understand the message, here he uses OMP to analyze the message). Then, the refusal message content expresses the references of unavailable servers (the reason of the refusal):

  <ICA_k, SA_i, Ø, refuse, ∂, fipa-sl, ontology, protocol >
  With $\partial \equiv (r_1,\ldots,r_m)$

The initiator does not wait for all answers because he must act rapidly, so he just waits for some answers for a very short period of time to make a decision.

4.5.3 Confirmation

An initiator has to confirm independently the agreed part of each contract k proposed to an agent ICA_k who represents an autonomous participant of the negotiation, the confirmation can be:

- ***Total:*** if the initiator agrees with the total response to the previous proposed contract ,

  <ICA_k, SA_i, Ø, confirm, Ø, fipa-sl, ontology, protocol >

- ***Partial:*** if the initiator agrees with a partial response to the previous proposed contract, the partial-confirm-proposal message content expresses the references of agreed tasks:

  <ICA_k, SA_i, Ø, partial-confirm-proposal, ∂, fipa-sl, ontology, protocol>
  With $\partial \equiv (g_1,\ldots,g_p)$

4.5.4 Modification request

If the DRT table is not yet empty (Saad et al., 2008a); the initiator asks the participants to propose a new distribution of services assignments which are canceled, the request-modification message content expresses the DRT table:

<SA_i, ICA_k, Ø, request-modification, ∂, fipa-sl, ontology, protocol>
With ∂ ≡ (DRT)

4.5.5 Modification proposition

According to our DRT algorithm, where we design a reassignment procedure strategy of servers to tasks, , taking into account not only the dynamic positions of ICA agents in their Workplans, but also their constraints, priorities, preferences and ontologies, according to their respective current positions. The proposition message content expresses for each participant k the new proposition of his remained Workplan according to his current state:

< ICA_k, SA_i, Ø, propose, ∂, fipa-sl, ontology, protocol >
With ∂ ≡ FinalWk (Owner: ICA_k, Final: $f_1,\ldots,f_{k_f}$)

Where $f_1,\ldots,f_{k_f}$ represent references of nodes which belong to the final Workplan of the agent ICAk.

3.5.6 Desist

After have sending the conformation. The participants (or the initiator) don't want to continue the negotiation process. Then, he decides to desist the process. In this case, if the DRT table is not empty, the initiator can resend another contract to the participants. the desist message content is as follow:

<SA_i, ICA_k, Ø, desist, ∂, fipa-sl, ontology, protocol>
With ∂ ≡ (DRT)

3.5.7 Not Understand

In our system the problem of heterogeneity may arise; when one of ICA_k agents receives the message and it don't understand the concepts. Then ICA Agent will send a message to the TA, setting the performative of the ACL message to NOT UNDERSTOOD. The TA is placed in the Semantic Layer of our system (SEL) (Saad, 2008c).

The TA Agent will examine the level of transibility between the ontologies correspondent. by applying the ontology mapping method. For this proposal TA access to the services provided by the KMSL (OntoSV), which are in this case helping in the existing heterogeneity problem, trying to map concepts of ontologies and thus looking for similarities. In order to facilitate the negotiation process (i.e, reduce the number of negotiation rules), the not understood message will to be, as follow:

< ICA_k, SA_i, Ø, not understood, ∂, fipa-sl, ontology, protocol>
With ∂= $(c_1,\ldots, c_n)$

3.5.8 Cancel

To avoid indefinite waiting for answers or for modifications, the initiator agent must make a decision at the end of a fixed period of time, illustrated by the last field of an agent message. Therefore he cancels the contract if there is no more solution (lack of resources, no available provider…) or he creates new ICA agents to execute the current contract:

< SA_i, ICA_k, Ø, cancel, ∂, fipa-sl, ontology, protocol >

5. Case Study

As we mentioned in the previous sections, one of the big problems to communication-based agents is that each one uses different terms with the same meaning or the same term for different meanings. Once we took this problem as a challenge, representing these differences in a common ontology becomes essential. Indeed, the use of a common ontology guarantees the consistency (an expression has the same meaning for all the agents) and the compatibility (a concept is designed, for the same expression, for any agent) of the information present in the system. However, it is not sure that all the agents will use a common ontology. Usually, each agent has its heterogeneous private ontology and it cannot fully understand other agent's ontology. Problems with heterogeneity of the data are already well known within the distributed database systems community. If common domain ontology is used, it seems easier to know that people are speaking about the same subject. However, even with a common domain ontology, people may use different terms to represent the same item, the representation can be either more general, or more specific and with more details.

In our work, to market its data, an information provider must solicit the system in order to register or update the services that it offers. A service is characterized by a cost, a response time and a data size. A service is also characterized by a time relevance that allows saving information locally for a certain time to reduce the transmission of data if that is possible. For that in the previous work (Zgaya, 2007a), we have developed two databases where the first is used to register the servers which want to propose their services through our system, and the second database plays the role of "buffer zone" contain static data to a certain degree, (Figure 7)

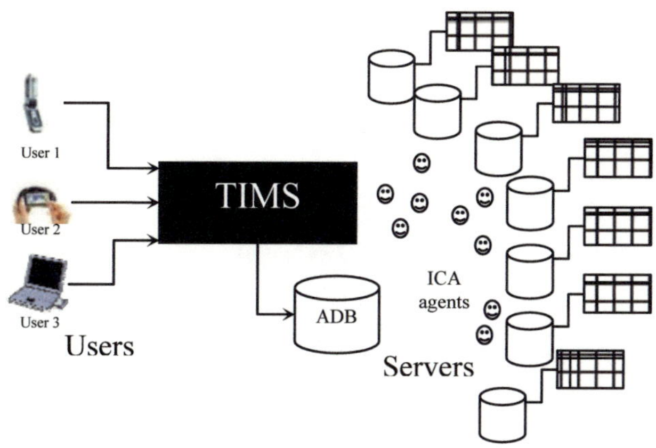

Fig. 7. Dynamic Information Archiving

We illustrated the first databases which use to register the providers of the services where each provider, wanting to offer its services through our system, must register all its services in this database. Previously, we have used the reference as the index for the services. Here, a supplier must register the label of each service proposed, its reference, the estimated response time, cost and size of data corresponding. It must also mention the address of his or its servers. The same service (same label) may be proposed by several suppliers with costs, response times and different sizes; for example when a provider S_{11}register its service (T_2) with the t=0,25second and cost= 5 point. There is the possibility that the providers S_5 and S_{20} have the same service where S_5 register it as (T_2) with the t=0, 15 second and cost=5 point in the register database. May the server S_{20} register the service with the label (T_2') with the t=0, 20 second and cost=4point. In this case, those providers use different terms with the same meaning. In this example, the simultaneous requests managed by the different IA agents are decomposed into a set of independent services which was sent to IdA agent. Thus, when the user searches service $T_{2,}$ the system will create the initial Workplans which contains the initial assignment solution of servers to tasks where $S_1,\ldots,S_{20}$ represent available servers containers on the network. Then, the final assignment solution of servers to tasks is deduced from initial Workplans generation and our genetic algorithm results, in our case S_5 will be in the final Workplans. The ICA agents can move in order to collect date according to the adopted contract model. Here, the move of an ICA1 agent into a server (S_5) on the network knowing that in JADE platform, containers must be created on machines to receive agents. The DRT algorithm is implemented in the context of a negotiation process between agents SA and ICA in order to negotiate dynamically best assignments of servers to tasks according to the new set of unavailable machines. I.e. when a server (S_5) is not available the SA begin the negotiation process where it proposes the new contract to ICA1 agent and this contract will contain the servers (S_{11} and S_{20}) whose propos the same service. In what follow, we present an example which show the execution of this contract where ICA1 agent received a proposition of the contract from SA agent. The propose message is, as follow:

```
(Propose
 :sender  (agent-identifier
        : name SA@home:1099/JADE
        : addresses(sequence    http://home:7778/acc))
 :receiver (set
        ( agent-identifier
        : name  ICA1@home:1099/JADE
        : addresses(sequence    http://home:7778/acc)))
 :content  "((OWNS (agent-identifier
         : name
          ICA1@home:1099/JADE
         : addresses (sequence   http://home:7778/acc))
        (services
         : servers (sequence
          http://home:7778/acc
           http://home:2588/acc
           http://home:2590/acc
           http://home:2592/acc
         http://home:2594/acc)
```

: duration 120)))"
: language fipa-sl
: ontology English-Transport-ontolog
: protocol Ontology-Negotiation-Protocol)

For S_{20} the answer will be not understand because he don't understand the message sends from SA agent although he has the same service which the user need. Indeed, problems of heterogeneity of the data are appearing here where server S_{20} has the service (T_2'). So, the answer will be with the message not understood. For that our DRT algorithm will use the QOM algorithm to solve this problem and to do the mapping between ontologies sure according to ontologies, constraints, priorities and preferences of the ICA agents in their final Workplans.

6. Conclusion and Future Work

In this chapter, we proposed an optimizing approach of the data flow management, in order to satisfy, in a better manner, customers' requests. The adopted approach decreases considerably computing time because Workplans are just deduced; they are computed when network traffic varies considerably.We have presented a new solution for the problem of language interoperability between negotiation agents, by incorporating architecture for Negotiation process with that uses an Ontology-based Knowledge Management System (NOKMS). The proposed solution prevents the misunderstanding during the negotiation process through the agents' communications. The architecture consists of three layers: (NL, SEL and KMSL). But in this work we talked about the first layer only (NL) that describes the negotiation process as well as illustrates the different messages types by using the different ontologies. Our proposed NOKMS improves the communications between heterogeneous negotiation mobile agents and the QoS in order to satisfy the transport customers. Indeed, the ICA agents can to ignore crashed nodes in their remained routes, so they have to avoid visiting them. This will be done by (DRT) algorithm for reassigning substitute servers tasks which need to be reassigned. This reassignment depends on the actual positions of ICA agents in their final Workplans. It depends also on their ontologies, constraints, priorities and preferences. The new assignment constitutes a contract between ICA agents and SA agents.

In a future work, we will try to apply our approach to contain the different systems which can negotiate at the same time and each of these systems has their ontologies (languages) and can offer different services. This can take place when ICAs know their final Workplans. The agents ICAs are supposed to visit their first nodes by the order as in their Workplans without problems before the declaration of all unavailable nodes. In this case, the proposed negotiation process allows us to reassign the nodes (i.e. new negotiation tour) by using our DRT algorithm. But when it rest another tasks in DRT table and there is not available nods in the same system then IS agent sends a new propose contract to a meta-system which in turn searches the suitable system to continuous the negotiation process. According to this new renegotiation process, it must to improve the DRT algorithm to adopt the novel ontology in the new system.

For the simulation part, we will create all our ontology structures by using Protégé which is an open-source development environment for ontologies and knowledge-based systems.

Protégé contains a large number of plug-ins that enabled the user to extend the editor's core functionality like the Bean Generator plug-in (JADE, 2002) which can be used for exporting ontology developed in Protégé to JADE ontology model. This was used to test capabilities of ontology based on Java class representation and FIPA-SL language (FIPA0008). As we had decided to use the JADE multi-agent environment (JADE site) for implementation of MTIS project (Saad et al., 2008c).The JADE framework is also able to integrate with web browsers and Java Applets, so the application could be translated into a web service in the future, enabling greater flexibility. Similarly, due to the underlying JADE infrastructure, the prototype may be run on multiple computers with little complication.

7. References

Abou Assali, A ; Lenne,D and Debray,B (2007): KoMIS: An Ontology-Based Knowledge Management System For Industrial Safety. (DEXA'2007). Regensburg, Germany

Bailin ,S ; Truszkowski. (2002). Ontology negotiation between intelligent information agents. The Knowledge Engineering Review,

Bravo, M.C; Perez, J;.Sosa,V.J; Montes, A; Reyes, G (2005): Ontology support for communicating agents in negotiation processes. Hybrid Intelligent Systems, 6-9 Novovmber.

Carey, M and Johnson, D,(1979) "Computers and Intractability: A Guide to the Theory of NP-Completeness", Freeman,.

Carzaniga, A; Picco, G.P and Vigna, G,(1997)"Designing distributed applications with mobile code paradigms", in Proc. of the 19th International Conference on Software Engineering (ICSE'97), Massachusetts, USA.

Davies, J; Studer, R; Warren ,P; (2006):Semantic Web Technologies: Trends and Research in Ontology-based Systems, April

Diggelen, J. Van; Beun, R.J.; Dignum, F.P.M.; Eijk, R.M. Van; Meyer, J-J.Ch. 2007. Ontology Negotiation in Heterogeneous Multi-agent Systems: the ANEMONE System ,IOS

Diggelen, J. Van ; Beun, R.J ; Dignum, F.P.M. ; Eijk, R.M. Van; Meyer, J-J.Ch(2004). Optimal Communication Vocabularies and Heterogeneous Ontologies , IOS Press 2005

Ehrig, M; Staab, S.(2004)

Efficiency of Ontology Mapping Approaches.

Falasconi, S; Lanzola, G; and Stefanelli, M. (1996) .Using ontologies in multiagent systems. In Proceedings of Tenth Knowledge Acquisition for Knowledge-Based Systems Workshop (KAW), Banff, Alberta, Canada,

Geiger, K, (1995):

Inside ODBC. Microsoft Press..

Green, S; Hurst, L; Nangle, B; Cunningham, P; Somers, F and Evans, R. (1997). "Software agents: A review", Technical report, TCS-CS-1997-06, Trinity College Dublin, Ireland

Gruber, Th.R. (1993): A Translation Approach to Portable Ontology Specification. Knowledge Acquisition Systems.

FIPA0081: FIPA ACL Message Structure Specification. http://www.fipa.org/specs/fipa00061/index.html .

FIPA0008: FIPA SL Content Language Specification http://www.fipa.org/specs/fipa00008/index.htm

Java Agent DEvelopment framework.
http://jade.titlab.com/doc
Jennings, N. R; Faratin ,P; A.R. Lomuscio, S. Parsons, C. Sierra, and M. Wooldridge. Automated haggling, (2000): Building artificial negotiators. In Pacific Rim International Conference on Artificial Intelligenc
Klein, M. (2001). Combining and relating ontologies: an analysis of problems and solutions. In IJCAI-2001Workshop on Ontologies and Information Sharing,pages 53–62, Seattle, WA.
Lander, S and Lesser, V; (1993). Understanding the role of negotiation in distributed search among heterogeneous agents. In Proceedings of the International Joint Conference on Artificial Intelligence
Maedche, A; Motik, B. (2003). Ontologies for Enterprise Knowledge Management ",IEEE Intelligent Systems,,26-33.
Malucelli, A., Oliveira, E.(2004). Ontology-Services Agent to Help in the Structural and Semantic Heterogeneity, In: Camarinha-Matos, L. (eds.) Virtual Enterprises and Collaborative Networks, Kluwer Academic Publishers, pp. 175-182,
Obitko, M; Marík ,V.(2004) OWL Ontology Agent based on FIPA proposal, Znalosti ;2004, Brno, Czech Republic,
Saad, S; Zgaya, H and Hammadi, S (2008a), Dynamic Reassigned Tasks during the Negotiation Process by Ontology Approach between Mobile Agents, IEEE, International Conference on Intelligent Agent Technology (IAT-08).Sydney, Australia.
Saad, S; Zgaya, H and Hammadi, S (2008b), Using Ontology to Solve the Negotiation Problems in Mobile Agent Information Systems. SMC, Singapore
Saad, S; Zgaya, H and Hammadi, S (2008c). The Flexible Negotiation Ontology-based Knowledge Management System: The Transport Ontology Case Study, In proceedings of the IEEE, The International Conference on Information & Communication Technologies: from Theory to Applications - ICTTA'08 - April 7 - 11, 2008 in Damascus, Syria
Sh.Ji , x; Qijia,T ; Liang,T, ;Yang,H;(2007): An Ontology Framework for EC Automated Negotiation Protocol. Networking, and Parallel/ Distributed Computing, 2007. SNPD 2007. July 30 2007-Aug.
Studer, R; Benjamins, V and Fensel, D. (1998) : Knowledge engineering, principles and methods. Data and Knowledge Engineering, 25(1-2):161–197,
Tamma ,V; and T.J.M. (2002a): An ontology model to facilitate knowledge sharing in multi-agent systems. In Knowledge Engineering Review. Bench-Capon,
Tamma, V; Wooldridge, M; Blacoe, I; and Dickinson, I.(2002b).An ontology based approach to automated negotiation. In Proceedings of the IV Workshop on Agent Mediated Electronic Commerce,
University of Amsterdam, Ontology Bean Generator for JADE, (2002)
http://www.swi.psy.uva.nl/usr/aart/beangenerator/,
Verrons ,M. H ; GeNCA. (2004) : un modèle général de négociation de contrats entre agents. PHD, France,
Zgaya, H (2007a): Conception et optimisation distribuée d'un système d'information d'aide à la mobilité urbaine : Une approche multi-agent pour la recherche et la composition des services liés au transport PHD, EC-Lille, France

Zgaya, H ; Hammadi, S and Ghédira, K , (2007b), Combination of mobile agent and evolutionary algorithm to optimize the client transport services, RAIRO.

Zgaya, H and Hammadi, S. (2007c), Multi-Agent Information System Using Mobile Agent Negotiation Based on a Flexible Transport Ontology. (AAMAS'2007), Honolulu, Hawai'i.

Zgaya, H ; Hammadi, S and Ghédira, K.(2005a) "Workplan Mobile Agent for the Transport Network Application", IMACS'2005, Paris,

Zgaya, H ; Hammadi, S and Ghédira, K.(2005b) "Evolutionary method to optimize Workplan mobile agent for the transport network application", IEEE SMC'2005, Hawaii, USA

Zhang, X; Lesser ,V; and Podorozhny,R (2005) Multi-dimensional, multistep negoriation for task allocation in a cooperative system. Autonomous Agents and Multi-Agent

14

Study on Product Knowledge Management forProduct Development

Chunli Yang[1], Hao Li[2] and Ming Yu[3]
[1]*China Center for Information Industry Development, Beijing, 100846, China*
[2]*Research Center for Medical and Health Management, School of Economics and management, Tsinghua University Beijing, 100084, China*
[3]*Department of Industry Engineering, Tsinghua University, Beijing, China*

1. Introduction

The goal of engineering product development in today's industry is to provide products meeting individual requirements at the lowest cost, the best quality and the shortest time. Abundant design knowledge is needed, and cases and designers' experiences should be utilized at most as possible. In addition, product development is becoming more often done collaboratively, by geographically and temporally distributed design teams, which means a single designer or design team can no longer manage the complete product development effort. Therefore it is necessary to collect and manage the design knowledge to support share and pass of them among designers. In some sense, quick capture and effective use of design knowledge are essential for successful product development.
The modern manufacturing environment and the new product development paradigms provide more chances with enterprises and customers to cooperate among different enterprises, different departments of a firm, enterprises and their customers, etc. Designers are no longer merely exchanging geometric data, but more general knowledge about design and design process, including specifications, design rules, constraints, rationale, etc (Simon Szykman, 2000). Product development is becoming increasingly knowledge intensive and collaborative. In this situation, the need for an integrated knowledge resource environment to support the representation, capture, share, and reuse of design knowledge among distributed designers becomes more critical.
A great deal of technical data and information including experience generated from product development is one of the most important resources of product knowledge. It is necessary to use knowledge based information management methods and technologies, which can dig and capture product knowledge from those resources supporting product development. The engineering design community has been developing new classes of tools to support product data management (PDM), which are making progress toward the next generation of engineering design support tools. However, these systems have been focusing primarily on database-related issues and do not place a primary emphasis on information models for artifact representation (Simon Szykman & Ram D. Sriram ,2000). Furthermore, although these systems can represent non-geometric information—for example, about design process,

manufacturing process, and bills of materials – representation of the artifacts is still generally limited to geometry. For example, PDM techniques focus on product data management but little product knowledge, and they are limited to capture, organization and transfer of product knowledge (Ni Yihua, Yang Jiangxin, Gu Xinjian,et,al, 2003). Moreover, they are unable to elicit knowledge from lots of product data and cannot satisfy the requirements of knowledge management in product development. In such cases, the need for building a kmowlege management system to support PLM (product lifecycle management) becomes more critical. Such kmowlege management system can not only represent the knowledge of product and product development processes, but also support firms to quickly identify, capture, store and transfer the knowledge, on which a better and more effective mechanism of knowledge accumulation and management is formed.
In response, the main purpose of this paper is to study product knowledge management methodologies, build an integrated knowledge management framework for decision-making, and develop a software prototype to support quick capture and reuse of knowledge during product development. The remaining part of this paper consists of five main sections: 2. Related research work; 3. Product knowledge management system (PKMS) framework; 4. Semantic object network model; 5. Product knowledge management process; 6. Design repository; 7. Implementation and application of PKMS; 8.Conclusions. Following on from a brief literature review to construct a PKMS research framework, a great portion of this paper focuses on the product knowledge management process, along with several illustrations of software prototype. The paper ends with concluding remarks.

2. Related research work

Product development is complex system engineering. It involves in representation, capture, and reuse of product knowledge. Recently, researches on knowledge representation, acquisition and management are emphasized increasingly.

2.1 Product knowledge representation

The knowledge representation is the core issue in AI and many representational methods such as logic and predicate mode, procedure mode, production system, semantic network, framework, knowledge unit, case base, and object orientation, etc. have been reported in AI to meet the requirements for the specific problems. Production system, semantic network, framework, case base, object orientation, and graph, etc. have been used to represent product knowledge in mechanical engineering, in which object orientation, rule-based, and hybrid representation schemes are popular.

2.1.1 Object orientation representation

X.F.Zha provided an integrated object model to represent product knowledge and data, which supports calculating and reasoning work in assembly oriented design processes (X.F. Zha,2001). The integrated object model employed an object orientation scheme and the knowledge P/T net formalisms to form a hierarchy of function-behaviour, structure, geometry and feature. Such model was used as a uniform description of assembly modelling, design and planning.
The SHARED object model is presented to realize conceptual design (S R Gorti &A Gupta,1998). It clearly defines relationships among objects. Object-oriented technology

makes it possible to naturally decompose design process and hierarchically represent design knowledge. S R. Gorti and etc (Simon Szykman &Ram D. Sriram ,2000). presented a flexibly knowledge representation model based on SHARED. It further extends object-oriented design technology, and represents knowledge of product and design process by combining products and their design processes according to the hierarchical structures. The model encapsulates design rationale by using structured knowledge code. Artifacts are defined as the composition of three kinds of objects: function, form and behavior. Form represents physical performance. Behavior represents consequence of operations.

A product modelling language is developed (Nonaka,1991). It defined products as object sets and relations. This product modeling language includes data language (DL) and design representation language (DPL). DL independent of any engineering environment is defined as basic framework of general object template and data structure. DPL provides methods of setting product model by combining DL with engineering environment. The method supports complex pattern matching algorithm based on graph and provides a neutral language to capture and exchange product information. It uses effective methods to store and reuse knowledge (Simon Szykman,2000).

Oliva R. Liu Sheng and Chih-Ping Wei proposed a synthesized object-oriented entity-relationship (SOOER) model to represent the knowledge and the imbedded data semantics involved in coupled knowledge-base/database systems (Sanja Vranes,1999). The SOOER model represents the structural knowledge using object classes and their relationships and encapsulates the general procedural, the heuristic and the control knowledge within the object classes involves.

XB, liU and Chunli YANG presented a product knowledge model which is built with object modelling techniques (XB, LIU & Chunli YANG,2003) . In order to easily realize knowledge management, the object model is mapped to the Relation Database.

2.1.2 Graph-based representation

In order to directly capture the relationships among design attributes (geometry, topology, features) and symbolic data representing other critical engineering and manufacturing data (tolerances, process plans, etc.), W.C. Regli presented a graphical structure called as a design signature, i.e. a hyper-graph structure H(V,E) with labeled edges is used to represent the a mechatronic design and its design attributes (W.C. Reglil, V.A. Cicirello,2000). All vertices representing design attributes are connected to the vertices representing the entities in the boundary model that attributes refer to. Such representation method can facilitate retrieval of models, design rules, constraints, cases, assembly dada, and experiences and identifying those products with similar structures or functions, which helps designers to better perform the variant designs based on cases.

Yu Junhe used structural hypergraph to describe the hierarchical structure of sets in a product family structure model. The evolving hypergraph networks represent the information on design processes, which can trace the historical information and facilitate retrival and reuse of the product information (YU JunHe, QI Guoning,WU Zhaotong, 2003).

Knowledge representation based on graph, such as knowledge map, concept map, hyper-graph and so on, belongs to the semantic network category, which has many characteristics, e.g. its structure is simple, easily readable, can truly describes the semantics of the natural language and has more precise mathematics bases. They will be used in many domains, especially in the knowledge representations based on Web, the topic map is the development tendency (Zhang lei &Hou dianshe, 1998).

2.1.3 STEP-based representation

Recently, as more CAD companies incorporate the ability to import and export STEP data, the use of the STEP AP 203 as a neutral format will leverage research efforts and maximize interoperability with existing CAD software used in industry. STEP provides a standard modeling method. Yang zijiang proposed a STEP-based organization, transfer and exchange mechanism for product information model (Yang Zijiang, Yang Xiaohu, Li Shanping, Dong Jianxiang, 2001). The NIST design repository also used STEP as representing the geometry information.

2.1.4 Generalized representation

Data, information and knowledge have some inner relationships. In order to effectively support product development, many researchers proposed that data, information and knowledge should represnt uniformily, thus a generalized knowledge representaion model was presented, which was organizaed, stored and managed by using database management systems. E.g. Cao Jian thought the data and knowledge invovled in the product development processes as the product knowledge (Cao jian, Zhang Youliang, Huang Shuangxi, Zhou Xinguang, 1999). Qi Yuansheng defined the generalized design knowedge as design information which was used to make decisions (Qi Yuansheng,Peng Hua, Guo Shunsheng, Yang Mingzhong, 2002). The generalized design informaion includes not only the formal design information and engineering information , such as industry documents, formulae, CAD data, tolerances, solutions,etc. , but also market information, forecasting information and some decision-making information. He used multi knowledge representaions including object-oriented, ontology, XML-based methods. The BEST's knowledge-representation language Prolog/Rex (Vranes^E and StanojevicÂ , 1994) attempts to combine rules, frames and logical expressions under a unique formalism.

All of the above mentioned knowledge representaion methods combine the product development and its charactristics. In addtion, they discribe design, design process and the used knowledge accroding bo the given domains. Their goals are to fast develop, design and manufacture good products. However, how to represent the design historical information, design rationale, expriences and other tacit knowledge needs to deep research. In addition, product knowledge has complicated semantics and heterogeneous constrains. Therefore product knowledge representation model should define and represent these semantics and constrains in order to subsequently share, transfer, and reuse product knowledge.

2.2 Product Knowledge Acquisition

Engineering product development is a knowledge intensive and creative action. The whole product development process will access and capture quite lots of knowledge about design and design process. However, the knowledge acquisition issues also become the bottleneck during the product development processes for lack of effective knowledge capture methods and techniques, e.g. only those salted "old designers" can do some product development activities well. Recently, in order to alleviate the knowledge acquisition issues, researches on knowledge acquisition are emphasized increasingly.

2.2.1 Design catalog
Design catalogue is used to capture and store engineering product design knowledge(Zhang han, Zhang yongqin,1999). Ontology is also employed to aid acquire product knowledge, since ontology provides an explicit scheme of structuring knowledge content according to coherent concepts. Designers can easily find the needed knowledge though ontology.

2.2.2 Ontologies
Soininen T. (Soininen T. ,2000)presented configuration ontology for representing knowledge on the component types in product configuration design. Recently most of design and manufacturing knowledge is stored in digital form in computer, therefore knowledge discover and data dig methods and tools are contributed to knowledge acquisition(Zhu cheng, Cao wenze,2002).

2.2.3 Multi knowledge-capturing schema
Generally, a multi knowledge-capturing schema is needed as product design requires many kinds of knowledge and one kind of knowledge acquisition method cannot capture all kinds of knowledge. Many kinds of knowledge acquisition method are integrated with work in product design process, which satisfies its requirements of knowledge (Zhang shu, Li aiping ,1999).

2.2.4 Web-based knowledge capture
In addition, web-based computer aided design technologies are becoming new product development methods driven by customer requirements, which needs to capture the relative knowledge through Internet/Intranet environment (Lai chaoan, Sun yanming, 2002). Web-based information platform provides abundant information resource for product innovation development. However, the traditional knowledge acquisition methods have not met the requirements of knowledge capturing, disposal, and use in the Internet/Intranet environment. So many researchers begin to study how to quickly acquire knowledge by Internet technologies.

A great deal of technical data and information including experience generated from product development exists in the form of files, communications, meeting notes and Emails, in which, design semantic information, such as design intent, design rationale, etc. is regarded as the important knowledge resource and the basis of new product development and the past product improvement. There are abundant product knowledge resource, but designers usually do not know where to find the right design knowledge, how to understand the original design purpose, how to reuse design methods, and so on. The main reason is that these technical data and information cannot be effectively organized, stored, and accumulated due to lack of methods and tools of knowledge acquisition, which leads to many efforts spent on retrieval.

3. Product knowledge management framework

To address those issues described above, we proposed the product knowledge management framework. It contains five main components: design repository (DR), OLAP, knowledge reduction, Case Based Reasoning (CBR), and machine learning, as shown in Fig.1.

3.1 Design Repository
DR (Design Repository) takes the role as a knowledge base where contains all the information and knowledge related to products. Furthermore, it is responsible for collecting, extracting, converting, cleaning, aggregation, and indexing the information and knowledge from various kinds of information and knowledge sources.
Knowledge in DR is organized into a subject-oriented and multi-dimensional knowledge model showed in Fig 2. Product design knowledge has five subjects: domain knowledge, product knowledge, design cases, knowledge of customer and market, and design methods. The subjects can be divided into sub-subjects according to requirements of product development.

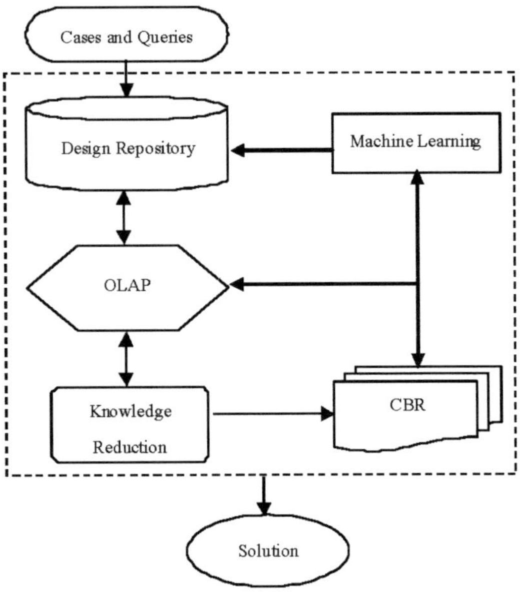

Fig. 1. Framework of Product Knowledge Management

3.2 OLAP technique
The purpose of OLAP in the framework is to facilitate timely access of the knowledge in DR though the application to roll up, drill down, slice, dice, and etc. knowledge to obtain further information. CBR takes advantages of OLAP techniques of its flexible and timely manipulate of data and its special functions, which may speed up attributes matching and cases searching.

3.3 Knowledge reduction
To retrieve a similar case, CBR attempts to match the similar condition between the new case and existing cases in a case-based repository. In traditional approaches, Nearest-Neighbor Retrieval (NNR) approach is used to compute the similarity between stored cases and the new case, based on features and variant weights of the cases. The NNR process examines the similarity for all cases in the case-based repository, which is time-consuming and inefficient when the scale of the case becomes large. In addition, traditional CBR is deficient for

case-reduction of information-preserving data, which results in redundant similarity testing and the computation time consuming (Huang C. C, Tseng T L.,2004). In order to avoid them, it is necessary to integrate rough set approach into CBR, in which knowledge reduction method can induce rules based on previous data in the cases to reduce the number of similarity testing and the computation time consuming (Huang C. C, Tseng T L.,2004). In order to avoid them, it is necessary to integrate rough set approach into CBR, in which knowledge reduction method can induce rules based on previous data in the cases to reduce the number of similarity testing cases and their attributes from OLAP module.

3.4 CBR

CBR model in this paper is extended to the R4 model, presented by Aamodt and Plaza, for satisfying the requirements of product agile development, as shown in Fig.2.
Case retrieval: Once a new inquiry has been input CBR module, it will be sent to OLAP which performs search and match to find the attributes that are similar to the inquiry's attributes in DR. OLAP will retrieve all the similar cases by drilling, slicing, and dicing the DR. Then knowledge reduction module reduces all the similar cases and their attributes so that NNR could avoid test redundant similarity cases and their attributes. After NNR examines the similarity for the reduced similar cases, finally CBR get the most similar case.
Case reuse: The retrieved case is combined with the new case—through REUSE — into a solved case, i.e. a proposed solution to the initial problem. Case revises: The new case is revised in structure or dimension according to the configuration rules and constraints. Then the revised case is tested for whether it meets the requirements, e.g. by being applied to the real environment or evaluated by customers, and repaired if failed. Case retains: Useful experience is retained for future reuse, and the DR is updated by a new case, or by modification of some existing cases.

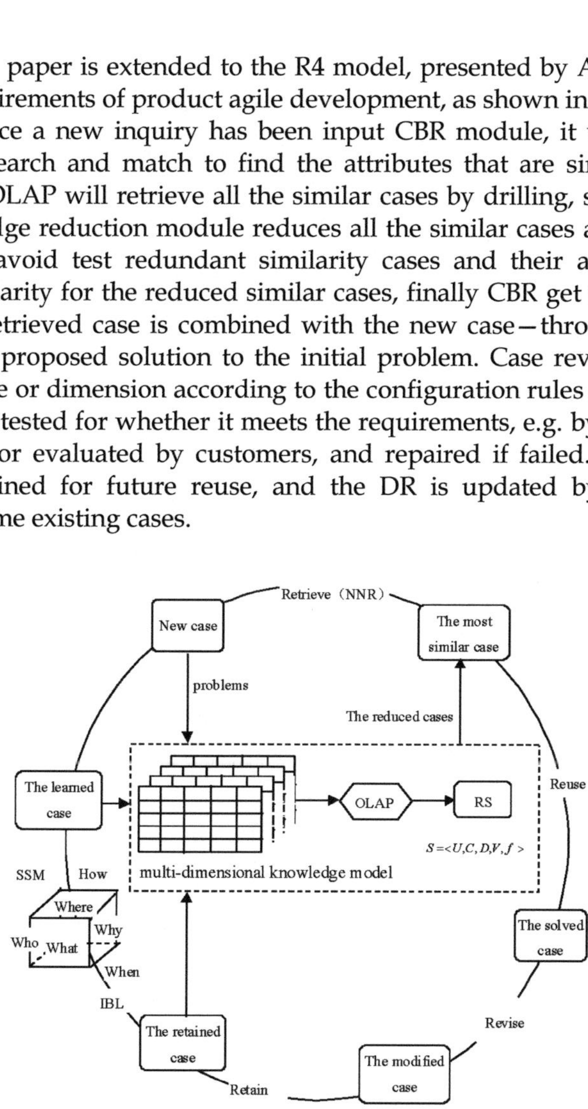

Fig. 2. CBR process model and machine learning process

3.5 Machine learning

Machine learning module is responsible for extracting process information and knowledge from CBR cycle and builds Solution Subject Model (SSM). SSM is stored as a kind of design rationale in DR. SSM includes all the background knowledge such as deliberating, reasoning, trade-off and decision-making in the CBR cycle of an artifact—information that can be valuable, even critical to various designers who deal with the artifact. Therefore, SSM contains a description of why it is revised the way it is, and more detail, it also includes how it is revised, who revised it, when it is revised, which part is revised, etc. SSM can be used as a basis to record the history of configuration and variant design process; to modify and maintain existing designs, or design similar artifacts.

4. Semantic object knowledge representation model

Knowledge in product customization design process is diverse. Design objects change dynamically with the change of the design process, and knowledge used during the whole process changes, too, even is iteratively used. Thus, product knowledge representation model should be constructed according to the features of product design and the process.

4.1 Semantic object network

From above analysis, semantic object network is used to represent knowledge on product customization design. Semantic object network is a kind of Semantic Networks (SNs), in which nodes are semantic objects. Semantic object networks link all information, documents and other descriptive knowledge related to the final products. Therefore, Semantic object networks are convenient for product structure and configuration management.

Semantic Object (SO) is a naming collection of attributes that sufficiently describes a distinct identity (Huang Wei, 2001). Attributes are described by attribute types, cardinality and domains. SO is divided into simple objects and composite objects according to attribute characters (Li SiQiang ,1999).

The nodes in Semantic object network represent SO, and directed arcs represent relations among nodes including Generalization Association (G), Aggregation Association (A), Composition Association (C), etc. AKO (a kind of), APO (a part of), and ACO (a composition of) respectively represents the G association, the A association, and the C association.

4.2 Domain knowledge semantic object network

Domain knowledge updates slowly. Designers usually use the definite domain knowledge for the specific tasks during product design process. According to this distinct character, domain knowledge semantic object networks are built, in which, all the semantic objects are basic objects and simple objects, as shown in Fig. 3.

Most of domain knowledge embodies in documents. Besides, some of domain knowledge embodies in program files, material, calculation methods, etc. Therefore, the semantic objects in domain knowledge semantic object networks are program objects, document objects, material objects, and calculation method objects. The document objects have three types: structured document objects, non-structured document objects and drawing document objects.

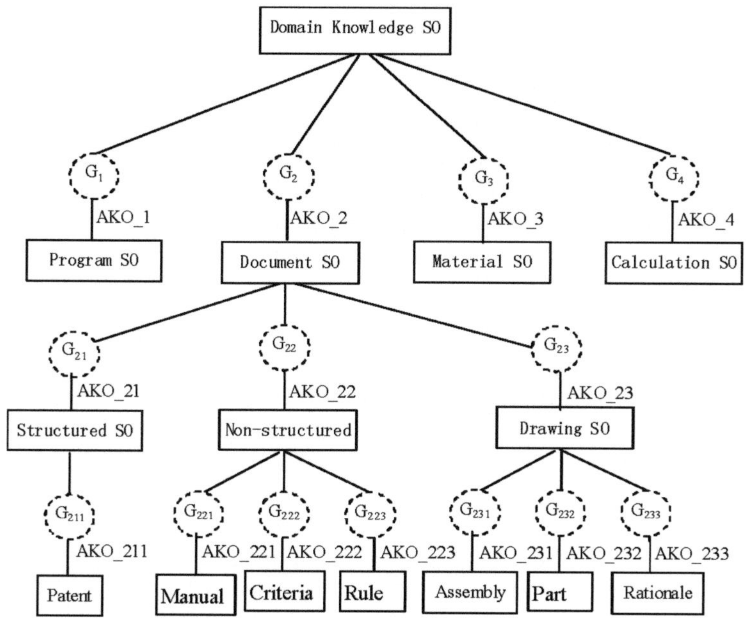

Fig. 3. Domain Semantic Object Networks

4.3 Product function semantic object networks

Product Function Semantic Object Networks (PFSONs) represent knowledge about product concept including customer requirements, product functional features, behavior knowledge, and design rationale. So, PFSONs are composed of four sub SNs: function, behavior, requirement, and design rationale, as is shown in Fig. 4.

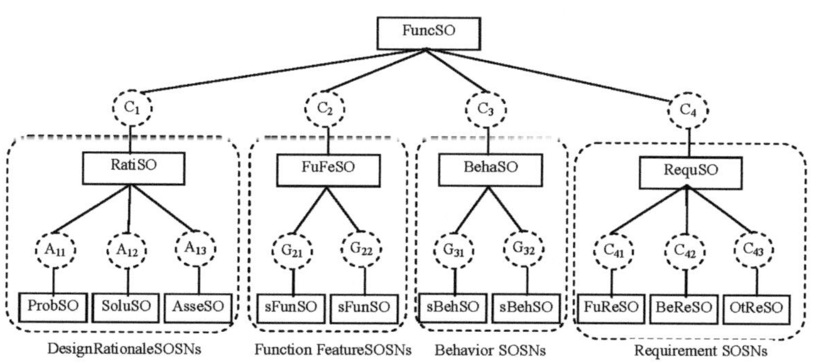

Fig. 4. Product function semantic object networks

Requirement Semantic Object (RequSO) is the collection of customers' requirements including structure, function, appearance, and other requirements. So RequSO includes structure requirement semantic object (StReSO), function requirement semantic object (FuReSO), appearance requirement semantic object (ApReSO), and other requirement semantic object (OtReSO). Function Feature Semantic Object (FuFeSO) represents knowledge of product function and engineering attributes. FuFeSO can be divided into sub FuFeSO (sFunSO). Behavior Semantic Object (BehaSO) specifies the response of an artifact to input conditions or behavioral states (or both). BehaSO can be divided into sub BehaSO (sBehaSO). Design rationale is a kind of process knowledge. It can encompass the documentation of the active processes of reasoning and decision making that led to the artifact design – including the justification for design decisions, records of design alternatives considered and tradeoffs evaluated, and details of the argumentation and communication processes associated with design work. So, design rationale semantic object (RatiSO) includes problem semantic object (ProbSO), solution semantic object (SoluSO), and evaluation semantic object (EvalSO).

4.4 Product configuration management semantic object networks

Configuration rule semantic objects (CRSO) are composed of valid configuration rule objects (ValidCRSO), variable configuration rule objects (VariableCRSO) and version configuration rule objects (VersionCRSO). Configuration constraint semantic objects (CCSO) are divided into variablesolving constraint objects (VSCSO), variable-judging constraint objects (VJCSO), logic constraint objects (LCSO). Product configuration management semantic objects (PCMSO) are composed of CRSO, CCSO and version semantic objects (VSO). Fig.5 presents the structure of PCMSO. Product structure management and configuration design are realized through versions management mechanism according to configuration rules and constraints.

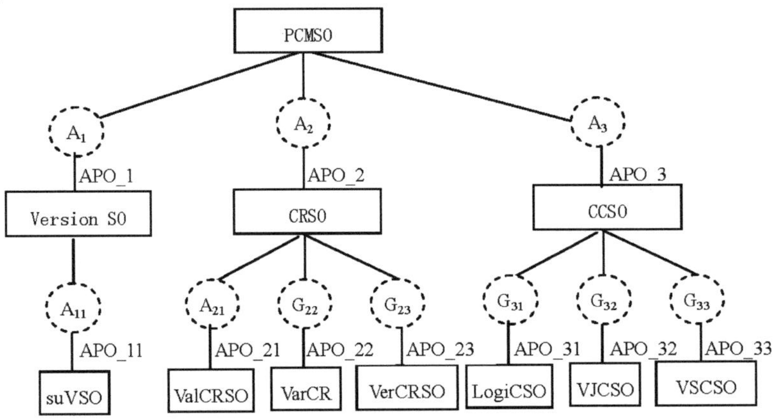

Fig. 5. Product configuration management semantic object networks

5. Product knowledge management process

The purpose of product knowledge management is to provide a mechanism to capture, organize, store, and reuse knowledge for product agile design. It aims to help designers timely find information and knowledge that is needed and enable the maximum reuse of existing knowledge resource in the development of a new product.

5.1 Knowledge analytical model

Product agile development is derived by customer needs. Thus the start point of it is to transform customer needs into engineering design attributes. These engineering design attributes, as the input conditions, will be input into CBR. The analytical model of product agile customization design is showed in Fig. 6.

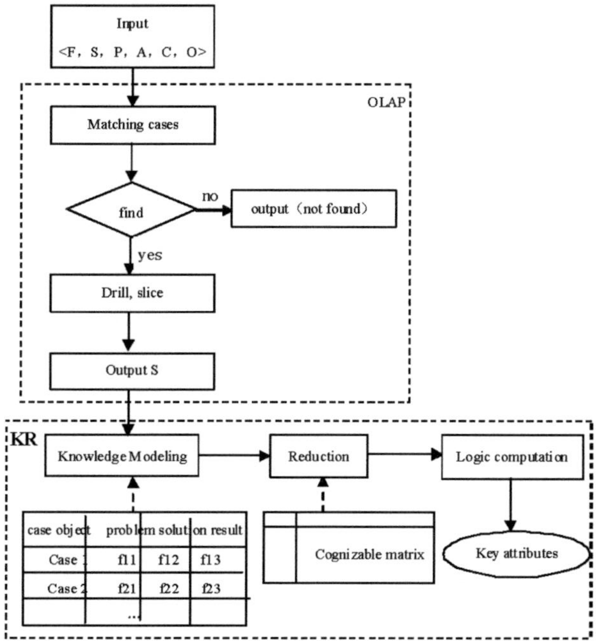

Fig. 6. Knowledge analytical

Firstly, input conditions, i.e. engineering design attributes, are input into CBR for retrieval the similar cases. The engineering design attributes are represented as an input model: I= (F, S, P, A, C, O). Where they separately denote function, structure, performance, appearance, cost, and other attributes. Then I will be sent to OLAP which performs search and match to find the model attributes that are similar to I in DR. OLAP would use multi-dimensional approach to obtain a specific data by going into proper dimension. OLAP will also drill down further for the differences that are found between the similar cases and I in order to get the best solution. Thirdly, knowledge reduction module reduces the similar cases got from OLAP. A case-reduction is defined as a minimal sufficient subset of a set of attributes, which has the same ability to discern concepts as when the full set of attributes is used. A knowledge model in rough set is defined as follows:

$S = \langle U, C, D, V, f \rangle$

Where

U: a finite set of cases

C: condition attributes set of the cases including problems and solutions

D: decision attributes

V: the value of attribute that a case contains

f: the function that designates the attributes values of each case in U

The case-reduction generation procedure is as follows:

Step1: Analyse the attributes of cases and build knowledge model in rough set for each case Step2: Establish concise matrix for each case according to logical algorithms Step3: Generate the core of the attributes, i.e. the key attributes that discern cases.

5.2 Knowledge acquisition

Knowledge acquisition is the key to the product knowledge management. Knowledge acquisition includes the capture of the existing knowledge and new knowledge. As mentioned above, product development generates a great deal knowledge resource. The existing knowledge is captured through extracting, aggregating, integrating and digging the database and knowledge bases, which store them. Then they are organized as the subject-oriented multi-dimensional knowledge model (SMM). New knowledge is acquired by machine learning module. The captured new knowledge is organized as SMM. SMM includes six dimensions: what (the object-old cases), where (the revised position of the old case), who (the reviser), when (the revising time), why (the reasons and motivations of revising), and how (the revising methods). SSM is stored together with the old case and the new case for designers to facilitate finding their relations.

5.3 Case example

A tied bill machine has various characteristics, for example it can automatically pack bank notes, can be adjusted the values of bank notes, has warning signals, packing time is less 30s, etc. Consumers may select the desired products based on their requirements (e.g. convenience, safe, price, functions, appearance, etc.). According to consumer requirements, the case retrieval conditions can be expressed as an input model: I= (F, S, P, A, C). Where, F denotes functions of the tied bill machine, fl denotes it can be adjusted the values of bank notes, f2 means it has warning signals; S is automatically packing or not (sl, automatically; s2, not automatically); P is the packing time (pl, packing time<30s; p2, packing time >30s,); A describes the size of the tied bill machine (al, small; a2, middle; a3, large); C represents the price of tied bill machine (cl, expensive; c2, middle; c3, cheap).
Let's assume DR contains six cases in current status and one customer's inquiry is I= (fl, f2, sl, pl, cl, al). OLAP 2D view is used to represent the cases, as shown in Fig.7., in which m1~m6 denote six solutions.

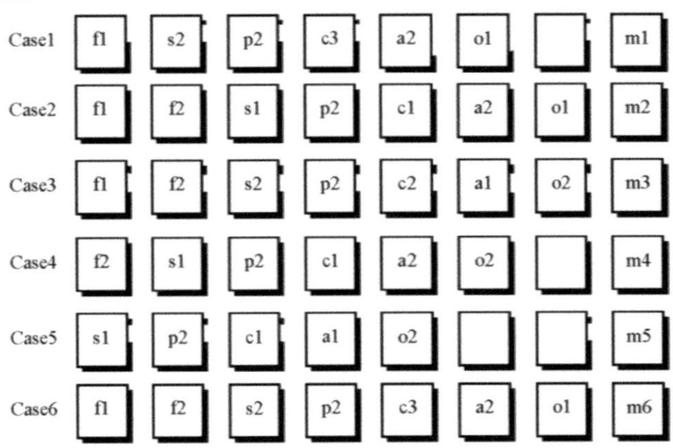

Fig. 7. OLAP 2D view

The inquiry (I) is sent to OLAP which finds all of the six cases contains the attributes that are similar to I. Therefore, the similar set is S (casel, case2, case3, case4, case5, case6). Afterwards, OLAP uses multi-dimensional approach (slice, roll up, drills down, etc.) to find the differences between each case and I in S by going into proper dimension. It discovers only casel has only one similar attribute, which is thought they have fewer similarities. So casel is deleted from S. Case6 has only two similar attributes, and it is also deleted from S. Other cases are closely matched between the attributes. So, the answer to the inquiry, the output of OLAP, is S (case2, case3, case4, case5).

It should be noted that the answer couldn't be 100% satisfied, since the packing time (p) is more than 30s. The similar cases are needed to modify. Packing time is directly related to the time of conveying bank notes and felting belts, orientation components, and the correctness of felting positions. In order to find the most similar case in S, a case-reduction method is used to reduce the number and the attributes of the cases in S that will be compared in CBR by NNR. Firstly, a general decision table (Table land Table 2) is incorporated with representing the relationship between condition attributes and decision attributes of the cases. Secondly, the procedure showed in Fig 4 determines the case-reduction and cases, as shown in Table 3. The attributes including felting method, orientation components, felting components, and compaction components are the key attributes that describe the cases. Thirdly, the approach of NNR is used to generate similarity between new cases and the final consistent data in DR.

The most similar case retrieved from NNR is combined with I in case retain, which means the belt component is needed to revise. SMM represents the process knowledge during the variant design of the belt component and the new case will be stored in DR.

Knowledge acquisition is the key to the product knowledge management. Knowledge acquisition includes the capture of the existing knowledge and new knowledge.

attributes		Values of the attributes	
a-structure of belt slot	0- knockdown	a-structure of belt slot	0- knockdown
b-felting method	0-five points	b-felting method	0-five points
c- orientation components	0-driven by electrical power	c- orientation components	0-driven by electrical power
d- felting components	0-driven by double wheels	d- felting components	0-driven by double wheels
e- compaction component	0-double shafts	e- compaction component	0-double shafts
f-width of belt	0-narrow	f-width of belt	0-narrow
g-felting time	0-≤10s	g-felting time	0-≤10s
h-accuracy of orientation	0-not accurate	h-accuracy of orientation	0-not accurate
l-felting location	0- not accurate	l-felting location	0- not accurate
m-feeding time	0-very long	m-feeding time	0-very long

cases	Condition domain						Decision domain			
U	a	b	c	d	e	f	g	h	l	m
1	0	0	0	0	1	1	0	0	0	0
2	0	1	1	1	1	0	1	1	1	1
3	0	1	0	1	0	1	2	1	2	0
4	1	1	1	1	0	1	2	1	2	1
5	0	0	1	1	0	1	0	1	2	0
6	0	1	1	1	0	1	2	2	0	1

case	Condition domain				Decision domain			
U	b	c	d	e	g	h	l	m
1	0	0	0	1	0	0	1	0
2	0	1	1	1	1	1	0	1
3	1	0	1	0	2	1	1	0
4	1	1	1	0	2	1	2	1
5	1	1	1	0	0	1	2	0

Table 1. THE DESCRIPTION OF CONDITION AND DECISION ATTRIBUTES

6. Design Repository

Design Repository (DR) takes the role as a knowledge base where contains all the information and knowledge related to products. Furthermore, it is responsible for collecting, extracting, converting, cleaning, aggregation, and indexing the information and knowledge from various kinds of information and knowledge sources.
The basic rules of knowledge organization are:

(1) constructing proper architectures in order to make knowledge base engine and inference engine quickly find the needed knowledge;
(2) knowledge must be easily maintained.

So the two following data structures are combined to organize design repository.

6.1 Doubly Linked List

Rules are organized by doubly linked list. Fig.8 .shows the structure of doubly linked list [8]. It has two pointers: prior and next. Prior links to the front node in doubly linked list and next links to the next node. The data domain includes three parts: rule number (no), rule presupposition (if) and result (then).

Prior	no	if	then	next

Fig. 8. Doubly linked list

6.2 Orthogonal Linked List

Semantic object network is a directed graph, so graph (a data structure) can be used to organize knowledge. Graph is composed of non-null nodes' set and arcs expressing relations among these nodes. Its definition is as follows [9]:

- G= (V, E)
- V= {vi | vi £ data object}
- E= {(vi, vj) | vi, vj £ V AP (vi, vj)}

G represents a graph; V, the set of nodes in the graph; E, the collection of ordered pairs of vertices, called arcs; P(vi, vj) describes a line connected vertex vi and vertex vj, that is to say an ordered pair (vi, vj) represents an arc. If a pair (vi, vj) £E composed of any two nodes is ordinal, i.e. lines between vertexes are directional, then the graph is called directed graph.
The information of a graph includes two parts: one is information of vertices in the graph, and the other is information of relations between vertexes or arc information. Therefore graph's storing structure should reflect these two parts' information.
Orthogonal linked list has two linked lists: vertices linked list and arc record linked list. Fig.9. (a) and (b) show the structures of vertices linked list and arc record linked list respectively. Each record in the vertices linked list has a pointer to the arc record linked list that contains the arc information of the node. In arc record linked list, tailvex and headvex represent the locations of arc tail vertex and arc head vertex respectively. Hlink and tlink are two pointers to the next arcs with the same arc head vertex and arc tail vertex respectively. Info points to the arc information. Arcs with the same arc head are in the same linked list; Arcs with the same arc tail are in the same linked list too. Their head nodes are vertices in the vertices linked list. Vertex stores the information on vertices, for example, name of the

Vertex domain	pointer	pointer
Vertex	firstin	firstout

(a) The structure of Vertices Linked List

Arc tail	Head	Information of lines	pointer	pointer
tailvex	headvex	Info	hlink	tlink

(b) The structure of Arc Record Linked List

Fig. 9. The structure of Vertices Linked List and Arc Record Linked List Fig.10. illustrates an orthogonal linked list representation of the graph of PCMSO in Figure 4.

vertex; firstin and firstout are two pointers to the first node with the node as the arc head or the arc tail respectively.

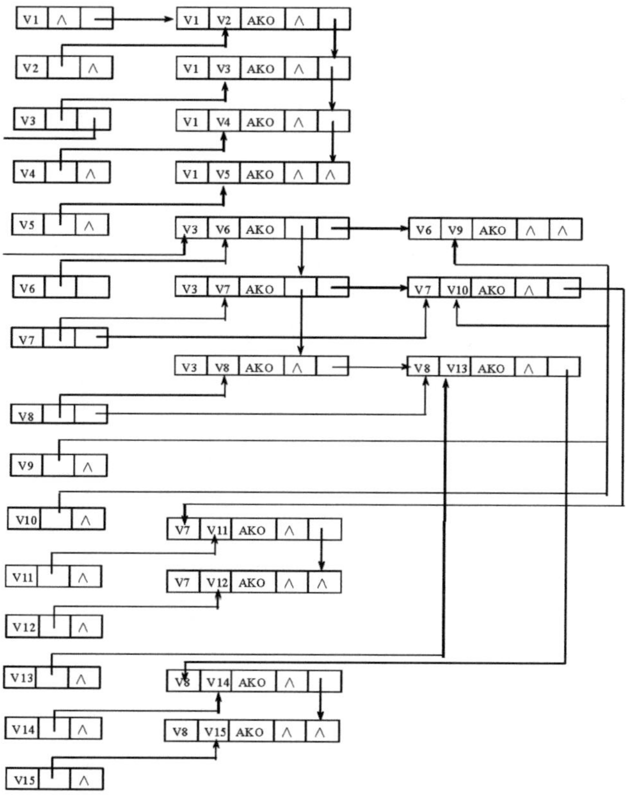

Fig. 10. The Orthogonal Linked List of PCMSOSNs

7. Implementation and application of PKM

According to the above methods, J2EE is utilized to construct a prototype of PKMS supporting the design process of the tied bill machines, in which, web and distributed

database technologies are used to realize the functions of searching, reasoning, browsing, and storing, updating and maintaining knowledge, as is shown in Fig.11.
In order to implement distributed computing technologies, simplify component model based on Internet and improve developing efficiency, J2EE is adopted to establish knowledge base engine, inference engine, updating module and maintaining module. For the sake of simplification, the four modules are built in a Java class package respectively. Servlets are used to exchange data with outer application systems. Searching engine and inference engine use stateless session beans to recall entity beans representing knowledge models. Searching engine and inference engine realize searching and reasoning. Stateless session beans can be shared among clients and cannot be maintained any status messages, so they meet the characteristic of multi-user concurrent access of web-based searching and reasoning. Updating module and user identification module must hold the status messages related to clients, therefore stateful beans are used to recall entity beans, which represent data of knowledge base, and visit the related knowledge in DR through JDBC.
The application tire fulfils the interfaces with product customization platform, CAD/CAM/CAE and etc. Querying requirements of designers are accepted through product customization platform interface. Knowledge on product model and structure is obtained through CAD/CAM/CAE interface. The knowledge is managed and maintained in the application tire.

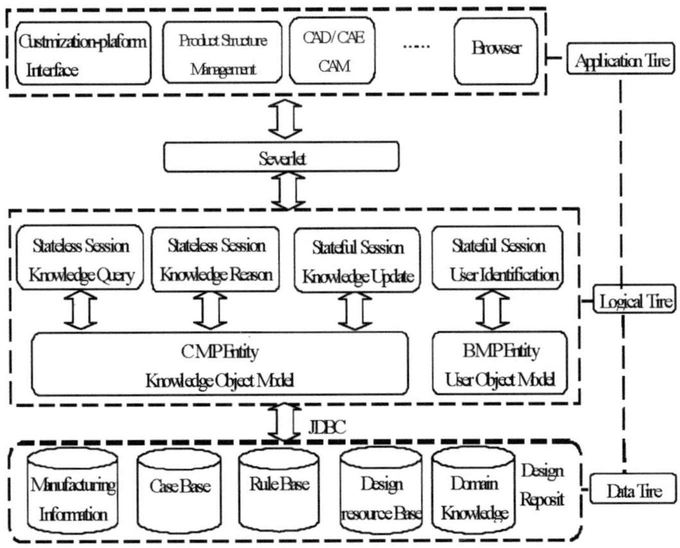

Fig. 11. Framework of Product Knowledge Management System

Fig.12. shows the interface. System has the functions of browsing, searching, updating and etc.
To address those issues described above, we proposed the product knowledge management framework. It provides PACD with an integrated knowledge environment. It uses
The design processes based on PKM are as follows:
(i)Function deployment: implementing function deployment to confirm the conditions of structure deployment according to user's demands;

(ii) Structure deployment: getting the structure tree based on the conditions of structure deployment, using CBR to obtain the similar cases and confirming BOM to finish the design of assembly model;
(iii)Variant design: variant design is necessary if similar cases cannot be acquired. The best variant design can be obtained from PKM;
(iv)New design: new design is needed if variant design cannot meet the needs. Function design, structure design can be implement based on the framework of product knowledge management system.

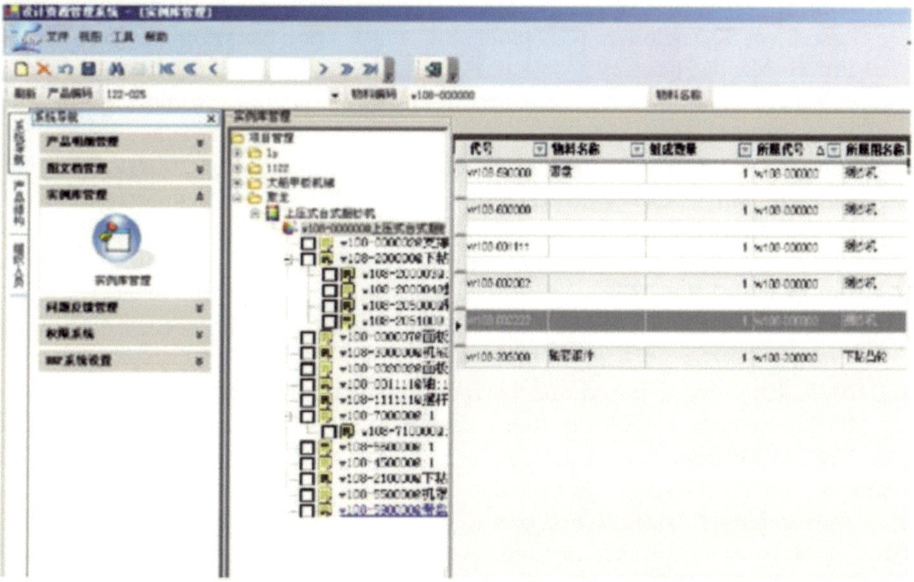

Fig. 12. The Interface of PKMS

8. Conclusions

At present, product knowledge management techniques have not been applied to the real product development process, and the existing document management tools and PDM cannot satisfy the rapid capture and reuse of knowledge during the product agile development processes. In this context, we proposed a product knowledge management framework with DR. A semantic object knowledge model can effectively organize various kinds of knowledge. Knowledge is organized into doubly linked list and orthogonal linked list.Designers could capture and reuse product knowledge by using the OLAP technique, knowledge reduction method, and CBR. Finally machine Learning could acquire new knowledge to make DR alive.

9. References

Cao Jian, Zhang Youliang, Huang Shuangxi, Zhou Xinguang.(1999). Study on Computer Supported Cooperative Design and Its Environment, *Computer Engineering and Applications*, No.5,39-41

Huang C. C, Tseng T L. (2004). Rough set approach to case-based reasoning application, *Expert Systems with Applications,* Vol. 26, 369-385

Huang Wei (2001). The analysis of Semantic Object Model, *Journal of Higher Correspondence Education (Natural Sciences),* Vol.13, No. 5, 40-43

Lai chaoan, Sun yanming (2002). Study on web-based mechanical knowledge acquisition method, *Mechanical design,* 33-36.

Li SiQiang (1999). Semantic Object Modeling Techniques, *Computer Application and Study,* No.5, 40-41

Ni Yihua, Yang Jiangxin, Gu Xinjian,ect on. (2003). Research on CAx Integrated Framework based on Knowledge. *Computer Integrated Manufacturing Systems-CIMS,* 2003, Vol.21, No. 3, 91-94.

Nonaka,I. (1991). The knowledge creating company, *Harvard Business Review.* No. 69, November-December, 96-104

Qi Yuansheng,Peng Hua, Guo Shunsheng, Yang Mingzhong.(2002). Study on the Management of Generalized Design Knowledge and Its Key Technology, *Machine Design,* No.8, 5-9

Simon Szykman. (2000). A web-based system for design artefact modelling. *Design Studies,* Vol.21, No. 2, 145-165

Simon Szykman, Ram D. Sriram .(2000). Design Repositories: Engineering Design's New Knowledge Base. *Intelligent Systems, IEEE,* 47-57.

X.F. Zha. (2001). Knowledge-based approach and system for assembly-oriented design, Part II: the system implementation. *Engineering Applications of Artificial Intelligence,* Vol.14 , 239-254.

Sanja Vranes. (1999). Design knowledge representation in Prolog/Rex. *Engineering Applications of Artificial Intelligence,* Vol.12, No. 7, 221-228.

Soininen T. (2000). An approach to knowledge representation and reasoning for product configuration tasks, *Finnish Academies of Technology,* 20-27.

S R Gorti, A Gupta. (1998). An object-oriented representation for product and design processes. *Computer-Aided Design,* Vol.30, No. 7, 489-501

W.C. Regli1, V.A. Cicirello. (2000). Managing digital libraries for computer-aided design. *Computer-Aided Design,* No. 32 : 119-132.

XB,LIU & Chunli YANG (2003). Method of Building Product Design Knowledge Base, *Computer Integrated Manufacturing Systems-CIMS,* Vol.9, No.8, 204-211

Yang Zijiang, Yang Xiaohu, Li Shanping, Dong Jianxiang.(2001). Research on STEP Feature Model and Its Application in the Integrated Environment of CM, *Journal of Computer Adied Design &Computer Graphics,* Vol.13, No.5, 438-443

Yu Junhe, Qi Guoning, Wu Zhaotong.(2003). Study on Product Family Structure Model based on Hypergraph, *China Mechanical Engineering,* Vol.14, No.2, 107-110

Zhang Lei, Hou Dianshe. (1998). The Problem Implementing a Conceptual Graph's Tool, *Journal of Xi'an Highway University,* Vol.18, No.2, 107-110

Zhu cheng, Cao wenze. (2002).Knowledge system modelling framework, *Computer engineering,* 3-5

Zhang han, Zhang yongqin.(1999). Deisgn catalog-based computer aided concept design system, Research on computer application, 24-26

Zhang shu, Li aiping (1999). Knowledge supply chain and technology innovation, *China mechanical engineering,* 224-227.

The Contribution of Technological Factors on Knowledge Sharing Quality among Government Officers in Malaysia

Mohd Bakhari Ismail and Zawiyah M. Yusof
Faculty of Information Science and Technology,
Universiti Kebangsaan Malaysia,
43600 Bangi Selangor.
Malaysia.

1. Introduction

Knowledge management is an emerging discipline with many ideas, discussions and researches that need to be explored (Beckman, 1999). It is multidisciplinary in nature dealing with managing knowledge in organizations (Andersson, 2000). The concept was coined by Karl Wiig during his keynote address for United Nation's International Labour Organization in 1986 (Beckman, 1999). To date, many researches on knowledge management in organizations have been executed worldwide. However, studies on knowledge sharing particularly in public sector in Malaysia are still handful (McAdam & Reid, 2000; Syed Ikhsan & Rowland, 2004). A number of studies in Malaysia limit their scope on antecedents of knowledge sharing or knowledge transfer (Ismail & Yusof, 2008; Syed Ikhsan & Rowland, 2004) from individual, organizational and technological perspectives. It is not evident that empirical research has been conducted to identify the relationship between technological factors and knowledge sharing quality in government agencies except that by Syed Ikhsan & Rowland (2004). However, the study was conducted on one agency only. Therefore, the results of the study could not be generalised to other government agencies.

Syed Ikhsan and Rowland (2004) suggest that public or private sector need to manage knowledge to ensure that the organization could take full advantage of organizational knowledge. Prevalently, the Ninth Malaysia Plan (2006) reported that there is lack of information/knowledge sharing among government agencies. Why? To answer the question, it is important to investigate factors that hinder public employees from sharing their knowledge particularly technological related factors. Thus, the objectives of this paper are:

- To investigate technological factors that influence knowledge sharing quality among government officers.
- To identify the most important technological factor that influence government officers' knowledge sharing quality.

In the following section, we present literature review related to the study. This is followed by the research theoretical framework, research methodology and discussion on the results. As conclusion, we summarize the main findings and discuss the limitations of the research.

2. Literature Review

2.1. Knowledge Management, Knowledge Sharing and Information Technology

Knowledge management is a process that encompasses three main elements: organizational learning, information management and information technology (Stoddart, 2001). Organizational learning is closely related to changing employees' attitude towards knowledge sharing whereas information management focuses on categorization, compilation and access to information and data in computer applications. Stoddart (2001) views information technology as tools to facilitate the flow of information and knowledge sharing. This indicates that information technology is part of knowledge management and it plays an important role in knowledge sharing.

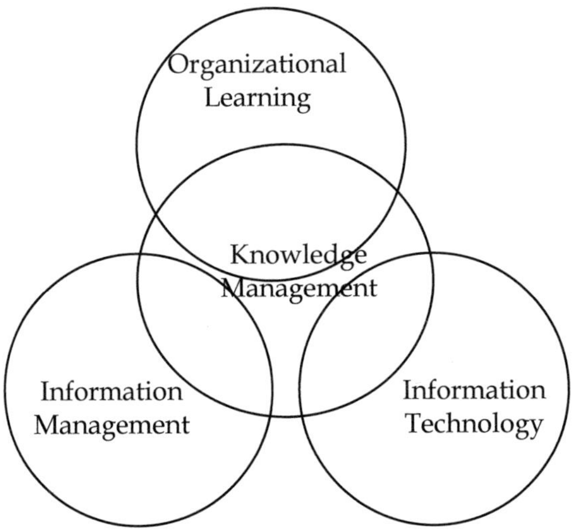

Fig. 1. Three elements of knowledge management (Stoddart, 2001)

Knowledge that is shared by individuals in organizations becomes organizational knowledge and could be described by four modes of knowledge exchange (Nonaka & Takeuchi, 1995; Sveiby, 1997). These are socialization, externalization, combination and internalization. Based on these modes, Van den Brink (2003) explains the knowledge sharing process that occurs in each mode as shown in Table 1.

The process of knowledge sharing could take place either through technology-mediated channel or non-technology mediated channel (Lee & Al-Hawamdeh, 2002). Technology-mediated channel could be in the form of video-conferencing, listservs, newsgroup, groupware, virtual team rooms, e-mail, voicemail, etc. (Lee & Al-Hawamdeh, 2002). Thus, the reliability of technology is paramount for knowledge sharing (Lee & Al-Hawamdeh, 2002) because it has become a facilitator for knowledge transfer (Roberts, 2000).

	Process	Knowledge sharing
1.	Tacit to tacit (Socialization)	Knowledge is shared during social interaction such as story telling that enable transfer of complex tacit knowledge from an technological to another.
2.	Tacit to explicit (Externalization)	Knowledge sharing happens when an individual try to communicate his/her tacit knowledge with others through for example writing ideas and thoughts in the form of theory.
3.	Explicit to explicit (Combination)	When knowledge is written in the form of documents, it is shared with other people. If they combine their knowledge, it will create new ideas that written on papers.
4.	Explicit to tacit (Internalization)	Human can get knowledge when rational behind a document is informed by other individuals.

Table 1. Knowledge sharing process and SECI modes adapted from Van den Brink (2003) and Nonaka & Takeuchi (1995)

2.2. Technological Factors and Knowledge Sharing

Technology is defined as material artefacts such as software and hardware used to perform duties in organization (Orlikowski, 1992). A lot of innovative software has been developed to enable knowledge sharing (Lee & Al-Hawamdeh, 2002) and as a result more than 1800 software products have been labelled as knowledge management solutions (Edgar, 1999).
According to (Orlikowski, 1992), the concept of technology comprises of two main elements i.e. scope and function. In terms of scope, there are two types of research. One, research that considers technology as 'hardware'; and two, views technology as 'social technology'. In terms of function, early research predicts technology as an objective while other research focuses on technology as a product which include people action on technology. The latest research refers technology as soft determinant in which technology is considered as external factor that has impact but controlled by human and organization.
Nevertheless, technology plays important role in knowledge management. Though it is not the centre of knowledge management, but it plays critical role as an enabler in increasing the level of knowledge sharing among employees (Andersson, 2000). Technology has always been the main variable in organizational theory (Orlikowski, 1992) and "*The fundamental requirement of knowledge sharing has always been technology*" (Lee & Al-Hawamdeh, 2002). It facilitates and accelerates the process of knowledge sharing both intra and inter-organizations beside plays an important transformational role in changing corporate culture to knowledge sharing (Gurteen, 1999). Information technology has the potential to affect the functions of coordination and communication within and inter organizations (Fountain, 2001). The role of information technology in knowledge sharing has been studied by communication theorists (Binz-Scharf 2003). For instance, Yates et al. (1999) research on how a new electronic medium being adopted and used by a firm to identify the types of communication shaped by groups based on their needs. These patterns change the social interaction between groups (Yates et al., 1999). Thus, to McDermott (1999) current development in information technology encourage organizations to think of new ways of sharing knowledge such as storing documents in a common knowledge base and use electronic networks to share knowledge within the entire organizations.

Despite the function of ICT as facilitator to knowledge transfer, a number of studies were conducted to identify technology-related factors that affect knowledge sharing behaviour. For instance, Riege (2005) lists 7 technological barriers that hinder people from sharing knowledge such as:

- Lack of information technology process and system integration which limit employees to work.
- Lack of internal and external technology support.
- Unrealistic expectation what technology can do and cannot do.
- Mismatch between technological needs, systems integration and information technology processes.
- Reluctant to use information technology because of not familiar to.
- Lack of training to get use to new information technology systems and processes.
- Lack of communication and usage of new system advantages compared to current system.

The high dependency on information technology has resulted in quick need for effective knowledge management (Sena & Shani, 1999). Organizations need to ensure the value of data is optimised when it is managed so that it can be shared by many applications and knowledge workers. In this regard, technology is to be exploited to disseminate information (English, 1996) as it could provide a bigger and deeper space to the creation, storing, transfer and application of knowledge in organization (Alavi & Leidner, 2001).

Based on Orlikowski (1992), technology in this paper is defined as Information Communication Technology (ICT) which includes software and hardware used by employees in organizations in executing their duties. Synthesizing from Orlikowski's concept of technology and the study by Syed Omar & Rowland (2004), three constructs are identified as technological factors that affect knowledge sharing quality among public sectors employees namely ICT infrastructure, ICT tools and ICT know-how.

a) ICT Infrastructure

The causal relationship between knowledge and technology has lead to the invention of computers (Binz-Scharf, 2003). The role of computer in enabling knowledge sharing is significant. Therefore, ICT infrastructure needs to be in place to facilitate the endeavour (Beckman 1999) especially to support the creation, structuring, penetration and usage of knowledge (Brink, 2003). It is impossible for organization to embark on knowledge sharing without proper ICT infrastructure (Hasanali, 2002) as its presence particularly in the form of new technology and systems could increase technological motivation to share knowledge (Hendriks, 1999). The effectiveness of knowledge management depends on the readiness of employees to share knowledge through computers that can be accessed by all employees in the organization (Syed Ikhsan & Rowland, 2004). The up to date ICT infrastructure could help employee create, transfer and share knowledge (Syed Omar & Rowland, 2004). Sometimes organizations have to overhaul completely their ICT infrastructure in order to make their employees share knowledge (Hasanali, 2002). In this paper ICT infrastructure is defined as up-to-date ICT infrastructure available in their organizations such as computers, networking, internet etc are considered by employees will affect their knowledge sharing quality. Hence, it is hypothesized that:

H_1: ICT infrastructure has a significant effect on knowledge sharing quality.

b) ICT Tools

According to Hasanali (2002), one of factors that contribute to the success of knowledge management is the used of simple technology. It is common that employees become frustrated if they have to clicks more than three times to find knowledge in the system. This indicates that ICT plays dominant role in knowledge management (Smith, 2001). Perhaps, to Anderson and Smith (1998), ICT functions that support knowledge sharing could be grouped into several segments as follows:

i) Office applications such as e-mail, message, calendar and timetable.
ii) Groupware that support teamwork and collaboration. It provides technological support to teamwork such as databases forum, sharing application, electronic meeting systems.
iii) Document systems that support document creation, storage and management life recycle. Printed document are being replaced by digital documents.
iv) Work process systems - ICT helps and monitors work flow generation and related work process. For example workflow management systems, process support systems and e-form.
v) Analytical systems that support analysis and translation of structured data for strategic planning and operation and decision making. For instance decision support systems and data warehouses.

In this paper, ICT tools or software available in the organization such as groupware, computer-based information systems etc. are considered by employees could affect their knowledge sharing quality. Hence, it is hypothesized that:

H_1: ICT tools have a significant effect on knowledge sharing quality.

c) ICT Know-how

Adequate ICT training is one of the factors that significantly contribute to the success of knowledge management (Hasanali, 2002). Adequate technology and well-trained people are important for knowledge management. A well-implemented technology with a well-trained people are important to make people work effectively and efficiently (Gurteen, 1999). As such, sufficient and appropriate ICT training to all employees has positive relationship with knowledge creation and knowledge transfer. Employees who are familiar with ICT are more ready and willing to share knowledge (Syed Omar & Rowland, 2004). In this paper ICT know-how is defined as the degree to which an employee considers their level of IT literacy would affect their knowledge sharing quality. Hence, it is hypothesized that:

H_3: ICT know-how has a significant effect on knowledge sharing quality.

2.4. Knowledge Sharing Quality

Van den Hooff et al. (2003) define knowledge sharing as a process where individual exchange knowledge (tacit or explicit) and together create new knowledge. Knowledge sharing is a process between individuals (Ryu et al.., 2003) which could not be seen directly nor observed. Knowledge sharing in a broader perspective refers to '*the communication of all types of knowledge*' either explicit knowledge or tacit knowledge (al-Hawamdeh, 2003). Knowledge sharing occurs when an individual is really interested in helping others to develop a new capability for action (Senge, 1990). Thus, knowledge sharing refers to the willingness of individuals in an organization to share whatever they possess or create with their colleagues (Gibbert & Krause, 2002).

However, it is often a question whether the knowledge shared is of quality. Knowledge sharing is meaningless unless the quality is guaranteed. However, much of previous studies focused on knowledge sharing behaviour instead of the quality. As such, it is deemed necessary to study the quality of knowledge shared rather than limiting to only knowledge sharing behaviour since quality knowledge is becoming the concern of matured community (Chiu et al., 2006). The quality of knowledge is measured in terms of relevancy, easy to understand, accuracy, completeness, reliability and timeliness (Chiu et al., 2006). The items are derived and modified from McKinney et al. (2002) and DeLone and McLean (2003).

3. Theoretical Framework and Hypotheses

The framework outlined in this paper is adapted from Syed Ikhsan and Rowland (2004) and Chiu et al. (2006). The former investigates the relationship between technological factors and knowledge transfer performance. While the latter focuses on knowledge sharing quality. In this study, the model is adapted and modified to identify the relationship between technological factors and knowledge sharing quality. The quality of knowledge shared becomes the main focus as knowledge sharing could occur anytime but the quality of knowledge shared is essential.

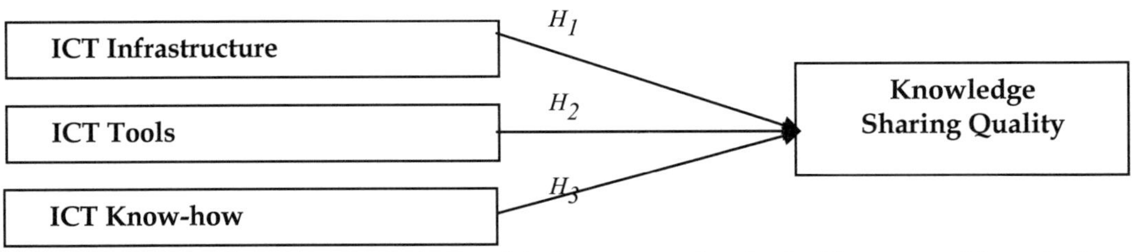

Fig. 1. Theoretical framework of relationship between technological factors and knowledge sharing quality

4. Method

4.1. Population and Sample

The population for the study are officers from the Management and Professional Group (MPG) in three government agencies in Putrajaya. These officers are middle managers positioned between top management (Premier Group) and supporting staff (Support Group). Middle managers are chosen since they are directly involved in policy making in the public sector human resource, financial management and socio-economic development of the country. Knowledge are aspired and created by middle managers who are the leaders of a working group or task force that mediate the exchange process between top management and supporting staff (Nonaka & Takeuchi, 1995). Moreover, knowledge is systematically generated at this level (McAdam & Reid, 2000). Policy making and business development are generated by the knowledge-based activities of government agencies (Husted *et al.*, 2005). The agencies are involved in public sector human resource management policies, public sector financial management policies and national socio-economic policies. In this study, stratified random sampling is used to select the sample. Questionnaires were distributed to 734 officers. The return rate is 61. 25% (450) and the number of questionnaires processed are 428. 22 questionnaires are not processed because of missing data is more than 10% (Hair et al., 2006).

4.2. Measurement

The measurement used in this study is adapted from Syed Ikhsan and Rowland (2004) (for technological factors); and Chiu et al. (2006) (for knowledge sharing quality). The measurements are modified to suit the public sector context. Technological factors consist of three constructs i.e. ICT infrastructure, ICT tools and ICT know-how. Each of these constructs contains three items. Six items are used to evaluate the response towards the quality of knowledge sharing. The respondents are asked whether they agree to the statements related to technological factors and knowledge sharing quality. All items are measured using a 5-point Likert scale ranging from 1=strongly disagree to 5=strongly disagree.

The questionnaire is pretested and refined to ensure its validity. The pre-test is carried out to ensure the clarity in wording, meaning and validity of the question. Two post-graduate students, four government officers and two experts in knowledge management and statistics were approached to comment on the wordings and questions. The comments provide a basis for improvement in construct measurement. After pre-testing, the refined instrument is pilot-tested with 48 officers to test the reliability of the constructs. The final instrument is then used in the study.

5. Findings and Discussion

5.1. Demographic Profile of the Respondents

The respondents' demographic characteristics are presented in the Table 1 below.

Demographic Characteristics and Classification		Frequency	Percentage
Gender	Male	195	45.6
	Female	233	54.4
Age	<26 years old	86	20.1
	26 to <30 years old	125	29.2
	30 to <35 years old	96	22.4
	35 to <40 years old	38	8.9
	40 to <45 years old	28	6.5
	45 to <50 years old	24	5.6
	≥ 50 years old	31	7.2
Level of Education	PhD	2	0.5
	Masters	106	24.8
	First Degree	317	74.1
	Others	3	0.7

Position Grade	54	26	6.1
	52	43	10.0
	48	74	17.3
	44	53	12.4
	41	232	54.2
Years of service in public sector	<1	90	21.0
	1-5	169	39.5
	6-10	55	12.9
	11-15	48	11.2
	16-20	17	4.0
	>20	49	11.4

Table 1. Respondents' demographic characteristics (n=428)

There were 195 (45.6%) male and 233 (54.4%) female respondents involved in the study. Most of them age between 26 to 40 years old (71.7%) and 66.6% are junior managers (grade 41 to 44). Almost all of the respondents have a first degree and 73.4% have less than 10 years work experience in public sector

5.2. Descriptive Profile of Technological Factors and Knowledge Sharing Quality

	Mean	Standard Deviation
ICT Tools	3.57	.727
ICT Infrastructure	4.05	.489
ICT Know-how	3.76	.578

Table 2. Descriptive profile of technological factors

The results indicate that ICT Infrastructure (mean=4.05, S.D=.489) is the most influential factors that affect the quality of knowledge sharing among government officers followed by ICT Know-how (mean=3.76, S.D=.578) and ICT Tools (mean=3.57, S.D=.727) as shown in Table 2.

	Mean	Standard Deviation
Relevancy	4.11	.462
Easy to understand	4.06	.418
Accuracy	3.85	.564
Completeness	3.67	.639
Reliability	3.95	.469
Timeliness	3.96	.452

Table 3. Descriptive profile of knowledge sharing quality

Table 3 shows the descriptive profile of knowledge sharing quality. The relevant knowledge sharing had the highest mean with a statistical value of 4.11 and standard deviation = 0.462 followed by easy to understand (mean 4.06, SD=0.418) and timeliness (mean 3.96, SD=0.452).

Based on the item mean scores, relevancy is considered as the most important dimension in knowledge sharing quality followed by easy to understand and timeliness of knowledge sharing quality construct.

5.3. Goodness of measure

Validity and reliability test are carried out to test the goodness of measure used in the study. Validity test is conducted by submitting data for factor analysis. Factors analysis is a data reduction technique and used to determine whether items are tapping into the same construct. During factor analysis, factors with eigen value of more than one would be retained for further analysis (Hair et al., 2006). To ensure consistency in measurement across time and various items in the instrument (Sekaran, 2005), reliability test was performed by obtaining Cronbach Alpha values.

a) Technological Factors

All the 9 items of technological factors are submitted for analysis using Principal Component Analysis (PCA). Initial results indicate that the KMO value is 0.654 which exceeds the recommended value of 0.6 (Kaiser, 1974; Pallant, 2001) and the Bartlett's Test of Sphericity is significant as shown in Table 4 below. The results (KMO and Bartlett's) suggest that the sampled data is appropriate to proceed with a factor analysis procedure.

Kaiser-Meyer-Olkin of Sampling Adequacy		0.654
Bartlett's Test of Sphericity	Approx. Chi Square	1891.250
	Df	36
	Significance	0.000

Table 4. KMO and Bartlett's test for technological factors instrument

Technological Factors	Component 1	Component 2	Component 3
I2. Computer-based information systems provide me with more up-to-date information than that available in manual files.	.892		
I3. Computer-based information systems make new information available to me that was not earlier available.	.883		
I1. My organization uses Groupware such as Lotus Notes, Microsoft Exchange to encourage the sharing of ideas.	.729		
J1. My organization has a very up-to-date ICT infrastructure which helps knowledge sharing.	**.505**	**.405**	
K2. Employees in my organization are given adequate training internally to use ICT tools.		.938	
K1. Employees in my organization are given adequate training internally to use computers.		.931	
K3. The technology know-how among employees is easily transferable.		.372	

J3. ICT facilitates my daily work			.938
J2. ICT can speed up my work in searching for information			.928
Cronbach Alpha	0.785	0.713	0.890
Eigenvalues	3.209	1.640	1.598
Percentage of common variance	26.951	23.043	21.646
Cumulative percentage	26.951	49.995	71.641

* cutt off point used is 0.30 since the sample is more than 350 (Hair et al.. 2006). All loadings less than 0.30 are not shown

Table 5: Factor analysis and reliability test result on technological factors instrument

Table 5 presents the results of initial varimax factor rotation of all variables for technological factors. All the 9 items loaded on three factors. Four items loaded in Factor 1 with a variance of 26.95, three items loaded on Factor 2 with 23.04 percent and two items loaded on Factor 3 with a variance of 21.65 percent. The total variance achieved is 71.64 percent. One item '*J1. My organization has a very up-to-date ICT infrastructure which helps knowledge sharing*' cross loaded on Factor 1 and Factor 2. In order for an item to be retained, the minimum cross-loading is at least 0.20 (Nunnally & Berstein, 1994). The item is dropped since the different of cross-loading between the two factors is less than 0.2.

The PCA is run again with 8 items without item 'J1'. The KMO value is 0.604 which is above the acceptable value of 0.6 (Kaiser, 1974; Pallant, 2001) and the Bartlett's Test of Sphericity is significant as shown in Table 6. The results show that factor analysis procedure could be performed and all the items loaded on three factors. Three items loaded in Factor 1 with a variance of 27.53, three items loaded on Factor 2 with 24.34 percent and two items loaded on Factor 3 with a variance of 23.78 percent. The total variance achieved is 75.65 percent as shown in Table 7. Reliability test is also performed again without item 'J1' and the results shows that all the Cronbach's Alpha value were between 0.730 to 0.890.

Kaiser-Meyer-Olkin of Sampling Adequacy		.604
Bartlett's Test of Sphericity	Approx. Chi Square	1723.708
	Df	28
	Significance	0.000

Table 6. KMO and Bartlett's test for technological factors instrument

Technological Factors	Component		
	1	2	3
I2. Computer-based information systems provide me with more up-to-date information than that available in manual files.	.905		
I3. Computer-based information systems make new information available to me that was not earlier available.	.897		
I1. My organization uses Groupware such as Lotus Notes, Microsoft Exchange to encourage the sharing of ideas.	.721		
K2. All employees in my organization are given adequate training internally to use ICT tools.		.946	

K1. All employees in my organization are given adequate training internally to use computers.		.939	
K3. The technology know-how among employees is easily transferable.		.378	
J3. ICT facilitates my daily work			.941
J2. ICT can speed up my work in searching for information			.929
Cronbach Alpha	0.799	0.730	0.890
Eigenvalues	2.817	1.638	1.596
Percentage of common variance	27.527	24.338	23.783
Cumulative percentage	27.527	51.865	75.648

* cutt off point used is 0.30 since the sample is more than 350 (Hair et al.. 2006). All loadings less than 0.30 are not shown

Table 7: Factor analysis and reliability test result on technological factors

b) Knowledge Sharing Quality

Principal Component Analysis (PCA) is also performed for the 6 items of knowledge sharing quality. The result shows that Kaiser-Meyer-Olkin of Sampling Adequacy (KMO) value is 0.813. This value is excellent because it exceeds the recommended value of 0.6 (Kaiser, 1974; Pallant 2001) and the Bartlett's Test of Spehericity is significant (0.000). The results (KMO and Bartlett's test) suggest that the sampled data is appropriate to proceed with a factor analysis procedure. The PCA extracted one distinct component with eigen values exceeding 1.0. Six items are loaded on a single factor with the variance of 53.65 percent. The Cronbach's Alpha value is 0.827 meeting the acceptable value 0.6 (Sekaran, 2005; Hair et al., 2006) and 0.70 (Nunnally 1978, Nunnally & Bernstein 1994). The results are presented in Table 8 and 9 below.

Kaiser-Meyer-Olkin of Sampling Adequacy		0.813
Bartlett's Test of Sphericity	Approx. Chi Square	878.067
	Df	15
	Significance	0.000

Table 8. KMO and Bartlett's test for trust instrument

Knowledge sharing quality	Component 1
Q3. Knowledge that I share with my colleagues in my organization is accurate.	.780
Q5. Knowledge that I share with my colleagues in my organization is reliable.	.773
Q6. Knowledge that I share with my colleagues in my organization is timely	.730
Q2. Knowledge that I share with my colleagues in my organization is easy to understand.	.723
Q4. Knowledge that I share with my colleagues in my organization is complete.	.695

Q1. Knowledge that I share with my colleagues in my organization is relevant to my job.	.689
Cronbach Alpha	0.827
Eigenvalues	3.29
Percentage of common variance	53.651
Cumulative percentage	53.651

Table 9. Factor analysis and reliability test result on knowledge sharing quality

Overall, the results statistically show that the instrument used in the study are valid and measure what it is supposed to measure. The instrument is reliable because of high consistencies with Cronbach Alpha were more than 0.70 for all the factors meeting the acceptable value of 0.70 (Nunnally, 1978, Nunnally & Bernstein, 1994).

5.4. Test of Relationship

In order to identify the relationship between technological factors and knowledge sharing quality, correlation analysis is conducted. Correlation analysis indicates the strength and direction of bivariate relationship between the independent and dependent variables. The result of correlation analysis of the study is shown in Table 8 below.

	Mean	Standard Deviation	ICT Tools	ICT Infra-structure	ICT Know-how
ICT Tools	3.57	.727	1.000		
ICT Infrastructure	4.05	.489	0.381**	1.000	
ICT Know-how	3.76	.578	0.221**	0.335**	1.000
Knowledge sharing quality	3.93	.367	0.224**	0.274**	0.339**

** $p < 0.01$

Table 10. Correlation analysis

The above results show that all the variables are significantly correlated with knowledge sharing quality. It indicates that ICT Know-how ($r=0.339$, $p<0.01$), ICT Infrastructure ($r=0.274$, $p<0.01$) and ICT Tools ($r=0.224$, $p<0.01$) have shown significant correlations with knowledge sharing quality among government officers. Cohen (1988) suggests guidelines in which the correlation between 0.10/-0.10 to 0.29/-0.29 is low, 0.3/-0.3 to 0.49/-0.49 is moderate and 0.5/-0.5 to 1/-1 is high. Based on the guidelines, ICT know-how has a moderate positive significant correlation with knowledge sharing quality whereas ICT Infrastructure and ICT Tools have low positive significant correlation with knowledge sharing quality.

In order to find the strongest predictor to knowledge sharing quality, a multiple regression is conducted. Multiple regressions also identify how much variance in knowledge sharing quality explained by technological factors. Table 11 show the results of multiple regression analysis.

	Dependent variable Knowledge sharing quality
Independent variables	(Beta Standardised Coefficient)
ICT Tools	0.111*
ICT Infrastructure	0.142**
ICT Know-how	0.267**
F value	25.82*
R^2	0.152
Adjusted R^2	0.148

** $p < 0.01$, * $p < 0.05$

Table 11. Results of regression analysis

The results of multiple regression show that technological factors have significant effects on knowledge sharing quality. The model is significant ($p<0.01$) with F-value of 25.82. The coefficient of determination (R^2) is 0.152, which indicates that 15.2% of the variance in knowledge sharing quality is explained by the independent variables (ICT Tools, ICT Infrastructure and ICT Know-how). The results indicate that ICT Know-how ($b=0.267$, $p<0.01$), is the most significant predictor of knowledge sharing quality followed by ICT Infrastructure ($b=0.142$, $p<0.01$) and ICT Tools ($b=0.111$, $P<0.05$) Therefore it can be concluded that all hypotheses (H_1, H_2 and H_3) are supported.

6. Conclusion

The findings of the study clearly indicate the achievement of the objectives for the study. Apparently, technological factors have significant positive relationship with knowledge sharing quality. ICT know-how is discovered as the strongest predictor of knowledge sharing quality among Malaysian government officers followed by ICT infrastructure and ICT tools. This shows the role of technology is crucial in knowledge management especially in facilitating and accelerating communications among employees. Simple technology, well-equipped ICT infrastructure and well-trained employees could foster better knowledge sharing. However, a well-equipped technology and easy to use ICT tools are meaningless unless employees know how to make use of it. It is the people that play a critical role. So it is crucial for the government of Malaysia to increase the ICT know-how of its employees in order to increase knowledge sharing quality. The emphasis on hardware and software ought to be balanced with ICT know-how.

Like any other study, this study also experiences some limitations. Firstly, the study is conducted in one location only i.e Putrajaya which is the administrative capital of Malaysian government. Future research will have to be conducted involving various government agencies at both state and district level. Secondly, the study embraces only quantitative approach. To understand better why employees are reluctant to share knowledge, particularly related to technological factors, qualitative approach should be considered. Thirdly, the unit of analysis are officers from middle management group. This is insufficient to draw comprehensive understanding of knowledge sharing in public sector in Malaysia. Thus, top management and supporting staff should be considered in future studies.

7. Rererences

Alavi, M and Leidner, D. E. (2001) Review: Knowledge management and knowledge management systems: Conceptual foundations and research issues. *MIS Quarterly* 25, 1, 107-132. ISSN: 0276-7783.

Al-Hawamdeh, S. (2003). *Knowledge Management Cultivating Knowledge Professionals.* Chandos Publishing. ISBN:1843340380. Oxford.

Andersson, K. (2000). Knowledge Technology Applications for Knowledge Management. Available in: http://uu.diva-portal.org/smash/get/diva2:170306/FULLTEXT01. Last accessed in: January 2007.

Beckman, T. J. (1999). The current state of knowledge management. In: *Knowledge management handbook,* Liebowitz, J. (Ed.), 1-11 to 1-22, CRC Press, ISBN:0849302382, Florida.

Binz-Scharf, M. C. (2008) Exploration and Exploitation: Knowledge Sharing In Digital Government Projects. Available in://www.unisg.ch/www/edis.nsf/wwwDisplayIdentifier/2828/$FILE/dis2828.pdf . Last accessed in: August 2008.

Chiu, C. M., Hsu, M.H. & Wang, E.T.G. (2006). Understanding knowledge sharing in virtual communities: An integration of social capital and social cognitive theories. *Decision Support Systems,* 42, 3, 1872-1888, ISSN: 01679236.

Cohen, J.W (1988). *Statistical Power Analysis for the Behavioural Sciences* (2nd Edition). Lawrence Erlbaum Associates, ISBN: 0805802835, Hillsdale, New Jersey.

DeLone, W.H. & Mc Lean, E.R (2003). The DeLone and Mc Lean model of information systems success: a ten year update. *Journal of Management Information Systems,* 19, 4, 9-30. ISSN: 07421222.

Edgar, S (1999). Knowledge management; has it changed my working life? Will it change yours? *Business Information Review,* 16, 3, 122-127, ISSN: 02663821

English, L. P. (1996). Turning information management into an effective business enabler. *Information Strategy: The Executive's Journal,* Winter, 12, 2, 16-27. ISSN: 0743-8613.

Fountain, J.E (2001). *Building The Virtual State: Information Technology and Institutional Change.* Brookings, ISBN: 0815700776, Washington, D.C.

Gibbert, M. & Krause, H. (2002) 'Practice exchange in a best practice marketplace', In: *Knowledge management case book: Siemen Best Practices,* Davenport, T.H and Probst, G.J.B. (Eds.), 89-107, Publicis Corporate Publishing, ISBN, Erlangen, Germany.

Gurteen, D. (1999). Creating a Knowledge Sharing Culture. Available in: http://www.gurteen.com/gurteen/gurteen.nsf/id/ksculture. Last accessed in: December 2008.

Hair, J.E., Anderson, R.E. Tatham, R.L. & Black, W.C. (2006). *Multivariate Data Analysis.* 5th Ed. Prentice Hall. ISBN: 0130329290, Upper Saddle River.

Hasanali, F. (2002) Critical Success Factors of Knowledge Management, Available in: http://www.providersedge.com/docs/km_articles/Critical_Success_Factors_of_KM.pdf. Last accessed in: May 2009.

Hendriks, P. (1999). Why Share Knowledge? The Influence of ICT on the Motivation for Knowledge Sharing. *Knowledge & Process Management,* 6, 2, 91-100, ISSN 1092-4604.

Ismail, M. B. & Yusof, Z. M. (2008). Factors affecting knowledge sharing in public organizations in Malaysia. In: *Proceedings of the Knowledge Management International Conference 2008,* Hashim, N.L. *et al.* (Eds.),165-171, Universiti Utara Malaysia, ISBN: 9789833827725, Sintok, Kedah.

Kaiser, H. (1974). An index of factorial simplicity. *Psychometrika,* 39, 31-36. ISSN 0033-3123.

Lee, C.K. & Al-Hawamdeh, S. (2002). Factors impacting knowledge sharing. *Journal of Information and Knowledge Management* 1, 1, 49-56, ISSN 0219-6492.

McAdam, R. and Reid, R. (2000). A comparison of public and private sector perception and use of knowledge management. *Journal of European Industrial Training,* 24, 6, 317-329, ISSN: 0309-0590.

McDermott, R. (1999). Why information technology inspired but cannot deliver knowledge management. *California Management Review* 41, 4, 103-117, ISSN: 0008-1256.

McKinney, V., Yoon, K. & Zahedi, F.M. (2002). The measurement of web-customer satisfaction: An expectation and disconfirmation approach. *Information Systems Research* 11, 3, 296-315, ISSN: 1047-7047.

Ninth Malaysia Plan (2006). Ninth Malaysia Plan 2006-2010. Available in: http://www.epu.jpm.my/rm9/html/english.htm. Last accessed in: December 2007.

Nonaka, I. and Takeuchi, H. (1995). *The knowledge-creating company: How Japanese companies create the dynamics of innovation,* Oxford University Press, ISBN: 0195092694, New York.

Nunnally, J.C. (1978). Psychometric Theory, McGraw Hill, ISBN: 0070474656, New York.

Nunnally, J.C., & Bernstein, I.H. (1994). Psychometric theory. McGraw-Hill, ISBN: 007047849X, New York.

Orlikowski, W.J. (1992). The duality of technology: Rethinking the concept of technology in organizations, *Organization Science* 3, 3, 398-427, ISSN 1047-7039.

Pallant, J. 2001. *A Step by Step Guide to Data Analysis Using SPSS for Windows,* Open University Press, ISBN: 0335208908, Buckingham,UK.

Riege, A. (2005). Three-dozen knowledge-sharing barriers managers must consider. *Journal of Knowledge Management:* 9, 3, 18-35, ISSN: 1367-3270.

Roberts, J. (2000). From know-how to show-how? Questioning the role of information and communication technologies in knowledge transfer. *Technology Analysis & Strategic Management* 12, 4, 429-443, ISSN 0935-7325.

Ryu, S., Hee, H. S. & Han, I. (2003). Knowledge sharing behavior of physicians in hospitals. *Expert systems with application 25,* 113-122, ISSN 0957-4174.

Sekaran, U. 2005. *Research methods for business – a skill building approach (4th edition).* John Wiley and Sons, ISBN 9814126748, New York.

Sena, J. A. & Shani, A.B. (1999). Intellectual Capital and Knowledge Creation: Towards an Alternative Framework. In: *Knowledge Management Handbook,* J. Liebowitz (Ed.), 8-1 to 8-7, CRC Press, ISBN: 0849302382, Boca Raton.

Senge, P. M. (1990). *The fifth discipline: the art and practice of the learning organization,* Currncy/Doubleday, ISBN: B000NY81VS, New York.

Smith, E.A. 2001. The role of tacit and explicit knowledge in workplace, *Journal of Knowledge Management,* 5, 4, 311-321, ISSN: 1367-3270.

Stoddart, L. (2001). Managing intranets to encourage knowledge sharing: opportunities and constraints, *Online Information Review,* 25, 1, 19-28. ISSN 1468-4527.

Sveiby, K. E (1997). The New Organisational Wealth, Managing and Measuring Knowledge-Based Assets, Berrett-Koehler, ISBN: 1576750140, San Fransisco.

Syed Ikhsan, S.O.S. and Rowland, F. (2004). Benchmarking knowledge management in a public organisation in Malaysia, *Benchmarking: An International Journal,* 11, 3, 238-266, ISSN 1463-5771.

Van den Brink, P. (2003). *Social, individual and technological conditions that enable knowledge sharing.* Available in: http://www.onthebrink.nl/eng/documenten/vandenbrink_dissertation.pdf. Last accessed in: June 2008.

Van den Hooff, B., Elving, W.J.L., Meeuwsen, J.M. & Dumoulin, C.M. (2003). Knowledge Sharing in Knowledge Communities, In: *Communities and Technologies*. Proceedings of the First International Conference on Communities and Technologies, Huysman, M, Wenger, E. & Wulf, V. (Eds.), 119-142, Kluwer Academic Publishers, ISBN: 1402016115, Deventer.

Yates, J., Orlikowski, W.J. & Okamura, K. (1999). Explicit and Implicit Structuring of Genres in Electronic Communication: Reinforcement and Change of Social Interaction. *Organization Science*, 10, 1, 83-103, ISSN 1047-7039.

16

Towards a Collection-Based Knowledge Representation: the Example of Geopolitical Crisis Management

Pr. Francis Rousseaux and Kevin Lhoste
University of Reims, Ecole Centrale d'Electronique
France

1. Introduction

Although the term "Geopolitics" has been invented in the 20th century, geopolitical crisis management is an old research field. From antiquity, deciders know that their country's geography has to be taken into consideration in political choices in order to protect the country from invasions (e.g. the Chinese great wall) or to guaranty the supply in natural resources. During those times the knowledge necessary to manage such geopolitical crisis was held by some specialists, working in the area for years and their expertise was lost in vain when they left that particular area.

In the 90's with the evolution of IT tools and emergence of artificial intelligence, militaries began to think about using those new tools for improving geopolitical crisis management by doing a quasi real time geopolitical risk evaluation in order to forecast what events are willing to happen and how to avoid it. The Cheops project was one of those tools. It was a success but was limited by its object-based knowledge representation and so one, of its goals which was to be able to incorporate the knowledge of experts to help a military attaché to take decisions and discuss it in human language was impossible to reach.

In order to improve the system a new form of knowledge representation had to be found between the too formal object representation which is too limiting in terms of creativity and no representation. We propose a form of representation well known in the artistic domain: the collection which can be an attempt to represent knowledge in a very open form.

It also led us to rethink the role the system has to play: the decider needs a system to make him more creative and imaginative in terms of hypothesis and that should be the canvas for his reflection.

We will illustrate our studies trough the design of real crisis management systems.

The following sections are organized as follows: section 2 presents the classical approach of risk and crisis management through the design of Cheops, section 3 introduce the concept of collection as an alternative to object based knowledge representations; section 4 present how can collections contribute to redesigning our crisis management systems; section 5 presents the results obtained and addresses the future work and section 6 conclude on the advantages of a collection based knowledge representation and its application in other domains.

2. Crisis management within classical knowledge representations: the Cheops project

2.1 The CHEOPS project

The CHEOPS Project was a geopolitical risk and crisis management system (Rousseaux, 1995). It was designed in 1997. Before the CHEOPS project, the knowledge necessary to manage such geo-political crisis was held by some specialists, working in the area for years and their expertise was lost in vain when they left that particular area. The CHEOPS project was a complete system aimed to use new tools offered by information technology like artificial intelligence, knowledge representation, geographical information systems (GIS) and databases to gather this knowledge and use it to help militaries to better understand the situation and to anticipate the events. This system also has to be multi user because crisis management is a typical a group activity.

The CHEOPS Project was based on a fictive crisis simulation in which a middle-east country (MEC) has some defence agreements with the French government. The French army has to defend MEC from any possible invasions from a foreign country but, at the same time, the French army must not take part in interior troubles resolution. So it is critical to determine if there are some threats against MEC; from where, who and what can be the consequences. In such an environment with lots of constraints from different types: geopolitical, economical, ethnical, etc… it is essential to act in the right manner at the right time.

In order to test the system in real conditions and to better understand needs and constraints, a scenario has been created as following: MEC is involved in a civil war where the rebels opposing the official government, are helped by a threatening neighbour country (TNC).

On the first day troubles appeared in some barracks, near the north frontier without having the possibility to know the causes of these troubles.

On the second day street Fights have been signalled in MEC capital near the national assembly, the consequence is that governmental troops have been sent from the north area to the capital.

On the third day, the airport of the capital has been bombed but the enemy fighter planes have not been identified. Experts are analysing bomb impact pictures. Rebels have old Soviet planes which would not have permitted them to commit this bombing.

2.2 Crisis management within an object-based knowledge representation

Before all it is essential to define what is a crisis. A crisis can be defined as a pool of events that, in a particular context will lead to some unwanted situation. In addition, we can define the crisis concept showing differences between permanent and crisis states. In the crisis state, the situation analysis is made harder because human discernment is wasted by stress, importance of stakes and indeed cost. The crisis generates a temporal paradox because its analysis and linked tasks, like communication or justification of choices, need time incompatible with crisis resolution. One man can not manage a whole crisis by himself like in the Marc Aurèle time. Only virtual or real human groups working together can face a dynamic and complex situation, and so it is a typical multi-participant activity. To meet this

multi participant requirement and match it with an IT based system, a multi-agent cooperation model has been realized.
In such multi-agent system, the challenge is to make human and artificial agents working together at the knowledge level (Newell, 1982). In addition, agents have to share the same knowledge which is on the basis of the crisis management.
To manage a situation with an "object" approach, the system matches any new event with a type event which has been identified from past events and crisis analysis and entered into the system. The same matching operation is done with situations: the system identifies the situation from all the events which happened in a given time and match it with a type situation. In order to predict the future situation, the system make analysis from past set of events entered in the system as ontologies and determines which one has the most probability to happen.
There are six main agents. The Military Attache (MA) collects information and sends argued reports on the situation (it is a human agent), the event database manager (EDM) classify each event, the map database manager (MDM) use a GIS to manage different maps, provides zoom and can put in relief thematic layers , the messenger (MSG) transmits messages (it is a human agent), the news report analyst (NRA) translates text news reports into the database format, the tactical simulator (TSIM) makes calculations and simulations in order to estimate current strength or necessary time to move units, and the arguer (ARGU) lets the user from tactical hypothesis to search corresponding events in the database and on the opposite, to analyse a pool of events in order to find strategic hypothesis.
Based on most of the activities on cooperation between human agents, we used the Maieutic approach (Plato, 1999) where the cooperation can be modelled with high level dialogues between agents.
Agents try to cooperate; they share a working memory where a history of their dialogues is recorded. In order to illustrate this model, we will use an artificial problem resolution dialogue between local crisis management computer agents.
The Table 1 presents an extract from the virtual dialog between agents. In this dialog we can see that the MA begins with an hypothesis: "interior troubles" because there are some hidden reasons that make him to prefer the hypothesis which does not need an intervention in order to avoid compromising. The arguer ARGU disagrees with MA hypothesis because he finds information that discredit MA event's classification. The MA is lead to test the ARGU hypothesis and ask him if he can show that rebels are implied in last events. ARGU does it and asks the tactical simulator (TSIM) to make a simulation of forces present in the north border area; the tactical simulator finds that the force ratio is highly in favour of the threatening neighbour country (TNC), ARGU reports to MA the situation.
The messenger (MSG) brings the confirmation that fighter planes which bombed the capital are a type of planes hold by TNC and so MA is lead to change his mind and to admit that passed events were not caused by some interior troubles but are evidence of an invasion in preparation.
This dialog is a part of a bigger one between all the agents managing all the events of the scenario.
A very interesting fact is that all this dialog between agents can fit into an inference's structure (Figure 1.) which is a well know graph in the social sciences domain (Simon & Lea, 1974; Michalski, 1986; Hoc, 1987) and can be easily be explored by IT tools.

1	MA: Did you receive the description of the events in the capital? It seems like the protestations are organized by some students from the opposition. This confirms that events in the barracks near the north border are probably just the consequence of a problem linked with the soldiers' salaries and so it is interior troubles…	**Build-Event** **Classify-Event** **Test-Type-Event** **Select-Hypothesis**
2	ARGU: I disagree, the cause of events in barracks is unknown because the M'Boutoul ethnic group implicated are with the rebels.	**Classify-Event**
3	MA: Can you show the possible role of rebels in recent events?	**Test-Type-Event**
4	ARGU: Yes! I can demonstrate it. (Demonstration following)	**Classify-Event** **Test-Type-Event**
5	MA: What are the consequences?	**Generate-Strategic-Hypothesis**
6	ARGU to TSIM: Can you make an estimation of forces present in the North area by taking the last events into consideration ?	**Generate-Strategic-Hypothesis**
7	TSIM to ARGU : Considering the rebel forces and TNC regiments the force ratio is unfavourable for MEC	**Generate-Strategic-Hypothesis**
8	ARGU to MA: If TNC rebels are implied, this means that an attack in the north area may happen at any time. The MEC defensive potential is low in this area	**Generate-Strategic-Hypothesis**
12	MSG intervention : I just received the news that we were waiting for : It is possible that fighter planes which have bombed the Capital Airport were from the Marchetti SF-260 type	**Build-Event**
13	MA to ARGU : You may be right	**Select-Strategic-Candidate-Hypothesis**
14	ARGU: Why this change of opinion ?	**Select-Strategic-Candidate-Hypothesis**
15	MA: Because the airport bombing has probably been committed by FTC who have this type of fighter planes, which means that a huge invasion may be in preparation	**Build-Event** **Classify-Event** **Test Event** **Select-Strategic-Candidate-Hypothesis**

Table 1. Extract from a dialog between agents in the problem resolution process.

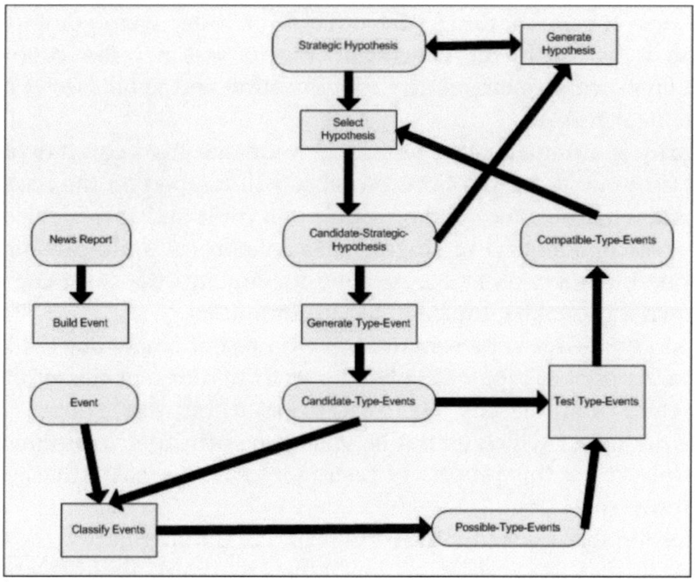

Fig. 1. Inference's structure.

The system is a success because it fulfilled its role: The human user is in permanent contradiction with an arguer agent who always tries to present other parts of the situation. The goal is to make the user sure of is decision and making him passing out non factual opinions based on hidden reasons. This is only possible if the arguer is replaced by a human. We could not manage with classical ontologies to make a virtual agent capable of questioning a human in his language (Turing, 1939; Turing, 1950) because it is a task which has to be realized at the knowledge level by an agent with high abstraction capabilities to figure out that a hypothesis is not reliable without testing all the possibilities. In addition, a computer, which use, logical relations to make hypothesis is limited in its hypothesis making process because all the situations are not logical. Given that this agent cannot be replaced by an artificial agent, the system has to be redesigned.

2.3 The perfect Arguer: between singularity and synthesis

We have seen that the way the system identify the events and synthesise them to hypothesis is essential. The identification of particular event can be called "singularity" identification as before any classification into the system each event is particular.

The study of *singularity* and *synthesis* is essential to understand how to improve our decision helping software. We have seen in the Cheops example that the essential missing element of the arguer is the possibility to question the military Attaché on his decisions i.e.: find singularities in the arguments and justifications of an hypothesis.

In terms of knowledge why humans are superior to the best computers? One of the possible explication is because humans know that they don't know. We can experience this in everyday life. For example we were walking on Vancouver's pier and looking at a motorized taxi boat which was sailing with a stream of water going from the hull. It came to our attention instantly leading us to discuss about the possible hypothesis on the function of this water stream. We wondered if it was an exit for water going into the boat or if it was a water cooling system for the motor. As the streams of water were going out synchronized with motor noise it led us to the conclusion that it was a water cooling system. This reasoning based on successive singularity identification and syntheses is a good model of what could be an ideal arguer.

Why this singularity is automatically identified? Neuroscientists could explain this because the brain makes continuous assumptions on what will happen on the next milliseconds. If something is unknown we cannot make assumption on it and it is viewed as a "potential threat". This process of identifying singularities salience is multi-dimensional: semantic, logic, spatiotemporal, emotional, etc.... As even for humans the exact cognitive process of salience is unknown it cannot be implemented in computers.

In an object based knowledge representation, if we present a new object to the computer it will compare it to the pool of type-object he knows from different classes on a certain base : lexical, logical etc... and classify the object based on this chosen parameter. The characteristics of the object which as not be chosen as principal will remains as particular properties of the object but this process of casting into a type make (that we could also call syntheses) transforms this object.

And so it is interesting to think about the counterpart of the singularity: the syntheses.

Singularity and synthesis share the facts that when we think about them, it lead to their spontaneous conversion. Thinking affects their nature by desingularization and immediate analysis. It can be compared in physics with quantum mechanics where it is impossible to know speed and position of a photon in the same time and without modifying it.

Synthesis come from Greek "sunthesis"= be together. But there is a multitude of forms of "being together" which co-exist. We can quote as examples: nature of the synthesized, its individualization mode, its causes, its origins or genesis, its future or horizon, its goals and modalities its structure and form, its organization and its composition, its operation, its exchanges and/or interactions with its environment, modalities of being together (in the time, the place or duration), its raison or utility its explication or justification...

As we can see, there is as many ways of being together that modes of not being together. Multiplicity of modes of being together is so huge that we are happy when we can justify the existence of one of them with a concordance of different species. Sometimes it is syntheses which are based and conjugate different modes of intellections. More often it is syntheses based on a mode of perception and a mode of intellection.

For the first type examples we can quote Cladistic which orders living organisms in phylogenies from species evolution before any "kind casting" based on aspectual similarities. For example based only on characteristics without any aspectual similarities we can compare monkeys, horses and lizard: they have 2 eyes, a tail but horses do not have 5 differentiated fingers on the anterior leg. This mode of classification is commonly used by actual biologist and it brings new point of view on aspectual similarities which only come with the filter of phylogenic bifurcations.

There are many second type examples: Computer simulations of plant growth are one of them. It interests researcher in sciences of complexity because in the same time it shows the shape and the ontogenesis of a given plant. For them such a simulation is better than a hand made drawing because they can be interpreted in terms of formal realism but also in terms of genetic plant simulation in his cycle of life. It is the same for the shell or the broccoli since we know fractal equations because their beauty can be seen in the same time by the perception and by a certain mathematical intellection.

We can find very convenient to put together different modes of justification for a same declared synthesis. But it also happens that we can take advantages from concurrent justifications. It is usual to find the simultaneous presence of the couple singularity-synthesis. This couple is it inseparable or does it constitute itself spontaneously when we see a synthesis which becomes analytic? How can what we experience can be converted in knowledge that we will know and that we will think we can use it when we want. ? How can singular immediate experiences contribute to build categories that we will use in future interpretative tasks? How to generalize singularities? The subject seams to be absurd because only particulars can be generalized: they cannot do anything more when they are frozen in a synthesis. Even the only one in its kind is not singular when it is ordered. Singularity and synthesis share the fact that they can be seen as disappearance for the first one when it become analytic and for the second one when it become particular.What can be the link between singularity and synthesis ? However a place exists for thinking together singularity and synthesis, this place is **the Collection.**

3. Collections as a new paradigm in our knowledge representation

From here, we will call *collection* this specific figure, which the present paragraph means to study. We will show that: This acceptation of the word collection is close to its usual meaning; That a collection differs from the notions of ensemble, class, series, set, group, or clutter but also from that of organic whole or family; That a collection is the institution of a metastable equilibrium between singularity and category, just as other concurrent fictions such as fashion, crises, choreographies, plans, liturgical cycles, scientific projects, or instrumental gestures.

3.1 The notion of collection

To begin better understand the concept of collection we can quote Gérard Wajcman's analyses (Criqui & Wajcman, 2004) on the status of excess in collections: "Excess in collections does not mean disordered accumulation; it is a constitutive principle: for a collection to exist—in the eyes of the collector himself—the number of works has to be greater than the number than can be presented and stored at the collector's home. Therefore someone who lives in a studio can very well have a collection: he only needs to have one piece that cannot be hanged in his studio. That is why the reserves are an integral part of a collection. Excess can also be noted at the level of the memorizing capacities: for a collection to exist, the collector just needs to be unable to remember all the artworks he possesses. The collector should not completely be the master of his collection".

A collection is far from a simple juxtaposition or reunion of individual elements. It is primarily a temporary correlate of an initiatory ritual made sacred by time. Adding works, or revisiting a collection keeps alterating and re-constituting it, leaving it always halfway between the original series of juxtaposed intimate moments and a permanently organized class of objects. Unlike an organic whole, a collection only exists for each of its parts, and unlike an ensemble, it does not exist as a normative or equalizing unity; it is productive if in tension between singularities and categorical structure.

As Gerard Wajcman writes, thinking probably of Gertrude Stein (Wajcman, 1999), " If nobody ever looks at "a collection," it is because it is not a collection of artworks, but an indefinite series of singular objects, an artwork + another artwork + another artwork..."

For the artist, the collection of his own works is like (In *The pastoral symphony* by André Gide) Matthew's herd: "Every painting on the easel, taken separately, is more precious to the painter than the rest of his collection". But in that case, the election of the next painting to be presented is naturally prescribed par the exhibit/procession. Series are never set a priori, and a specific painting never make us forget the rest of the collection.
The collector, at this point, is interested about what his collection lacks, about its virtual development. It is through the repetition of intimate lived moments that a collection is created. By this gesture is instituted not only the same, which unifies the collection through the similarities supposedly going through the collected objects, but also the object nature of the specific things that constitute the collection.
Collecting is therefore part of an initiatory journey, between what was lived and what can be communicated, and thus becomes a sacred activity, just as creating. The process of reconstitution regenerates the coherence of the collection. If the reconstitution is not well done, the collection can soon be abandoned, or dispersed. A collection ceases to exist as something else than a mundane correlate as soon as the collector ceases to be interested in its development. Then he stops repeating the acquiring gesture or the reconstituting gesture for himself or his intimate friends.
These two gestures have the same meaning. The reconstitution gives better balance to the heavy tendencies of the collection, makes new relationships appear between artworks, and institutes new similarities which later influence the logic of acquisition. New objects become part of the collection as "different," and they become "same" only later, because they have in common to be different, thus being part of what Jean-Claude Milner calls a paradoxical class. It is rather easy to spot individual cases of collections that were abandoned.
The synthetic nature of an ensemble of objects presented to be seen as a collection is different from the nature of the ensemble that is constituted and shown by the collector. Indeed, the collector does not juxtapose objects; he puts together elements of remembrance, to be prompted by objects. Walter Benjamin, quoted by Jean-Pierre Criqui (Benjamin, 1989) writes: "Everything that is present to memory, to thought, to consciousness becomes a base, a frame, a pedestal, a casket for the object possessed. The art of collecting is a form of practical recollection, and, of all the profane manifestations of proximity, it is the most convincing."

3.2 Collections and Knowledge management in IT

Collections as an alternative to formal ontologies appear as a metastable equilibrium coming from a productive tension between categorical structures and singularities. If in everyday life, collection can be distinguished from list, ensemble, class, series, set, group or clutter but also from that of organic whole or family, from lineage, cohort or procession it is by the mode where it donated.
The donation of the collection (to the visitor or to the collector, if it is in acquiring or recolletion) appears under the paradox that a donation as a whole coherent is impossible excepted in the reducing mode of collection management. Because in this mode even a clutter can be seen as a coherent whole because all the objects have in common to be different forming what Jean-Claude Milner calls a paradoxal class.
In other words we can see the collection as a coherent whole but only if we renounce to one of its properties: the impossibility to experience anything else that the sheep apart from the herd, always more precious than the rest of the flock together.

What are the consequences of those considerations in the applicative domain of information systems and of decision helping and content-based browsing software?
Collection manifests a mode of synthesis characterized by a possibility to be reconstructed from only one look of the shepherd (collector or visitor) on one of its constituting part. This characteristic clearly distinguish collection from class, or from category where the observation of one prototype or one example is incapable of specifying alone a reconstitution
So *collections* can be defined as IT objects; considered as lists or ensembles grouping objects in synthetetic position of "being together" – ---(onto-chrono)logical, synoptic and other- inside the IT environment for a given level. Those same objects are considered at any time as being susceptible of reconstitution on another level of the IT environment.
This schizophrenia of the environment is a characteristic of IT tools for collection management or for helping content-based browsing. It benefits to the user, powerful artisan of singular recollections that he do constantly.

3.3 Figural Collections as a new form of knowledge representation

For Piaget (Piaget & Inhelder, 1980), the main difference between collections and classes is that a collection exists only because of the union of its elements in space whereas elements of a class can be separated in space without changing class properties. For example: cats have in common certain properties whereas other properties are common with other animals but in this definition of a class there is no property or relation linked with space: cats can be dispersed in space randomly or in groups, it will not modify the class properties. On the opposite, a collection like a collection of paintings is a whole: a painting cannot be removed from the collection without modifying the collection itself. We can also distinguish figural collections and non-figural collection. A figural collection is a figure itself, not mandatory linked with relations between its elements. In this project we will focus on these figural collections which are the only ones which can represent spatio-temporal dependence needed in the crisis management.
As a model of a figural collection we studied what can be the analogies between a collection of paintings in a museum and a collection of geopolitical events. In a museum the main agent is the curator; his role is to manage the collection. The subject of the collection has been previously defined (e.g.: impressionist paintings) and he has to buy new paintings to keep the collection up to date, to arrange and rearrange spatially the collection in the way it is displayed to the public (with the help of other agents who put the paintings in place), he can also conduct research on archives of the collection (with archivist agents) and rearrange the collection between the displayed collection and the collection's archives or reserves (with reservist agents). As we have seen before, a collection is a whole and the collection's archives or reserves of the collection have the same importance as the displayed part. The following table shows possible analogies between museum's curator and collection's curator in a geo-political risk and crisis management system.

	Museum	Geo-political crisis management
1	Manage the collection of Paintings	Manage the collection of Events
2	Buy or sell paintings to keep collection up to date	Integrate new events in the collection
3	Arrange and rearrange spatially the collection for public (humans)	Arrange and rearrange spatially events in the system interface for public (human and artificial agents)
4	Conduct research on archives (with archivists) to find new information on paintings	Conduct research on archives(with archivists) to find new links between events and situations or new information
5	rearrange the collection between the displayed collection and the collection's archives or reserves to refresh the collection	rearrange the collection between the displayed collection and the collection's archives or reserves to bring creativity by showing new embryos of hypothesis

Table 2. Analogies between curator's role in a museum and in a geo-political crisis management system

Every museum has a displayed part of the collection and a part of the collection in the reserves. The coherence of the collection is guaranteed by the collector or the curator.
The way the collection is displayed is crucial because it is more than paintings put together. Each painting has its meaning for the collection just displayed with others. When displayed in a certain way the paintings tell a story and bring some feelings; displayed in another way they will also tell another story and bring other feelings. It will be the same for the geo-political crisis: displayed in a certain way events will tell a certain story and bring hypothesis of what will happen. The user interacts with the collection to arrange and re-arrange it accordingly.

4. Use of collections for redesigning our critical decision helping systems

Within the new knowledge representation the system can play a new role: it can be seen as a creativity helper. We renounced to build an arguer making hypothesis at the knowledge level. We decided to build a system which suggests embryos of hypothesis in displaying events and information in different ways, helping user's creativity.
As we have seen before a computer can not be creative as humans in terms of hypothesis and maieutic questioning but it can be better than humans for calculations (e.g. : path length, time to area etc…), data fusion/aggregation. We choose to use this repartition for studying how collections can improve our critical decision making.
We called our new system iCheops (iCheops, 2008) because we are using the "Web 2.0 revolution" and its new tools (API's Application Programming Interface) that let developers to bring easily new functionalities that where very complicated to implement few years before. We can quote as example the implementation of the GIS (Geographical Information System) which on the original Cheops project required more than 70% of the total resources of the project (High definition satellite maps of each zone add to be purchased individually,

digitalized and objects add to be manually encoded into the GIS format) and that now can be easily replaced by the Google Maps API (Google Map API, 2009).

4.1 Architecture of the system

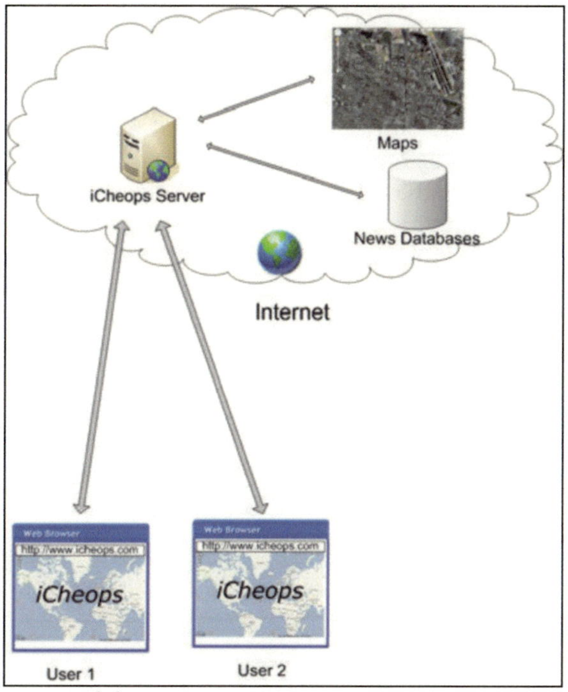

Fig. 2. General Architecture of the system

The architecture is a typical web application architecture were many users can access to the system without any previous installation. The system is also interoperable and can be access by any machine (computer, PDA, Smartphone) which has a web browser. The iCheops system is installed on a web server and so can access autonomously to many data sources (e.g.: Google maps, news databases, governmental websites, etc...). The two demonstrators we will present later in this section are developed in AJAX (Asyncronous Javascript And XML). The main interest of this technology is to bring desktop like functionalities to the web sites. In terms of HCI (Human Computer Interface), Ajax brings more flexibility and interactivity. All the elements of a classical desktop interface (sliders, splash screens, dropping menus, etc...) can be implemented. Ajax also let developers to design new types of application, closing the gap between the desktop and the web.

The iCheops community of agents is the following:

The Military Attaché (MA) (is a human agent) is the curator of the collection: he chooses which events he wants to put in his collection and on which he want to conduct analyses. He has also the role of configuring the behavior of software agents; more than one Military Attaché can modify the same collection. The News Crawler (NC) is always running in background and feed the event database with news retrieved from different news databases (e.g. : Reuters, AFP, le monde, the New York Times, etc...). The archivist agent (ARCH) conduct research on past crisis: it can correlate specified events with past events and show it to the military Attaché who can decide to put them also on the map. A Fusion/Aggregation agent (F/A) can help the military attaché to conduct analysis on a collection of event; this agent can also crawl the web to search for links between objects. A text translator (TT) can be mobilized by every agent in order to translate data into military Attaché's language. A time manager (CHRONOS) can replay cognitive process of past crisis. The Map Overlay Manager (MOM) displays the part of the map needed by the user. Normally this process is automatic through the Google Map API but in certain cases if the user wants a custom map overlay the MOM agent will overlay it accordingly. MOM has also in charge to overlay different types of information custom information coming from the user (icons, comments etc..) but it can also propose the different overlays available for the concerned area according to the data available in his database (e.g.: power grid, density of population etc...). If MOM does not have the information needed the user can ask a Map crawler (MC) to propose him different sets of data to incorporate to the map or to help him to find data sources. The tactical simulator (TSIM) makes calculations and simulations in order to estimate current strength or necessary time to move units.

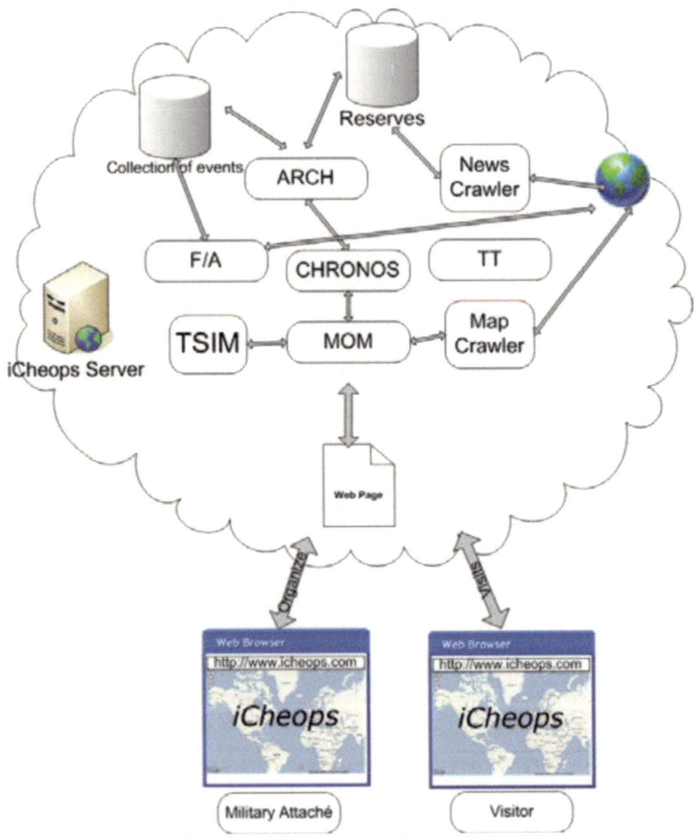

Fig. 3. iCheops Agent simplified cooperation model

There is two main modes in iCheops: The curator mode for the military attaché and the visitor mode. The curator can do everything and can plan a visit spatiotemporal visit for a visitor. The visitor can visualize the visit proposed by the curator but can do also his own visit in the collection of events and can put annotations for the curator. Like in a museum there is also a physical distinction between the displayed collection and the reserves: the two sets of events are in two different databases.

We build two demonstrators each one implementing a part of the iCheops system:

A first one Geonews is dealing with databases, data fusion/aggregation, time management, crisis anticipation and we choose to use it for research about crisis management at the knowledge level.

A second one Netsensor deals more specifically with Human Computer Interface and visualization. A client who sells sensor networks for Unattended Ground Sensors (UGS) needed to demonstrate capabilities of its systems. We choose to use this opportunity to build the MOM (Map Overlay Manager) and the TSIM (Tactical Simulator) agents for iCHEOPS.

4.2 The Geonews demonstrator

In crisis management, information spatialization, evaluation, as well as data fusion/aggregation, time management, resources mobilization, real time analysis is a proactive analysis. In order to be able to demonstrate those features we choose to make a system that displays spatially news from internet websites to manage this collection of news and to do some analysis on it.

The objective is to show the events in time and space and to do some basic processing in order to find similar events in an area and to find if there is a possible threat in this area.

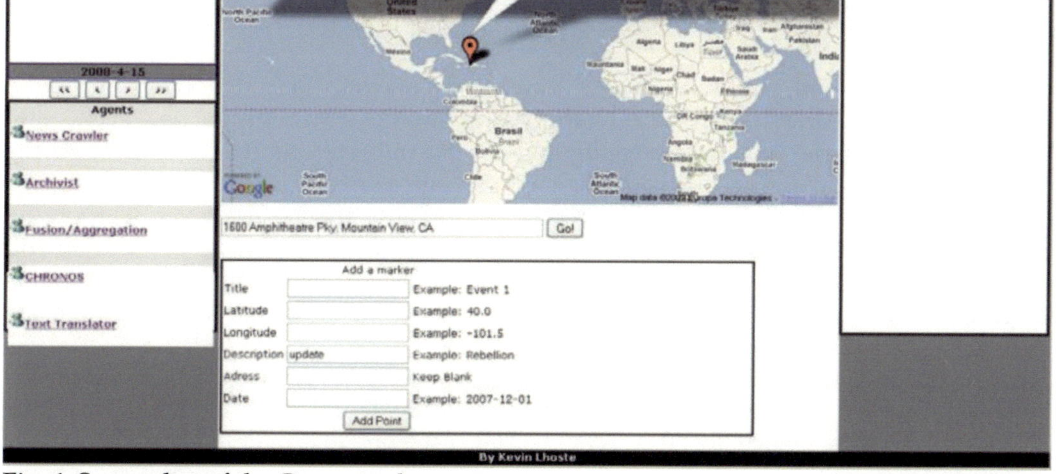

Fig. 4. Screenshot of the Geonews demonstrator

A database contains a huge collection of events. Because it is for a proof of concept, the event descriptions have been extracted from free online newspapers. Each event has been tagged with a geographic position (latitude, longitude), a date and a time. The user can select spatially or temporally the events to display. Each user (military attaché) can create its own collection of events. The user can also add manually an event into the database. Basic operations can be done on the user's collection: add an event, remove an event, visualize the event on the map and select some event to do data fusion.)

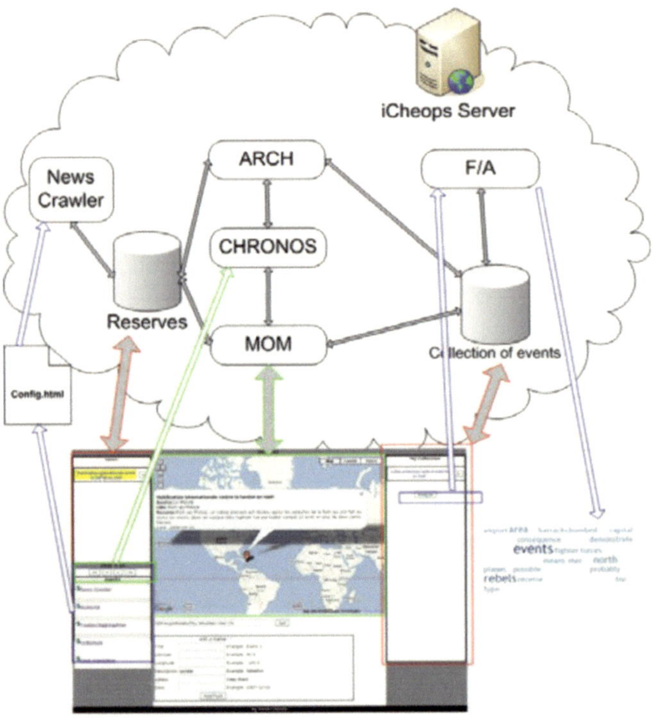

Fig. 5. The Geonews simplified agent cooperation model

Figure 5 presents an simplified agent cooperation model. Only the most important interactions have been represented. A News Crawler crawl the web adding new events into the reserves database. NC can be configured by the military attaché (MA) through the config.html file (e.g. : topics, languages, keywords, data sources to include). All the agents can be configured in the same way. When the military attaché navigates temporarily through events the CHRONOS agent is called (green arrow on Figure 5) CHRONOS will interact with the Map Overlay Manager to display spatially and temporarily the events contained in the reserves. MA can choose to add an event in his collection through the archivist agent (ARCH).

The data fusion made by the Fusion / Aggregation agent (F/A) on the collection of events is quite simple: a list of "irrelevant" words has been made according to the language of the database, which is French for this project. This list contains, determinants, pronouns, connectors and auxiliary verbs. Then a loop counts the number of occurrences of each word and the words are displayed as a tag cloud (figure 6) where the words with the most occurrences are displayed in a bigger font.

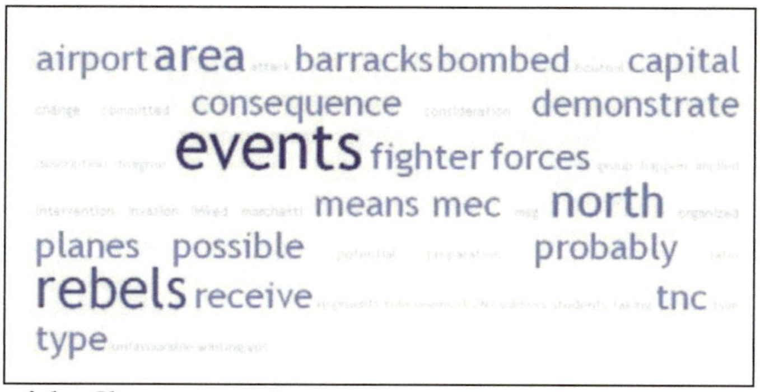

Fig. 6. Tag cloud of the Cheops scenario

4.3 The Netsensor demonstrator

The market of UGS (Unattended Ground Sensors) is very competitive and in order to make the difference with competitors, it is important to be very innovative. Before the Netsensor project, the client used to present his products to military agencies on a map background but it was not interactive at all. For each presentation he had to do screenshots and overlay sample pictures of the products.

We developed an online application where he can simulate the behavior of the UGS systems and interact with them. For example we can choose the geographical place, the number and the type of sensors to put their range, the attenuation of radio range and detection range induced by the terrain topography. Then we can simulate the trajectory of enemies and see how each sensor detect the enemy.

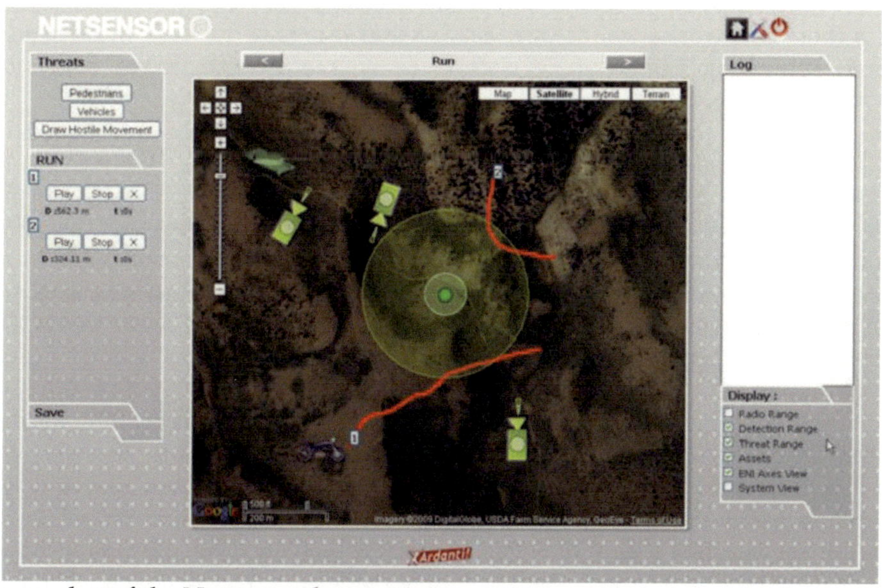

Fig. 7.Screenshot of the Netsensor demonstrator

The system is decomposed in 2 modes: one for editing scenarios and one for running in commercial demonstrations still on the model of museum with the making of the collection and its visit.
The tactical simulator (TSIM) is capable of doing calculation in real time on the time to move units, the estimated distance from the enemies to the base, the time before possible attack etc. Data concerning enemy speed is store in a database of enemies' possible properties. With the help of the Map Overlay Manager (MOM) the user can place an enemy icon and trace its trajectory and he will see the enemy moving according to its speed.
Technically a table in the database contains the general properties of the application (e.g.: password, scenarios, users, default parameters for each sensors) and each scenario is associated with a table of the database containing all the properties of the particular scenario (e.g.: number of sensors, enemies, trajectories of the enemy, enemy speed). When the user runs the scenario, a timer is started in order to refresh the page at fixed interval of time, for showing enemy progression in live. MOM let also the user overlay different layers of information (radio range, detection range, assets etc…) that he can choose to display or hide at any time. If an enemy crosses a detection area of a sensor an alert is sent as a form of a popup.

5. Results and perspective of evolution

As the iCheops is not finished yet we can not make real studies of performances on real examples of crisis management but we can evaluate the utility and creativity of the two demonstrators we developed.
Geonews appeared to be a very interesting tool because when we use it we can see instantly the potential that have spatiotemporal representation and also representation of knowledge in collections.
When we read a newspaper we can forget very easily events and also it is very difficult to link different event in a context. Newspapers are mostly organized in an object-like form : in categories (business, world, technology, etc....) and it is hard to cross those categories to understand something in its whole context as well as it is hard to cross correlates information from different newspapers.
Our demonstrator let the user browse all the events on a certain area of the world and he can see how different data sources speak about this zone. It is essential in order to understand easily the geopolitics of a certain area. The Text Translator agent which will be developed in a next version will be useful for completing the achievement of this goal.
In addition nowadays with globalization an event can have consequences globally and it is also interesting to be able to see what can be the perimeter of consequences of an event. With the fusion/aggregation agent of Geonews we can put in relief some words related to some concepts and it is designed to encourage the user to continue his search by giving him new path to explore. As an example we used the F/A agent with the food crisis in Haiti and the tag cloud linked this event to the FMI and to other food crisis happening in the world.
The principle of organizing relevant events in a collection appears to be very interesting because this collection is not a replacement of our memory but it is an active canvas for our cognition. As a parallel we can quote the organization of human memory: it is usual to think that we forgot something and like Proust's madeleine by the taste it lead us to a remembrance of a past event associated with this Madeleine. This madeleine is the element

of remembrance but this Madeleine is significant only for the one who experienced the situation and is not always understandable. It is a good justification of why our collection knowledge representation can be a canvas for those elements of remembrance.

For its evolution we will improve data fusion and aggregation. But we would like to avoid as much as possible classical "knowledge gathering" tools using linguistics. Linguistic and natural language processing can be useful in some case to represent knowledge but we would like to use it as metadata and not as the main knowledge gathering technique.

We would like to try some simple techniques that have been applied in the domain of arts (Pachet & Cazaly, 2000) to search some similarities in an event collection and then to sort events in heaps in function of the principal component. We also would like to work on 3D representations of the collection of events in order to see if it can improve the "feeling of knowledge" and the understanding of the whole situation.

Netsensor is an industrial success because it gives a competitive advantage to our client. In the same time it helped us better understand constraints and capabilities of web based tactical simulator. The possibilities are huge because we can find a large amount of useful data on the web that we can overlay through the Google Map API. It demonstrates also the power of web based tool because, compared to the original Cheops project where more that 70% of resources was used for the GIS, here we could focus on principal aspects(user interface, databases, crisis management,…) of the project by using no resources for the GIS itself. Some limitations appeared also during the development we can quote for example the interactions between agents which are more complicated to organize than in classical desktop software. Some agents are scripts running in background of the server and other ones are scripts executed when the user load a page. With the uncertain network transfer time it is also difficult to do some real time synchronizing. It raises also the concerns of data security which are important in geopolitics. We need to find a good compromise between security of data and time to decrypt it. This algorithm should be adaptive in function of sensitivity of data: if some data are not critical we should be able to send it with a minimum encryption which increases the speed of the system.

In terms of evolution next versions will use the Google Earth API which is now in 3D and what will improve the simulation by adding another dimension which is critical. This big step will be a real challenge because 3D simulations are much more difficult to implement.

For the general iCheops project, the next step will be to integrate the two demonstrator in iCheops and trying to find new models to organize the community of agents and their interactions. As the concept of collection is a form of emergence we will study if we can apply some results coming from the field of ecology (Van Peach, 2002) or system biology which study emergence of organization in populations (e.g. :bacteria).

We will also work on the concept 3D collections in order to see in which extent the third dimension can improve knowledge representations.

6. Conclusion

In this chapter we demonstrated that the concept of collection can be used as a knowledge representation and its implementation in IT can improve tools that were very difficult to implement in object-based knowledge representation. It appeared to be a good alternative to classical object-based knowledge representation.

This collection-based knowledge representation can be used in many domains where a object-type matching loses a part of the object. We can find many examples in different domains: In digital data management it can be more relevant to manage a whole collection of files than to match it with their type. For example, it is too limiting to match a song with a music style and it limits the choice of the listener (Pachet & Cazaly, 2000).
A lot still has to be done but the matter is scientifically rich enough to let a great deal of researchers in multidisciplinary domains to bring their contribution. This subject is a challenge for us because beyond technological and scientific aspects invites us to think about our intelligence and the way we are representing the world.

7. References

Benjamin W. (1989), *Paris, capitale du XIXe siècle.*, Le Cerf, ISBN : 2-204-03157-7, Paris

Criqui J-P. & Wajcman G. (2004), L'intime – le collectionneur derrière la porte, In: *Catalogue de l'exposition inaugurale de la Maison rouge*, Fage, Paris

Google Map API (2009), Examples and documentation available at http://code.google.com/apis/maps/documentation/

Hoc J.M. (1987), Psychologie Cognitive de la Planification, PU of Grenoble, ISBN: 2706102802 , Grenoble

iCheops Project (2008), Demonstrators available at
http://www.icheops.com

Michalski R.S.(1986), Inference-based Theory of Learning , International Meeting on Advances in Learning, Les Arcs, August 1986.

Newell A. (1982), The knowledge Level, Artificial Intelligence, Vol. 18, p.87-127

Pachet F. & Cazaly D. (2000), A Taxonomy of Musical Genres, *Proceedings of Content-Based Multimedia Information Access* (RIAO)

Piaget J. & Inhelder B. (1980), *La genèse des structures logiques élémentaires*, Delachaux et Niestlé, ISBN: 2-603-00838-2, Neuchâtel

Plato (1999), L'Apologie de Socrate, Flammarion, ISBN: 2-0807-0848-1

Rousseaux F. (1995), Contribution à une méthodologied'acquisition des connaissances pour l'ingénierie des SIC: l'exemple de Cheops pour l'aide à la gestion de crises collectives à caractère géographique, *Mémoire d'habilitation à diriger des recherches, rapport de recherche LAFORIA*

Simon H., Lea G. (1974), Problem Solving and Rule Induction: A Unified View, In: *Knowledge and Cognition* , Gregg L-G. (ed.), pp. 105-28, Lawrence Erlbaum, 1974.

Turing A. (1939) , Systems of Logic based on Ordinals, *Proceedings of the London Mathematical Society*, n°45

Turing A. (1950), Computing Machinery and Intelligence, Mind LIX, n°236

Van Peach H. (2002), Complexity and Ecosystem Management: The Theory and Practice of Multi-Agent Systems: Marco A. Janssen (editor), Edward Elgar, Cheltenham UK and Northampton MA, USA in association with the International Society for Ecological Economics, 2003, ISBN: 1843760614,

Wajcman G. (1999)., Collection, Nous, ISBN : 2913549047, Paris